Special Education and the Law

Third Edition

To Debbie and Debbie
With all of our love, now, always, and forever

Special Education and the Law

A Guide for Practitioners

Third Edition

Allan G. Osborne, Jr.

Charles J. Russo

Foreword by Richard D. Lavoie

CORWIN
A SAGE Company

CORWIN
A SAGE Company

FOR INFORMATION:

Corwin
A SAGE Company
2455 Teller Road
Thousand Oaks, California 91320
(800) 233-9936
www.corwin.com

SAGE Publications Ltd.
1 Oliver's Yard
55 City Road
London EC1Y 1SP
United Kingdom

SAGE Publications India Pvt. Ltd.
B 1/I 1 Mohan Cooperative Industrial Area
Mathura Road, New Delhi 110 044
India

SAGE Publications Asia-Pacific Pte. Ltd.
3 Church Street
#10-04 Samsung Hub
Singapore 049483

Executive Editor: Arnis Burvikovs
Associate Editor: Desirée A. Bartlett
Editorial Assistant: Ariel Price
Production Editor: Melanie Birdsall
Copy Editor: Cate Huisman
Typesetter: C&M Digitals (P) Ltd.
Proofreader: Ellen Howard
Indexer: Jean Casalegno
Cover Designer: Anupama Krishnan

Printed in the United States of America

Library of Congress Cataloging-in-Publication Data

Osborne, Allan G. author.
Special education and the law : a guide for practitioners / Allan G. Osborne, Jr., Charles J. Russo. — Third Edition.

pages cm
Includes bibliographical references and index.

ISBN 978-1-4833-0314-7 (pbk.)

1. Special education—Law and legislation—United States. I. Russo, Charles J. author. II. Title.

KF4209.3.O82 2014
344.73′0791—dc23   2013049068

This book is printed on acid-free paper

MIX
Paper from responsible sources
FSC® C012947

17 18 10 9 8 7 6 5 4 3

Contents

Foreword

In the 1980s, I served as Educational Director at a residential independent school for students with learning disorders. Early one September afternoon, I received a telephone message from a young teacher who resigned from our program to take a job at a local public school as an elementary school teacher.

Her message stated that although she had been in her new position for only a few days the teacher recognized that she had two students in her class who would benefit from our specialized (and very expensive!) curriculum. The teacher was meeting with the parents the next day and wanted me to know that she would be referring them to me.

Fortunately, I was able to contact the teacher and dissuade her from her plan before she committed the act of professional suicide.

The young, well-intentioned teacher had no understanding of the legal implications of her actions. She had little appreciation of the fact that even as a young, fledgling teacher she *spoke* for *the school system* and her recommendation would have committed her school to paying for the costs of the services that we provided as an "outside agency."

It was then that I realized that most teachers have little understanding of (or appreciation for) the complex laws and regulations that impact on special education teachers. This situation has improved a bit in recent years due to the legal courses offered in university teacher-training programs, but I continue to observe that many building-level educators find "legalities" an inconvenient and bothersome obstacle.

On the contrary, these legislative regulations and mandates form the template for 21st century special education.

Enter Allan Osborne and Charlie Russo.

In the latest edition of *Special Education and the Law: A Guide for Practitioners*, the Drs. Osborne and Russo provide teachers and administrators with an updated and understandable guide to the intricate and often perplexing laws that regulate our field today. Their impeccable research and user-friendly writing style make this book a must for administrators' and teachers' professional bookshelves.

It is important for practitioners to recognize that the legal mandates and requirements—although troublesome and time-consuming—are designed to protect and defend the special needs students that we serve daily in the classroom.

Prior to 1975, these students had no specific rights or safeguards. Their services were delivered at the whim of each municipality, and programs for special needs students were tantamount to holding patterns where these students were occupied with haphazard and objective-less curricula. Further, resources intended for these programs were often instead used as "spare parts" for the regular education programs. . . . If the Science Department needed additional furniture, equipment, or funds, it was simply taken from the special education program. Special needs teachers had no guidance or accountability and parents had no rights or due process. The authors of the 1975 legislation referred to a "papier mache" mentality in special education where teachers were expected to keep their students busy, happy . . . and invisible.

The laws outlined in this invaluable book have changed all that. These students, their families and their teachers have specific, enforceable rights to receive a "free appropriate public education" that enables the students to reach their fullest potential and become contributing members of our society. In the words of President William J. Clinton, "In these troubled, challenging times, we simply do not have a single person to waste."

From a practical, day-to-day viewpoint, I will grant that these regulations create an additional layer of paperwork, meetings, and requirements that can occupy a troubling percentage of a teacher's time and energy. But if teachers come to truly understand the nature, history, and nuances of these laws, they can become more effective and impactful advocates for their students and their families.

Again, the laws were not created to be an obstacle to service delivery in special education. Rather, they were designed to serve as a vehicle to outline, protect, and preserve the rights of these students.

The pioneers in our field fought long and hard to establish these rights. As 21st century special educators, it is our responsibility to understand and utilize these laws to level the playing field for students whose abilities are compromised through no fault or choice of their own.

Dr. Osborne and Dr. Russo provide the information that enables administrators and teachers to view education legislation as an opportunity . . . and not an obstacle.

—*Richard D. Lavoie, M.A., M.Ed.*
Consultant and Author, *It's So Much Work to Be Your Friend:
Helping the Child With Learning Disabilities Find Social Success*

Preface

In 1975 Congress enacted sweeping legislation known as the Education for All Handicapped Children Act mandating a free appropriate public education (FAPE) in the least restrictive environment for all eligible students with disabilities tailored to their unique needs as reflected in their individualized education programs (IEPs). Most recently reauthorized in 2004, this comprehensive law, now known as the Individuals with Disabilities Education Act (IDEA), drastically altered the continuum of programs that states, through local school board officials, must provide to students with disabilities. Over the years, the IDEA and its regulations have generated more litigation than any other educational legislation in the history of American public schools. Moreover, the IDEA and its regulations created a web of legal obligations about which educators constantly need to be updated.

Since the last edition of this book was published in 2007, federal and state courts have resolved well over 900 cases in disputes involving special education. While the majority of these judgments are consistent with prior case law, many deal with new issues or matters specific to the 2004 IDEA amendments. In the third edition, we have added discussions based on the cases that have broken new ground. Further, we have updated our discussions of other issues to include specific citations to more recent, and arguably more relevant, case law. We have updated the "Frequently Asked Questions" and "Recommendations" sections of each chapter to reflect changes in case law.

Past editions included a chapter on procedural issues that included a section on parental rights. We separated out this section and incorporated it as part of a new chapter on student and parent rights. We have also added a new chapter on the rights of students with disabilities under Section 504 of the Rehabilitation Act and the Americans with Disabilities Act. This chapter includes a discussion on the U.S. Department of Education's 2013 guidance on providing access to athletic programs for students with disabilities.

Given the far-reaching scope of the IDEA and its regulations, this edition examines how federal and state courts continue to interpret the statute and its regulations, addressing the delivery of special education and related services to students with disabilities. The book is organized around the major procedural and substantive issues in special education law. Specifically, the book examines the substantive and procedural requirements that the IDEA, its regulations, and litigation have placed on school officials. Among the major topics that this book addresses are the rights of students with disabilities to a FAPE, procedural due process, proper placement, the receipt of related services, discipline, and remedies if school officials fail to adhere to the IDEA. In addition, the book traces the legal history of special education while briefly discussing other statutes that affect the delivery of special education services.

This book is not by any means intended to replace the advice and counsel of school board attorneys. Rather, this book is designed to help make school officials, especially at the building level, more aware of the requirements of the laws governing special education, in the hope that doing so will put them in a better position to implement the myriad legal requirements. Still, we caution readers always to consult their school board attorneys when difficult situations arise.

Chapter 1 provides a historical perspective on the special education movement. It begins with an overview of the various sources of law in order to place the rest of the book in its proper legal context. The chapter then discusses the forces that led to the development of special education legislation in the United States and goes on to review the various laws that currently affect the delivery of special education services and the rights of children with disabilities.

The second chapter presents information about the rights of students to receive special education and related services. The chapter reviews information on who is eligible to receive services, along with the legal requirements for providing a FAPE in the least restrictive environment. The chapter next discusses the components of a FAPE and the factors that IEP teams must consider when making placements. The chapter adds discussions about when school boards must provide private day school and residential school programs and when extended school year programs are warranted.

Students with disabilities are entitled to receive related, or supportive, services to the extent that these services are necessary for them to benefit from their special education programs. Chapter 3 offers detailed information concerning the supportive services that qualify as related services and the circumstances under which they must be provided. Further, the chapter examines issues surrounding assistive technology and transition services.

The IDEA gives parents and students very specific rights throughout the entire process. Addressing these, the fourth chapter examines issues such as the IDEA's notification and consent requirements as well as parental rights regarding the development of IEPs for their children. The chapter also explores the rights of noncustodial parents and of students when they reach the age of majority while including a detailed section on the law regarding educational records.

One of the IDEA's unique features is its elaborate due process safeguards. These safeguards are designed to ensure that students with disabilities receive the FAPE that they are guaranteed by the law. The fifth chapter outlines the procedural steps that educators must follow to properly identify, assess, and place children with disabilities. Moreover, the chapter discusses the responsibilities of educators in the development of IEPs and the procedures they must follow when changing student placements.

Unfortunately, since students with disabilities, like their peers without disabilities, sometimes misbehave, they are not immune to being disciplined. Nonetheless, the disciplinary sanctions meted out must not deprive students with disabilities of the FAPE they are guaranteed by the IDEA. Chapter 6 discusses the special procedures that school officials must adhere to when disciplining special education students.

When Congress enacted the IDEA, it envisioned a system whereby school officials and parents would work together to plan and develop students' IEPs. However, insofar as Congress was not naïve and realized that disputes would arise, it included procedures in the statute relating to dispute resolution. These procedures are reviewed in Chapter 7.

Parents have recourse when school board officials fail to provide the FAPEs mandated by the IDEA. Since the enactment of the IDEA, the courts have provided parents with compensatory remedies in addition to prospective relief. Chapter 8 outlines the remedies available to parents when their school boards fail to live up to their responsibilities. This chapter includes information about awards of tuition reimbursement, compensatory educational services, and attorney fees, plus a general discussion of punitive damages.

The new Chapter 9 presents information on Section 504 and the Americans with Disabilities Act, two civil rights statutes that prohibit discrimination against individuals with disabilities. Like the content of the other chapters, this material analyzes the statutes, their regulations, and case law. The topics include providing reasonable accommodations to students with disabilities, testing and evaluation considerations, participation in sports and extracurricular activities, and antidiscrimination provisions of these laws.

Rounding out the book, Chapter 10 briefly reflects on practical issues in dealing with the legal system. Most notably, this chapter reviews the subject of preventative law and dispute resolution. Further, the chapter offers insights for school officials about the value of having a good attorney who is knowledgeable about special education and about how to locate such a professional.

The book includes a brief glossary of terms that are neither defined nor explained in the text. Rather, the glossary is designed to define the legal terms with which the reader may be unfamiliar. During the past few decades, terminology in special education has changed. Much of the old terminology today may be considered politically incorrect. This has provided us with a challenge in that older court decisions used the terminology that was prevalent at the time the decisions were made. Rather than translate those terms ourselves, and risk misinterpretation, in many instances we have chosen to describe students as they were labeled in the original court documents. We ask readers to understand that the terminology is that of the courts and not ours. Finally, we list Internet resources at the end of the book, including websites of state departments of education, special education services, and education law in the hope that these will be useful to readers.

Acknowledgments

We could not have written or revised a book of this magnitude without the support, encouragement, and assistance of many friends, colleagues, and family members. Thus, while it may be almost impossible to acknowledge all who have in some way influenced us and so contributed to this book, we would at least like to extend our gratitude to those who have had the greatest impact in our lives. This group includes all who have contributed to our knowledge and understanding of the subject matter of this book, most notably our many friends and colleagues who are members of the Education Law Association. These professionals have not only consistently shared their knowledge with us but also, more important, provided constructive criticism and constantly challenged our thinking.

We are also most fortunate to have worked with a group of professionals who understand the importance of our work and provide us with the resources to continue our research. The contributions of many colleagues and former colleagues from the Quincy Public Schools and the University of Dayton can never be adequately acknowledged.

I (Allan Osborne) wish to thank all of the administrators and teachers in the Quincy Public Schools with whom I had the pleasure of working for 24 years. I would especially like to extend a very warm thank you to the faculty, parents, and students of the Snug Harbor Community School in Quincy, Massachusetts, for their support during my tenure there. I wish to thank two good friends and colleagues: Dennis Carini, for providing me with advice, motivation, and many light moments when they were most needed; and the late Carol Shiffer, who, by example, taught me to face illness bravely.

I also wish to thank my friend and former doctoral mentor, Dr. Phil DiMattia of Boston College, for first encouraging me to investigate many of the issues addressed in this book and for continuing to challenge my thinking.

Finally, a very special thank you to Dr. Edwin Alyea of the Dana-Farber Cancer Institute and Dr. Timothy Ernst and Melissa Hopp-Woolwine of Charles River Oncology for keeping me healthy during these past five years.

At the University of Dayton, I (Charlie Russo) would like to express my thanks to Dr. Dave Dolph, Chair of the Department of Educational Leadership; Deans Kevin Kelly and Paul McGreal of the School of Education and Health Sciences and the School of Law, respectively, at the University of Dayton; and my colleague, Fr. Joseph Massucci, for their ongoing support and friendship. I also extend a special note of thanks to my assistant, Ms. Elizabeth Pearn, for her valuable assistance in helping us process the manuscript for publication.

I would like to extend my special thanks to two of my former professors and long-term friends from my student days at St. John's: Many thanks to the late Dr. David B. Evans, who, even while I was an undergraduate, taught me a great deal about the skills necessary to succeed in an academic career. I must also express my deep appreciation to my doctoral mentor and close friend, Dr. Zarif Bacilous, for helping me to complete my studies and enter the academy as he continues to offer his sage counsel.

We would both like to thank our acquisitions editor at Corwin, Arnis Burvikovs, and his predecessors, Robb Clouse and Lizzie Brenkus, for their support as we conceptualized and wrote all three editions of this book. It is a pleasure working with such outstanding professionals and their colleagues at Corwin. They certainly helped to make our jobs easier. Further, we would like to acknowledge the superb job of our copyeditor, Cate Huisman, in meticulously going over the manuscript and preparing it for publication. Special thanks is given to Emily Ferguson, University of Dayton School of Law class of 2015, for researching the websites listed in the resources at the end of the book.

On a more personal note, we both extend our appreciation to our parents, the late Allan G. and late Ruth L. Osborne along with the late Helen J. and late James J. Russo. We can never adequately express our gratitude to our parents but recognize the profound influence that they have had over us during the course of our lifetimes.

I (Charlie Russo) would like to extend a special note of thanks and appreciation to my two wonderful children, David Peter and Emily Rebecca. These two bright and inquisitive children, and their spouses, Li Hong Russo and Adriel Kong, respectively have grown to be wonderful young adults who provide me with a constant source of inspiration and love. We also appreciate watching our first grandchild James Robert, born to David and Li Hong, as he reaches milestones in his young life as a constant reminder that those of us who are educators have dedicated ourselves to the pursuit of improving schooling for all children.

Our wonderful wives, the two Debbies, have been the major influence in our lives and professional careers. Our best friends, our loving wives encourage us to write and have shown great patience as we ramble on endlessly about litigation in special education and other topics. We would not be able to do all that we do if it were not for their constant love and support. Thus, we dedicate this book to them with all of our love.

—*A.G.O.*

—*C.J.R.*

Publisher's Acknowledgments

Corwin would like to thank the following individuals for taking the time to provide their editorial insight and guidance:

Dr. Elizabeth Alvarez, Principal
Chicago Public Schools
Chicago, IL

Jo-Anne Goldberg, Director of Special Education
    and the Child Study Team
Mainland Regional High School
1301 Oak Avenue
Linwood, NJ

Diane P. Smith, School Counselor
Smethport Area School District
Smethport, PA

Dr. Karen L. Tichy, Associate Superintendent
    for Instruction and Special Education
Archdiocese of St. Louis
St. Louis, MO

About the Authors

Allan G. Osborne, Jr., Ed.D., is the former principal of the Snug Harbor Community School in Quincy, Massachusetts. Retired after 34 years as a special education teacher and school administrator, he currently spends his time writing and teaching graduate courses in school law and special education law and volunteering, along with his wife, at the Dana-Farber Cancer Institute in Boston. He received his doctorate in educational leadership from Boston College. Allan Osborne has authored or coauthored numerous articles, monographs, textbooks, and textbook chapters on special education law, along with textbooks on other aspects of special education. A past president of the Education Law Association (ELA) and recipient of the McGhehey Award for lifetime achievement in educational law, he has been a frequent presenter at ELA conferences and writes the "Students with Disabilities" chapter of the *Yearbook of Education Law,* which is published by ELA. Allan Osborne is on the editorial advisory committee of *West's Education Law Reporter* and is coeditor of the "Education Law Into Practice" section of that journal. He also serves as an editorial consultant for many other publications in education law, administration, and special education.

Charles J. Russo, J.D., Ed.D., the Joseph Panzer Chair in Education in the School of Education and Health Sciences and Director of the Ph.D. Program in Educational Leadership, as well as Adjunct Professor of Law in the School of Law at the University of Dayton, Ohio, earned his J.D. and Ed.D. at St. John's University in his native New York City. The 1998–1999 president of the Education Law Association and 2002 recipient of its McGhehey (Lifetime Achievement) Award, he is the author of more than 250 articles in peer-reviewed journals and the author, coauthor, editor, or coeditor of more than 50 books. He has been the editor of the *Yearbook of Education Law* for the Education Law

Association since 1995, has written or coauthored more than 900 publications, is the editor of two academic journals, and serves as a member of more than a dozen editorial boards. He has spoken and taught extensively on issues in education law in the United States and in 26 other nations on all six inhabited continents. In recognition of his work in education law in other countries, he received an honorary Ph.D. from Potchefstroom University, now the Potchefstroom Campus of North-West University, in Potchefstroom, South Africa, in May of 2004 and a Certificate of Achievement from the Australia & New Zealand Education Law Association in 2009.

Other Corwin Books by Allan G. Osborne, Jr. and Charles J. Russo

The Legal Rights and Responsibilities of Teachers: Issues of Employment and Instruction

Discipline in Special Education

Section 504 and the ADA

Essential Concepts and School-Based Cases in Special Education Law

Special Education Law

An Introduction

A major challenge facing educators today is addressing the educational needs of students with disabilities. Amazingly, though, school officials were not always concerned with the needs of children with special needs.

In fact, unlike today, until well into the 19th century, most public schools in the United States did virtually nothing to meet the educational needs of students with disabilities. Special schools and classes began to emerge for children who were visually and hearing impaired as well as for those with physical disabilities during the latter half of the 19th century; children who were considered to be retarded, or who had emotional problems and/or serious physical disabilities, were still largely ignored.

Even so, an almost 100-year-old opinion from the Supreme Court of Wisconsin is representative of attitudes of the time. In language that is unthinkable today, the court affirmed the exclusion of a student whose paralysis caused him to speak hesitatingly and drool uncontrollably even though he had the academic ability to benefit from school because "his physical condition and ailment produce[d] a depressing and nauseating effect upon the teachers and school children."[1]

During the late 19th and early 20th centuries, educational reformers developed classes for students who were, in the language used at the time, mentally retarded. Even so, these programs were segregated, typically offered little for children with physical disabilities, and were often taught by personnel who were insufficiently prepared for their jobs. Moreover, much of the progress that occurred in the early part of the century came grinding to a halt with the onset of the Great Depression in 1929. Fortunately, during the latter half, or more precisely, the final third, of the 20th century, American educational leaders, lawmakers, and others recognized the need to meet the educational needs of students with disabilities.

In light of the framework of statutes, regulations, and cases protecting the rights of students with disabilities and their parents, the first of the three sections in this chapter presents a brief overview of the American legal system by discussing the sources of law. Even though some might perceive this material as overly legal, this part of the chapter is designed to help readers who may be unfamiliar with the general principles of education law so that they may better understand both the rest of the book and the legal system that shapes special education. The second section briefly examines the history of the movement in pursuit of equal educational opportunities for students with disabilities, highlighting key cases that shaped legal developments in this area. The final part of the chapter offers an overview of major federal legislation safeguarding the educational rights of children with disabilities and their parents; this part of the chapter also acknowledges that the states have adopted similar laws.

Sources of Law

Simply put, the U.S. Constitution is the law of the land. As the primary source of American law, the Constitution provides the framework within which the entire legal system operates. To this end, all actions taken by the federal and state governments, including the creation of and amendments to state constitutions, which are supreme within their states as long as they do not contradict or limit rights protected under their federal counterpart, statutes, regulations, and common law, are subject to the Constitution as interpreted by the Supreme Court.

As important as education is, it is not mentioned in the Constitution. According to the Tenth Amendment, "The powers not delegated to the United States by the Constitution, nor prohibited by it to the States, are reserved to the States respectively, or to the people."[2] Therefore, education is primarily the concern of the states. The federal government can intervene in disputes arising under state law, as in *Brown v. Board of Education* (*Brown*),[3] where state action deprived individuals of rights protected under the Constitution. More precisely, in *Brown,* the Supreme Court struck down state-sanctioned racial segregation in public schools, because it violated the students' rights to equal protection under the Fourteenth Amendment by denying them equal educational opportunities. The Court was able to intervene in what was essentially a dispute under state law because once states create, and open, public schools, the Fourteenth Amendment dictates that they be made available to all children on an equal basis.

Along with delineating the rights and responsibilities of Americans, the Constitution establishes the three coequal branches of government that exist on both the federal and state levels. The legislative, executive, and judicial branches of government, in turn, give rise to the three other sources of law.

The legislative branch "makes the law." In other words, once a bill completes the legislative process, it is signed into law by a chief executive, who has the authority to enforce the new statute. Federal statutes are located in the United States Code (U.S.C.) or the United States Code Annotated (U.S.C.A.), the latter being a version that is particularly useful for attorneys and other individuals who work with the law, because it provides brief summaries of cases that have interpreted these statutes. This book cites the U.S.C. rather than the unofficial U.S.C.A., since the U.S.C. is the official source of federal statutes. The statutes are identical in both locations. State laws are identified by a variety of titles.

Keeping in mind that statutes provide broad directives, the executive branch "enforces" the law by providing details in the form of regulations. For example, a typical compulsory attendance law requires that "except as provided in this section, the parent of a child of compulsory school age shall cause such child to attend a school in the school district in which the child is entitled to attend school."[4] Insofar as statutes are typically silent on such matters as curricular content and the length of the school day, these elements are addressed by regulations that are developed by administrative personnel who are well versed in their areas of expertise. Given the extensiveness of regulations, it is safe to say that the professional lives of educators, especially in public schools, are more directly influenced by regulations than by statutes. Federal regulations are located in the Code of Federal Regulations (C.F.R.). State regulations are identified by a variety of titles.

From time to time the U.S. Department of Education, and particularly its Office of Special Education Programs, issues policy letters, typically in response to inquiries from state or local education officials, either to clarify regulations or to interpret what is required by federal law.[5] These letters are generally published in the Federal Register and are often reproduced by loose-leaf law-reporting services.

The third and final source of law is judge-made or common law. *Common law* refers to judicial interpretations of issues as judges "interpret the law" by examining issues that may have been overlooked in the legislative or regulatory process or that may not have been anticipated when statutes were enacted. In its landmark judgment in *Marbury v. Madison*,[6] the Supreme Court asserted its authority to review the actions of other branches of American government. While there is an occasional tension between the three branches of government, the legislative and executive branches generally defer to judicial review and interpretations of their actions.

Common law is rooted in the concept of precedent, the proposition that a majority ruling of the highest court in a given jurisdiction, or geographic area over which a court has authority, is binding on all lower courts within its jurisdiction. Put another way, a ruling of the Supreme Court is binding throughout the nation, while a decision of a state's highest court is binding only in that state. Persuasive precedent, a ruling from another jurisdiction, is actually not precedent. In other words, when a judge in Massachusetts, for instance, seeks to resolve a novel legal issue, the jurist would typically review precedent from other jurisdictions to determine whether it has been addressed elsewhere. However, since a court is not bound to follow precedent from a different jurisdiction, the advice from other jurisdictions remains persuasive in nature.

The federal courts and most state judicial systems have three levels: trial courts, intermediate appellate courts, and courts of last resort. In the federal system, trial courts are known as federal district courts; state trial courts employ a variety of names. Each state has at least one federal trial court, and some densely populated states, such as California and New York, have as many as four. Federal intermediate appellate courts are known as circuit courts of appeal; as discussed below, there are 13 circuit courts; state intermediate appellate courts employ a variety of names. The highest court of the land is the U.S. Supreme Court; while most states refer to their high courts as supreme courts, here, too, a variety of titles is in use.

Trial courts typically involve one judge and a jury. The role of the judge, as trier of law, is to apply the law by resolving such issues as the admissibility of evidence and proper instructions for juries on how to apply the law in the disputes under consideration. All federal judges are appointed for life based on the advice and consent of the U.S. Senate. State courts vary as judges are appointed in some jurisdictions and elected by popular vote in others.

Juries function as triers of fact, meaning that they must weigh the evidence, decide what happened, and render verdicts based on the evidence presented at trial. As triers of fact in special education cases, juries (or, in nonjury trials, judges) review the records of administrative, or due process, hearings and additional evidence, and hear the testimony of witnesses. In a distinction with a significant difference, parties who lose civil suits are rendered *liable*, while those who are found to be at fault in criminal trials, a matter well beyond the scope of this book, are described as *guilty*.

Other than in a few select areas, such as constitutional issues and special education, which is governed by the Individuals with Disabilities Education Act (IDEA),[7] few school-related cases are directly under the jurisdiction of the federal courts. Before disputes can proceed to federal courts, cases must generally satisfy one of two broad categories. First, cases must involve diversity of citizenship, namely that the plaintiff and defendant are from two different jurisdictions, and the amount in controversy must be at least $75,000; this latter requirement is imposed because of the high costs associated with operating the federal court system.[8] Second, disputes must involve a federal question, meaning that cases must be over the interpretation of the U.S. Constitution, federal statutes, federal regulations, or federal crimes.

The party that is not satisfied with the outcome of a trial court ordinarily has the right to seek discretionary review from an intermediate appellate court. Figure 1.1 illustrates the locations of the 13 federal judicial circuits in the United States. Under this arrangement, which is designed, in part, for administrative ease and convenience in the sense that parties should not have to travel too far when contesting their cases, each circuit is composed of a number of states. By way of illustration, the Sixth Circuit consists of Michigan, Ohio, Kentucky, and Tennessee.

Figure 1.1 Federal Circuit Courts of Appeal

State courts with three-tiered systems most often refer to this intermediate appellate level as a court of appeals. Intermediate appellate courts typically consist of three judges and ordinarily review cases for errors in the record of a trial court. This means that appellate panels usually inquire into such matters as whether a trial court judge properly admitted or excluded evidence from trial. Appellate courts generally prefer to examine issues of law, leaving them undisturbed unless they are clearly erroneous, and ordinarily do not review the facts unless there are strong reasons to do so.

A party not satisfied with the ruling of an intermediate appellate court may seek further discretionary review from the high court in the jurisdiction. In order for a case to reach the U.S. Supreme Court, a party must file a petition seeking a writ of *certiorari* (literally, to be informed). In order to be granted a writ of *certiorari,* at least four of the Court's nine Justices must agree to hear an appeal. Insofar as the Court receives in excess of 7,000 petitions per year and takes, on average, fewer than 100 cases, it should be clear that the Supreme Court will accept relatively few disputes. A denial of a writ of *certiorari* is of no precedential value and merely has the effect of leaving a lower court's decision unchanged. It is generally easier for discretionary appeals in state judicial systems to reach their courts of last resort, typically composed of five, seven, or nine members, especially where state law is at issue.

Opinions of the Supreme Court can be located in a variety of sources. The official version of Supreme Court opinions is the United States Reports (abbreviated to U.S. in legal citations). The same text, with additional research aids, is located in the Supreme Court Reporter (S. Ct.) and the Lawyer's Edition, now in its second series (L. Ed. 2d). Federal appellate cases are found in the Federal Reporter, now in its third series (F.3d) while federal trial court rulings are in the Federal Supplement, now in its second series (F. Supp. 2d). Some cases decided by the federal appellate courts are published in the Federal Appendix (F. App'x). However, these cases have not been released by the courts for official publication and so are not considered to be precedent setting. Even so, these opinions can be instructional as persuasive precedent. State cases are published in a variety of publications, most notably in West's National Reporter system, which breaks the country up into seven regions: Atlantic, North Eastern, North Western, Pacific, South Eastern, South Western, and Southern.

Prior to being published in bound volumes, most cases are available in so-called slip opinions, from a variety of loose-leaf services, and from electronic sources. Statutes and regulations are also available in similar readily accessible formats. Legal materials are also available online from a variety of sources, most notably Westlaw and LexisNexis. State laws and regulations are generally available online from each state. (See the list of state websites in Resource B at the end of the book.)

Legal citations are easy to read. The first number in a citation is the volume number where a case, statute, or regulation is located; the abbreviation refers to the book or series in which the material may be found; the second number indicates the page on which a case begins or the section number of a statute or regulation; the last part of a citation includes the name of the court, for lower court cases, and the year in which the dispute was resolved. For example, the citation for *Board of Education of the Hendrick Hudson Central School District v. Rowley*, 458 U.S. 176 (1982), the first Supreme Court case involving special education, reveals that it can be found on page 176 of volume 458 of the United States Reports. The earlier case between the parties, *Rowley v. Board of Education of the Hendrick Hudson Central School District*, 632 F.2d 945 (2d Cir. 1980), which was decided by the Second Circuit in 1980, begins on page 945 of volume 632 in the Federal Reporter, second series. Similarly, the Individuals with Disabilities Education Act (IDEA), 20 U.S.C. § 1400 *et seq.* (2012) can be found starting in section 1400 of Title 20 of the U.S. Code.

History of the Equal Educational Opportunity Movement

Prior to 1975, no federal statute obligated states to provide comprehensive special education programming for students with disabilities. Previously, some states enacted legislation offering special education services to students with disabilities, but these jurisdictions were in the minority. Before the enactment of these state laws, as discussed at the outset of this chapter, school boards routinely excluded students with disabilities. When such practices were challenged, the courts largely upheld the exclusionary practices but the status quo changed in the early 1970s. Yet, federal involvement in special education came only after a long battle by advocates for individuals with disabilities to gain equal rights and was spurred on as a direct result of the civil rights movement.

The impetus for ensuring equal educational opportunities for all American children can be traced to the Supreme Court's opinion in *Brown*.[9] Although equal access to education was resolved in the context of school desegregation, in *Brown* a unanimous Court set the tone for later developments, including those leading to protecting the rights of students with disabilities, in asserting that "education is perhaps the most important function of state and local governments."[10] The Court added that "in these days, it is doubtful that any child may reasonably be expected to succeed in life if he is denied the opportunity of an education. Such an opportunity, where the State has undertaken to provide it, is a right that must be made available to all on equal terms."[11] The language of *Brown* has often been either quoted directly or paraphrased by innumerable other courts in cases where parties sought equal educational opportunities for students with disabilities.

> Education is perhaps the most important function of state and local governments. . . . In these days, it is doubtful that any child may reasonably be expected to succeed in life if he is denied the opportunity of an education. (*Brown v. Board of Education*, 347 U.S. 483 (1954), p. 493)

Unfortunately, immediately following *Brown* the rights of individuals with disabilities continued to be overlooked. Throughout the 1950s, more than half of the states had laws calling for the sterilization of individuals with disabilities, while other jurisdictions limited their basic rights, such as voting, marrying, and obtaining drivers' licenses. By the 1960s, the percentage of children with disabilities who were served in public schools began to rise; while 12% of the students in public schools in 1948 had disabilities, the number of students with disabilities increased to 21% by 1963 and to 38% by 1968.[12] As of July 1, 1974, the federal Bureau for the Education of the Handicapped reported that about 78.5% of America's 8,150,000 children with disabilities received some form of public education. Of these students, 47.8% received special education and related services, 30.7% received no related services, and the remaining 21.5% received no educational services at all.[13]

A major push for the development of special education came as a result of judicial actions that set the stage for statutory developments. Rather than trace the full history of this litigation, this brief review focuses on arguably the two most significant cases that contributed to developments aimed at protecting the rights of students with disabilities. These disputes, although decided in trial courts, are considered landmark cases because they provided the impetus for Congress to pass sweeping legislation safeguarding the rights of students with disabilities, regardless of the severity or nature of their conditions.

Pennsylvania Association for Retarded Children v. Pennsylvania (*PARC*)[14] helped to establish the conceptual bases for what developed into the IDEA. In *PARC*, advocates filed suit in a federal trial court against the Commonwealth of Pennsylvania on behalf of all individuals who were considered mentally retarded and who were between the ages of 6 and 21 and were excluded from the public schools. Commonwealth officials sought to justify the exclusions by relying on four statutes that relieved local school boards of any obligation to educate children whom school psychologists certified as uneducable and untrainable, allowed officials to postpone the admission to children who had not attained a mental age of five years, excused children from compulsory attendance if they were found unable to profit from education, and defined compulsory school age as 8 to 17 (but used these limits to exclude children who were considered mentally retarded but were not between those ages). The plaintiffs challenged the constitutionality of the statutes seeking to enjoin their enforcement.

PARC was resolved via a consent decree, meaning that the parties essentially reached a settlement on their own that the court later approved. Pursuant to the decree, no children who were classified as mentally retarded, or who were thought to have been mentally retarded, could be assigned to or excluded from special education programs without due process. This meant that placements in regular school classrooms were preferable to ones in more restrictive settings for children with disabilities and that these children could neither be denied admission to public schools nor be subjected to changes in educational placements unless they, through their parents, received procedural due process. The court added not only that all children can learn in school settings but also that officials in Pennsylvania were obligated to provide each student who was considered mentally retarded with a free appropriate public education along with training programs appropriate to their capacities.

Similarly, in *Mills v. Board of Education of the District of Columbia* (*Mills*),[15] the parents of seven named exceptional children filed a class action suit in a federal trial court on behalf of perhaps as many as 18,000 students with disabilities who were not receiving programs of specialized education. Most of the children, who were minorities, were classified as having behavior problems or being mentally retarded, emotionally disturbed, and/or hyperactive. The plaintiffs sought a declaration of their rights and an order directing the school board to provide a publicly supported education to all students with disabilities. The court rejected the board's claims that insofar as it lacked the resources for all of its students, it could deny services to children with disabilities.

Unlike *PARC*, which was a consent decree, *Mills* was a decision on the record, meaning that the court reached its judgment after a trial on the merits of the dispute. The court found that the U.S. Constitution, coupled with the District of Columbia Code and its own regulations, required school officials to provide a publicly supported education to all children, including those with disabilities. The court ruled that the school board had to expend its funds equitably so that all students would receive an education consistent with their needs and abilities. If sufficient funds were not available, the court directed officials to distribute existing resources in such a manner that no child would have been entirely excluded and the inadequacies would not have been allowed to bear more heavily on one class of students. In addition, the court ordered the board to provide due process safeguards before any children were excluded from the public schools, were reassigned, or had their special education services terminated.

At the same time, the *Mills* court outlined elaborate due process procedures that helped to form the foundation for the due process safeguards that were included in the IDEA. Since *Mills* originated in Washington, D.C., it was likely among the more significant influences moving federal lawmakers to act to ensure adequate protection for children with disabilities when they adopted Section 504 of the Rehabilitation Act of 1973 and the IDEA.

In light of legal developments following *PARC* and *Mills,* the remainder of this book reviews major developments designed to safeguard the education rights of children with disabilities. In the wake of the literally thousands of suits that have been filed in federal and state courts, the chapters review selected cases under appropriate headings throughout the book rather than as separate entries.

Legislative Mandates

Special education in the United States is governed by four major federal statutes—the IDEA,[16] Section 504 of the Rehabilitation Act (Section 504),[17] the Americans with Disabilities Act (ADA),[18] and the No Child Left Behind Act (NCLB)[19]—and numerous state laws. The federal laws are summarized in Table 1.1. After highlighting key features of the IDEA, this chapter provides an overview of Section 504 before taking a brief look at the ADA and NCLB. The remainder of the book, other than Chapter 9, which examines key provisions of Section 504 and the ADA, focuses on the IDEA, paying particular attention to its application by school administrators.

Individuals with Disabilities Education Act

Most of the remainder of this book focuses on the IDEA. Accordingly, this section serves as a brief overview of this comprehensive statute. In 1975 Congress enacted Public Law (P.L.) 94–142, the 142nd piece of legislation introduced during the 94th Congress, formerly known as the Education for All Handicapped Children Act. Following its initial revision in 1986, in 1990 Congress further amended this landmark statute, renaming it the Individuals with Disabilities Education Act (IDEA). The IDEA underwent additional major changes in 1997. Most recently, President George W. Bush signed the Individuals with Disabilities Education Improvement Act of 2004 into law; it became fully effective on July 1, 2005. For the sake of clarity, this book refers to the IDEA by this title throughout.

Section 504 has fairly broad standards, but the IDEA does not; in order to qualify for services under the IDEA, children with disabilities must meet four statutory requirements. First, children must be between the ages of 3 and 21.[20] Second, children must have specifically identified disabilities.[21] Third, children must be in need of special education, and fourth, in need of related services when necessary to benefit from their special education.[22] The criterion that children must be in need of special education means that they require specially designed instruction to receive a free appropriate public education (FAPE)[23] in the least restrictive environment (LRE)[24] conforming to individualized education programs (IEPs).[25] Even though the IDEA includes related services,[26] defined as "developmental, corrective, and other supportive services,"[27] as part of its definition of a FAPE, students do not have to need related services to qualify under the statute. Rather, related services are provided in conjunction with special education to assist students in receiving educational benefit from their programs, but not all students covered by the IDEA need or receive related services.[28]

The IDEA includes an elaborate system of procedural safeguards to protect the rights of children with disabilities and their parents.[29] The IDEA requires school officials to provide written notice and obtain parental consent prior to evaluating children,[30] making initial placements, or initiating changes in placements.[31] Moreover, the parents of children with disabilities must be afforded opportunities to participate in the development of the IEPs for and placement of their children.[32] Once placed, the status of all children must be reviewed at least annually[33] and reevaluated at least once every three years unless their parents and local school officials agree that reevaluations are unnecessary.[34] Further, the IDEA includes provisions, supplemented by the Family Educational Rights and Privacy Act[35] and its regulations,[36] as well as the IDEA's own regulations,[37] preserving the confidentiality of all information used in the evaluation, placement, and education of students.

Table 1.1   The IDEA and Its Amendments

Year	Public Law	Statute	Title
1970	91–230	84 Stat. 175	Education of the Handicapped Act
1974	93–380	88 Stat. 580	Education Amendments of 1974
1975	94–142	89 Stat. 773	Education of All Handicapped Children Act
1986	99–372	100 Stat. 796	Handicapped Children's Protection Act of 1986
1986	99–457	100 Stat. 1145	Education of the Handicapped Amendments of 1986
1990	101–476	104 Stat. 1103	Individuals with Disabilities Education Act
1997	105–17	111 Stat. 37	Individuals with Disabilities Education Act Amendments of 1997
2004	108–446	118 Stat. 2647	Individuals with Disabilities Education Improvement Act of 2004

Section 504 of the Rehabilitation Act of 1973

The Rehabilitation Act of 1973, which traces its origins back to 1918, a time when the American government sought to provide rehabilitation services for military veterans of World War I, was the first federal civil rights law protecting the rights of individuals with disabilities.[38] Pursuant to Section 504,

> No otherwise qualified individual with a disability in the United States . . . shall, solely by reason of her or his disability, be excluded from the participation in, be denied the benefits of, or be subjected to discrimination under any program or activity receiving [f]ederal financial assistance.[39]

Section 504, which is predicated on an institution's receipt of "federal financial assistance," applies to virtually all schools, because this term is interpreted so expansively[40] and offers broad-based protection to individuals under the more amorphous concept of impairment rather than disability. It is important to keep in mind that even though Section 504 covers children, employees, and others who may visit schools, this book focuses on the rights of students. Section 504 defines an individual with a disability as one "who (i) has a physical or mental impairment which substantially limits one or more of such person's major life activities, (ii) has a record of such an impairment, or (iii) is regarded as having such an impairment."[41] The regulations define physical or mental impairments as including

> (A) any physiological disorder or condition, cosmetic disfigurement, or anatomical loss affecting one or more of the following body systems: neurological; musculoskeletal; special sense organs; respiratory, including speech organs; cardiovascular; reproductive, digestive, genito-urinary; hemic and lymphatic; skin; and endocrine; or

> (B) any mental or psychological disorder, such as mental retardation, organic brain syndrome, emotional or mental illness, and specific learning disorders.[42]

A note accompanying this list indicates that it merely provides examples of the types of impairments that are covered; it is not meant to be exhaustive.

In order to have a record of impairment, individuals must have a history of, or been identified as having, a mental or physical impairment that substantially limits one or more major life activities. As defined in one of Section 504's regulations, individuals who are regarded as having impairment are those who have

(A) a physical or mental impairment that does not substantially limit major life activities but that is treated by a recipient as constituting such a limitation; (B) a physical or mental impairment that substantially limits major life activities only as a result of the attitudes of others toward such impairment; or (C) none of the impairments . . . but is treated by a recipient as having such an impairment.[43]

"'Major life activities' means functions such as caring for one's self, performing manual tasks, walking, seeing, hearing, speaking, breathing, learning, and working."[44] Once students are identified as having impairments, the next step is to evaluate whether they are "otherwise qualified." In order to be "otherwise qualified" under Section 504, as the term is applied to students, children must be "(i) of an age during which non-handicapped persons are provided such services, (ii) of any age during which it is mandatory under state law to provide such services to handicapped persons, or (iii) [a student] to whom a state is required to provide a free appropriate public education [under the IDEA]."[45] Students who are "otherwise qualified," meaning that they are eligible to participate in programs or activities despite the existence of their impairments, must be permitted to take part as long as it is possible to do so by means of "reasonable accommodation[s]."[46]

Once identified, qualified students are entitled to appropriate public educations, regardless of the nature or severity of their impairments. In order to guarantee that school officials make appropriate educations available to all children, Section 504's regulations include due process requirements for the evaluation and placement of students that are similar to, but not nearly as detailed as, those under the IDEA.[47]

In making modifications for students, educators must provide aid, benefits, and/or services that are comparable to those available to children who do not have impairments. Qualified students must thus receive comparable materials, teacher quality, length of school term, and daily hours of instruction. Moreover, programs for qualified children should not be separate from those available to students who are not impaired unless such segregation is necessary for their educational programming to be effective. While school officials are not prohibited from offering separate programs for students who have impairments, these children cannot be required to attend such classes unless they cannot be served adequately in settings with their peers.[48] If separate programs are offered, facilities must, of course, be comparable.[49]

Reasonable accommodations may involve minor adjustments such as permitting a child to be accompanied by a service dog,[50] modifying a behavior policy to accommodate a student with an autoimmune disease who was disruptive,[51] or providing a hearing interpreter.[52] On the other hand, school officials do not have to grant all requests for accommodations.

For example, in addition to the cases discussed below under the defenses to Section 504, a federal trial court in Missouri ruled that school officials did not have to maintain a "scent-free" environment for a child with severe asthma because she was not otherwise qualified to participate in its educational program.[53]

Examples of academic modifications include permitting children longer periods of time to complete examinations or assignments, using peer tutors, distributing outlines in advance, permitting children to obtain copies of notes from peers, employing specialized curricular materials, and/or permitting students to use laptop computers to record answers on examinations. In modifying facilities, school officials do not have to make all classrooms and/or areas of buildings accessible; it may be enough to bring services to children, such as offering a keyboard for musical instruction in an accessible classroom rather than revamping an entire music room for a student who wishes to take piano classes.

In a related concern, Section 504's only regulation directly addressing private schools declares that institutional officials may not exclude students on the basis of their conditions if the children can, with minor adjustments, be provided with appropriate educations.[54] Additionally, this regulation dictates that private schools "may not charge more for the provision of an appropriate education to handicapped persons than to nonhandicapped persons except to the extent that any additional charge is justified by a substantial increase in cost to the recipient."[55] Therefore, private school officials may be able to charge additional costs to parents of children with impairments.

Even if children appear to be "otherwise qualified" school officials can rely on one of three defenses to avoid being charged with noncompliance with Section 504, as described below. This represents a major difference between Section 504 and the IDEA, since no such defenses are applicable under the latter. Another major difference between the laws is that the federal government provides public schools with direct federal financial assistance to help fund programs under the IDEA but offers no financial incentives to aid institutions, public and nonpublic, as they seek to comply with the dictates of Section 504.

The first defense under Section 504 is that school officials can be excused from making accommodations that result in "a fundamental alteration in the nature of [a] program."[56] The second defense permits educational officials to avoid compliance if a modification imposes an "undue financial burden"[57] on institutions or entities as a whole. The third defense is that otherwise qualified students with disabilities can be excluded from programs if their presence creates a substantial risk of injury to themselves or others.[58] For example, a child with a severe visual impairment could be excluded from using a scalpel in a biology laboratory. However, in order to comply with Section 504, school officials would likely have to offer a reasonable accommodation, such as providing a computer-assisted program to achieve an instructional goal similar to the one that would have been achieved in a laboratory class.

Finally, Section 504, which is enforced by the Office of Civil Rights, requires recipients of federal financial aid to file annual assurances of compliance; provide notice to students and their parents that their programs are nondiscriminatory; engage in remedial actions where violations are proven; take voluntary steps to overcome the effects of conditions that resulted in limiting the participation of students with disabilities in their programs; conduct self-evaluations; designate staff members, typically at the central office level, as compliance coordinators; and adopt grievance procedures.[59]

Admissions Evaluations

Some public (and many nonpublic) schools may require students with disabilities to take admissions examinations and/or be interviewed prior to acceptance or placement in order to evaluate whether these applicants are otherwise qualified; provisions in Section 504 address this situation. The regulations cover four areas: preplacement evaluations, evaluations, placements, and reevaluations.[60]

As to preplacement evaluations, the regulations require school officials to evaluate all children who, because of their conditions, need or are believed to need special education or related services. Educators must complete these evaluations before taking any actions with respect to the initial placements of children in regular or special education as well as before any subsequent significant changes in placements.

The evaluation provisions in Section 504's regulations require school officials to follow procedures similar to those under the IDEA. More specifically, officials must validate tests and other evaluation materials for the specific purposes for which they are to be used, and the tests must be administered by trained personnel in conformance with the instructions provided by their publishers. Officials must tailor these materials to assess specific areas of educational need and cannot use materials designed to provide a single general intelligence quotient. Also, officials must select and administer these materials in ways to best ensure that when tests are administered to students with impaired sensory, manual, or speaking skills, the results accurately reflect the students' aptitude or achievement level or whatever other factor the test purports to measure, rather than reflecting their impaired sensory, manual, or speaking skills, except where those skills are the factors that the tests purport to measure.

When educators apply placement procedures to students under Section 504, their interpretations of data must consider information from a variety of sources, including the students' aptitude and achievement test scores, teacher recommendations, physical conditions, social and cultural backgrounds, and adaptive behaviors that have been documented and carefully considered. In addition, not only must any such decisions be made by groups of persons, including individuals who are knowledgeable, but all children must be periodically reevaluated in a manner consistent with the dictates of the IDEA.

Under Section 504, officials in schools with policies relying on examinations or interviews may be required to provide reasonable accommodations to applicants who are impaired. While school officials are not required to alter the content of examinations or interviews, they may have to make accommodations in how tests are administered or interviews are conducted. In other words, officials would not be required to make examinations easier so that students who simply lacked the requisite knowledge could pass them, but would have to alter the conditions under which the tests were administered, or interviews were conducted, so that students with impairments with the requisite knowledge and skills to pass or express themselves fully could do so despite their conditions.

The accommodations that educators provide for examinations may be as simple as providing quiet rooms without distractions, essentially private rooms away from others, for students who suffer from attention deficit hyperactivity disorder, or procuring the services of readers or Braille versions of examinations for applicants who are blind. Moreover, students with physical impairments may require special seating arrangements, scribes to record answers to questions, and/or computers to record answers on examinations.

In like manner, whether as part of examinations or admissions interviews, students who are hearing impaired might be entitled to the services of sign language interpreters to communicate directions that are normally given orally. At the same time, school officials may be required to provide students with learning disabilities with extra time to complete examinations or make computers available to children who are more comfortable with computers than with traditional paper-and-pencil tests.

Prior to receiving accommodations, students must prove that they have needs for accommodations, such as learning disabilities[61] that necessitate their taking additional time to complete examinations. The purpose of providing the extra time is to allow students who might have difficulty processing information sufficient opportunity to show that they are capable of answering the questions.

Unlike the IDEA, which imposes an affirmative obligation on school officials to identify, assess, and serve children with disabilities, under Section 504, students, and/or their parents, are responsible for making school officials aware of their impairments and need for accommodations for such activities as testing or interviewing. Accordingly, administrators can request proof that students have impairments in need of accommodations in order for the students to demonstrate knowledge and skills on examinations. In such situations, students, through their parents, should suggest which accommodations would be most appropriate. In considering whether students are entitled to accommodations, officials must make individualized inquiries. School officials would violate Section 504 if they refused to make testing accommodations or made modifications only for students with certain specified disabilities.

Section 504 Service Plans

As noted, students who qualify under Section 504 are entitled to reasonable accommodations allowing them to access school programs. Making accommodations may involve alterations to physical plants, such as building wheelchair ramps or removing architectural barriers, so that students may physically enter and get around school buildings. School officials may be required, under some circumstances, to provide accommodations such as allowing students to bring service animals into classrooms,[62] but officials are not required to provide accommodations going beyond what can be considered to be reasonable. To this end, school officials are not required to make accommodations that are excessively expensive, that expose staff members to excessive risk, or that require them to make substantial modifications to the missions or purposes of their programs.

In another departure from the IDEA, neither Section 504 nor its regulations mandate the creation of written agreements with regard to student accommodations or specify the content of such documents. Even so, school officials in many districts meet with parents to formalize the accommodations and services that they provide to eligible students. These written agreements are euphemistically referred to as Section 504 service plans. In practical terms, school officials should be sure to include the following components in each written Section 504 service plan:

- **Demographic Data**—the student's name, date of birth, school identification number, grade, schools attended, teacher, names of parents or guardians, addresses, telephone numbers, and the like
- **Team Members**—a listing of all team members who contributed to the development of the service plan and their respective roles
- **Impairment**—a detailed description of the student's impairment and its severity, along with an explanation of how it impedes the student's educational progress
- **Accommodations and Services**—a detailed description of the accommodations and services to be offered under the plan, including the frequency of services, where they are to be provided, and by whom they are to be provided

In addition, officials should attach the evaluative reports or assessments that helped to determine the nature of the student's impairment and the need for accommodations and services.

Americans with Disabilities Act

Patterned largely after Section 504 of the Rehabilitation Act, the Americans with Disabilities Act,[63] enacted in 1990, protects individuals with disabilities by imposing far-reaching obligations on private sector employers, public services and accommodations, and transportation. As indicated in its preamble, the purpose of the ADA is "to provide a clear and comprehensive national mandate for the elimination of discrimination against individuals with disabilities."[64] This clarifies that the ADA intends to extend the protections afforded by Section 504 to private programs and activities that are not covered by Section 504 because they do not receive federal funds.

The ADA provides a comprehensive federal mandate to eliminate discrimination against people with disabilities and to provide "clear, strong, consistent and enforceable standards"[65] to help accomplish this goal. The ADA's broad definition of a disability is comparable with the one in Section 504: "(a) a physical or mental impairment that substantially limits one or more of the major life activities; (b) a record of such an impairment; or (c) being regarded as having such an impairment."[66] As with Section 504, "major life activities" include caring for oneself, hearing, walking, speaking, seeing, breathing, and learning. The ADA, like Section 504, does not require individuals to have certificates from doctors or psychologists in order to be covered by its provisions.

The ADA specifically excludes a variety of individuals, of whom few are likely to be students but some may be school employees, most notably those who use illegal drugs.[67] The ADA specifically excludes transvestites;[68] homosexuals and bisexuals;[69] transsexuals, pedophiles, exhibitionists, voyeurs, and those with sexual behavior disorders;[70] and those with conditions such as psychoactive substance use disorders stemming from current illegal use of drugs.[71] Further, the ADA modifies Section 504 since it covers individuals who are no longer engaged in illegal drug use, including those who have successfully completed drug treatment or have otherwise been rehabilitated and those who have been "erroneously" regarded as being drug users.[72] The ADA permits drug testing by employers to ensure that workers are complying with the Drug-Free Workplace Act of 1988.[73] Although it permits employers to prohibit the use of illegal drugs or alcohol in the workplace, the ADA is less clear over the status of alcoholics, as it appears that the protections afforded rehabilitated drug users extend to recovering alcoholics.

There are five major Titles in the ADA. Title I, which addresses employment in the private sector, is directly applicable to private schools. Like Section 504, this Title requires school officials to make reasonable accommodations for otherwise qualified individuals once administrators are aware of individuals' conditions; this means that in order to be covered by the ADA, students and staff need to inform education officials of their conditions and provide specific suggestions on how their needs can be met.

Title II of the ADA covers public services of state and local governments for both employers and providers of public services, including transportation, and most notably education, as part of the law applies to public schools. Since the reasonable accommodations specifications in these provisions imply academic program accommodations, they can be applied to permit qualified students with disabilities to participate in school activities.

Title III of the ADA, which expands the scope of Section 504, deals with public accommodations, covering both the private and public sectors. This Title includes private businesses and a wide array of community services, including buildings, transportation systems, parks, recreational facilities, hotels, and theaters.

Title IV of the ADA deals with telecommunications, specifically voice and nonvoice systems. Title V, the ADA's miscellaneous provisions, stipulates not only that the law cannot be construed as applying a lesser standard than that under Section 504 and its regulations but also that qualified individuals are not required to accept services that do not meet their needs. In addition, the ADA employs defenses that parallel those in Section 504.

The ADA's impact on schools is most significant in the areas of reasonable accommodations for employees and academic programs for students. Since schools are subject to many ADA-like regulations through the rules enacted pursuant to Section 504, officials can avoid difficulties with the ADA by keeping proactive policies and procedures in place to ensure reasonable accommodations. School boards should designate ADA compliance officers who keep up-to-date on current ADA regulations and policies in the areas of employment and academic inclusion. In sum, if board officials have faithfully implemented Section 504 and its regulations, in most instances they should not have difficulties with the ADA.

No Child Left Behind Act

Perhaps the most controversial federal education law in recent memory is the No Child Left Behind Act (NCLB),[74] enacted in 2002. The NCLB, which is actually an extension of the original Elementary and Secondary Education Act of 1965, has had an impact on the delivery of special education services.

The key elements in the NCLB are to improve the academic achievement of students who are economically disadvantaged; assist in preparing, training, and recruiting highly qualified teachers (and principals); provide improved language instruction for children of limited English proficiency; make school systems accountable for student achievement, particularly by imposing standards for annual yearly progress for students and districts; require school systems to rely on teaching methods that are research-based and that have been proven effective; and afford parents better choices while creating innovative educational programs, especially where local school systems are unresponsive to parents' needs.[75] As part of the process of complying with the IDEA and the NCLB, school officials must "take measurable steps to recruit, hire, train, and retain highly qualified school personnel to provide special education and related services"[76] for students with disabilities.

The IDEA and the NCLB are both similar and dissimilar. The laws are alike to the extent that both address the needs of students with disabilities, albeit in varying degrees, through state agencies and local school systems; focus on student achievement and outcomes; emphasize parental participation; and require the regular evaluation or assessment of students and staffs. On the other hand, the laws have some significant differences. The most important difference between the two statutes is that IDEA focuses on the performance of individual students in an array of areas, while the NCLB is more interested in systemwide outcomes.

One of the IDEA's most controversial additions, its definition of "highly qualified" teachers,[77] which also applies to related services personnel and paraprofessionals,[78] parallels the language of the NCLB. In order to be classified as "highly qualified," a standard based on state rather than federal law, subject area teachers in public schools must not only be certified fully in special education or pass state-designed special education licensure examinations, but must also possess bachelor's degrees and demonstrate knowledge of each subject for which they are the primary instructors.[79]

New special education teachers have up to two years after they are hired to become approved as "highly qualified" in different subjects as long as they are fully certificated in at least one. The IDEA adds that while teachers who meet its definition of highly qualified also qualify for this title under the NCLB,[80] the law does not create a private right of action permitting judicial enforcement to ensure that children are taught by such teachers.[81] Put another way, parents cannot file suits to ensure that their children are taught by teachers who meet the "highly qualified" standards under the IDEA and the NCLB. The IDEA's regulations specify that the requirements concerning how to be categorized as highly qualified are inapplicable to teachers in private schools.[82]

State Statutes

Insofar as education is a state function, special education is governed by state statutes as well as the federal laws discussed above. While each state's special education laws must be consistent with federal laws, differences do exist. Most jurisdictions have laws that are similar in scope, and even language, to the IDEA. However, some states have provisions in their legislation that go beyond the IDEA's substantive and procedural requirements, setting higher standards of what constitutes appropriate educations for students with disabilities. Further, most states have established procedures for implementing programs associated with special education that either are not explicitly covered by federal law or that have been left to the states' discretion, such as defining the qualifications and preparation of hearing officers. If, or when, conflicts develop between provisions of federal law and state laws, federal law is supreme.

A comprehensive discussion of the laws of each of the 50 states, the District of Columbia, and U.S. possessions and territories is beyond the scope of this book. Indeed, entire books could be written on the special education laws of each state. The purpose of this book is to provide information on the federal mandate, the law encompassing the entire nation. Educators are cautioned that they cannot have a complete understanding of special education law if they are not familiar with state law and so should seek out sources of information on pertinent state laws as supplements to this book.

FREQUENTLY ASKED QUESTIONS

Q: Why was the IDEA passed in the first place?

A: When the IDEA was initially passed in 1975, many states lacked statutes addressing the educational rights of students with disabilities. Congress found that many students with disabilities were excluded from public schools and that those who did attend did not always receive appropriate educations. Prior to the enactment of the IDEA, advocates for students with disabilities had won some significant judicial victories against states and school boards. The IDEA was passed, in part, in response to early litigation designed to provide services for students with disabilities while also providing them with equal educational opportunities.

Q: What is the difference between federal and state laws governing special education?

A: State statutes must, of course, be consistent with federal laws but can provide students with disabilities with additional rights and protections. If conflicts arise between state and federal laws, the latter govern under the supremacy clause of the U.S. Constitution. Therefore, it is important for school officials to be familiar with both federal and state laws designed to protect the educational rights of students with disabilities.

Q: Why are some students with disabilities covered only by Section 504 and not the IDEA?

A: According to the IDEA, in order to be eligible, students with disabilities must have specifically identifiable disabilities, be between the ages of 3 and 21, and need special education and related services as a result of their disabilities. Thus, if students have disabilities not requiring special education, they lack entitlements to the rights and protections of the IDEA. Even so, students who are otherwise qualified may be eligible for protections against

(Continued)

(Continued)

discrimination under Section 504 if their impairments impact their ability to be educated and their needs can be met through reasonable accommodations.

Q: What is the purpose of the IDEA's regulations?

A: The IDEA provides general guidelines explaining the services that state and local school boards must provide. The regulations, which are written by the U.S. Department of Education and subject to public comment, are more specific, reflecting the statute, and in many cases are identical to it in actual wording. Even so, the regulations typically provide more detailed step-by-step guidance on how the dictates of the IDEA, in a manner consistent with other statutes, are to be implemented.

Q: Why is it important to be familiar with the outcome of judicial opinions?

A: As comprehensive as the IDEA and its regulations are, their authors recognized that they could not possibly have anticipated every conceivable situation that could have arisen. Thus, insofar as many of the IDEA's provisions are open to interpretation when applied to specific sets of facts, its creators provided for judicial review. Courts interpret how the IDEA is to be applied in unique factual settings. Studying judicial opinions affords school officials and attorneys better understandings of how the courts have interpreted the law and so make them better prepared to implement the IDEA's mandates in their board policies and practices.

Recommendations

Even though educators wisely rely largely on their attorneys when dealing with technical aspects of disputes involving special education, they should acquaint themselves with both the federal and state legal systems. By familiarizing themselves with their legal systems, educators can assist their attorneys and school boards because such a working knowledge can help to cut to the heart of issues and help to avoid unnecessary delays. Still, school officials need to do the following:

- Provide regular professional development sessions for professional staff and board members to help them to have a better understanding of how their legal systems operate. Doing so can help staff and board members to recognize the significant differences and interplay between and among Section 504 and the IDEA, as well as other federal and state disability-related laws, so as to better serve the needs of children with disabilities and their parents.

- Offer similar informational sessions for parents and qualified students to help ensure that they are aware of their rights.
- Develop written handout materials explaining how federal and state disability laws operate, including detailed information on eligibility criteria under such key statutes as the IDEA and Section 504.
- Make sure that board policies and procedures relating to the delivery of special education and related services are up-to-date. Among the policies that boards adopt are those dealing with parental involvement and notification as well as mechanisms designed to provide parents with information on regular bases such as progress reports and report cards.
- Prepare checklists to help ensure that staff members are responding to parental requests in a timely and appropriate manner.
- Consider whether students with disabilities who do not qualify for services under the IDEA require reasonable accommodations under Section 504 and/or the ADA.
- Take steps to ensure that students with disabilities are not subjected to differential treatment because of their disabilities or because of their need for accommodations.
- Ensure that compliance officers regularly monitor or audit educational programming to make sure that it meets the dictates of the IDEA, Section 504, the ADA, and the NCLB, as well as other applicable federal and state laws.
- Recognize that in light of the complexity of disability law, it is important to rely on the advice of attorneys who specialize in education law, especially special education. If school officials are unable to find attorneys on their own, they should contact their state school boards and administrator associations, bar associations, or professional groups such as the Education Law Association or National School Boards Association.

Endnotes

1. State v. Board of Education of City of Antigo, 172 N.W. 153 (Wis. 1919). Earlier, in perhaps the first reported case involving a student with a disability, *Watson v. City of Cambridge*, 32 N.E. 864 (Mass. 1893), the Supreme Judicial Court of Massachusetts upheld a school committee's right to exclude a student for being too "weak-minded" to attend school.
2. U.S. Constitution, Amendment X.
3. 347 U.S. 483 (1954).
4. Ohio Rev. Code § 3321.03 (2001).
5. Zirkel, P. A. (2003). Do OSEP policy letters have legal weight? *Education Law Reporter, 171,* 391–396.
6. 5 U.S. 137 (1803).

7. 20 U.S.C. §§ 1400–1482 (2012). The IDEA's regulations can be found at Assistance to the States for the Education of Children with Disabilities, 34 C.F.R. §§ 300.1–300.818 (2013).
8. 28 U.S.C. § 1332.
9. 347 U.S. 483 (1954).
10. *Id.* at 493.
11. *Id.*
12. Zettel, J. J., & Ballard, J. (1982). Introduction: Bridging the gap. In J. Ballard, B. A. Ramirez, & F. J. Weintraub (Eds.), *Special education in America: Its legal and governmental foundations* (pp. 1–9). Reston, VA: The Council for Exceptional Children.
13. House Report No. 332, 94th Congress (1975).
14. 334 F. Supp. 1257 (E.D. Pa. 1971), 343 F. Supp. 279 (E.D. Pa. 1972).
15. 348 F. Supp. 866 (D.D.C. 1972).
16. 20 U.S.C. §§ 1400–1482 (2012).
17. 29 U.S.C. § 794 (2012).
18. 42 U.S.C. §§ 12101–12213 (2012).
19. 20 U.S.C. §§ 6301–7941 (2012).
20. 20 U.S.C. § 1412(a)(1)(A).
21. 20 U.S.C. § 1401(3)(A)(i).
22. 20 U.S.C. § 1401(3)(A)(ii).
23. 20 U.S.C. § 1401(9).
24. 20 U.S.C. § 1412(5).
25. 20 U.S.C. §§ 1401(14), 1414(d).
26. 20 U.S.C. § 1401(3)(A)(ii).
27. 20 U.S.C. § 1401(26)(A).
28. In *Irving Independent School District v. Tatro*, 468 U.S. 883, 894 (1984), the Supreme Court explained that school board officials are not obligated to provide related services to students unless they need those services to benefit from their special educations.
29. 20 U.S.C. § 1415.
30. 20 U.S.C. § 1414(a)(1)(d)(i)(I).
31. 20 U.S.C. § 1415(b)(3)(A).
32. 20 U.S.C. §§ 1414(d)(1)(B)(i), 1414(f).
33. 20 U.S.C. § 1414(d)(4).
34. 20 U.S.C. §§ 1414(a)(2)(A), (B)(ii).
35. 29 U.S.C. § 1232g.
36. 34 C.F.R. § 99.1 *et seq.*
37. 34 C.F.R. § 300.611 *et seq.*
38. Scotch, R. K. (2001). *From good will to civil rights: Transforming federal disability policy.* Philadelphia, PA: Temple University Press.
39. 29 U.S.C. § 794(a).
40. Bob Jones University v. United States, 461 U.S. 574 (1983).
41. 29 U.S.C. § 706(7)(B).
42. 34 C.F.R. § 104.3(j)(2)(i).
43. 34 C.F.R. § 104.3(j)(2)(iv).
44. 34 C.F.R. § 104.3(j)(2)(ii).
45. 34 C.F.R. § 104.3(k)(2).
46. 34 C.F.R. § 104.39.

47. 34 C.F.R. § 104.36.
48. 34 C.F.R. § 104.4(b)(3).
49. 34 C.F.R. § 104.34(c).
50. Sullivan v. Vallejo City Unified School District, 731 F. Supp. 947 (E.D. Cal. 1990).
51. Thomas v. Davidson Academy, 846 F. Supp. 611 (M.D. Tenn. 1994).
52. Barnes v. Converse College, 436 F. Supp. (D.S.C. 1977).
53. Hunt v. St. Peter School, 963 F. Supp. 843 (W.D. Mo. 1997).
54. 34 C.F.R. § 104.39(a).
55. 34 C.F.R. § 104.39(b).
56. Southeastern Community College v. Davis, 442 U.S. 397, 410 (1979).
57. *Id.* at 412.
58. School Board of Nassau County v. Arline, 480 U.S. 273 (1987).
59. 34 C.F.R. § 104.5.
60. 34 C.F.R. § 104.35.
61. Argen v. New York State Board of Law Examiners, 860 F. Supp. 84 (W.D.N.Y. 1994).
62. Sullivan v. Vallejo City Unified School District, 731 F. Supp. 947 (E.D. Cal. 1990). For a commentary on this topic, see Zirkel, P. A. (2010). Service animals in public schools. *West's Education Law Reporter, 257,* 525–535.
63. 42 U.S.C. §§ 12101–12213 (2012).
64. 42 U.S.C. § 12101.
65. 42 U.S.C. § 12101(b)(2).
66. 42 U.S.C. § 12102(2).
67. 42 U.S.C. § 12210.
68. 42 U.S.C. § 12208.
69. 42 U.S.C. § 12211(a).
70. 42 U.S.C. § 12211(b).
71. 42 U.S.C. § 12211(c).
72. 42 U.S.C. § 12110.
73. 41 U.S.C. § 701.
74. 20 U.S.C. §§ 6301–7941 (2012).
75. Wenkart, R. D. (2003). The No Child Left Behind Act and Congress' power to regulate under the Spending Clause. *Education Law Reporter, 174,* 589–597.
76. 20 U.S.C. § 1412 (a)(14)(D).
77. 20 U.S.C. §§ 1402(10), 1412 (a)(14).
78. 20 U.S.C. § 1412 (a)(14)(B).
79. 20 U.S.C. § 1402(10).
80. 20 U.S.C. § 1402 (10)(F).
81. 20 U.S.C. § 1412(a)(14)(E).
82. 34 C.F.R. § 300.18(g).

Rights to a Free Appropriate Public Education

The Individuals with Disabilities Education Act (IDEA),[1] which provides students with disabilities with unprecedented access to public education, directs all school boards in the United States to provide each child with special needs with a free appropriate public education (FAPE) in the least restrictive environment. The IDEA requires teams of educators and parents to describe what is to be provided to ensure students a FAPE, including needed special education and related services, in individualized education programs (IEPs). Even though the IDEA now provides a definition of a FAPE,[2] neither the Congress nor the U.S. Department of Education has yet established substantive standards by which to judge the adequacy of special education services.

In *Board of Education of the Hendrick Hudson Central School District v. Rowley,*[3] its first case interpreting the IDEA, the Supreme Court held that a child with hearing impairments was entitled to personalized instruction and support services sufficient to permit her to benefit from the instruction that she received. Yet, in denying the parental request for a sign language interpreter, the Justices cautioned lower courts not to impose their views of preferable educational methods on school officials.[4] Not surprisingly, courts are frequently called on to consider the level of services required to meet the IDEA's minimum standards.

This chapter reviews eligibility requirements for special education and related services, an important matter, since issues often arise over whether students have met the requirements to be placed in one of the IDEA's disability categories in order to qualify for services. This chapter also delineates the rights of children to access services and programs regardless of whether they attend public or nonpublic schools.

Free Appropriate Public Education

The components of a FAPE are summarized in Figure 2.1.

According to the IDEA, each child with a disability is entitled to a FAPE. The statute states that

The term "free appropriate public education" means special education and related services that—

(A) have been provided at public expense, under public supervision and direction, and without charge;

(B) meet the standards of the State educational agency;

(C) include an appropriate preschool, elementary school, or secondary school education in the State involved; and

(D) are provided in conformity with the individualized education program required under [this law].[5]

In order to qualify under the IDEA, children with disabilities must meet four statutory requirements. First, children must be between the ages of 3 and 21;[6] under this provision, children remain 21 until the day before they turn 22, unless state law extends this limitation. Second,

Figure 2.1 Components of a Free Appropriate Public Education

- **Specifically Designed Instruction**—personalized instruction designed to meet the unique needs of students with disabilities
- **Appropriate Peer Group**—students should be educated, whenever possible, with peer groups including children of approximately the same age and developmental level
- **Least Restrictive Environment**—to the maximum extent feasible, students with disabilities must be educated with peers who are not disabled
- **Educational Benefit**—special education and related services should be designed to assist students in making meaningful progress toward the goals and objectives of their IEPs
- **Procedural Requirement**—IEPs must be developed in accordance with all of the requirements of the IDEA and state law
- **Related Services**—supportive services must be provided if they are necessary for students to benefit from their educational programs
- **Assistive Technology**—assistive technology services and devices must be provided when necessary for students to receive educational benefit
- **Public Expense**—programs and all of their components must be provided at no cost to students or their parents

children must have specifically identifiable disabilities. The IDEA defines children with disabilities as having

> mental retardation, hearing impairments (including deafness), speech or language impairments, visual impairments (including blindness), serious emotional disturbance (referred to in this chapter as "emotional disturbance"), orthopedic impairments, autism, traumatic brain injury, other health impairments, or specific learning disabilities.[7]

The third and fourth requirements under the IDEA, which must be taken together, are that qualified children, "by reason thereof, need . . . special education and related services."[8] This means that children must receive a FAPE in the least restrictive environment that is directed by the contents of their IEPs.

The IDEA uses the term *special education and related services* in its definition of a FAPE. Even so, children with disabilities do not necessarily have to need related services in order to be eligible for special education services under the IDEA. Children are entitled to related services only when they need such developmental, corrective, or supportive services in order to benefit from their special education. The Supreme Court ruled in *Irving Independent School District v. Tatro*[9] that the statute does not obligate school boards to provide related services to students with disabilities who do not need such services to benefit from their special education. For this reason, it is unnecessary for students to need related services to qualify under the IDEA as long as they require special education. By the same token, students are not entitled to related services if they do not require special education. Put another way, related services are provided to some students with disabilities in conjunction with special education, but not all students who receive IDEA services need or are entitled to related services.

The 2004 version of the IDEA[10] made a significant change with regard to the category of students with learning disabilities. The IDEA changed the evaluation procedures for these children by no longer requiring educators to consider whether these students have severe discrepancies between achievement and intellectual ability in oral expression, listening comprehension, written expression, basic reading skills, reading comprehension, mathematical calculation, or mathematical reasoning.[11] Instead, as part of their evaluation procedures, school personnel may use processes, known as Response to Intervention, to consider whether children respond to scientific, research-based interventions.[12] Students who fail to respond to the interventions called for in the IDEA may be considered eligible for special education services.

The 2004 amendments to the IDEA also added language addressing the needs of children aged 3 through 9:

> The term "child with a disability" for a child aged 3 through 9 (or any subset of that age range, including ages 3 through 5), may, at the discretion of the State and the local educational agency, include a child—
>
> (i) experiencing developmental delays, as defined by the State and as measured by appropriate diagnostic instruments and procedures, in 1 or more of the following areas: physical development; cognitive development; communication development; social or emotional development; or adaptive development.[13]

The IDEA defines an IEP as "a written statement for each child with a disability that is developed, reviewed, and revised in accordance with section 1414(d) of this title."[14] Section 1414(d) outlines all of the components of IEPs, including students' current levels of performance, annual goals, and short-term objectives, as well as the specific educational services that children are to receive.[15]

The IDEA and its regulations require school board officials to provide a continuum of alternative placements for all students with disabilities. In practice, this range of options progresses from full inclusion in a regular education classroom, to inclusion with supplementary assistance such as an aide, to partial inclusion—meaning that children split time between regular classrooms and resource room placements,[16] to self-contained or individualized placements;[17] the IDEA prefers to have all four of these options provided in the local neighborhood schools that children would otherwise have attended, unless other arrangements are required to provide FAPEs. The more restrictive settings on the continuum range from special day schools to hospital or home-bound instruction (which should not be confused with homeschooling) to residential placements.[18]

While the IDEA states a preference for the four options to be offered in the local neighborhood schools that children with disabilities would attend,[19] the statute offers little guidance in defining what may be considered appropriate. The IDEA's regulations indicate that an appropriate education consists of special education and related services that are provided in conformance with children's IEPs.[20] Since neither the IDEA nor its regulations include a precise definition of the term *appropriate*, it is necessary to turn to judicial interpretations for guidance on the meaning of FAPE.

The *Rowley* Standard

In *Board of Education of the Hendrick Hudson Central School District v. Rowley (Rowley)*,[21] the Supreme Court offered what amounts to a minimal definition of a FAPE. *Rowley* involved parents who challenged school officials after they refused to provide their hearing-impaired kindergarten-aged daughter with a sign language interpreter. A hearing officer and lower courts ordered board officials to provide an interpreter for the child on the basis that an appropriate education was one that would have afforded her the opportunity to achieve at a level commensurate with that of her peers who were not disabled.

The Supreme Court, in pointing out that the child in *Rowley* was achieving passing marks and advancing from grade to grade without the sign language interpreter, reversed in favor of the board. In deciding that the child was not entitled to an interpreter, the Court ruled that an appropriate education was one that is formulated pursuant to all of the IDEA's procedures and is "sufficient to confer some educational benefit"[22] on children with disabilities, a standard that courts continue to apply.[23] To the extent that the child in *Rowley* received "some educational benefit" without the sign language interpreter, the Court reasoned that educators were not required to provide her with one, even though she might have achieved at a higher level had she received this additional assistance.[24]

An appropriate education is one that is formulated in accordance with all of the IDEA's procedures and is "sufficient to confer some educational benefit" on children with disabilities.

As noted, *Rowley* established a minimum standard for what constitutes a FAPE under federal law. Even so, one state, West Virginia, has gone so far as to enact a statute specifying that no "state rule, policy, or standard . . . nor any county board rule, policy, or standard governing special education may exceed the requirements of federal law or regulation."[25] Conversely, courts in North Carolina,[26] New Jersey,[27] Michigan,[28] and California[29] found that those states had higher standards of appropriateness at the time the decisions were issued. Further, in the case from New Jersey, the Third Circuit explained that the higher state standards replaced the federal requirements, because one of the essential elements of the IDEA is that special education programs must "meet the standards of the state educational agency."[30]

Shortly after *Rowley*, lower courts began to expand their interpretations of the "some educational benefit" criterion, asserting that an appropriate education for students with disabilities requires more than just minimal or trivial benefits.[31] While the initial cases reflected the judicial position that minimal benefits met this standard, later disputes explained that the IDEA required more. For example, in a case from North Carolina, the Fourth Circuit affirmed that *Rowley* permits courts to make case-by-case evaluations of the substantive standards needed to meet the criterion that IEPs must be reasonably calculated to enable students to receive educational benefits.[32] The student here made only minimal progress, a situation that the court thought was insufficient in view of his intellectual potential. The court stated that Congress certainly did not intend for board officials to provide a program for the child that produced only trivial academic advancement. In another case, the same court maintained that insofar as a goal of four months' progress during an academic year was unlikely to allow a student who had learning disabilities to advance from one grade to the next with passing marks, it was insufficient to provide her with an appropriate education.[33]

The Third Circuit, in a case from New Jersey, indicated that in order to comply with *Rowley's* mandate, an IEP must confer an educational benefit that is appropriate, meaning that it is likely to produce progress, not trivial educational advancement.[34] In a case from Pennsylvania, the same court later reiterated that insofar as the IDEA calls for more than just trivial educational benefit, Congress intended to provide students with disabilities with educational services that would result in meaningful benefits.[35] A federal trial court in Georgia added that the educational benefit must be appreciable.[36]

Similar cases expanded on the concept that students must make more than trivial academic gains. In reversing an order from a federal trial court in New York, the Second Circuit explained that because school board officials are not required to maximize the potential of students with disabilities, IEPs only had to meet the "some educational benefit" criterion.[37] In contrast, the Eleventh Circuit, in a case from Florida, determined that appropriate educations may be defined as those wherein students make measurable and adequate gains in classrooms.[38] The Eleventh Circuit later noted that a child's having demonstrated serious behavioral problems at home did not render his special education program inappropriate.[39] In this latter case, which also arose in Florida, the court rejected the parental argument that the child's placement was inadequate because the student could not generalize learned skills across settings. The court was convinced that generalization across settings is not required to show educational benefit. The court also discounted a parental argument that the IEP was insufficient on the ground that it failed to provide respite care for the family, given that the parents were unable to demonstrate how this would have provided an educational benefit for their child. Further, the Fifth Circuit upheld a proposed IEP from a school board in Texas, concluding that a student received significant benefit from his special education program because he not only achieved passing grades but also demonstrated an increased ability to focus on tasks.[40] In like manner, the Eighth Circuit observed that where a student from Missouri achieved passing grades and improved his reading skills, his IEP was appropriate.[41]

Indicators of Educational Benefit

In *Rowley*, the Supreme Court held that the program provided to a student with disabilities who attends school predominantly in a regular classroom setting should enable the child to achieve passing marks and advance from one grade to the next. However, other courts responded that promotion to the next grade by itself is not proof that students received an education that was appropriate.[42] For instance, in a case from North Carolina, the Fourth Circuit decided that promotion alone, especially in conjunction with test scores revealing minimal progress, did not satisfy *Rowley's* standard of "some educational benefit."[43] Subsequently, the same court found that passing marks and annual grade promotions were important considerations under the IDEA but that achieving each did not automatically mean that a student received an appropriate education.[44] In other words, courts do not view so-called social promotions as indictors of students having received FAPEs.

Along similar lines, while some courts view the fact that students earned high school diplomas as evidence that they received appropriate educations,[45] not all courts agree. For example, the highest court of Massachusetts remarked that a student's having graduated and received a high school diploma did not mean that he received an appropriate education. The court thus rescinded the diploma that was awarded to an 18-year-old student who was unable to adapt to life in a sheltered workshop or to live independently after graduation.[46] The court was of the opinion that awarding a diploma to the student, who was unable to earn one under normal requirements even by the age of 22, was substantively inappropriate. The critical factor in such cases is whether the students legitimately earned diplomas by satisfactorily completing all requirements. Thus, school boards cannot absolve themselves of their obligation to educate children with disabilities through the age of 21 by issuing diplomas that students have not earned by meeting the usual prerequisites.

In considering whether proposed IEPs are appropriate, evidence of students' academic progress is relevant in evaluating whether children received FAPEs in the past.[47] Courts have agreed that past progress in the same or similar programs, along with evidence that the progress should continue, indicated that the programs would confer educational benefit,[48] even if it is incremental in nature.[49] Likewise, courts have concurred that the continuation of IEPs that failed to produce educational benefits in the past would be inappropriate.[50] One court even acknowledged that an IEP that reduced services was insufficient to confer a FAPE when the child had not received meaningful educational benefits.[51] On the related topic of regression, courts tend to interpret declines in student performances after the discontinuation of services or programs as indicators that the education that was provided following the cessation of services was not meaningful.[52]

Generally speaking, the progress of special education students should be comparable with the advances that similarly situated children achieve.[53] To this end, courts decreed that progress should be measured in terms of the ability of students as children with disabilities.[54] A federal trial court in Texas was satisfied that a student who stayed within two grade levels of her peers was making meaningful academic progress.[55] Similarly, an appellate court in Virginia affirmed that although a child did not advance at the same rate as his peers, there was no reason to change his placement because his progress was real and measurable.[56] Yet, lack of progress does not necessarily mean that students' programs are inappropriate. The courts recognize that some students are not motivated and that other factors, such as substance abuse, poor conduct, failure to complete homework, and absenteeism may contribute to a student's lack of success.[57] In order to evaluate whether meaningful or significant progress has occurred, the courts may rely on objective data, including test scores and the opinions of experts in the field, such as psychologists and educational diagnosticians.

In assessing whether children made progress under their IEPs, courts consider an array of indicators such as standardized test scores, report card grades, anecdotal teacher assessments, and evaluations of students' growth in the areas addressed by their IEP goals and objectives.[58] Even so, the Third Circuit cautioned that good grades earned in special education classes should not be viewed the same way as grades earned in mainstream classrooms.[59] In reversing an order from the federal trial court in New Jersey, the appellate panel expressed concern that there could be a disconnect between educators' assessments of students in special education as opposed to general education settings, insisting that course grades alone could not be used to evaluate whether a special education program provided educational benefits. In other words, since the criteria for awarding grades in special education classes may not be the same as in general education classes, the grades in each cannot be considered to be equivalent.

IEPs are prospective. Still, courts or hearing officers can examine IEPs retrospectively. Since due process appeals and judicial actions generally occur after IEPs were to have been implemented, those reviewing IEPs have the benefit of history in evaluating their appropriateness. How much weight subsequent history should be given was the subject of a great deal of debate in a case from New Jersey. Affirming that the school board's actions could not have been judged exclusively in hindsight, a divided Third Circuit explained that such a finding must be based on whether a child's IEP was appropriate when developed, not on whether he actually received benefit as a result of a placement.[60] The court also commented that student gains could be attributed to other factors besides their educational programs. The dissent argued that evidence of what actually happened was material even though it might not have impacted the final outcome.

In judging IEPs prospectively, that is, considering whether they were reasonably calculated to confer educational benefit at the time they were proposed, courts evaluate whether the services and supports proposed are sufficient to meet student needs.[61] To do so, courts consider the services proposed in IEPs in light of students' identified disabilities and deficits.[62] Courts approve proposed IEPs when educators can show that the IEPs have been individually tailored to meet students' unique needs, contain appropriate goals and objectives, and include strategies to address students' weaknesses. In this respect, when educators and parents disagree over proper methodology, courts typically defer to the expertise of school officials.[63]

Failure to Implement an IEP Fully

IEPs are essentially roadmaps of the services school board officials intend to provide to students with disabilities. Unfortunately, for various reasons, good intentions sometimes go awry, and educators are not always able to fully implement an agreed-upon IEP. While on the surface it may appear that the failure to implement an IEP fully would result in an IDEA violation, courts have not always agreed. In one of the first cases to address the issue, the Ninth Circuit noted that minor discrepancies between the services outlined in an Oregon student's IEP and those actually provided did not necessarily result in a denial of a FAPE.[64] However, courts have agreed that the failure to implement a material portion of an IEP is an IDEA violation.[65] To assess whether the failure to implement all services called for in IEPs translates into denials of a FAPE, courts review whether children still received sufficient educational benefit without the missing services.[66]

Failure to Identify a Placement Location in an IEP

An array of courts have addressed whether placements refer to the programs and services provided rather than specific locations where IEPs are implemented[67] and whether a school board's failure to name a placement location in an IEP may justify parents' rejection of that IEP.[68] The Fourth Circuit, in a dispute from Virginia, acknowledged that an IEP that fails to identify the school at which special education services will be provided is not sufficiently specific for parents to evaluate its appropriateness.[69] The Second Circuit reached the opposite result.[70] According to the court, since the term *education placement* refers only to the general type of educational program in which a child is placed, rather than a specific school, an IEP designed for a student in New York that failed to identify the school where services would be implemented was not defective.

Least Restrictive Environment

The IDEA requires all states and local education agencies to educate students with disabilities in the least restrictive environment (LRE).[71] This provision applies across the continuum of placement alternatives discussed earlier. Specifically, the IDEA obliges states to establish procedures assuring that students with disabilities are educated, to the maximum extent appropriate, with peers who do not have disabilities. Further, children can be placed in special classes or separate facilities, or otherwise be removed from the general education environment, only when the nature or severity of their disabilities is such that instruction in general education classes cannot be achieved satisfactorily, even with supplementary aids and services.[72]

These provisions apply to students who attend private schools, institutions, or other care facilities at public expense as well as to children who attend public schools.[73] Since educational agencies are mandated to spend only a proportionate amount of federal funds on students who attend private schools at parental expense, the degree to which such children can be educated in inclusionary settings at their private schools may be limited.[74] In addressing the provision of a FAPE for students with disabilities, courts must consider the IDEA's LRE provisions in tandem with the services students need. Factors that the courts consider in identifying LREs are listed in Figure 2.2.

In two important cases, federal appellate courts directed school boards to place students with disabilities in regular settings as opposed to segregated special education classrooms. Both courts agreed that educators must consider a variety of factors when formulating the LRE for children with disabilities. In *Oberti v. Board of Education of the Borough of Clementon School District*,[75] a case from New Jersey, the Third Circuit adopted a two-part test, originally proposed by the Fifth Circuit,[76] for assessing compliance with the

Figure 2.2 Determining the Need for a More Restrictive Placement

Students may require more restrictive placements when

- They failed to progress in their then-current placements, even with the use of supplemental aids and services.
- The cost of maintaining them in less restrictive environments is unreasonable.
- They require specialized environments to receive FAPEs.
- They need specialized techniques or resources that are unavailable in regular public school programs.
- They have low-incidence–type disabilities requiring contact with peers who have similar disabilities.
- They need 24-hour programs of instruction and care.
- They require consistency of approaches between their home and school environments.
- They need total immersion in programs in order to make progress.
- Their presence in the less restrictive environments is disruptive to the educational process of peers.
- Their potentially dangerous behavior puts themselves and/or others at risk of harm.

LRE mandate. The first element of the test asks whether children with disabilities can be educated satisfactorily in regular classrooms with the use of supplementary aids and services. The second part of the test addresses what occurs in situations arising if placements outside of regular classrooms are necessary. This inquiry takes into account what educators must consider to determine whether children were mainstreamed to the maximum extent appropriate.

As the Ninth Circuit summarized in *Sacramento City Unified School District Board of Education v. Rachel H.*,[77] educators must consider four factors in making placements: the educational benefits of placing children with disabilities in regular classrooms, the nonacademic benefits of such placements, the effect that the presence of students with disabilities would have on teachers and other children in classes, and the costs of inclusionary placements. IEP teams must take all of these factors into account in making placement decisions for students with disabilities.

Inherent in these tests is the principle that educators must make reasonable efforts to place students with disabilities in fully inclusive settings by providing them with supplementary aids and services to ensure their success.[78] Even with the focus on inclusion, not all students with disabilities must be placed in regular education classes. Courts have approved segregated settings over parental objections[79] where IEP teams demonstrated that students with disabilities could not have functioned in regular classrooms or would not have benefited in such settings, even with supplementary aids and services.[80] In one case, originating in California, the

Ninth Circuit affirmed that the LRE for a student with multiple disabilities was a special education class with some mainstreaming since he was non-verbal, could only respond to "yes–no" questions, and did not interact with peers.[81]

Courts have been reluctant to order inclusionary placements for students who exhibit disruptive behaviors.[82] The bottom line is that inclusionary placements should be the settings of choice, with segregated settings contemplated only if fully inclusive placements failed despite the best efforts of educators, or there is overwhelming evidence that they are not reasonable.

Entitlement to Services

The IDEA makes it clear that all eligible children are entitled to receive FAPEs regardless of the severity of their disabilities. In the seminal case of a child from New Hampshire with severe disabilities, *Timothy W. v. Rochester, N.H., School District*, the First Circuit decided that the IDEA's language is unequivocal and neither includes exceptions for those with severe disabilities nor requires students to demonstrate the ability to benefit from services in order to be eligible.[83] This case is thus known for introducing the concept of "zero reject," meaning that once children are identified as being in need of IDEA services, they must be served. The court also defined education in a broad sense, encompassing training in basic life skills.

In *Honig v. Doe*,[84] the Supreme Court pointed out that even students with disabilities who are dangerous cannot be denied the IDEA's educational benefits. Yet, as noted, not all students with disabilities need be educated within public school settings. While the IDEA and its regulations allow residential or private placements of students at no cost to them or their parents,[85] the law does not cover children who have problems with drug addiction or sexual aggression unless they meet the criteria for one of the IDEA's disability categories.[86]

> The IDEA makes it clear that all eligible children are entitled to receive a FAPE regardless of the severity of their disabilities.

The IDEA requires states, through local education agencies, to provide special education services to students between the ages of 18 and 21 if education services are offered to peers of the same age who are not disabled.[87] The Ninth Circuit ruled that a statute enacted in Hawaii,[88] barring students from attending public schools after the last days of the school years in which they turned 20, violated the IDEA even though it applied to both general and special education students.[89] Since the state's education department operates a network of adult-education schools, which the court ascertained constituted secondary education, the panel insisted that it must also provide IDEA services to students with disabilities aged 20 and 21. Even so, students may not continue to receive services through the age of 21 if special education is no longer necessary or if they have completed their formal educations. For example, a federal trial court in Michigan upheld a school board's permitting a student with disabilities to graduate and terminating his eligibility for special education services; the school board pointed out that he had received a FAPE and adequate transition services.[90] The court was of the opinion that insofar as the student completed all of his graduation requirements and had shown exceptional performance in mainstream classes, he was no longer eligible to receive special education services.

As straightforward as the IDEA and its regulations seem to be, controversy continues over who is eligible for special education and related services. A great deal of the debate has evolved over the specified disability categories that are defined in the IDEA and its regulations. As reflected in the following sections, controversial eligibility suits examined the delivery of special education and/or related services to students attending private schools at the options of their parents, prompting Congress to address this issue in the IDEA's most recent amendments.

Eligibility

Students who may be identified under any of the categories of disabilities listed in the IDEA are eligible for services as long as their educational performances are adversely affected by their disabilities. Individual states may specify disability categories in addition to those listed in the IDEA or may provide special education services on a noncategorical basis. In *Rowley*, the Supreme Court, while reasoning that the IDEA required only a level of services to confer "some educational benefit" on students, suggested that children who achieved passing grades as they advanced from one grade to the next received educational benefit.

One of the more controversial disability categories listed in the IDEA addresses students with emotional disturbances.[91] In order to be classified as having emotional disturbances, students' educational performances must be adversely affected by their conditions. The definition in the IDEA's regulations[92] lists characteristics of serious emotional disturbance as an inability to learn that cannot be explained by other factors, an inability to build and maintain interpersonal relationships, inappropriate behavior or feelings under normal circumstances, a general pervasive mood of unhappiness or depression, or a tendency to develop physical symptoms or fears.[93] This definition includes schizophrenia but specifically excludes "children who are socially maladjusted, unless it is determined that they are seriously emotionally disturbed."[94]

Courts reached mixed results when evaluating whether students qualify for services under the category of seriously emotionally disturbed. In an illustrative case from Virginia, the Fourth Circuit affirmed that a student was not seriously emotionally disturbed.[95] The court relied on the testimony of three psychologists who examined the student, accepting their opinions that he was not seriously emotionally disturbed. The court pointed out that a drop in the student's grades was directly attributable to his truancy,[96] drug and alcohol use,[97] and delinquent behavior rather than any emotional disturbance. The Eighth Circuit commented that the factor that controls eligibility under the IDEA is not whether a student's problem is educational or noneducational. Rather, the court contended that the issue was whether the child's behavior needed to be addressed in order for her to learn.[98] In reversing an order from the federal trial court in Minnesota, the appellate panel concluded that because the student had social and emotional problems preventing her from receiving educational benefit, she was entitled to receive special education services in a residential setting.[99]

In another case, the Second Circuit ruled that a student from New York whose inability to learn could not have been explained solely by intellectual, sensory, or health factors, and whose emotional difficulties adversely affected her educational development, was entitled to special education.[100] The record reflected that the student exhibited a pervasive mood of unhappiness, depression, and despondency, as evidenced by a suicide attempt. The court was convinced that under normal circumstances the child exhibited inappropriate behavior, such as lying, cutting classes, failing to complete assignments, stealing, and being defiant. In addition, the Sixth Circuit was of the view that a student from Tennessee who had average intelligence, but demonstrated a long history of academic failure, difficulty making and maintaining friendships, and the inability to create normal social bonds, was seriously emotionally disturbed and entitled to services under the IDEA.[101] Conversely, the Ninth Circuit affirmed that a student from California who suffered from post-traumatic stress syndrome was not emotionally disturbed because she was able to develop and maintain satisfactory relationships, and her condition did not adversely affect her educational performance.[102]

A growing area of concern involves children who are diagnosed as having attention deficit disorder (ADD) or attention deficit hyperactivity disorder (ADHD), conditions that are identified in the IDEA's regulations under "other heath impairment." In order to be covered by the IDEA, such students must demonstrate

> limited strength, vitality, or alertness, including a heightened alertness to environmental stimuli, that results in limited alertness with respect to the educational environment, that—

(i) Is due to chronic or acute health problems such as asthma, attention deficit or attention deficit hyperactivity disorder, diabetes, epilepsy, a heart condition, hemophilia, lead poisoning, leukemia, nephritis, rheumatic fever, sickle cell anemia, and Tourette syndrome; and

(ii) Adversely affects a child's educational performance.[103]

In a case from Texas, the Fifth Circuit affirmed that a student who had ADHD but earned passing grades and scored successfully on state tests was ineligible for special education even though the ADHD adversely affected his educational performance.[104] On the other hand, the Eighth Circuit affirmed that a student from Missouri, whose hyperactivity, impulsivity, and inattention severely impaired his ability to learn, qualified for special education.[105] Further, a federal trial court in California was convinced that a student whose lack of motivation was attributed to his ADHD was eligible for special education because his condition adversely affected his educational performance.[106]

A concern arises because school nurses typically administer medication to students with ADHD who must take their prescriptions during school days. The Eighth Circuit, in two separate cases from Missouri, agreed that school officials did not violate the rights of students with disabilities who were diagnosed as having ADHD by refusing to administer Ritalin to them in dosages that exceeded the amount called for in the *Physician's Desk Reference*,[107] a book that doctors commonly rely on in prescribing medications.[108] The IDEA now prohibits education officials from requiring parents to obtain prescriptions for their children for substances such as Ritalin under the Controlled Substances Act as a condition of attending classes, being evaluated, or receiving special education services.[109]

In a matter related to other health impairments, it is well settled that students with AIDS, hepatitis B, or similar illnesses are entitled to FAPEs under the IDEA or Section 504 of the Rehabilitation Act[110] and that their parents are not required to disclose their illnesses to school officials as a precondition for admission or continued enrollment.[111] In addition, children with AIDS cannot be classified as other health impaired unless their diseases have progressed and have an effect on their ability to perform in school. A state court in New York declared that an unidentified student did not qualify as disabled merely due to having AIDS, but such a child could become eligible for services under the IDEA as the disease progressed.[112] The court observed that in order to qualify as having a disability under the IDEA, a child's educational performance had to have been adversely affected as a result of limited strength, vitality, or alertness due to having AIDS. Similarly, a federal trial court in Illinois declared that the IDEA applied to students with AIDS only if their physical conditions adversely affected their ability to learn and to complete required classroom work.[113]

In both of these cases, as well as in other litigation involving students with AIDS, the courts made it clear that federal law protects the rights of children who are in need of special education services.

> It is well settled that students with AIDS, hepatitis B, or similar illnesses are entitled to FAPEs under the IDEA or Section 504.

In a related vein, students with disabilities cannot be excluded from public schools due to their health problems, even when they are afflicted with contagious diseases, if the risk of transmission of the illnesses is low. Exclusions due to health problems would violate Section 504, the Americans with Disabilities Act,[114] and/or the IDEA. In such a dispute, the Second Circuit affirmed that students who were carriers of the hepatitis B virus could not be excluded from their public schools in New York or segregated within them because of their medical conditions.[115] In like fashion, a state court in Illinois posited that a student with hepatitis B was entitled to an education in a regular setting.[116] Both courts agreed that the risk of transmission was low and could be reduced further through the use of proper prophylactic procedures.

The analyses in the cases involving hepatitis can also be applied to litigation focusing on children with AIDS and other infectious diseases. To this end, the Eleventh Circuit vacated an earlier order to the contrary in asserting that before a student can be excluded from school, a court must evaluate whether reasonable accommodations can reduce the risk of transmission.[117] The student was classified as mentally retarded and excluded from the public schools in Florida, in part because she was incontinent and drooled. On remand, the trial court decided that insofar as the risk of transmission from the student's bodily secretions was remote, she was to be admitted to a special education classroom.

School boards traditionally have used a discrepancy criterion to identify students as having specific learning disabilities. Under this criterion, students may be considered to have learning disabilities if there is a statistically significant gap between their intellectual potential and academic achievement.[118] When Congress amended the IDEA in 2004, it stipulated that board officials may not be required to use the discrepancy model when evaluating whether children have specific learning disabilities as defined by the statute.[119] Rather, states must allow educators to use what has become known as the Response to Intervention (RTI) model. The RTI model permits school personnel to decide whether students have specific learning disabilities by assessing their response to scientific, research-based intervention strategies. The Ninth Circuit declared that the Hawaii Department of Education violated this provision when officials failed to use the RTI model instead of the severe discrepancy criterion to evaluate whether a child with dyslexia qualified for special education services.[120] In doing so the court struck down a state regulation in force at the time that conditioned eligibility for special education on the existence of a severe discrepancy between academic achievement and intellectual ability. This does not mean that the discrepancy model may not be used, but it may not be the exclusive method IEP teams employ to establish eligibility for students suspected of having learning disabilities.

Extracurricular Activities

Students with disabilities are entitled to participate in nonacademic and extracurricular services such as counseling, athletics, transportation, health services, recreational activities, special interest groups, and clubs on an equal basis with their peers who are not disabled.[121] While the judiciary has refused to permit students with disabilities to take part in activities from which they cannot benefit unless unreasonable modifications are made,[122] the courts have allowed children to take part if the required modifications are reasonable.[123] The Supreme Court of Minnesota decided that IEP teams must consider whether an extracurricular or nonacademic activity is appropriate for students with disabilities along with which supplementary aids and services are appropriate and necessary for their being involved in these activities.[124]

Another difficulty for children with disabilities often occurs because, insofar as they repeat grades, they are often older than other students at the same grade level. While most courts have upheld age requirements,[125] others have granted waivers for athletic participation.[126] A question that remains is whether students with disabilities who fail courses can retain their eligibility to participate under "no pass, no play" rules. The answer is likely to depend on the individual circumstances of given situations. If students fail as a direct result of their disabilities or due to inappropriate IEPs, courts may well agree that enforcement of such rules is discriminatory.[127]

Nontraditional Program Schedules and Extended School Year Programs

In most states, students typically attend school 6 hours a day, 180 days a year, for 12 years. Even so, courts agree that students with disabilities are entitled to programming arrangements and schedules that deviate from this pattern if this is necessary for them to receive FAPEs. Since the IDEA requires IEPs to be tailored to meet the needs of individual students,[128] this provision sometimes requires nontraditional schedules for the delivery of services.

> Courts agree that students with disabilities are entitled to educational
> programming that extends beyond the parameters of traditional school
> years if the combination of regression during vacation periods and
> recoupment time prevents meaningful progress.

Since students with disabilities sometimes repeat grades, a number of children may require more than 12 years to complete their general programs of study. In an older case from Oklahoma, the Tenth Circuit affirmed that students with disabilities are entitled to more than the standard 12 years of schooling if necessary.[129] School officials terminated educational services for the student in this case after she completed 12 years of school, when she reached her 21st birthday, even though she was classified as a tenth grader. The court ordered the board to provide the student with two more years of schooling. More recently, the Eleventh Circuit affirmed that an 18-year-old from Georgia with a third-grade reading level due to his learning disabilities was entitled to additional services, since school officials failed both to evaluate his progress for more than five years and to implement his IEP in a timely fashion.[130] The panel agreed that awarding the student a placement in a private school for about five years or until he graduated high school, whichever came first, was appropriate, since this would have put him in the situation he would have been in but for the failure of officials to provide him with the educational benefits that he should have received had they placed him properly at the outset. Conversely, the Tenth Circuit affirmed the denial of compensatory services to a student from New Mexico who dropped out of school and demonstrated her unwillingness to return.[131] The court noted that she could have received the services she sought simply by reenrolling.

As discussed below, courts agree that students with disabilities are entitled to educational programming extending beyond the parameters of traditional school years if the combination of regression during vacation periods and recoupment time prevents meaningful progress. Further, the IDEA's regulations direct officials to provide extended school year services only if IEP teams are convinced that such programming is necessary for the provision of FAPEs.[132] Extended school year programs are required only to prevent regression, not to advance skills in IEPs that students have not yet mastered.[133] If students with disabilities need educational programs extending beyond regular school years, such services must be provided at public expense.[134]

Extended school year programs are generally necessary when students regress and the time needed to recoup lost skills interferes with their overall progress toward attaining their IEP goals and objectives. Courts agree that policies or practices serving to limit programs for students with disabilities to 180 days violate the IDEA.[135] In one case, the Sixth Circuit held that a child from Kentucky with cerebral palsy who also had delayed cognitive and communication development was not entitled to an extended school year placement, because his parents were unable to demonstrate that such a program was essential to avoid more than adequately recoupable regression.[136] The court decided that although the parents may have wished for a more extensive placement for their son than the IDEA required, the student was not entitled to such a placement because school officials developed an appropriate IEP placing him in an inclusive setting with special education support and assistive technology adaptations.

In order for students to qualify for extended school year placements, the regression they experience must be greater than that which normally occurs during school vacations. In a leading case, the Fifth Circuit affirmed that a child from Texas was not entitled to an extended school year placement unless regression was severe or substantial.[137] More recently, federal trial courts in California[138] and New Hampshire[139] reiterated essentially the same position in agreeing that students' being academically behind was not a valid reason to require their boards to provide them with extended school year placements.

At the same time, due to the nature of their disabilities, students who may be unable to tolerate long periods of instruction may require shortened school days. In apparently the only reported case dealing with the issue, the Fifth Circuit affirmed that a school board in Texas was not required to provide a full day of educational programming for a student with multiple disabilities whose educational programming consisted of basic sensory stimulation, since it was not in his best interest.[140] Due to the child's inability to sustain a response to prolonged stimulation, the court agreed with special educators in his district that there was no reason to provide him with a full school day since it was inappropriate to do so.

Private and Residential School Placements

The courts continue to recognize that the IDEA's preference for full inclusion is not feasible for all students with disabilities.[141] Consequently, the IDEA and its regulations require school officials to offer a continuum of placement alternatives to meet the educational needs of children with disabilities.[142] In this regard, public school officials may be required to place children in nonpublic schools when boards lack appropriate placements[143] such as when a student has a low-incidence disability and there are not enough children with the same type of disability within a system to warrant the development of a program.[144] These courts acknowledged that inasmuch as boards in smaller districts probably cannot afford to develop specialized programs, they must look elsewhere for placements.

If private day or residential school placements are necessary for educational reasons, they must be made at no cost to students or their parents. States or local school boards may share the cost of placements with other agencies but may not assign any financial responsibility to parents. It is well settled that policies requiring parents to pay a portion of the costs of residential placements are unacceptable.[145]

States have adopted different regulations regarding residential placements. To the extent that a number of jurisdictions provide some, if not all, of the funding for residential placements, state agencies sometimes become involved in these placement decisions. Once placed, students with disabilities do not necessarily need to remain in private day or residential programs indefinitely. Since one of the IDEA's major goals is to have students with disabilities educated in fully inclusive settings, children should be returned to such placements as soon as it is feasible to do so.

Courts may order residential placements for students with severe, profound, or multiple disabilities[146] if they need 24-hour-per-day programming or consistency between their school and home environments. Residential placements may also be necessary for students who have significant behavioral disorders,[147] are emotionally disturbed,[148] or require total immersion in educational environments in order to progress.[149] For example, the Sixth Circuit ruled in favor of parents from Ohio who unilaterally placed their child, who had behavioral disabilities, in a private residential facility.[150] The court approved of the placement since the child's behavior and grades improved in the school. Further, it is conceivable that children who are dangerous to themselves and/or others may be sent to residential facilities. For instance, in a case from Puerto Rico, the First Circuit decided that a student's need for constant supervision and an in-school psychologist necessitated a private school placement.[151]

If students need residential placements for purely educational reasons, school boards must bear their entire cost and cannot require parents to contribute toward payment.[152] On the other hand, if placements are made for other than educational reasons, such as for medical, behavioral, or social purposes, or are essentially custodial in nature,[153] then school systems may be required to pay only for the educational components of the residential settings[154] and may enter into cost-share agreements with other agencies. Boards may not even be required to pay the educational costs of residential placements that are made predominantly for noneducational reasons if they are able to show that they could provide FAPEs locally.[155] However, the issue is complicated, because students' educational disabilities are often inextricably intertwined with their noneducational problems. In such instances, the Fifth Circuit directed lower courts within its jurisdiction to examine each part of student placements in evaluating which costs boards must bear.[156] Even so, courts have ordered boards to assume all costs of residential placements when student needs are intimately intertwined and it is not realistically possible to assign financial responsibility to appropriate agencies.[157]

Disputes often arise over whether residential placements are being made for medical, rather than educational, reasons. These disputes occur most often in the context of placements in psychiatric facilities. Under the IDEA, school boards are not required to pay medical expenses for students other than those for diagnostic or evaluative purposes.[158] Also, psychiatric facilities often are characterized as hospitals, since psychiatrists are medical doctors. Moreover, students with physical disabilities are frequently placed in facilities where a number of services of a medical nature are offered. As some of the cases cited herein demonstrate, it is often impossible to separate out the various services provided by rehabilitation facilities and assign the costs accordingly. Whether programs taken as a whole are considered to be medical or educational depends on the extent and purpose of the provided medical services.

Child Find

The IDEA and its regulations require states, through local educational agencies or school boards, to identify, assess, and serve all children with disabilities,[159] regardless of the severity of their disabilities. This mandate includes homeless children, wards of the state, and, as discussed below in more detail, children whose parents have placed them in private schools, including religiously affiliated elementary and secondary schools.[160] Regarding private school students, the IDEA's regulations place the child find obligation on the school boards in the districts where the private schools are located rather than the ones in which the children and their families reside.[161]

School officials cannot ignore signs that children may have disabilities.[162] Be that as it may, disputes have arisen under the child find provision centering over when school personnel knew, or should have recognized, that children possibly had disabilities. It is a common practice for educators to employ various types of remedial strategies to assist struggling children before referring them for special education. In fact, in a case from Pennsylvania, the Third Circuit recognized that such tactics often are warranted, particularly with young children.[163] Given the IDEA's emphasis on educating students in the least restrictive environment, referring a student for a special education evaluation should not be a teacher's first response when a child encounters difficulties. On the other hand, waiting too long to evaluate a student when other remedial tactics fail to produce results can deny a FAPE.[164]

The task of identifying children in need of services is generally delegated to individual school boards. In order to locate young children who may have disabilities, board officials typically disseminate information about the services available to qualified students via school websites, newspaper articles, radio announcements, and advertisements on cable television. In addition, many officials may leave information pamphlets in locations frequented by parents of young children such as pediatricians' offices, day care centers, and shopping malls.

Early identification and assessment of children with disabilities is a related service under the IDEA.[165] In providing this service, many school boards offer annual screenings for preschool- and kindergarten-aged children. While the kindergarten screening process is generally conducted as part of normal registration activities, educators usually set up special dates to screen preschool-aged children. Parents who suspect that their young children may be disabled can ask for screenings by appointment at any time during school years.

Students in Private Schools

Students with disabilities who attend religiously affiliated nonpublic schools may be entitled to services under the IDEA and/or Section 504.[166] Accordingly, this section primarily reviews issues that may arise when educators in public schools seek to provide special education services to children who attend religiously affiliated nonpublic schools.

Issues surrounding the delivery of special education services to children who attend religiously affiliated nonpublic schools often involve the Establishment Clause of the First Amendment to the U.S. Constitution,[167] according to which "Congress shall make no law respecting an establishment of religion, or prohibiting the free exercise thereof. . . ." Even so, this section does not engage in a full discussion of the lengthy and complex history of litigation involving the limits of aid to religious schools under the Establishment Clause. Rather, it is sufficient to acknowledge that insofar as the Supreme Court first enunciated the Child Benefit Test, which permits a variety of forms of aid to children in nonpublic schools[168] on the basis that the aid is directed at children (and their families), not their schools, it has had a checkered history. Put another way, depending on the composition of the Court, some Justices have been more supportive of the Child Benefit Test than others. Further, virtually all litigation involving the Establishment Clause has been examined in light of the tripartite test enunciated by the Supreme Court in *Lemon v. Kurtzman* (*Lemon*).[169] Under this seemingly ubiquitous test,

> every analysis in this area must begin with consideration of the cumulative criteria developed by the Court over many years. Three such tests may be gleaned from our cases. First, the statute must have a secular legislative purpose; second, its principal or primary effect must be one that neither advances nor inhibits religion; finally, the statute must not foster "an excessive government entanglement with religion."[170]

The low point of the Child Benefit Test occurred in 1985, when, in *Aguilar v. Felton*,[171] the Supreme Court banned the onsite delivery of remedial Title I services in religiously affiliated nonpublic schools in New York City.

The Court struck down the program even in the absence of any allegations of misconduct or misappropriation of public funds, based on the fear that having public school educators provide services in religious schools might have created "excessive entanglement" between the government and religion. Consequently, since school boards still had to provide services at public schools or neutral sites, many students who attended religiously affiliated nonpublic schools were denied equal educational opportunities under Title I.

The landscape with regard to state aid to K–12 education began to shift in 1993, when the Supreme Court revitalized the Child Benefit Test in *Zobrest v. Catalina Foothills School District* (*Zobrest*).[172] In *Zobrest* the Court ruled that the Establishment Clause did not bar a public school board from providing the onsite delivery of the services of a sign language interpreter for a student who attended a sectarian high school. The Court reasoned that insofar as the interpreter was essentially a conduit through whom information passed, the onsite delivery of such assistance did not violate the Establishment Clause.[173] Four years later, in *Agostini v. Felton*,[174] following up on *Aguilar*, the Court essentially lifted the ban against the onsite delivery of services to students who attended religiously affiliated nonpublic schools in New York City, since appropriate safeguards were in place.[175]

> Regulatory modifications to the IDEA that were adopted in 1999, and which changed little in the 2004 amendments, created a dilemma. The regulations, and earlier case law, made it clear that children in religious schools are entitled to receive some special education services, but the laws set funding restrictions in place that limited the amount of services that these children can receive onsite in their religious schools.

Later, in *Mitchell v. Helms*,[176] the Supreme Court, in a plurality, meaning that it lacked the necessary five-Justice majority needed to make it binding precedent, upheld the constitutionality of Chapter 2, now Title VI, of the Elementary and Secondary Education Act, a far-reaching federal statute permitting the loan of state-owned instructional materials such as computers, slide projectors, television sets, tape recorders, maps, and globes to nonpublic schools. In the part of the case most relevant to special education, but which was not appealed to the Supreme Court, the Fifth Circuit[177] upheld state laws from Louisiana permitting the onsite delivery of special education services to children who attended faith-based schools while granting them free transportation to and from school.

A major statutory change occurred in 1997 when Congressional reauthorization of the IDEA included provisions clarifying the obligations of public school systems to provide special education and related services to students in nonpublic schools. Unfortunately, neither Congress nor the courts conclusively answered questions about the delivery of special education for children in religiously affiliated nonpublic schools. Regulatory modifications adopted in 1999, which changed little in the 2004 amendments, created a dilemma. The regulations, and earlier case law, made it clear that children in religious schools were entitled to receive some special education services. Yet, the laws set funding restrictions in place that limited the amount of services that these children can receive onsite in their religious schools. The net result is that these students are likely to receive fewer services if public school officials follow the letter of the law and do not make additional services available to qualified students in religious schools.

The IDEA[178] and its regulations[179] make it clear that children whose parents voluntarily enroll them in nonpublic schools are entitled to some level of special education services.[180] Further, the IDEA permits the onsite delivery of special education for students with disabilities whose parents have placed them in "private schools," including religious, elementary, and secondary schools,[181] as long as safeguards are in place to avoid "excessive entanglement" between public school systems and religious institutions. This approach is consistent with settled law that public school personnel can conduct diagnostic tests onsite in religiously affiliated nonpublic schools to evaluate whether children are eligible for services in programs that are supported by public funds.[182]

The regulations incorporate statutory changes and provide guidance on meeting the IDEA's requirements while borrowing from preexisting Education Department General Administrative Regulations (EDGAR regulations).[183] The EDGAR regulations require school boards to provide students in nonpublic schools with opportunities for equitable participation in federal programs.[184] This means that students in nonpublic schools are entitled to opportunities to participate in federal programs that are comparable in quality to those available to children in public schools.[185] In developing programs, public school personnel must consult with representatives of the nonpublic schools to consider which students will be served, how their needs will be identified, what benefits they will receive, how the benefits will be delivered, and how the programs will be evaluated.[186]

Private School Students Defined

Public school officials must locate, identify, and evaluate all students with disabilities who attend "private schools" within their jurisdictions, including children whose parents place them in nonpublic schools.[187] This means that boards must develop plans to permit these students to participate in programs carried out pursuant to the IDEA.[188] The regulations define students in nonpublic schools as those whose parents have voluntarily enrolled them in such schools or facilities.[189] This definition does not include students whose school boards have placed them in private facilities at public expense in order to provide each of them with a FAPE.

Spending Restrictions

The IDEA and its regulations limit the amount of money that school boards must spend in providing services to students in nonpublic schools.[190] The total is limited to a proportionate amount of the federal funds received based on the number of students in nonpublic schools in relation to the overall number of pupils in districts.[191] Boards are not prohibited from using state funds to offer more than the IDEA calls for since the regulation establishes only a minimum amount that they must spend on qualified children.[192]

Under its regulations, IDEA funds cannot be used to benefit private schools.[193] More specifically, public funds cannot be used to offer impermissible aid to religious institutions by financing existing instructional programs, otherwise providing them with direct financial benefits such as money, or organizing classes based on students' religions or schools they attend.[194] Even so, the regulations allow boards to employ public school personnel in these nonpublic schools as long as they are not supplanting services that are normally provided by those institutions.[195] The regulations further permit boards to hire personnel from nonpublic schools to provide services outside of their regular hours of work as long as they are under the supervision and control of officials from the public schools.[196] Finally, property, equipment, or supplies purchased with IDEA funds can be used onsite in nonpublic schools only for the benefit of students with disabilities.[197]

Comparable Services

According to the IDEA's regulations, students who attend private schools do not have individual rights to receive some or all of the special education and related services that they might have received in public schools.[198] This does not mean that children in private schools are denied all services under the IDEA. Rather, the regulations give public school officials the authority to develop service plans and to decide which students from private schools will be served.[199] The regulations also require public school officials to ensure that representatives of private or religious schools have the opportunity to attend such meetings or participate by other means, such as individual or conference calls.[200]

Students in private schools are entitled to receive services from personnel who meet the same standards as educators in public schools,[201] even if they receive different amounts of services than their peers in public schools.[202] Since students with disabilities who attend private schools are not entitled to the same amount of services as similarly situated peers in public schools, the regulations do not require the development of IEPs. Instead, the regulations obligate school officials to develop service plans describing the aid that they will provide to students.[203] Even so, service plans must not only meet the same content requirements as IEPs but must also be developed, reviewed, and revised in a manner consistent with the IEP process.[204]

Delivery of Services

The regulations reiterate that services may be offered onsite in religiously affiliated nonpublic schools.[205] In order to differentiate between public and private schools, the regulations specifically use the phrase "including religious schools" to reflect the fact that religiously affiliated nonpublic schools are included within the IDEA's framework.[206] Although public boards may provide onsite services in nonpublic schools, they are not required to do so.[207]

If it is necessary for children to receive benefits from services that are not offered onsite, and students must be transported to alternate locations to receive them, school boards must provide transportation between the students' schools or homes to sites where they receive services[208] and from the service sites to their private schools or homes, depending on the time of day.[209] Yet, boards are not required to transport private school students from their homes to their private schools.[210] In addition, it is important to recognize that the cost of transportation may be included in calculating the minimum amount of federal funds that boards must spend on students in nonpublic schools.[211]

Dispute Resolution

The IDEA's procedural safeguards are generally inapplicable to complaints that boards failed to deliver services to students in nonpublic schools.[212] The due process provisions do apply to complaints that boards failed to comply with the child find requirements applicable to students in nonpublic schools[213] and to complaints pursuant to allegations arising in connection with state administration of special education.[214]

Child Find in Private Schools

The 2004 modification of the IDEA and its regulations direct officials in public schools to identify children with disabilities whose parents enrolled them in private schools (including religious, elementary, and secondary schools) in their districts rather than simply those who live within school districts.[215] Under these provisions, public school officials must provide accurate counts to state education agencies of the number of children from private schools who are evaluated, determined to have disabilities, and served.[216]

These changes also require school boards to employ child find activities for students in private schools that are similar to those used to identify children who attend public schools.[217] Further, the cost of such activities does not count in calculating whether school systems exceeded the amount that they spent in serving students who attend private schools.[218]

FREQUENTLY ASKED QUESTIONS

Q: Are school boards required to provide students with disabilities the best possible education regardless of cost?

A: No, the IDEA does not require school boards to provide students with disabilities with the best education possible regardless of cost, although state law may dictate that they do so. This is based on the notion that states can provide more but not less service than the IDEA mandates. Under the IDEA, school boards are obligated to provide educational programs that confer some educational benefit on students; benefits cannot be minimal or trivial, but the program provided does not need to be ideal.

Q: Are school boards required to adopt methodologies preferred by students' parents?

A: No, courts have consistently agreed that the choice of methodology is up to school board officials. Thus, educators may choose from among competing methodologies and are not required to adopt the parents' choice. Educators are not even required to adopt what may be considered to be the best approach as long as their chosen methods are generally accepted in the professional community.

Q: Are school boards required to educate all students with disabilities in inclusionary settings?

A: No, the IDEA is clear that inclusion is a goal, not a mandate, requiring that students be educated in the least restrictive environment. For some students the least restrictive environment may be substantially separate programs. Even so, school board officials may educate students with disabilities in more restrictive settings only when such placements are necessary to provide children with FAPEs. Officials also must provide reasonable supplementary aids and services that allow students to be educated in the less restrictive environments.

Q: When are school boards required to pay for residential placements?

A: School boards are required to pay for residential placements when they are necessary for educational reasons. Boards are not obligated to pay the room and board portion of such placements when they are made for noneducational reasons. Often, boards can share the costs of residential placements with other agencies.

Q: When are school boards required to provide educational services beyond the traditional school year?

A: Students with disabilities are entitled to programming beyond traditional school years if they suffer regressions during school breaks that combined

(Continued)

(Continued)

with the time required to recoup lost skills, substantially interfere with the attainment of educational goals. When the cumulative effects of regression and recoupment time result in little or no educational gains over a period of time, students may be entitled to extended school year placements.

Q: What responsibility do school boards have for students who attend private schools at their parents' expense?

A: School boards are required to spend a proportionate share of the federal money they receive on students with disabilities who attend private schools, including those in religiously affiliated schools. School board representatives must consult with officials from private schools to decide how these funds will be spent. Since students in private schools do not have an individual right to receive special education and related services at public expense, they lack the right to receive the same level of services that they would have received in public schools.

Recommendations

Before turning to specific recommendations, it almost goes without saying that school officials should be honest, good listeners who provide support for parents. Still, in offering hope to parents, school officials should be realistic about the status of children and keep parents up to date at all times. Moreover, to the extent that all children with disabilities are entitled to IEPs to direct their schooling, educators should do the following:

- Work to provide all students (including, with limits, children whose parents place them in private and religiously affiliated nonpublic schools) with FAPEs in the LREs. Thus, in seeking to become knowledgeable about all aspects of the IDEA, educational leaders must seek regular professional development opportunities for themselves and members of their staffs.
- Address the educational needs of students on their individual merits, since all children have unique talents, abilities, and needs. Even in recognizing that a continuum of placements is available, educators must make genuine efforts to serve the needs of all children, meaning that students should be provided with all the necessary related and support services.
- Keep in mind that state standards, only a few of which provide greater protection than the IDEA, must be taken into consideration when evaluating whether placements are appropriate. If higher state standards are in place, they must be met.

- Avoid segregating special education students by placing them in LREs.
- Balance appropriate levels of specialized services and placements in inclusionary settings.
- Take nonacademic benefits into consideration when justifying inclusive settings, even if students' academic progress does not come as quickly as it would in segregated placements.
- Be careful to avoid, whenever possible, using private day or residential schools in lieu of inclusive placements for children with low-incidence–type disabilities.
- Recall that if needed, placements in residential facilities, or year-round placements, must be made at no cost to parents. Moreover, educators would be wise to consider ways of sharing the cost of such placements with other agencies, particularly when residential placements are required for reasons not strictly educational.
- Use a variety of criteria, such as standardized test scores, anecdotal teacher reports, report card grades, and portfolios in addressing whether the services provided are conferring an educational benefit on students.
- Recall that insofar as students with disabilities who attend religiously affiliated nonpublic schools may be entitled to some services under the IDEA and/or Section 504, liaisons should be appointed to work with staff members in these schools.
- Take steps to ensure the early identification of all children with special needs, regardless of where they attend school.
- While good educational practices, coupled with the IDEA's LRE mandate, dictate that teachers should attempt remedial strategies prior to referring students who are having difficulty to special education, evaluations must be conducted when it becomes clear that these measures are not working.

Endnotes

1. 20 U.S.C. §§ 1400–1482 (2012). The IDEA's regulations can be found at Assistance to the States for the Education of Children with Disabilities, 34 C.F.R. §§ 300.1–300.818. (2013).
2. 20 U.S.C. § 1401(9).
3. 458 U.S. 176 (1982).
4. "We previously have cautioned that courts lack the 'specialized knowledge and experience' necessary to resolve 'persistent and difficult questions of educational policy. . . .' Therefore, once a court determines that the requirements of the Act have been met, questions of methodology are for resolution by the States [through school officials]." *Id.* at 208.
5. 20 U.S.C. § 1401(9).
6. 20 U.S.C. § 1412(a)(1)(A).

7. 20 U.S.C. § 1401(3)(A)(i).
8. 20 U.S.C. §§ 1401(3)(A)(ii), (B)(ii).
9. 468 U.S. 883, 894 (1984). "Only those services necessary to aid a child [with disabilities] to benefit from special education must be provided."
10. The IDEA was reauthorized and amended in 2004 by the Individuals with Disabilities Education Improvement Act of 2004, now codified at 20 U.S.C. §§ 1400–1485.
11. 20 U.S.C. § 1401(30).
12. 20 U.S.C. § 1401(c)(5)(F).
13. 20 U.S.C. § 1401(3)(B)(i).
14. 20 U.S.C. § 1401(14).
15. 20 U.S.C. § 1414(d)(1)(A)(i).
16. A.B. *ex rel.* D.B. v. Lawson, 354 F.3d 315 (4th Cir. 2004).
17. Lt. T.B. *ex rel.* N.B. v. Warwick School Committee, 361 F.3d 80 (1st Cir. 2004).
18. 34 C.F.R. § 300.115(b)(1).
19. The IDEA states a preference for students to be educated in their neighborhood schools. Even so, courts consistently agree that the IDEA does not mandate placement in these settings. *See, e.g.,* White v. Ascension Parish School Board, 343 F.3d 373 (5th Cir. 2010); Lebron v. North Penn School District, 769 F. Supp. 2d 788 (E.D. Pa. 2011).
20. 34 C.F.R. § 300.17.
21. 458 U.S. 176 (1982).
22. *Id.* at 200.
23. A.B. *ex rel.* D.B. v. Lawson, 354 F.3d 315 (4th Cir. 2004).
24. Although the IDEA has been amended since *Rowley,* its standard has not been altered. *See* J.L., M.L., K.L. v. Mercer Island School District, 592 F.3d 938 (9th Cir. 2010) (reiterating that recent amendments to the IDEA have not superseded *Rowley's* definition of a FAPE).
25. W. Va. Code Ann. §18-20-5(3) (West 2013).
26. Burke County Board of Education v. Denton, 895 F.2d 973 (4th Cir. 1990).
27. Geis v. Board of Education of Parsippany–Troy Hills, 774 F.2d 575 (3d Cir. 1985).
28. Barwacz v. Michigan Department of Education, 681 F. Supp. 427 (W.D. Mich. 1988).
29. Pink v. Mt. Diablo Unified School District, 738 F. Supp. 345 (N.D. Cal. 1990).
30. Geis v. Board of Education of Parsippany-Troy Hills, 774 F.2d 575, 581 (3d Cir. 1985), *citing* then 20 U.S.C. § 1401(18)(B), currently codified at 20 U.S.C. § 1401(9)(B). *See also* David D. v. Dartmouth School Committee, 775 F.2d 411 (1st Cir. 1985) (affirming that Massachusetts had a standard higher than the one established by the IDEA). Massachusetts has since revised its standard to more closely conform to the federal requirements; *see* Mass. Gen. Laws ch. 71B, § 1 (2012); Wanham v. Everett Public Schools, 550 F. Supp. 2d 152 (D. Mass. 2008).
31. Osborne, A. G. (1992). Legal standards for an appropriate education in the post-*Rowley* era. *Exceptional Children, 58,* 488–494. *See also* M.C. v. Central Regional School District, 81 F.3d 389 (3d Cir. 1996), *cert. denied,* 519 U.S. 806 (1996).
32. Hall v. Vance County Board of Education, 774 F.2d 629 (4th Cir. 1985).
33. Carter v. Florence County School District Four, 950 F.2d 156 (4th Cir. 1991), *affirmed on other grounds sub nom.* Florence County School District Four v. Carter, 510 U.S. 126 (1993).

34. Board of Education of East Windsor Regional School District v. Diamond, 808 F.2d 987 (3d Cir. 1986).

35. Polk v. Central Susquehanna Intermediate Unit 16, 853 F.2d 171 (3d Cir. 1988).

36. Chris C. v. Gwinnett County School District, 780 F. Supp. 804 (N.D. Ga. 1991).

37. Walczak v. Florida Union Free School District, 142 F.3d 119 (2d Cir. 1998).

38. J.S.K. v. Hendry County School Board, 941 F.2d 1563 (11th Cir. 1991).

39. Devine v. Indian River County School Board, 249 F.3d 1289 (11th Cir. 2001).

40. Teague Independent School District v. Todd D., 999 F.2d 127 (5th Cir. 1993).

41. Fort Zumwalt School District v. Clynes, 119 F.3d 607 (8th Cir. 1997), *cert. denied sub nom* Clynes v. Fort Zumwalt School District, 523 U.S. 1137 (1998). *See also* M.M. *ex rel.* L.M. v. District 0001 Lancaster County Schools, 702 F.3d 479 (8th Cir. 2012) (affirming that a student who advanced from year to year and was gaining educational skills received a FAPE).

42. Osborne, A. G. (1992). Legal standards for an appropriate education in the post-*Rowley* era. *Exceptional Children, 58,* 488–494.

43. Hall v. Vance County Board of Education, 774 F.2d 629 (4th Cir. 1985).

44. In re Conklin, 946 F.2d 306 (4th Cir. 1991).

45. *See, e.g.,* Klein Independent School District v. Hovem, 690 F.3d 390 (5th Cir. 2012).

46. Stock v. Massachusetts Hospital School, 467 N.E.2d 448 (Mass. 1984).

47. Thompson R2-J School District v. Luke P., 540 F. Supp. 2d 1143 (10th Cir. 2008); CJN v. Minneapolis Public Schools, 323 F.3d 630 (8th Cir. 2003), *cert. denied sub nom* Nygren v. Minneapolis Public Schools, Special School Dist. No. 1, 540 U.S. 984 (2003).

48. D.B. *ex rel.* Elizabeth B. v. Esposito, 675 F.3d 260 (1st Cir. 2012); Sebastian M. v. King Philip Regional School District, 685 F.3d 79 (1st Cir. 2012); D.B. *ex rel.* Elizabeth B. v. Esposito, 675 F.3d 260 (1st Cir. 2012); Bonnie Ann F. v. Calallen Independent School District, 835 F. Supp. 340 (S.D. Tex. 1993), *affirmed* 40 F.3d 386 (5th Cir. 1994) (mem).

49. *See, e.g.,* R.P. *ex rel.* C.P. v. Prescott Unified School District, 631 F.3d 1117 (9th Cir. 2011); Adam J. v. Keller Independent School District, 328 F.3d 804 (5th Cir. 2003); James and Lee Ann D. *ex rel.* Sarah D. v. Board of Education of Aptakisic-Tripp Community Consolidated School District No. 102, 642 F. Supp. 2d 804 (N.D. Ill. 2009).

50. Richardson Independent School District v. Michael Z., 580 F.3d 286 (5th Cir. 2009); Draper v. Atlanta Independent School System, 518 F.3d 1275 (11th Cir. 2008); Nein v. Greater Clark County School Corporation, 95 F. Supp. 2d 961 (S.D. Ind. 2000); Ojai Unified School District v. Jackson, 4 F.3d 1467 (9th Cir. 1993).

51. Woods *ex rel.* T.W. v. Northport Public Schools, 487 F. App'x 968 (6th Cir. 2012).

52. Johnson v. Lancaster-Lebanon Intermediate Unit 13, Lancaster City School District, 757 F. Supp. 606 (E.D. Pa. 1991).

53. School Board of Campbell County v. Beasley, 380 S.E.2d 884 (Va. 1989).

54. Lessard v. Wilton Lyndeborough Cooperative School District, 518 F.3d 18 (1st Cir. 2008); Jaccari J. v. Board of Education of Chicago, 690 F. Supp. 2d 687 (N.D. Ill. 2010); K.S. *ex rel.* P.S. v. Fremont Unified School District, 679 F. Supp. 2d 1046 (N.D. Cal. 2009), *affirmed* 426 F. App'x 536 (9th Cir. 2011); Mavis v. Sobol, 839 F. Supp. 968 (N.D.N.Y. 1994).

55. Socorro Independent School District v. Angelic Y., 107 F. Supp. 2d 761 (W.D. Tex. 2000).

56. White v. School Board of Henrico County, 549 S.E.2d 16 (Va. Ct. App. 2001).

57. *See, e.g.,* Hinson v. Merritt Educational Center, 579 F. Supp. 2d 89 (D.D.C. 2008); P.K. and P.K. *ex rel.* P.K. v. Bedford Central School District, 569 F. Supp. 2d 371 (S.D.N.Y. 2008); Hampton School District v. Dobrowolski, 976 F.2d 48 (1st Cir. 1992).

58. *See, e.g.,* R.P. *ex rel.* R.P. and C.P. v. Alamo Heights Independent School District, 703 F.3d 801 (5th Cir. 2012); K.E. *ex rel.* K.E. and T.E. v. Independent School District No. 15, 647 F.3d 795 (8th Cir. 2011); S.H. v. Fairfax County Board of Education, 875 F. Supp. 2d 633 (E.D. Va. 2012); R.H. *ex rel.* Emily H. v. Plano Independent School District, 607 F.3d 1003 (5th Cir. 2010).

59. D.S. v. Bayonne Board of Education, 602 F.3d 553 (3d Cir. 2010).

60. Fuhrmann v. East Hanover Board of Education, 993 F.2d 1031 (3d Cir. 1993).

61. *See, e.g.,* Klein Independent School District v. Hovem, 690 F.3d 390 (5th Cir. 2012); D.S. v. Bayonne Board of Education, 602 F.3d 553 (3d Cir. 2010); A.M. *ex rel.* Marshall v. Montrovia Unified School District, 627 F.3d 773 (9th Cir. 2010); Jortness v. Neenah Joint School District, 507 F.3d 1060 (7th Cir. 2007).

62. *See, e.g.,* J.G. and J.G. v. Briarcliff Manor Union Free School District, 682 F. Supp. 2d 387 (S.D.N.Y. 2010).

63. *See, e.g.,* Ridley School District v. M.R., 680 F.3d 260 (3d Cir. 2012); Carlson v. San Diego Unified School District, 380 F. App'x 595 (9th Cir. 2010); Lessard v. Wilton Lyndeborough Cooperative School District, 518 F.3d 18 (1st Cir. 2008); Poway Unified School District v. Cheng, 821 F. Supp. 2d 1197 (S.D. Cal. 2011); D.G. *ex rel.* P.O. v. Cooperstown Central School District, 746 F. Supp. 2d 435 (N.D.N.Y. 2010); Greenwood v. Wissachickon School District, 571 F. Supp. 2d 654 (E.D. Pa. 2008), *affirmed* 374 F. App'x 330 (3d Cir. 2010).

64. Van Duyn v. Baker School District, 502 F.3d 811 (9th Cir. 2007).

65. *See, e.g.,* Sumter County School District 17 v. Heffernan, 642 F.3d 478 (4th Cir. 2011); Banks v. District of Columbia, 720 F. Supp. 2d 83 (D.D.C. 2010).

66. *See, e.g.,* Woods *ex rel.* T.W. v. Northport Public Schools, 487 F. App'x 968 (6th Cir. 2012); Sumpter County School District 17 v. Hefferman, 642 F.3d 478 (4th Cir. 2011); Doe v. Hampden-Wilbraham Regional School District, 715 F. Supp. 2d 185 (D. Mass. 2010).

67. For a discussion of this topic, see the "Change in Placement" section of Chapter 5.

68. Osborne, A.G. (2010). Are school districts required to identify placement locations for the delivery of services in IEPs? *Education Law Reporter, 261,* 497–514.

69. A.K. *ex rel.* J.K. v. Alexandria City School Board, 484 F.3d 672 (4th Cir. 2007). *But see* Shaw v. Weast, 364 F. App'x 47 (4th Cir. 2010) (affirming that a school board did not deny a FAPE by failing to name a specific school in an IEP); K.J. *ex rel.* B.J. v. Fairfax County School Board, 361 F. App'x 435 (4th Cir. 2010) (affirming that the failure to name a specific placement in writing did not violate the IDEA because it did not result in a loss of an educational opportunity). It must be noted that because they were not officially published, the latter two cases are not considered to be precedent setting.

70. T.Y. v. New York City Department of Education, 584 F.3d 412 (2d Cir. 2009). *Accord* M.N. and H.N. *ex rel.* J.N. v. New York City Department of Education, 700 F. Supp. 2d 356 (S.D.N.Y. 2010). *See also* Brad K. *ex rel.* Jennifer K. v. Board of Education of Chicago, 787 F. Supp. 2d 734 (N.D. Ill. 2011).

71. 20 U.S.C. § 1412(a)(5)(A).

72. Osborne, A. G., & DiMattia, P. (1994). The IDEA's least restrictive environment mandate: Legal implications. *Exceptional Children, 61,* 6–14.

73. *See, e.g.,* J.G. and R.G. *ex rel.* N.G v. Kiryas Joel Union Free School District, 777 F. Supp. 2d 606 (S.D.N.Y. 2011).

74. 20 U.S.C. § 1412(a)(10)(A)(i).

75. 995 F.2d 1204 (3d Cir. 1993). *Accord* P. *ex rel.* Mr. P. v. Newington Board of Education, 546 F.3d 111 (2d Cir. 2008).

76. Daniel R.R. v. State Board of Education, 874 F.2d 1036 (5th Cir. 1989). Other circuits also have adopted the Fifth Circuit's test. *See, e.g.,* L.B. and J.B. *ex rel.* K.B. v. Nebo School District, 379 F.3d 966 (10th Cir. 2004); Greer v. Rome City School District, 950 F.2d 688 (11th Cir. 1991).

77. 14 F.3d 1398 (9th Cir. 1994), *cert. denied,* 512 U.S. 1207 (1994).

78. *See, e.g.,* G.B. and L.B. *ex rel.* N.B. v. Tuxedo Union Free School District, 751 F. Supp. 2d 552 (S.D.N.Y. 2010).

79. *See, e.g.,* B.S. *ex rel.* R.S. and P.S. v. Placentia-Yorba Linda Unified School District, 306 F. App'x 397 (9th Cir. 2009); Beth B. v. Van Clay, 282 F.3d 493 (7th Cir. 2002).

80. *See, e.g.,* J.H. *ex rel.* A.H. and S.H. v. Fort Bend Independent School District, 482 F. App'x 915 (5th Cir. 2012); A.G. v. Wissahickon School District, 374 F. App'x 330 (3d Cir. 2010); L.E. *ex rel.* E.S. v. Ramsey Board of Education, 435 F.3d 384 (3d Cir. 2006); T.W. *ex rel.* McCullough v. Unified School District No. 259, 136 F. App'x 122 (10th Cir. 2005); Capistrano Unified School District v. Wartenberg, 59 F.3d 884 (9th Cir. 1995); K.I. *ex rel.* Jennie I. v. Montgomery Public Schools, 805 F. Supp. 2d 1283 (M.D. Ala. 2011); J.S. *ex rel.* Y.S. v. North Colonie Central School District, 586 F. Supp. 2d 74 (N.D.N.Y. 2008); Dick-Friedman *ex rel.* Friedman v. Board of Education of West Bloomfield Public Schools, 427 F. Supp. 2d 768 (E.D. Mich. 2006)

81. A.M. *ex rel.* Marshall v. Monrovia Unified School District, 627 F.3d 773 (9th Cir. 2010). *See also* Board of Education of Township High School District No. 211 v. Ross, 468 F.3d 267 (7th Cir. 2007) (affirming that a special class placement was the least restrictive environment for a student who was not making meaningful progress in a mainstream program); Manchester School District v. Christopher B., 807 F. Supp. 860 (D.N.H. 1992) (finding that mainstreaming was not appropriate for a 15-year-old student who was reading on a first-grade level).

82. *See, e.g.,* L.G. *ex rel.* E.G. v. Fair Lawn Board of Education, 486 F. App'x 967 (3d Cir. 2012); Clyde K. v. Puyallup School District No. 3, 35 F.3d 1396 (9th Cir. 1994).

83. 875 F.2d 954 (1st Cir. 1989), *cert. denied,* 493 U.S. 983 (1989).

84. 484 U.S. 305 (1988).

85. 34 C.F.R. §§ 300.104, 300.115(b)(1).

86. Wenkart, R. D. (2000). Juvenile offenders: Residential placement and special education. *Education Law Reporter, 144,* 1–13. *See* P.C. and M.C. *ex rel.* K.C. v. Oceanside Union Free School District, 818 F. Supp. 2d 516 (E.D.N.Y. 2011)

(ruling that a student whose academic and behavioral difficulties were attributed to heavy drug abuse was not entitled to special education); Mr. and Mrs. N.C. *ex rel.* M.C. v. Bedford Central School District, 473 F. Supp. 2d 532 (S.D.N.Y. 2007), *affirmed* 300 F. App'x 11 (2d Cir. 2008) (agreeing that a student's drug use and aggressive behavior by themselves were not enough to qualify him for special education).

87. 20 U.S.C. § 1412(a)(1)(B).

88. Hawaii Revised Statutes § 302A–1134(c (2010).

89. E.R.K. v. Hawaii Department of Education, 728 F.3d 982 (9th Cir. 2013). *See also* Helms v. Independent School District, 750 F.2d 820 (10th Cir. 1984) (affirming that a school board could not terminate special education services for a student with disabilities who had completed 12 years of school but was not yet 21 since it provided more than12 years of education to nondisabled students who repeated a grade).

90. Chuhran v. Walled Lake Consolidated School, 839 F. Supp. 465 (E.D. Mich. 1993). *See also* T.M. and J.M. *ex rel.* Kingston City School District, 891 F. Supp. 2d 289 (N.D.N.Y. 2012) (ruling that a student who had earned a standard high school diploma was no longer eligible for IDEA services).

91. 20 U.S.C. § 1401(3)(A).

92. Assistance to the States for the Education of Children with Disabilities, 34 C.F.R. §§ 300.1–300.818 (2006).

93. 34 C.F.R. § 300.8(c)(4).

94. 34 C.F.R. § 300.8(c)(4)(ii). *See* Mr. and Mrs. N.C. *ex rel.* M.C. v. Bedford Central School District, 473 F. Supp. 2d 532 (S.D.N.Y. 2007), *affirmed* 300 F. App'x 11 (2d Cir. 2008) (holding that a student's drug use and aggressive behavior could be characterized as social maladjustment, not emotional disturbance).

95. Springer v. Fairfax County School Board, 134 F.3d 659 (4th Cir. 1998).

96. *See also* W.G. and M.G. *ex rel.* K.G. v. New York City Department of Education, 801 F. Supp. 2d 142 (S.D.N.Y. 2011) (finding that a student's academic problems were due to truancy); Nguyen v. District of Columbia, 681 F. Supp. 2d 49 (D.D.C. 2010) (deciding that the factor that most affected a student's educational performance was his nonattendance); Loch v. Board of Education of Edwardsville Community School District #7, 573 F. Supp. 2d 1072 (S.D. Ill. 2008), *affirmed* 327 F. App'x 647 (7th Cir. 2009) (agreeing that a student who achieved well until she stopped attending school and completing her assignments did not need special education).

97. *See also* P.C. and M.C. *ex rel.* K.C. v. Oceanside Union Free School District, 818 F. Supp. 2d 516 (E.D.N.Y. 2011) (ruling that a student who began to fail only after he started abusing drugs was not seriously emotionally disturbed).

98. Independent School District No. 284 v. A.C., 258 F.3d 769 (8th Cir. 2001).

99. *See also* Eschenasy v. New York City Department of Education, 604 F. Supp. 2d 639 (S.D.N.Y. 2009).

100. Muller v. Committee on Special Education of the East Islip Union Free School District, 145 F.3d 95 (2d Cir. 1998).

101. Babb v. Knox County School System, 965 F.2d 104 (6th Cir. 1992).

102. R.B. *ex rel.* F.B. v. Napa Valley Unified School District, 496 F.3d 932 (9th Cir. 2007).

103. 34 C.F.R. § 300.8(c)(9).

104. Alvin Independent School District v. A.D. *ex rel.* Patricia F., 503 F.3d 378 (5th Cir. 2007). *See also* Lyons v. Smith, 829 F. Supp. 414 (D.D.C. 1993) (maintaining that evidence supported the school board's contention that ADHD did not adversely affect a child's academic performance since he did superior schoolwork).

105. Hansen v. Republic R-III School District, 632 F.3d 1024 (8th Cir. 2011).

106. M.P. *ex rel.* Peyman v. Santa Monica Malibu Unified School District, 633 F. Supp. 2d 1089 (C.D. Cal. 2008).

107. PDR Staff (2013). *Physicians Desk Reference*. Montvale, NJ: PDR Network.

108. Davis v. Francis Howell School District, 138 F.3d 754 (8th Cir. 1998); DeBord v. Board of Education of the Ferguson-Florissant School District, 126 F.3d 1102 (8th Cir. 1997).

109. 20 U.S.C.A. § 1412(a)(25).

110. Rehabilitation Act, Section 504, 29 U.S.C. § 794 (2006).

111. Russo, C. J. (2011). HIV/AIDS and K–12 education: Neither out of sight nor out of mind. *Education Law Reporter, 267,* 1–20.

112. District 27 Community School Board v. Board of Education of the City of New York, 502 N.Y.S.2d 325 (N.Y. Sup. Ct. 1986).

113. Doe v. Belleville Public School District No. 118, 672 F. Supp. 342 (S.D. Ill. 1987).

114. Americans with Disabilities Act, 42 U.S.C. §§ 12101–12213 (2006).

115. New York State Association for Retarded Children v. Carey, 612 F.2d 644 (2d Cir. 1979).

116. Community High School District 155 v. Denz, 463 N.E.2d 998 (Ill. App. Ct. 1984).

117. Martinez v. School Board of Hillsborough County, Fla., 861 F.2d 1502 (11th Cir. 1988), *on remand* 711 F. Supp. 1066 (M.D. Fla. 1989).

118. Minor discrepancies or those that can be corrected in the regular classroom do not qualify students for special education. *See* C.M. *ex rel.* Jodi M. v. Department of Education, State of Hawaii, 476 F. App'x 674 (9th Cir. 2012); Hood v. Encinitas Union School District, 486 F.3d 1099 (9th Cir. 2007); Nguyen v. District of Columbia, 681 F. Supp. 2d 49 (D.D.C. 2010).

119. 20 U.S.C. § 1414(b)(6); 34 C.F.R. § 300.307(a)(1).

120. Michael P. v. Department of Education, 656 F.3d 1057 (9th Cir. 2011).

121. 34 C.F.R. § 300.107.

122. Rettig v. Kent School District, 788 F.2d 326 (6th Cir. 1986), *cert. denied,* 478 U.S. 1005 (1986).

123. Crocker v. Tennessee Secondary School Athletic Association, 735 F. Supp. 753 (M.D. Tenn. 1990), *affirmed sub nom.* Metropolitan Government of Nashville and Davidson County v. Crocker, 908 F.2d 973 (6th Cir. 1990) (mem.).

124. Independent School District No. 12, Centennial v. Minnesota Department of Education, 788 N.W.2d 907 (Minn. 2010).

125. McPherson v. Michigan High School Athletic Association, 119 F.3d 453 (6th Cir. 1997); Pottgen v. Missouri State High School Athletic Association, 40 F.3d 926 (8th Cir. 1994).

126. Washington v. Indiana High School Athletic Association, 181 F.3d 849 (7th Cir. 1999), *cert denied,* 528 U.S. 1046 (1999); Bingham v. Oregon School Activities Association, 37 F. Supp. 2d 1189 (D. Or. 1999).

127. Osborne, A. G., & Battaglino, L. (1996). Eligibility of students with disabilities for sports: Implications for policy. *Education Law Reporter, 105,* 379–388.
128. 20 U.S.C. §§ 1401(14), 1414(d).
129. Helms v. Independent School District, 750 F.2d 820 (10th Cir. 1984).
130. Draper v. Atlanta Independent School System, 518 F.3d 1275 (11th Cir. 2008).
131. Garcia v. Board of Education of Albuquerque Public Schools, 520 F.3d 1116 (10th Cir. 2008).
132. 34 C.F.R. § 300.106(a)(2).
133. McQueen v. Colorado Springs School District No. 11, 419 F. Supp. 2d 1303 (D. Colo. 2006), *reversed and remanded on other grounds* 488 F.3d 868 (10th Cir. 2007) (reversing because the parents had not exhausted administrative remedies).
134. 34 C.F.R. § 300.106(b)(1)(iii).
135. Crawford v. Pittman, 708 F.2d 1028 (5th Cir. 1983); Georgia Association of Retarded Citizens v. McDaniel, 716 F.2d 1565 (11th Cir. 1983); Battle v. Pennsylvania, 629 F.3d 269 (3d Cir. 1980).
136. Kenton County School District v. Hunt, 384 F.3d. 269 (6th Cir. 2004).
137. Alamo Heights Independent School District v. State Board of Education, 790 F.2d 1153 (5th Cir. 1986). *See also* Board of Education of Fayette County v. L.M., 478 F.3d 307 (6th Cir. 2007) (noting that a student's regression was not severe enough to warrant extended school year services); Kenton County School District v. Hunt, 384 F.3d 269 (6th Cir. 2004) (observing that parents had not demonstrated that extended school years services were required to avoid more than adequately recoupable regression); MM v. School District of Greenville County, 303 F.3d 523 (4th Cir. 2002) (affirming that extended school year services are necessary only when the benefits students gain during school years are significantly jeopardized if they do not receive services during the summer).
138. Moser v. Bret Harte Union High School District, 366 F. Supp. 2d 944 (E.D. Cal. 2005).
139. J.W. v. Contoocook Valley School District, 154 F. Supp. 2d 217 (D.N.H. 2001).
140. Christopher M. v. Corpus Christi Independent School District, 933 F.2d 1285 (5th Cir. 1991).
141. Hartmann v. Loudon County Board of Education, 118 F.3d 996 (4th Cir. 1997); Poolaw v. Bishop, 67 F.3d 830 (9th Cir. 1995). For a discussion of *Hartmann, see* Osborne, A. G. (1998). *Hartmann v. Loudoun County:* Another round in the inclusion controversy. *Education Law Reporter, 125,* 289–302.
142. 34 C.F.R. § 300.115(a).
143. 20 U.S.C. § 1412(a)(10)(B); 34 C.F.R. § 300.325; Cleveland Heights-University Heights City School District v. Boss, 144 F.3d 391 (6th Cir. 1998); Board of Education of Community Consolidated School District No. 21, Cook County v. Illinois State Board of Education, 938 F.3d 712 (7th Cir. 1991), *cert. denied* 502 U.S. 1066 (1992).
144. Colin K. v. Schmidt, 715 F.2d 1 (1st Cir. 1983).
145. Parks v. Pavkovic, 753 F.2d 1397 (7th Cir.1985).
146. Gladys J. v. Pearland Independent School District, 520 F. Supp. 869 (S.D. Tex. 1981).
147. Brown v. Wilson County School Board, 747 F. Supp. 436 (M.D. Tenn. 1990).
148. Chris D. v. Montgomery County Board of Education, 743 F. Supp. 1524 (M.D. Ala. 1990).

149. Abrahamson v. Hershman, 701 F.2d 223 (1st Cir. 1983).
150. Knable v. Bexley City School District, 238 F.3d 755 (6th Cir. 2001).
151. Zayas v. Commonwealth of Puerto Rico, 378 F. Supp. 2d 13 (D.P.R. 2005), *affirmed* 163 F. App'x 4 (1st Cir. 2005).
152. Parks v. Pavkovic, 753 F.2d 1397 (7th Cir.1985).
153. Dale M. *ex rel.* Alice M. v. Board of Education of Bradley-Bourbonnais High School District No. 307, 237 F.3d 813 (7th Cir. 2001).
154. McKenzie v. Jefferson, EHLR 554:338 (D.D.C. 1983).
155. Shaw v. Weast, 364 F. App'x 47 (4th Cir. 2009); Ashland School District v. Parents of Student R.J., 588 F.3d 1004 (9th Cir. 2009); Ashland School District v. Parents of Student E.H., 587 F.3d 1175 (9th Cir. 2009); A.S. v. Madison Metropolitan School District, 477 F. Supp. 2d 969 (W.D. Wis. 2007).
156. Richardson Independent School District v. Michael Z., 580 F.3d 286 (5th Cir. 2009).
157. *See, e.g.,* Vander Malle v. Ambach, 667 F. Supp. 1015 (S.D.N.Y. 1987); North v. District of Columbia, 471 F. Supp. 136 (D.D.C. 1979).
158. 20 U.S.C. § 1401(a)(26).
159. 20 U.S.C. § 1412(a)(3); 34 C.F.R. § 300.111. *See* Department of Education, State of Hawaii v. Cari Rae S., 158 F. Supp. 2d 1190 (D. Haw. 2001).
160. 20 U.S.C. §§ 1412(a)(3)(A), 1412(a)(10)(A)(ii)(I).
161. 34 C.F.R. § 300.131.
162. N.G. v. District of Columbia, 556 F. Supp. 2d 11 (D.D.C. 2008).
163. D.K. *ex rel.* Stephen K. v. Abington School District, 696 F.3d 233 (3d Cir. 2012). *See also* Board of Education of Fayette County, Kentucky v. L.M., 478 F.3d 307 (6th Cir. 2007).
164. G."J"D. *ex rel.* G.D. and M.D. v. Wissahickon School District, 832 F. Supp. 2d 455 (E.D. Pa. 2011); D.B. v. Bedford County School Board, 708 F. Supp. 2d 564 (W.D. Va. 2010); El Paso Independent School District v. Richard R., 567 F. Supp. 2d 918 (W.D. Tex. 2008).
165. 20 U.S.C. § 1401(26).
166. Russo, C. J., Osborne, A. G., Massucci, J. D., & Cattaro, G. M. (2009). *The Law of Special Education and Non-Public Schools*. Lanham, MD: Rowman & Littlefield Education.
167. Russo, C. J., Osborne, A. G., Massucci, J. D., & Cattaro, G. M. (2011). The legal rights of students with disabilities in Christian schools. *Journal of Research in Christian Education, 20*(3), 254–280.
168. Everson v. Board of Education, 330 U.S. 1 (1947).
169. 403 U.S. 602 (1971).
170. *Id.* at 612–613 (internal citations omitted).
171. 473 U.S. 402 (1985).
172. 509 U.S. 1 (1993).
173. Osborne, A. G. (1994). Providing special education and related services to parochial school students in the wake of *Zobrest. Education Law Reporter, 87,* 329–339.
174. 521 U.S. 203 (1997).
175. Osborne, A. G., & Russo, C. (1997). The ghoul is dead, long live the ghoul: *Agostini v. Felton* and the delivery of Title I services in nonpublic schools. *Education Law Reporter, 119,* 781–797.
176. 530 U.S. 793 (2000), *on remand,* 229 F.3d 467 (5th Cir. 2000).

177. Helms v. Picard, 151 F.3d 347 (5th Cir. 1998).
178. 20 U.S.C. § 1412(a)(10).
179. 34 C.F.R. § 300.132.
180. Mawdsley, R. D. & Osborne, A. G. (2007). Providing special education services to students in religious schools. *Education Law Reporter, 219,* 347–367.
181. 20 U.S.C. § 1412(a)(10)(A)(i)(III). Although the term *nonpublic schools* is preferred to *private schools,* the latter is the term used in the IDEA.
182. Wolman v. Walter, 433 U.S. 229 (1977); Meek v. Pittenger, 421 U.S. 349 (1975).
183. 34 C.F.R. § 76.1 *et seq.*
184. 34 C.F.R. § 76.651(a)(1).
185. 34 C.F.R. § 76.654(a).
186. 34 C.F.R. § 76.652(a)(1)–(5).
187. 34 C.F.R. § 300.131(a).
188. 34 C.F.R. § 300.132.
189. 34 C.F.R. § 300.130.
190. 34 C.F.R. § 300.133.
191. 20 U.S.C. § 1412(a)(10)(A)(i)(I),(II).
192. 34 C.F.R. § 300.133(d).
193. 34 C.F.R. § 300.141.
194. 34 C.F.R. § 300.143.
195. 34 C.F.R. § 300.142(a).
196. 34 C.F.R. § 300.142(b).
197. 34 C.F.R. § 300.144(c).
198. 34 C.F.R. § 300.137(a).
199. 34 C.F.R. § 300.137(b)(2).
200. 34 C.F.R. § 300.137(c)(2).
201. 34 C.F.R. § 300.138(a)(1).
202. 34 C.F.R. § 300.138(a)(2).
203. 34 C.F.R. § 300.138(b)(1).
204. 34 C.F.R. § 300.138(b)(2).
205. 34 C.F.R. § 300.139(a).
206. 34 C.F.R. § 300.139(a).
207. Board of Education of the Appoquinimink School District v. Johnson, 543 F. Supp. 2d 351 (D. Del. 2008); Bristol Warren Regional School Committee v. Rhode Island Department of Education and Secondary Educations, 253 F. Supp. 2d 236 (D.R.I. 2003).
208. 34 C.F.R. § 300.139(b)(1)(i)(A).
209. 34 C.F.R. § 300.139(b)(1)(i)(B).
210. 34 C.F.R. § 300.139(b)(1)(B)(ii).
211. 34 C.F.R. § 300.139(b)(2).
212. 34 C.F.R. § 300.140(a); Gabel *ex rel.* L.G. v. Board of Education of the Hyde Park Central School District, 368 F. Supp. 2d 313 (S.D.N.Y. 2005).
213. 34 C.F.R. § 300.140(b).
214. 34 C.F.R. § 300.140(c).
215. 20 U.S.C. § 1412 (a)(10)(A)(I); 34 C.F.R. § 300.131(a).
216. 34 C.F.R. § 300.131(b)(2).
217. 34 C.F.R. § 300.131(c).
218. 34 C.F.R. § 300.131(d).

3

Related Services, Assistive Technology, and Transition Services

Key Concepts in This Chapter

- When Related Services Must Be Provided
- Types of Related Services Required
- Role of Assistive Technology Devices and Services
- Transitioning Students to Postschool Activities

The Individuals with Disabilities Education Act (IDEA)[1] requires school boards to provide related, or supportive, services to students with disabilities who need such services to assist them in benefiting from their special education programs.[2] The IDEA defines related services as transportation and such developmental, corrective, and supportive services as speech-language pathology and audiology services, interpreting services, psychological services, physical and occupational therapy, recreation (including therapeutic recreation), social work services, school nurse services, counseling services (including rehabilitation counseling), orientation and mobility services, and medical services for diagnostic and evaluation purposes.[3] Thus, by definition, related services are adjuncts to special education services.

The list of related service is exemplary, not exhaustive, even though Congress placed limits on what can be related services. Medical services are exempted unless they are specifically for diagnostic or evaluative purposes. Further, the 2004 IDEA amendments clarified that the term *related services* does not include surgically implanted medical devices or their replacements.[4] Moreover, the regulations specify that optimization of the functioning, maintenance, or replacement of these devices is beyond the scope of school board responsibilities.[5] This does not mean that school personnel lack all responsibility for monitoring devices or making sure that they function properly.[6] While these provisions were included to address board responsibilities regarding cochlear implants, they apply to other surgically implanted devices as well.[7]

In *Irving Independent School District v. Tatro*,[8] the Supreme Court placed two important limitations on the obligations of school boards to provide related services. First, the Court insisted that "to be entitled to related services, a child must be [disabled] so as to require special education."[9] The Court pointed out that absent a disability requiring special education, "the need for what otherwise might qualify as a related service does not create an obligation under the Act."[10] Second, the Court noted that only services necessary to aid children with disabilities in benefitting from special education must be provided, regardless of how easily such services could be furnished. Thus, students who receive free appropriate public educations (FAPEs) from their special education without related services are not entitled to receive such services. Even though the IDEA does not require school boards to provide related services to students who are not receiving special education, as is explained in more detail in Chapter 9, Section 504 may require boards to furnish such services as reasonable accommodations to students with disabilities that may not necessarily entitle them to special education.

> Supportive services may be deemed related services if they assist students with disabilities to benefit from special education. Related services may be provided by persons of differing professional backgrounds with a variety of occupational titles.

The IDEA's regulations define each of the identified related services in detail.[11] To the extent that these definitions are not exhaustive, any services, other than those that are specifically exempted, may be considered related services if they can assist students with disabilities in benefiting from special education. For example, services such as artistic and cultural programs or art, music, and dance therapy could be related services under the appropriate circumstances.[12] These related services may be provided by persons of differing professional backgrounds with a variety of occupational titles.

The 1990 IDEA amendments added definitions of assistive technology devices and services. The 1997 and 2004 versions of the IDEA clarified and expanded these definitions. Assistive technology devices are items, pieces of equipment, or product systems used to increase, maintain, or improve the functional capabilities of individuals with disabilities. These devices may include commercially available, modified, or customized equipment[13] but, as with related services, do not include a surgically implanted medical device.[14] Assistive technology services are designed to help individuals in the selection, acquisition, or use of assistive technology devices.[15] Assistive technology services include evaluations of the needs of children, provision of assistive technology devices, training in their use, coordination of other services with assistive technology, and maintenance and repair of devices.[16]

Interestingly, assistive technology is not specifically included in the definition of either special education or related services, but does fit within the definition of special education as specially designed instruction, and within the definition of related services as a developmental, corrective, or supportive service. Rather than include assistive technology within either of these two definitions, Congress chose to create it as a category separate from both special education and related services. Accordingly, assistive technology can be a special education service, a related service, or simply a supplementary aid or service.[17] This is significant because school boards have the duty to provide supplementary aids and services to students with disabilities to allow them to be educated in the least restrictive environment (LRE).[18]

At the same time, the IDEA requires school boards to provide transition services to students with disabilities to promote movement from school to postschool activities such as employment, vocational training, and independent living. Transition services include related services, instruction, community experiences, and the acquisition of daily living skills.[19] School officials must include statements in the individualized education plans (IEPs) of students identifying needed transition services beginning before they turn 16 years of age.[20]

There has been much litigation, including two cases that reached the Supreme Court, over the related services provisions of the IDEA. Against this background, the first part of this chapter reviews and analyzes litigation over related services. The next two sections address the requirements for providing assistive technology and transition services. The final portion of the chapter offers guidelines for educational personnel in situations where school boards must provide related services or assistive technology.

Related Services

Figure 3.1 summarizes when related services are required. Subsequent sections within this part detail the case law surrounding the different kinds of services schools must make available.

Figure 3.1   When Are Related Services Required?

Related services are required for students with disabilities when

- They are necessary for students to gain access to special education programs or the services outlined in their IEPs.
- They are needed for students to remain physically in educational programs.
- They are necessary for students to make meaningful progress toward the goals and objectives of their IEPs.
- Students' needs are so intertwined that they require integrated programs of special education and related services.
- Students' progress toward the goals and objectives of their IEPs depends on the resolution of other needs.

Transportation

It almost goes without saying that students cannot benefit from their IEPs if they cannot get to school. For this reason, transportation is probably the most common related service that school boards offer to students with disabilities. Transportation is typically provided in district-owned and operated vehicles, in vehicles owned and operated by private service providers, and/or via public transportation; in rare instances, boards may enter into contracts with parents to transport their children to school. School officials need to make special transportation arrangements when students are unable to access their usual modes of transportation. The term *transportation,* as used in the IDEA and its regulations, embodies travel to and from school, between schools, and around school buildings. Specialized equipment, such as adapted buses, lifts, and ramps, is required when needed to provide the transportation.[21]

The term *transportation* includes transit from a house to a vehicle. . . . As important as this related service is, though, door-to-door transportation is required only when a student is unable to get to school without such assistance.

An early case from Rhode Island demonstrates that the term *transportation* includes transit from a house to a vehicle. When school officials refused to provide assistance for a child who, because he was physically challenged, was unable to get from his home to a school bus without help, his father drove him to school for a period of time. Once the child's father could no longer take him to school, the child stopped attending classes. The situation was finally rectified, but the court, declaring that transportation clearly was the responsibility of the school committee,[22] awarded the parents compensation for their efforts in taking their son to school.[23] As important as this related service is, though, door-to-door transportation is required only when students are unable to get to school without such assistance.[24]

If IEP teams place students in private schools, then these children are entitled to transportation.[25] Should students attend residential private schools, they must be transported between their homes and schools for usual vacation periods. Regardless, one court affirmed that a student was not entitled to additional trips home for therapeutic purposes even though improved family relations was a goal of his IEP.[26] The court maintained that a hearing officer did not abuse his discretion in deciding that parents were not entitled to reimbursement for more than three annual round trips from their home in Florida to a treatment facility in Georgia, because the school board had met its obligation to provide transportation for the child.

Under the IDEA, an alteration in the delivery of related services can be a change in placement. As discussed in greater detail in Chapter 5, changes in placement occur when students' programs are altered in such a way that their IEPs cannot be implemented as written or their learning is affected. Even so, in a case from Pennsylvania, the Third Circuit conceded that a minor adjustment to a child's transportation plan did not constitute a change in placement.[27] Recognizing that transportation could have an effect on a student's learning, the court found that an adjustment that added 10 minutes to the child's trip home from school did not impact his learning. At the same time, transportation arrangements cannot be unreasonable. For instance, a federal trial court in Virginia ordered board officials to make better arrangements for a student whose ride took more than 30 minutes even though she lived only six miles from her school.[28]

School boards may not be required to provide transportation when parents elect to send their children to schools other than the ones recommended by school personnel. In such a case, a state court in Florida declared that a board was not obligated to transport a student to a geographically distant facility after she was enrolled there at her parents' request. The court observed that transportation was unnecessary, since the student could have received an appropriate education at a closer facility.[29]

In today's world, many students do not return home after school; instead, they go to afterschool caretakers. In a case originating in Texas, the

Fifth Circuit determined that students with disabilities are entitled to be transported to caretakers even when those caretakers live out of a district's attendance boundaries.[30] The court indicated that the parental request for transporting their son, who had multiple disabilities, to his caretaker was reasonable and did not place a burden on the board.

On the other hand, the Eighth Circuit reasoned that a special education student from South Dakota was not entitled to be dropped off at a day care center that was outside of a school's attendance area. Here the school board's policy for all students dictated that children could be dropped off only within their school's attendance boundary. The court, viewing the board policy as facially neutral, adding that the parental request was based on her personal convenience and not her son's educational needs, affirmed that the board did not violate the IDEA by refusing to transport the child to his day care center.[31] More recently, the federal trial court in Maine reached the same outcome. The court agreed that a hearing officer and a federal magistrate properly denied a mother's request that her son, who had a severe learning disability, be allowed to ride a public school bus home and be met by another adult, since she could not be there to meet him when he returned from school.[32] The court specified that the mother was not entitled to have her request granted because it was motivated by her child care arrangements with her ex-husband, with whom she shared custody, rather than her son's educational needs.

As reflected in the previous paragraph, divorced parents reach a variety of shared custody agreements. In some circumstances, children reside with each parent on a rotating basis under joint custody arrangements. In a case illustrating an arrangement of this type, where a father lived outside of a district's boundaries, a commonwealth court in Pennsylvania commented that a school board was required to provide transportation on the weeks when the child lived with his mother but not on the weeks when he lived with his father.[33] The court wrote that the additional requested transportation did not address the boy's special needs, but rather served only to accommodate the parents' domestic situation.

In addition to providing specialized equipment that may be needed to transport students safely, a case from Michigan demonstrates that school boards may have to provide aides on vehicles. A federal trial court ordered a board to provide a trained aide to attend a student, who was medically fragile, when he was being transported.[34] The court thought that under the IDEA, students with disabilities were entitled to transportation and incidents thereto.

Counseling, Psychological, and Social Work Services

The IDEA's regulations define *counseling* as a service provided by a qualified social worker, psychologist, guidance counselor, or other qualified person.[35] The definition of *psychological services* includes psychological counseling,[36] while the definition of *social work services* includes group and individual counseling.[37] On the other hand, the regulations neither use nor define the term *psychotherapy*. This is important, because while boards in most public school systems provide students with in-house counseling, psychological services, and social work services, there are many situations that call for such services to be provided by an outside vendor. School district employees and families would benefit from clarity in this regard.

> Counseling, psychological, and social work services clearly are required related services only when needed by a student with a disability to benefit from special education. These may be required as related services for students with emotional difficulties who may not be able to benefit from their special education programs until their emotional problems are addressed.

One of the controversies that developed over the medical exclusion clause of the related services mandate concerns psychotherapy. Counseling, psychological, and social work services are clearly required related services only when students with disabilities need them to benefit from special education. While psychotherapy can be classified as a psychological service, in some situations it falls within the medical exclusion. Whether psychotherapy is a psychological or medical service depends on individual state laws governing psychotherapy. Put another way, some state laws stipulate that only psychiatrists can provide psychotherapy, while other states allow clinical psychologists to provide psychotherapy. Insofar as psychiatrists are licensed physicians, psychotherapy is an exempted medical service in states that allow only psychiatrists to provide it.

The distinguishing criterion regarding whether psychotherapy is a related service or an exempted medical service is how it is defined in a state law, not by whom it is actually provided. In Illinois, for instance, where state law allows nonpsychiatric professionals to provide psychotherapy, a federal trial court decided that a school board was responsible for the costs of psychotherapy even though the psychotherapy was actually provided by a psychiatrist.[38] The court ruled that the criterion, that schools were not required to provide services that must be performed by a physician, did not mean that services that could be provided by a nonphysician, but were in actuality provided by a physician, were excluded. Still, the court indicated that the board was obligated to pay for the services only to the extent of the costs of their being performed by a nonphysician.

Counseling, psychotherapy, or social work services may be required as related services for students with emotional difficulties who may be unable to benefit from their special education programs until their emotional problems are addressed. The Supreme Court of Montana, turning to the dictionary for a definition of the term *psychotherapy*, found that according to *Webster's*, *psychotherapy* is a psychological service. Thus, the court treated psychotherapy as a related service.[39] The federal trial court in New Jersey also categorized psychotherapy as a counseling or psychological service, pointing out that it was a required related service.[40]

Federal trial courts in Illinois[41] and Massachusetts,[42] along with the Third Circuit,[43] agreed that psychotherapy is a required related service because it assists some children in benefiting from their educational programs. Further, in Illinois, a federal trial court mandated that although psychotherapy is related to mental health, it may be required before a child can derive benefits from education. Similarly, the Third Circuit was persuaded that psychotherapy was an essential service that allowed an emotionally disturbed student in New Jersey to benefit from his educational program.

Since counseling is generally not considered to be a medical service, it may not be an exempted service. For example, the federal trial court in Connecticut was of the opinion that psychological and counseling services that a student with disabilities needed to benefit from his special education program were not embraced within the exempted medical services clause.[44] The court posited that insofar as the therapy services offered as part of a residential placement were essential to render the child educable, they were required related services.

An important element in the requirement to provide related services is that they must be necessary for students to benefit from special education services. In a case addressing this issue, the Fourth Circuit remarked that counseling services were not required for a student from Virginia who made great improvement under an IEP that did not include counseling.[45]

If a therapeutic service can be classified as psychiatric, courts are likely to declare that it falls within the medical exception. The federal trial court for the District of Columbia decreed that the school board was not required to pay for the residential component costs of a placement in a psychiatric hospital and school, because the primary reasons for the child's placement were medical, not educational.[46] In like fashion, a federal trial court in Illinois concluded that psychiatric services are exempted medical services, because psychiatrists are licensed physicians.[47] At least four other courts agreed that insofar as psychiatric facilities are medical facilities, school boards are not required to pay for the services that they offer.[48] By the same token, the federal trial court in Connecticut asserted that psychiatric supervision to manage a student's medication regimen was an exempted medical service.[49]

Psychiatric and other medical services are required as related services when they are for diagnostic or evaluative purposes. In the first of two cases from Tennessee, a federal trial court held that an evaluation by a neurologist was a related service.[50] Five years later, another court acknowledged that the limited medical services a student received in a residential rehabilitation facility could not have been used to characterize her entire program as medical.[51] The court contended that because medical services were provided to monitor and adjust the child's medication, they were for diagnostic and evaluative purposes. Similarly, the federal trial court in Connecticut, recognizing that a student had not made academic progress, ordered a school board to conduct a psychiatric evaluation to evaluate his need for counseling.[52] Further, the federal trial court in Hawaii was of the view that hospitalization costs were a significant part of a student's diagnosis and evaluation as having a disability. Even though the student was hospitalized in response to a medical crisis, the court directed state officials to pay for the hospitalization, because it was an integral part of her overall evaluation.[53]

Whether placement in a facility that provides psychiatric services is primarily for medical or educational reasons may affect the costs that school boards are required to pay. Two cases from the Ninth Circuit, resolved only months apart, illustrate this point. In *Clovis Unified School District v. California Office of Administrative Hearings*,[54] where a student was admitted to an acute care psychiatric hospital when the residential school she attended could no longer control her behavior, her parents unsuccessfully asked their school board to pay for this placement. In comparing the placement to one for a student suffering from a physical illness, the court thought that it had been made for medical reasons. The court was further convinced that the student's room and board costs were medically related, not educationally related, because the hospital did not provide educational services. In *Taylor v. Honig*,[55] also from California, after a student was placed in a residential school and psychiatric hospital for assaulting a family member, the court found that the residential facility was a boarding school that had the capacity to offer necessary medical services. According to the court, since the placement was made for primarily educational reasons, it was appropriate under the IDEA.

Physical, Occupational, and Speech Therapy

Occupational therapy (OT) refers to services to improve, develop, or restore functions impaired or lost through illness, injury, or deprivation or to improve the ability of students to perform tasks for independent functioning.[56] OT also includes services to prevent the impairment or loss of functions through early intervention.

The IDEA's regulations define physical therapy (PT) simply as the services provided by a qualified physical therapist.[57] Speech-language pathology includes the identification, diagnosis, and appraisal of speech or language impairments and the provision of appropriate services for the habilitation or prevention of communication impairments.[58]

A federal trial court in New York ordered a school board to provide OT over the summer months when it realized that a student would have regressed in the areas of upper body strength and ambulation skills.[59]

The court added that the child's ability to perform classroom work and to function in the classroom would have been adversely affected without the summer therapy. Conversely, the federal trial court for the District of Columbia believed that a proposed placement for a student with multiple disabilities was inappropriate, since it did not provide for an integrated OT program as called for in her IEP.[60] The court maintained that the child did not need the program because she would not have benefited from her special education program even with this service. Even so, the amount of OT that students receive must be sufficient to confer *educational* benefit. In a case addressing this issue, a federal trial court in California upheld a hearing officer's order directing a school board to provide additional OT to a student who had delays in all areas of development.[61]

Many school boards use the services of OT therapy assistants to provide services. A federal trial court in Tennessee upheld this practice on the basis that the assistants were well trained and helped the child to make progress.[62] In addition, the court suggested that school boards are not required to maximize a student's gains.

In a case from Pennsylvania, the Third Circuit decided that PT is an important facilitator of classroom learning for some children.[63] Noting that the IDEA calls for an education that provides meaningful benefit, the court observed that physical therapy is an essential prerequisite for learning for some students with severe disabilities.

Insofar as the inability to communicate can effectively interfere with learning, speech and language therapy, when needed, is considered a related service. Although there has been no major litigation involving the need for speech or language therapy, it is safe to say that courts would likely require its delivery. Most school boards provide extensive speech and language therapy services; in some states it is considered to be a special education service rather than a related service.

Recreation and Enrichment Programs

The IDEA specifically identifies recreation and therapeutic recreation as related services.[64] The definition of recreation in the IDEA's regulations includes assessment of leisure function, recreation programs in schools and community agencies, and leisure education, along with therapeutic recreation.[65] Moreover, the IDEA's regulations specify that school boards must provide nonacademic and extracurricular services and activities to the extent necessary to afford students with disabilities opportunities for participation equal to those given to their peers without disabilities.[66] Nonacademic and extracurricular services and activities may include lunch, recess, athletics, recreational activities, special interest groups or clubs, employment, and many of the items listed as related services. These activities must be provided in inclusive settings to the maximum extent appropriate.[67]

If students with disabilities are unable to participate in general extra-curricular programs, school officials may need to provide them with special activities.[68] Also, students who meet the eligibility requirements for participation in general extracurricular programs cannot be denied access to them under Section 504 of the Rehabilitation Act.[69] School officials may thus need to provide reasonable accommodations to allow students with disabilities to participate in general extracurricular programs. For example, courts may waive eligibility rules that might prevent students from participating due to their disabilities.[70]

> School officials may need to provide reasonable accommodations to allow students with disabilities to participate in general extracurricular programs. If students with disabilities are unable to participate in general extracurricular programs, school officials may need to develop special activities for these children.

A state court in Michigan affirmed that a school board had to provide a summer enrichment program to a student with autism where testimony revealed that he needed a program that included outdoor activities.[71] The court directed the board to act in judging that the requested program fell within the parameters of special education and related services since physical education is included in the definition of special education, and recreation is a related service.

In like fashion, a federal trial court in Ohio issued a preliminary injunction ordering a school board to include participation in interscholastic athletics in a student's IEP. The court relied on evidence that the student's participation in sports resulted in academic, physical, and personal progress.[72] On the other hand, a state court in New York refused to obligate a board to provide an afterschool program when such participation was unnecessary for the student to receive a free appropriate public education (FAPE).[73]

School Nurse Services

According to the IDEA's regulations, school nurse services are those performed by qualified school nurses and are designed to enable students with disabilities to receive a FAPE.[74] There has been controversy over the provision of health-related services in the schools because of the medical exclusion clause. To the extent that a number of medical procedures can be performed by registered nurses, questions have arisen as to whether selected nursing services fall within the definition of school health services or are exempted medical services. Figure 3.2 clarifies the difference between health services (which are required) and medical services (which are not required), as defined by the IDEA and interpreted by the courts.

> Absent a disability requiring special education, the need for related services does not create an obligation under the IDEA. School officials must provide only those services that are necessary to aid students in benefiting from special education.

The United States Supreme Court, in *Irving Independent School District v. Tatro*,[75] held that catheterization was a required related service for a student in Texas who could not voluntarily empty her bladder due to spina bifida. Acknowledging that the student had to be catheterized every three to four hours, the Court pointed out that services designed to allow a child to remain in class during the school day, such as catheterization, are no less related to the effort to educate than those that allowed her to reach, enter, or exit the school. The Court was satisfied that insofar as the catheterization procedure could have been performed by a school nurse or trained health aide, Congress did not intend to exclude it as a medical service, thereby clarifying when related services must be provided to students with disabilities. The Court ruled that absent a disability requiring special education, the need for related services did not create an obligation under the IDEA and that school officials must provide only those services that are necessary to aid students in benefiting from special education. The Court emphasized that a life support service would not be a related service if it did not need to be provided during school hours.

Figure 3.2   Difference Between Medical and Health Services

Medical services are those that can legally be provided only by licensed physicians. Under the IDEA, school boards are not responsible for providing medical services except when such services are required for diagnostic or evaluative purposes as part of the multidisciplinary evaluations that students undergo in the process of deciding whether they are eligible for special education and related services.

Health services are those that can be performed by school nurses, trained health aides, or other trained laypersons. Typically, students receive these services as part of the school nursing services provided by their boards. Other health procedures are included as long as they do not, by law, have to be provided by licensed physicians.

The Ninth Circuit affirmed that the school board in Hawaii was obligated to provide a student with cystic fibrosis with health services attendant to a tracheotomy tube even though the tube became dislodged occasionally and needed to be reinserted and mucus had to be suctioned from her lungs periodically.[76] Again, where these procedures could have been performed by a school nurse or trained layperson, the court treated them as required related services.

Pursuant to an order from a federal trial court in Illinois, school boards must also provide nursing services during transportation.[77] Previously, a federal trial court in Michigan noted that a board was required to provide an aide on a school bus to attend to a medically fragile student.[78] The court observed that the provision of an aide or other health professional did not constitute an exempted medical service.

It is well settled that services that can be provided by school nurses, health aides, or even trained laypersons fall within the IDEA's mandated related services clause. Even so, many students who attend school are fragile due to medical conditions, requiring the constant presence of nurses. The question has arisen as to whether school boards are required to pay for the services of full-time nurses for single students. Courts, in the past, have disagreed over whether full-time nursing services were more akin to exempted medical services than to required health services.[79]

The Supreme Court settled the controversy over school nursing services in 1999 in *Cedar Rapids Community School District v. Garret F.* (*Garret F.*).[80] In affirming that a school board in Iowa was required to provide full-time nursing services for a student who was quadriplegic, the Court reasoned that although continuous services may be more costly and may require additional school personnel, this did not render them more medical. Recognizing that cost was not a factor in the definition of related services, the Court concluded that even costly related services must be provided to help guarantee that students with significant medical needs are integrated into the public schools. *Garret F.* clearly has the potential to have a major impact on school board budgets in light of the costs associated with the delivery of nursing services, whether for one child or groups of students.[81]

Diagnostic and Evaluative Services

The proper diagnosis and evaluation of students suspected of having disabilities is an important component of the special education process. Medical evaluations can be part of that process. The IDEA makes it clear that medical services can be related services when used for that purpose.[82]

In a case from Tennessee, a federal trial court declared that a school board had the duty to pay for a pediatrician-ordered neurological and psychological evaluation for a student.[83] School personnel had requested that the pediatrician evaluate the child, who had a seizure disorder, visual difficulties, and learning disabilities, after his behavior and school performance deteriorated. The pediatrician referred the child to a neurologist who subsequently referred him to a psychologist. When a dispute arose over who was responsible for paying for the neurological and psychological evaluations, the court maintained that insofar as the child's needs were intertwined, these evaluations were necessary for him to benefit from his special education. In language that should be of interest to school officials elsewhere, the court explained that the child's parents could have been required to use their health insurance to pay for the evaluations as long as they did not incur any costs in doing so. Since the parents' policy placed a lifetime cap on psychological services that would have been reduced by the amount of the evaluation bill, the court decided that the board was responsible for payment. While no such cap existed for neurological services, the court indicated that the parents were required to use their insurance for that evaluation.

The term *diagnostic and evaluative services* does not refer only to assessments that may be conducted as part of initial evaluations. According to a federal trial court in Tennessee, the ongoing monitoring of a student's condition could fall within the realm of diagnostic and evaluative services.[84] The court pointed out that insofar as the medical services at issue, which were designed to monitor and adjust the student's medication, were for diagnostic and evaluation purposes, the school board was responsible for paying for them.

As indicated, the Ninth Circuit upheld an order directing the school board in Hawaii to pay for hospitalization costs that were a significant part of a student's diagnosis and evaluation as disabled.[85] The dispute arose after the child's stay in the hospital triggered, and was an integral part of, her diagnosis and evaluation. The court ascertained that pre-placement medical costs limited to diagnosis and evaluation are recoverable where a student is subsequently found to have qualified for special education services.

Substance Abuse Prevention and Treatment

Conceding that Congress did not intend to create a federal claim for every activity or type of conduct that could impede the ability of students to take advantage of educational opportunities, a federal trial court in California refused to interpret drug prevention treatment as a related service under the IDEA.[86] The case arose after a student who attended a private school ingested an illegal substance and his parents unsuccessfully alleged that educational officials tolerated the use of illegal drugs on campus.

School boards are not required to provide substance abuse programs under the related services mandate if these intervention programs follow a medical model.[87] The federal trial court in New Jersey decreed that a substance abuse program does not fall within the domain of related services that must be provided under the IDEA, even though it would benefit learning.[88] When a special education student who attended a private school was expelled for drug possession, officials informed his parents that their son could return if he attended a substance abuse program. After the board refused to pay for the program, the parents unsuccessfully filed suit. The court rejected the parental claim because the student was not entitled to public payment for the program, since it was medical to the extent that it consisted of psychiatric counseling, physical examinations, and administration of medication.

A substance abuse program that is not primarily medical could be a required related service. The IDEA's regulations make it clear that insofar as counseling, psychological, and social work services are required related services, a substance abuse program primarily utilizing one of these services could be a required related service.

Habilitation Services

The Fourth Circuit affirmed that in-home habilitation services do not fall within the definitions of special education and related services.[89] Parents had requested the services, which were primarily designed to help control their son's behavior at home, when he returned to the family home in North Carolina after attending a residential program. The court noted that the child made educational progress without the requested services. On the other hand, a federal trial court in Georgia posited that vision therapy is a required related service because the student's vision problems impacted his future ability to benefit from special education.[90] In affirming the initial order, the Eleventh Circuit agreed that without the vision therapy, the child's problems would have become much worse.

Cochlear Mapping

The IDEA now includes an exception to exclude surgically implanted medical devices or their replacements from its definition of related services.[91] Following the passage of the amendments adding this exception, the U.S. Department of Education promulgated regulations excluding cochlear mapping from the definition of related services.[92] Shortly after the implementation of those regulations, a federal trial court in Tennessee ruled that a school board was not required to pay for cochlear mapping, observing that the IDEA's regulations made it clear that programming of cochlear implants was not a service that school boards must provide.[93]

In a suit challenging the regulations regarding cochlear mapping, the federal trial court in the District of Columbia insisted that the regulation did not contravene the clear meaning of the IDEA.[94] The court acknowledged that Congress had not spoken directly to the question of whether cochlear mapping constituted a related service but, nevertheless, thought that the department was entitled to deference regarding its position, since it represented a permissible construction of the statute. The District of Columbia Circuit affirmed, agreeing that the regulations embodied a permissible construction of the IDEA, because they were rationally related to the underlying objectives of the statute.

Physical Plant Alterations

Boards may be required to alter the physical plants of schools in order to allow students with disabilities to participate fully in and benefit from their educational programs. Most of these alterations allow access to school buildings. A case from Texas reflects the notion that modifications may be required to allow students to remain in classrooms. A federal trial court ordered a board to provide an air-conditioned classroom for a student who, due to brain injuries that he suffered in an accident, could not regulate his body temperature and thus required a temperature-controlled environment at all times.[95] While the board provided the student with an air-conditioned Plexiglas cubicle, and he achieved satisfactory academic progress, he had a limited ability to socialize and participate in group activities. The court pointed out that the use of the cubicle violated the LRE mandate, because it caused the student to miss out on the class participation and group interactions that were important to his education.

At the same time, boards are not required to make alterations to all school buildings within their districts in order to make them accessible to students with disabilities. In an illustrative case, the Eighth Circuit affirmed that a board in Minnesota complied with the IDEA by offering parents a placement for their daughter in an accessible school that was reasonably close to the family home.[96] The parents filed suit on behalf of their daughter, who used a wheelchair, seeking to require the board to modify her neighborhood school to make it accessible. The record revealed that three other schools in the district were wheelchair accessible and that the board offered the parents a placement for their daughter in one that was four miles from her home. The court upheld this arrangement, recognizing that by busing the student to a nearby school, board officials provided her with a fully integrated education and that nothing in the IDEA required officials to place her in the school closest to her home.

Parent Training and Counseling

As defined in the IDEA's regulations, parent training and counseling means assisting parents to understand the special needs of their children and provide them with information about child development.[97] Courts sometimes order residential placements for students who require consistency and support that is not available in the home environment. Less restrictive placements can be appropriate if parents are trained to deal with their children appropriately in their homes, using techniques similar to those that are used at school. Yet, avoidance of a residential placement is not the sole criterion for providing parent training and counseling.

A federal trial court in Texas wrote that an appropriate placement could be provided within a public school setting for a student with severe disabilities if her parents received training and counseling, thereby averting the need for a residential placement.[98] The court observed that the child required a highly structured educational program that needed to be maintained year-round. In order to preserve that structure after school hours, the court ordered board officials to provide the child's parents with training in behavioral techniques. In addition, the court directed educational officials to offer counseling to help relieve the stress of the burdensome demands that the child's disability placed on her parents. Similarly, a federal trial court in Alabama ordered a board to provide training and counseling to the parents of a student who exhibited academic and behavioral problems.[99] Stating that the student's overall IEP was not appropriate, the court noted that educators ignored a crucial component of a behavioral control program by failing to counsel and instruct the parents in how to reinforce the training the child received at school in their home.

As with all special education and related services, school boards are not required to provide an optimal level of parent training and counseling. Recognizing that a school board was not obligated to provide every possible service or the very best education that might be desired, a federal trial court in Texas found that an IEP that reduced the amount of scheduled at-home parent training sessions did not deny a child with multiple disabilities a FAPE.[100]

Along the same line, a federal trial court in Connecticut held that the IDEA did not require a school board to provide a 24-hour crisis plan, respite care for the family, and an in-home mentor in the IEP of a student who had a long history of behavior problems.[101] The court agreed with a hearing officer that these services were not related services under the IDEA, and that they were not necessary since the student had made academic progress without them.

Residential Placements and Lodging

Many students with disabilities require placements in residential schools or facilities in order to receive a FAPE. In some cases, residential placements are called for, because children need instructional services on a round-the-clock basis in order to receive an appropriate education. In other situations, students who do not necessarily require 24-hour-per-day instruction must remain at such schools on a residential basis, since they are the only facilities that can provide an appropriate education and are not within commuting distance of the students' homes. Under these circumstances, school boards must still pay for the room-and-board portion of residential placements, as such arrangements are considered to be a related service.

According to the IDEA's regulations, if a residential program "is necessary to provide special education and related services to a child with a disability, the program, including nonmedical care and room and board, must be at no cost to the parents of the child."[102] This regulation applies whether the residential portion of the placement is needed for educational reasons or access reasons. When students are placed in residential facilities that have a psychiatric component, the medical and educational components often can be intricately intertwined. Nevertheless, in a case from Texas, the Fifth Circuit explained that courts must examine each part of placements and weed out the costs that are reimbursable from those that are not.[103]

Boards may be required to provide off-campus lodging to students with disabilities if appropriate arrangements cannot be made for them to live at their schools and the schools are located too far from home to commute.[104] This can occur when the schools that students attend either do not offer residential components or do not have any room for children in their residential programs but have openings in their day programs.

Residential placements are not considered to be related services if their sole purpose is to provide confinement. Explaining that it stretches the IDEA too far to classify confinement as a related service, the Seventh Circuit decided that a student from Illinois whose problems were not primarily educational did not require a residential placement at public expense.[105]

Teacher Training

Realizing that the IDEA's list of related services is not all-inclusive, the Supreme Court of South Dakota refused to order a school board to include specific teacher training in the IEP of a student with autism.[106] In so doing, the court rejected the mother's request to include a provision in her son's IEP calling for his teachers to be trained in a specified instructional methodology. The court affirmed that insofar as teacher competency is in the control of school administrators, a parent cannot dictate how teachers are to be prepared or how their competency is to be measured.

Assistive Technology

Assistive technology may be provided as a special education service, a related service, or a supplementary aid and service. Assistive technology is required when it is necessary for students to receive FAPEs under the standard established by the Supreme Court in *Board of Education of the Hendrick Hudson School District v. Rowley*.[107] Further, because assistive technology may allow many students with disabilities to benefit from education in less restrictive settings, it may be required under the IDEA's LRE mandate. Still, school boards are not required to provide assistive technology when students are able to receive meaningful educational benefit, and thus a FAPE, without this service.[108]

> Assistive technology may allow many students with disabilities to benefit from education in less restrictive settings.

IEP teams must consider whether children require assistive technology devices and services in order to receive FAPEs.[109] If teams determine that students need assistive technology, then they must write this into the students' IEPs. Even so, the IDEA does not require teams to document that they considered providing students with assistive technology devices and services but did not think that they were needed.

The IDEA specifically requires school boards to ensure that assistive technology devices and services are made available to students if either or both are required as part of the children's special education, related services, or supplementary aids and services.[110] The IDEA calls for the use of school-provided assistive technology devices in the homes of students if their IEP teams decide that they need access to assistive technology in order to receive a FAPE.[111]

In explanatory material accompanying the 1999 IDEA regulations, the Department of Education made it clear that school boards are not required to provide personal devices, such as eyeglasses, hearing aids, and braces that students would require regardless of whether they attended school.[112] In one case the federal trial court in Connecticut ruled that a school board was not obligated to provide a myoelectric prosthesis for a student who was born with an amputated arm below her left elbow.[113] Of course, nothing prohibits boards from providing students with these items. Further, based on federal regulations, students with disabilities are entitled to have access to any general technology that is available to peers who are not disabled. When students with disabilities require accommodations in order to use general technology, educators must make sure to provide these modifications.[114]

In an illustrative case, a federal trial court in Pennsylvania declared that a school board's provision of assistive technology to a student with multiple disabilities was inadequate.[115] The court was of the view that the student required a laptop computer with appropriate software but that school personnel wasted nearly a year before obtaining and setting up the device. Further, the court faulted the board's chosen software program and keyboarding instruction. In Maryland, the federal trial court upheld a hearing officer's order directing board officials to provide a student with appropriate software to use at home and school along with instruction about its use.[116] Of course, school personnel often have a variety of options when selecting the type of assistive technology to provide for students. As with the delivery of special education services, the choice of methodology is up to educators.[117]

A case from New York highlights the point that an assistive technology device should aid students in receiving a FAPE by mitigating the effects of their disabilities but should not circumvent the learning process. Although a student with learning disabilities that affected his ability in mathematics was allowed to use a calculator, educators denied his request to use a more advanced calculator on the ground that doing so would have circumvented the learning process. The Second Circuit affirmed a New York hearing offer's adjudication that officials provided the student with appropriate assistive technology and that the more advanced calculator was not needed.[118]

In order to provide appropriate assistive technology, school personnel must conduct timely evaluations to assess student needs.[119] An assistive technology evaluation should identify students' areas of need and assess whether assistive technology is needed to provide educational benefits.[120] On the other hand, since assistive technology is required only when needed for students to receive a FAPE, it is unnecessary to assess children for assistive technology when it is clear that they can receive meaningful educational benefit without assistive technology.[121]

School boards have the duty to provide assistive technology, when needed, and must train all stakeholders to use the devices. However, boards cannot be rendered liable if students fail to take advantage of what has been offered. Courts have refused to impose liability on boards when educators supply appropriate assistive technology but students do not use the devices or services.[122] Even so, it is important for boards to provide appropriate training for students and teachers in the use of devices, assist them in using technology properly, and provide follow-up support. If students fail to use the supplied technology due to a lack of training, boards will be accountable.

Transition Services

Pursuant to the IDEA, school boards must provide transition services to students with disabilities in order to facilitate their passages from school to postschool activities.[123] Transition services not only involve instruction and training but may also encompass related services.[124] While transition plans must be included in the IEPs of all students once they reach the age of 16, the First Circuit affirmed that this requirement does not mandate a stand-alone plan.[125] The court agreed that an IEP developed by a school in

New Hampshire that integrated transition services throughout a child's program met the IDEA's standard.

The federal trial court in Connecticut reasoned that a 20-year-old student was entitled to instruction in community and daily living skills because this instruction fell within the ambit of transition services.[126] In Pennsylvania, a federal trial court, observing that transition services should be designed to prepare a student for life outside the school system, recognized that providing him with only vocational evaluations and training was insufficient, as these services did not meet all of his needs.[127]

In Hawaii, the federal trial court approved a coordinated set of activities that were clearly designed to promote a student's movement from school to postschool activities. These activities, which were written into the student's IEP, were aimed at assisting him in completing high school, becoming part of his community, exploring careers and colleges, and meeting with vocational counselors.[128] Similarly, a federal trial court in Louisiana found that transition plans detailing desired adult outcomes, including school action steps and family action steps, were appropriate.[129]

A federal trial court in Wisconsin approved an IEP containing detailed transition statements, including suggested courses of study, instruction, employment, postschool adult living, daily living, community experiences, functional vocational assessments, and related services. Conversely, the federal trial court in Hawaii rejected a transition plan that failed to include measurable postsecondary goals and did not include a statement of transition services needed to assist the student in reaching those goals as failing to comply with the IDEA's requirements.[130]

FREQUENTLY ASKED QUESTIONS

Q: Medical services are exempted from the related services provision of the IDEA. When do health-related services become medical services?

A: Medical services, by definition, are those that by law, can be provided only by licensed physicians. State law is important in this regard since it typically dictates the requirements for persons who provide specified services. For example, in some states only psychiatrists may provide psychotherapy while in others clinical psychologists or licensed clinical social workers may do so.

Q: Why are school boards required to provide health services?

A: Health services may be equated to modifications to physical plants that allow students with disabilities to access educational programs: Many

(Continued)

(Continued)

students cannot be physically present in classrooms without these services. For instance, students who require catheterization every three to four hours may be unable to attend school for a typical six-hour day unless school officials provide catheterization.

Q: Are school boards required to provide substance abuse programs to students with disabilities who have drug or alcohol problems?

A: Since school boards are required to provide counseling and social work services, substance abuse programs utilizing counseling or social work models could be required as a related service. However, boards are not responsible for any such programs that follow a medical model.

Q: When are school boards obligated to provide special transportation for students with disabilities?

A: School boards must provide special transportation arrangements when the disabilities of students call for such services. If students are able to access regular transportation, special transportation is not required. For example, students with hearing impairments, under most circumstances, should be able to ride regular school buses. On the other hand, students in wheelchairs may need vehicles equipped to accommodate their wheelchairs.

Q: Are school boards required to provide transportation to day care centers or other afterschool caretakers?

A: School boards are required to provide transportation to day care centers or other afterschool caretakers for students with disabilities to the same extent that they provide such transportation to students who are not disabled. Boards should develop policies regarding transportation to locations other than the homes of students. School officials must apply these policies equally to all students, regardless of the students' disability status.

Q: Are school boards required to provide students with special extracurricular activities?

A: Under Section 504, students with disabilities are entitled to access regular extracurricular activities as long as they are otherwise qualified to participate in them with reasonable accommodations. If participation in extracurricular activities assists students in benefiting from their special education programs, such activities can be a required related service. School officials may need to provide special programs if students are unable to participate in regular extracurricular offerings.

Q: Under what circumstances are school boards required to provide assistive technology to students with disabilities?

A: School boards are required to provide assistive technology when it is necessary for students to receive educational benefit from their special education programs. When boards are able to provide FAPEs without assistive technology, they are not required to add assistive technology to student IEPs.

Q: What types of transition services are school boards required to provide to students over the age of 16?

A: The purpose of transition services is to help students with disabilities move from school to postschool activities. As with special education and related services, the provision of transition services is individualized and must be tailored to the unique needs of each individual student. Transition plans should include goals and objectives along with the specific services to be provided to meet these goals and objectives.

Recommendations

In addition to special education, school boards must provide students with disabilities with related services when such services are necessary for students to benefit from their special education programs. The only limitation that has been placed on what may be considered related services is that medical services are exempted unless they are for diagnostic or evaluative purposes. Not surprisingly, the large amount of litigation that has ensued in disputes over the IDEA's related services provisions offers school officials considerable guidance. The recommendations below have been developed from that litigation.

School boards must provide assistive technology services and devices to students who require such services and devices to receive educational benefit from their special education programs. While the purpose of assistive technology is to mitigate some of the effects of students' disabilities, it should not allow students to bypass the learning process.

At the same time, school boards must include transition services in the IEPs of students with disabilities that are in place when they turn 16 years of age. The types of transition plans provided are likely to vary depending on the unique needs of each student but should be sufficient to help them to transition from school to postschool activities.

When dealing with children who have IEPs, school officials should

- Provide related services to students who are receiving special education if such services are necessary for the children to receive educational benefits.
- Consider whether students who are not receiving special education may be entitled to related services under Section 504.
- Provide students with disabilities with services of a life-support nature if necessary during the school day.
- Deliver medical services for children if such services are needed for diagnostic or evaluative purposes.
- Provide students with all necessary school health services that can be performed by school nurses, health aides, or other trained laypersons.
- Provide full-time nurses to help guarantee that children with significant medical needs are integrated into the public schools.
- Check to see whether students who require extensive health-related services are eligible for Medicaid benefits that could offset the costs of many expensive health-related services.
- Investigate the option of using parental health insurance, particularly for diagnostic and evaluative services; at the same time, recall that parents cannot be required to use their health insurance if doing so incurs a cost to them in the form of a reduction in benefits, a cap on benefits, or increased premiums.
- Provide psychotherapy, social work services, or counseling when the resolution of emotional concerns is a prerequisite to helping children make successful progress toward their IEP goals.
- Be diligent in ascertaining exactly what the primary reason for residential placements is, since components of residential placements that are noneducational in nature may not be the responsibility of school boards.
- Provide special transportation when students are unable to access standard modes of transportation.
- Avoid excessively long bus or van rides to schools since these can be considered unreasonable and transportation arrangements must be reasonable.
- Make provisions for children whose disabilities prevent them from getting to and from their transportation vehicles.
- Provide students with transportation to and from their residential facilities.
- Establish neutral policies regarding transportation of all children to day care centers or afterschool caretakers.
- Ensure that students with disabilities are given the same considerations as peers who are not disabled regarding transportation outside of a school's attendance boundaries.

- Provide aides on vehicles, if necessary, to ensure safe passage for children who are medically fragile.
- Alter physical plants to allow students with disabilities to participate fully in and benefit from their educational program; keep in mind that another option may be to transport students to nearby schools that are accessible if the required alterations would be excessively costly.
- Provide parents with training so that there is consistency between the techniques used in school and at home; this option may be a viable alternative to residential placements.
- Pay room and board expenses for children if the only facilities that can provide a FAPE are not within commuting distance from the students' homes.
- Provide full access to sports or other extracurricular activities whenever students qualify for participation.
- Include participation in sports or other extracurricular activities in IEPs if these activities may assist students in benefiting from their educational programs.
- Provide assistive technology to children with disabilities when needed, recalling that school boards are not required to provide personal devices that children would require regardless of whether they attended school.
- Develop transition plans for students who are close to exiting educational systems; plans should include goals and objectives and list the services that will be provided to meet those goals and objectives.

Endnotes

1. 20 U.S.C. §§ 1400–1482 (2012). The IDEA's regulations can be found at Assistance to the States for the Education of Children with Disabilities, 34 C.F.R. §§ 300.1–300.818 (2013).
2. 20 U.S.C. §§ 1400(c)(5)(D), (d)(1)(A), 1401(3)(A)(i).
3. 20 U.S.C. § 1401(26)(A).
4. 20 U.S.C. § 1401(20)(B).
5. 34 C.F.R. § 300.34(b).
6. 34 C.F.R. § 300.34(b)(2).
7. Russo, C. J., Osborne, A. G., & Borreca, E. A. (2006). *What's changed? A side-by-side analysis of the 2006 and 1999 Part B regulations.* Horsham, PA: LRP Publications.
8. 468 U.S. 883 (1984).
9. *Id.* at 894.
10. *Id.*
11. 34 C.F.R. § 300.34.
12. *See, e.g.,* K.C. *ex rel.* Her Parents v. Nazareth Area School District, 806 F. Supp. 2d 806 (E.D. Pa. 2011) (finding that the board had provided appropriate executive functioning coaching for the student's needs).

13. 20 U.S.C. § 1401(1)(A).
14. 20 U.S.C. § 1401(1)(B).
15. Osborne, A. G. (2012). Providing assistive technology to students with disabilities under the IDEA. *Education Law Reporter, 280,* 519–533.
16. 20 U.S.C. § 1401(2).
17. 34 C.F.R. § 300.105(a).
18. 20 U.S.C. §§ 1401(33), 1412(a)(5).
19. 20 U.S.C. § 1401(34).
20. 20 U.S.C.A. § 1414(d)(1)(A)(i)(VIII).
21. 34 C.F.R. § 300.34(c)(16)(iii).
22. In several New England states, such as Rhode Island, school boards are known as school committees.
23. Hurry v. Jones, 560 F. Supp. 500 (D.R.I. 1983), *affirmed in part, reversed in part* 734 F.2d 879 (1st Cir. 1984). *See also* District of Columbia v. Ramirez, 377 F. Supp. 2d 63 (D.D.C. 2005) (directing the board to provide an aide to convey a student from his apartment to his school bus).
24. Malehorn v. Hill City School District, 987 F. Supp. 772 (D.S.D. 1997).
25. Union School District v. Smith, 15 F.3d 1519 (9th Cir. 1994).
26. Cohen v. School Board of Dade County, 450 So. 2d 1238 (Fla. Dist. Ct. App. 1984).
27. DeLeon v. Susquehanna Community School District, 747 F.2d 149 (3d Cir. 1984).
28. Pinkerton v. Moye, 509 F. Supp. 107 (W.D. Va. 1981).
29. School Board of Pinellas County v. Smith, 537 So. 2d 168 (Fla. Dist. Ct. App. 1989).
30. Alamo Heights Independent School District v. State Board of Education, 790 F.2d 1153 (5th Cir. 1986).
31. Fick *ex rel.* Fick v. Sioux Falls School District, 337 F.3d 968 (8th Cir. 2003).
32. Ms. S. *ex rel.* L.S. v. Scarborough School Committee, 366 F. Supp. 2d 98 (D. Me. 2005).
33. North Allegheny School District v. Gregory P., 687 A.2d 37 (Pa. Commw. Ct. 1996).
34. Macomb County Intermediate School District v. Joshua S., 715 F. Supp. 824 (E.D. Mich. 1989).
35. 34 C.F.R. § 300.34(c)(2).
36. 34 C.F.R. § 300.34(c)(10)(v).
37. 34 C.F.R. § 300.34(c)(14)(ii).
38. Max M. v. Thompson, 566 F. Supp. 1330 (N.D. Ill. 1983), 585 F. Supp. 317 (N.D. Ill. 1984), 592 F. Supp. 1437 (N.D. Ill. 1984), 592 F. Supp. 1450 (N.D. Ill. 1984), 629 F. Supp. 1504 (N.D. Ill. 1986).
39. In re A Family, 602 P.2d 157 (Mont. 1979).
40. T.G. and P.G. v. Board of Education of Piscataway, 576 F. Supp. 420 (D.N.J. 1983).
41. Gary B. v. Cronin, 542 F. Supp. 102 (N.D. Ill. 1980).
42. Doe v. Anrig, 651 F. Supp. 424 (D. Mass. 1987).
43. T.G. and P.G. v. Board of Education of Piscataway, 576 F. Supp. 420 (D.N.J. 1983), *affirmed* 738 F.2d 425 (3d Cir. 1984).
44. Papacoda v. State of Connecticut, 528 F. Supp. 68 (D. Conn. 1981).

45. Tice v. Botetourt County School Board, 908 F.2d 1200 (4th Cir. 1990). *See also* W.T. and K.T. *ex rel.* J.T. v. Board of Education of School District of New York, 716 F. Supp. 2d 270 (S.D.N.Y. 2010) (deciding that a child did not require counseling to make academic progress).

46. McKenzie v. Jefferson, EHLR 554:338 (D.D.C. 1983).

47. Darlene L. v. Illinois Board of Education, 568 F. Supp. 1340 (N.D. Ill. 1983).

48. Tice v. Botetourt County School Board, 908 F.2d 1200 (4th Cir. 1990); Clovis Unified School District v. California Office of Administrative Hearings, 903 F.2d 635 (9th Cir. 1990); Doe v. Anrig, 651 F. Supp. 424 (D. Mass. 1987); Metropolitan Government of Nashville and Davidson County v. Tennessee Department of Education, 771 S.W.2d 427 (Tenn. Ct. App. 1989).

49. M.K. *ex rel.* Mrs. K. v. Sergi, 554 F. Supp. 2d 201 (D. Conn. 2008).

50. Seals v. Loftis, 614 F. Supp. 302 (E.D. Tenn. 1985).

51. Brown v. Wilson County School Board, 747 F. Supp. 436 (M.D. Tenn. 1990).

52. J.B. v. Killingly Board of Education, 990 F. Supp. 57 (D. Conn. 1997).

53. Department of Education, State of Hawaii v. Cari Rae S., 158 F. Supp. 2d 1190 (D. Haw. 2001).

54. 903 F.2d 635 (9th Cir. 1990).

55. 910 F.2d 627 (9th Cir. 1990).

56. 34 C.F.R. § 300.34(c)(6).

57. 34 C.F.R. § 300.34(c)(9).

58. 34 C.F.R. § 300.34(c)(15).

59. Holmes v. Sobol, 690 F. Supp. 154 (W.D.N.Y. 1988).

60. Kattan v. District of Columbia, 691 F. Supp. 1539 (D.D.C. 1988).

61. Glendale Unified School District v. Almasi, 122 F. Supp. 2d 1093 (C.D. Cal. 2000).

62. Metropolitan Nashville and Davidson County School System v. Guest, 900 F. Supp. 905 (M.D. Tenn. 1995).

63. Polk v. Central Susquehanna Intermediate Unit 16, 853 F.2d 171 (3d Cir. 1988).

64. 20 U.S.C. § 1401(26)(A).

65. 34 C.F.R. § 300.34(c)(11).

66. 34 C.F.R. § 300.107.

67. 34 C.F.R. § 300.117.

68. *See Dear Colleague Letter*, Assistant Secretary for Civil Rights, U.S. Department of Education, available at http://www2.ed.gov/about/offices/list/ocr/letters/colleague-201301-504.pdf.

69. Rehabilitation Act, Section 504, 29 U.S.C. § 794 (2006).

70. Osborne, A. G., & Battaglino, L. (1996). Eligibility of students with disabilities for sports: Implications for policy. *Education Law Reporter, 105*, 379–388.

71. Birmingham and Lamphere School Districts v. Superintendent of Public Instruction, 328 N.W.2d 59 (Mich. Ct. App. 1982).

72. Kling v. Mentor Public School District, 136 F. Supp. 2d 744 (N.D. Ohio, 2001). *See also* Independent School District No. 12, Centennial v. Minnesota Department of Education, 788 N.W.2d 907 (Minn. 2010) (directing an IEP team to evaluate whether an extracurricular or nonacademic activity was appropriate for a student with disabilities and which supplementary aids and services were appropriate and necessary for participation in these activities).

73. Roslyn Union Free School District v. University of the State of New York, State Education Department, 711 N.Y.S.2d 582 (N.Y. App. Div. 2000).
74. 34 C.F.R. § 300.34(c)(13).
75. 468 U.S. 883 (1984).
76. Department of Education, State of Hawaii v. Katherine D., 531 F. Supp. 517 (D. Haw. 1982), *affirmed* 727 F.2d 809 (9th Cir. 1983). Hawaii has only one school board for the entire state.
77. Skelly v. Brookfield LaGrange Park School District 95, 968 F. Supp. 385 (N.D. Ill. 1997).
78. Macomb County Intermediate School District v. Joshua S., 715 F. Supp. 824 (E.D. Mich. 1989).
79. Osborne, A. G. (1999). Supreme Court rules that schools must provide full-time nursing services for medically fragile students. *Education Law Reporter, 136,* 1–14.
80. 526 U.S. 66 (1999).
81. For a commentary on this case *see* Russo, C. J. (1999). *Cedar Rapids Community School District v. Garret F.*: School districts must pay for nursing services under the IDEA. *School Business Affairs, 65*(6), 35–38.
82. 34 C.F.R. § 300.34(c)(5).
83. Seals v. Loftis, 614 F. Supp. 302 (E.D. Tenn. 1985).
84. Brown v. Wilson County School Board, 747 F. Supp. 436 (M.D. Tenn. 1990).
85. Department of Education, State of Hawaii v. Cari Rae S., 158 F. Supp. 2d 1190 (D. Haw. 2001).
86. Armstrong *ex rel.* Steffensen v. Alicante School, 44 F. Supp. 2d 1087 (E.D. Cal. 1999).
87. Wenkart, R. D. (2000). Juvenile offenders: Residential placement and special education. *Education Law Reporter, 144,* 1–13.
88. Field v. Haddonfield Board of Education, 769 F. Supp. 1313 (D.N.J. 1991).
89. Burke County Board of Education v. Denton, 895 F.2d 973 (4th Cir. 1990).
90. DeKalb County School District v. M.T.V. *ex rel.* C.E.V., 413 F. Supp. 2d 1322 (N.D. Ga. 2005), *affirmed* 164 F. App'x 900 (11th Cir. 2006).
91. 20 U.S.C. § 1401(20)(B).
92. 34 C.F.R. § 300.34(b).
93. A.U. *ex rel.* N.U. and B.U. v. Roane County Board of Education, 501 F. Supp. 2d 1134 (E.D. Tenn. 2007).
94. Petit v. U.S. Department of Education, 578 F. Supp. 2d 145 (D.D.C. 2008), 756 F. Supp. 2d 11 (D.D.C. 2010), *affirmed* 675 F.3d 769 (D.C. Cir. 2012).
95. Espino v. Besteiro, 520 F. Supp. 905 (S.D. Tex. 1981).
96. Schuldt v. Mankato Independent School District No. 77, 937 F.2d 1357 (8th Cir. 1991).
97. 34 C.F.R. § 300.34(c)(8).
98. Stacey G. v. Pasadena Independent School District, 547 F. Supp. 61 (S.D. Tex. 1982), *vacated and remanded on other grounds* 695 F.2d 949 (5th Cir. 1983).
99. Chris D. v. Montgomery County Board of Education, 753 F. Supp. 922 (M.D. Ala. 1990). *See also* P.K. and T.K. *ex rel.* S.K. v. New York City Department of Education, 819 F. Supp. 2d 90 (E.D.N.Y. 2011) (declaring that not providing parent training and counseling to the parents of a student with severe autism was likely to lead to regression).

100. Clear Creek Independent School District v. J.K., 400 F. Supp. 2d 991 (S.D. Tex. 2005).
101. M.K. *ex rel.* Mrs. K. v. Sergi, 554 F. Supp. 2d 201 (D. Conn. 2008).
102. 34 C.F.R. § 300.104.
103. Richardson Independent School District v. Michael Z., 580 F.3d 286 (5th Cir. 2009).
104. Union School District v. Smith, 15 F.3d 1519 (9th Cir. 1994); Ojai Unified School District v. Jackson, 4 F.3d 1467 (9th Cir. 1993).
105. Dale M. v. Board of Education of Bradley-Bourbonnais High School District No. 307, 237 F.3d 813 (7th Cir. 2001).
106. Sioux Falls School District v. Koupal, 526 N.W.2d 248 (S.D. 1994).
107. 458 U.S. 176 (1982).
108. Smith v. District of Columbia, 846 F. Supp. 2d 197 (D.D.C. 2012); J.C. *ex rel.* Mr. and Mrs. C. v. New Fairfield Board of Education, 2011 WL 1322563 (D. Conn. 2011); High v. Exeter Township School District, 2010 WL 363832 (E.D. Pa. 2010); School Board of Lee County v. M.M. *ex rel.* M.M.II, 2007 WL 983274 (M.D. Fla. 2007).
109. 34 C.F.R. § 300.324(a)(2)(v). For a comprehensive treatment of this topic, see Osborne, A. G. (2012). Providing assistive technology to students with disabilities under the IDEA. *Education Law Reporter, 280*, 519–533.
110. 34 C.F.R. § 300.105(a).
111. 34 C.F.R. § 300.105(b).
112. Assistance to the States for the Education of Children with Disabilities: Appendix B., 64 Fed. Reg. 12,405, 12,540 (Mar. 12, 1999).
113. J.C. *ex rel.* Mr. and Mrs. C. v. New Fairfield Board of Education, 2011 WL 1322563 (D. Conn. 2011).
114. *Id.*
115. East Penn School District v. Scott B., 1999 WL 178363 (E.D. Pa. 1999).
116. Board of Education of Harford County v. Bauer, 2000 WL 1481464 (D. Md. 2000).
117. Miller v. Board of Education of the Albuquerque Public Schools, 455 F. Supp. 2d 1286 (D.N.M. 2006), *affirmed* 565 F.3d 1232 (10th Cir. 2009).
118. Sherman v. Mamaroneck Union Free School District, 340 F.3d 87 (2d Cir. 2003).
119. Woods *ex rel.* T.W. v. Northport Public Schools, 2011 WL 1230813 (W.D. Mich. 2011), *affirmed* 487 F. App'x 968 (6th Cir. 2012); Jaccari J. v. Board of Education of Chicago, District N. 209, 690 F. Supp. 2d 687 (N.D. Ill. 2010); Blake C. *ex rel.* Tina F. v. Department of Education, State of Hawaii, 593 F. Supp. 2d 1199 (D. Haw. 2009); Kevin T. v. Elmhurst Community School District No. 205, 2002 WL 433061 (N.D. Ill. 2002); School Board of Independent School District No. 11 v. Pachl, 2002 WL 32653752 (D. Minn. 2002).
120. A.L. *ex rel.* L.L. v. Chicago Public School District No. 299, 2011 WL 5828209 (N.D. Ill. 2011).
121. Grant *ex rel.* Sunderlin v. Independent School District No. 11, 2005 WL 1539805 (D. Minn. 2005).
122. T.G. *ex rel.* Mr. & Mrs. T.G. v. Midland School District, 848 F. Supp. 2d 902 (C.D. Ill. 2012); C.G. *ex rel.* E.B. v. Pittsfield Central School District, 2010 WL 1533392 (W.D.N.Y. 2010); Schroll v. Board of Education Champaign Community Unit School District #4, 2007 WL 2681207 (C.D. Ill. 2007).

123. 20 U.S.C. § 1414(d)(1)(A).
124. 20 U.S.C. § 1401(34); 34 C.F.R. § 300.43.
125. Lessard v. Wilton Lyndeborough Cooperative School District, 518 F.3d 18 (1st Cir. 2008).
126. J.B. v. Killingly Board of Education, 990 F. Supp. 57 (D. Conn. 1997).
127. East Penn School District v. Scott B., 1999 WL 178363 (E.D. Pa. 1999).
128. Browell v. LeMahieu, 127 F. Supp. 2d 1117 (D. Haw. 2000).
129. Pace v. Bogulusa City School Board, 137 F. Supp. 2d 711 (E.D. La. 2001), *affirmed* 325 F.3d 609 (5th Cir. 2003).
130. Carrie I. *ex rel.* Greg I. v. Department of Education, State of Hawaii, 869 F. Supp. 2d 1225 (D. Haw. 2012).

Parent and Student Rights

In enacting the Individuals with Disabilities Education Act (IDEA),[1] Congress intended to make parents partners in the development of appropriate educational programs for their children, whether in their schools or homes.[2] In order to accomplish this goal, Congress granted parents unprecedented substantial procedural due process rights. Among the far-reaching rights that the IDEA affords parents is

> an opportunity for the parents of a child with a disability to examine all records relating to such child and to participate in meetings with respect to the identification, evaluation, and educational placement of the child, and the provision of a free appropriate public education to such child, and to obtain an independent educational evaluation of the child.[3]

According to the IDEA, the term *parent* means

(A) a natural, adoptive, or foster parent of a child (unless a foster parent is prohibited by State law from serving as a parent);

(B) a guardian (but not the State if the child is a ward of the State);

(C) an individual acting in the place of a natural or adoptive parent (including a grandparent, stepparent, or other relative) with whom the child lives, or an individual who is legally responsible for the child's welfare; or

(D) except as used in sections 1415(b)(2) of this title and 1439(a)(5) of this title, an individual assigned under either of those sections to be a surrogate parent.[4]

State laws may further refine, or place additional restrictions on, who may be considered to be a parent. For example, the Ninth Circuit held that in California the definition of parent includes a guardian "appointed by the juvenile court to have legal authority for making educational decisions" on behalf of a child.[5]

The courts recognize the importance Congress placed on parental participation.[6] Accordingly, case law makes it clear that school officials must offer parents opportunities to participate meaningfully in the development of Individual Education Programs (IEPs) for their children. In one such case, the Sixth Circuit affirmed the relevant part of an earlier order finding that educators in Tennessee violated the rights of a child and his parents by having predetermined not to offer him intensive applied behavioral analysis.[7] However, in a case from Louisiana, the Fifth Circuit clarified that the right to provide meaningful input does not grant parents veto power over the decisions of IEP teams or the right to dictate outcomes.[8]

At the same time, while courts have not insisted on absolute compliance with the letter of the law regarding parental rights, they have diligently upheld parental rights in the special education process. The courts typically allow school board proposals to stand if procedural violations do not prejudice the process and do not result in a detriment to students, but they do not tolerate egregious violations of parental rights.[9]

Parental Rights

In order to help achieve the main goal of the IDEA, providing a free appropriate public education (FAPE) to all students with disabilities, Congress included significant parental rights in the statute so that parents could advocate on behalf of their children. Although most of the due process rights in the IDEA are for the benefit of children, the Supreme Court ruled that parents have rights of their own independent of those of their children.[10]

Since the IDEA grants numerous rights throughout all aspects of the special education process, student and parental rights are inherent in discussions throughout this book. This chapter focuses on the general rights of students and parents such as the right to be notified of school board actions regarding the provision of FAPEs. The chapter also includes an extensive discussion of student and parent rights with regard to school records.

Parental Notification

It almost goes without saying that parents cannot exercise rights of which they are unaware. The IDEA obligates school boards to inform parents fully of their rights once per year.[11] In addition, the IDEA directs education officials to notify parents on the initial referrals or their first request for evaluations of their children, on the first occurrence when they file IDEA-related complaints, and when they make such requests.[12] The IDEA and its regulations also permit school officials to place notice of the procedural safeguards on their websites.[13]

Insofar as the failure of school officials to inform parents of their rights has limited parental ability to participate in the education of their children, this has led to significant amounts of litigation. Case law acknowledges that the purpose of notifying parents of their rights is to provide them with sufficient information to protect their rights, allow them to make informed judgments, and fully participate in due process hearings, if necessary.[14]

> The purpose of notifying parents of their rights is to provide them with sufficient information to protect those rights, allow them to make informed judgments, and fully participate in due process hearings, if necessary.

The IDEA's regulations identify seven key elements that parental notice must contain. Notice must

- Describe the actions that school officials proposed or refused to initiate.
- Explain why officials proposed to or refused to act.
- Describe each evaluation, procedure, assessment, record, and/or report that officials used as bases for their proposed or refused actions.
- Include reminders that parents retain their procedural safeguards along with information about where they may obtain descriptions of those safeguards.
- Identify sources for parents to contact if they need assistance in understanding the contents of notice.

- Describe the other options that officials considered and the reasons why the other options were not pursued.
- Be in a language that is understandable to the general public and in the parents' native language unless it is otherwise clearly not feasible to do so. If the native language or other mode of parental communication is not a written language, education officials must ensure that notice is translated orally or by other means to parents in their native language or other mode of communication, that the parents understand the notice, and that there is written evidence that educators satisfied these requirements.[15]

A federal trial court in Illinois declared that a school board's failure to notify a student's parents about meetings at which their son's educational placement was discussed, about their right to review psychological evaluations, and about their right to obtain an independent evaluation violated the IDEA.[16] The court found that these procedural violations effectively denied the parents the opportunity to participate in the development of their child's IEP. In another case, the Fourth Circuit affirmed that the failure of a school board in North Carolina to notify parents of their rights resulted in its failure to provide a FAPE under the standards established by the Supreme Court.[17] The lower court had discovered that board officials consistently failed to comply with federal and state statutes requiring them to notify the parents of their rights. The panel reasoned that this failure relegated parental participation to little more than acquiescence to the actions of school officials.

More recently, when an IEP team in Delaware adjourned a conference and reconvened later without providing 10 days' written notice of the second meeting, the Third Circuit affirmed that the alleged notice violations did not impair parental ability to participate in IEP meetings.[18] In a case from Tennessee, the Sixth Circuit decided that school officials did not violate a mother's rights when they conferred on an assessment report since she participated fully in the IEP process and was actively involved in evaluating her daughter's eligibility for IDEA services.[19]

The IDEA's notice requirements are designed to provide parents with the information necessary to allow them to participate actively in the educational planning process for their children. When parents in the District of Columbia challenged the notice provided by their school board, a federal trial court observed that the notice was statutorily sufficient.[20] The court was satisfied that the notices informed parents about the board's proposed placements for their child and why school officials selected that placement. The court remarked that the information that officials supplied adequately provided the parents with the opportunity to have a meaningful role in the decision-making process and to draw informed conclusions about whether the proposed placement would have conferred an appropriate education on their child. Conversely, the federal trial court in Arizona rejected notice as insufficient because it failed to detail the reasons for a school board's proposed action.[21]

Naturally, misleading notice or a failure to provide notice is problematic for school boards. The federal trial court for the District of Columbia maintained that misleading notice violated the procedural rights of parents under the IDEA.[22] The court conceded that although school officials notified the parents that they had 15 days to request a due process hearing, this action was inappropriate because the IDEA did not authorize them to impose such a unilateral time limitation. In a case from Texas, the court held that a board's failure to provide a father with written notice of its refusal to evaluate his child constituted a procedural violation of the IDEA.[23]

A case from Maryland illustrates the principle that notice must be kept up to date. On discovering that school board officials provided parents with an outdated booklet that did not reflect changes in federal and state law regarding procedural safeguards, the federal trial court decreed that they violated the IDEA.[24] The court determined that the fact that the parents' attorney was aware of those changes did not relieve the board of its obligation to provide them with adequate, up-to-date notice. Figure 4.1 lists the content that notice to parents must include.

Figure 4.1   Required Content of Notice to Parents

- A description of the action(s) that school board officials proposed or refused to initiate
- An explanation of why school board officials proposed to do something or refused to act
- Descriptions of all evaluations, procedures, assessments, records, or reports that school board officials used as bases for their proposed or refused actions
- A reminder that the IDEA protects parents and their children
- Information about where parents may obtain a copy of their procedural safeguards
- A list of sources for parents to contact if they need assistance in understanding the contents of the notice
- A description of the other options that IEP teams considered and reasons why the other options were not pursued
- A description of other relevant factors concerning the actions of refusals to act by school board officials
- A written explanation in the parents' native language or other mode of communication and in a language that is understandable to the general public or presented orally, if necessary

Parental Consent

School boards must obtain informed consent from parents before school personnel can conduct evaluations to determine if children qualify for special education and prior to providing special education and related services.

The IDEA requires school board officials to obtain informed consent from parents before personnel can conduct evaluations to determine whether children qualify for special education and prior to providing special education and related services.[25] If parents refuse or otherwise fail to provide consent for evaluations of their children, and officials believe that evaluations are warranted, educators may use the IDEA's due process hearing mechanism to seek to override the lack of parental consent unless doing so is inconsistent with state law.[26] In this respect, a federal trial court in Texas reasoned that a hearing officer had the authority to override a mother's refusal to consent to an evaluation of her child for learning disabilities.[27] The IDEA does not, though, allow boards to seek overrides of parents' refusal for services,[28] including circumstances when they choose to homeschool their children rather than submit to services.[29]

Effect of Procedural Errors

Procedural errors by school officials do not necessarily render their recommendations concerning IEPs inappropriate. The Supreme Court, in *Board of Education of the Hendrick Hudson Central School District v. Rowley*,[30] held that in order to be appropriate, IEPs must be developed in accordance with the procedures outlined in the IDEA. Courts examine the effect of violations to evaluate whether, and to what extent, the violations interfere with the development of IEPs for students. If school officials violate the letter of the law but their errors do not interfere with parental participation in the IEP process, courts generally do not invalidate IEPs. If violations prevent active parental participation in the development of IEPs, though, these errors are generally sufficient to have IEPs invalidated.

> Egregious disregard for the IDEA's basic provisions provides courts with sufficient bases to invalidate proposed IEPs.

Egregious disregard for the IDEA's basic provisions provides courts with sufficient bases to invalidate proposed IEPs. The Fourth Circuit affirmed that a school board in West Virginia that failed both to conduct an annual review of a student's program as required by law, and to involve his parents in the IEP process, did not provide an appropriate education.[31]

The Sixth Circuit was of the opinion that strict compliance with the IDEA's procedural safeguards is the best way to ensure that its substantive provisions are enforced.[32] Despite this analysis, the court did not treat the failure of school officials from Ohio to provide the parents with written notice as prejudicial because the mother received adequate oral notice and participated in the IEP conference. Similarly, a federal trial court in New York asserted that a school board's violation of the letter of the law did not prejudice a student or his parents in any way because the latter were involved in planning and executing their child's IEP.[33] Further, the Eleventh Circuit noted that deficiencies in the notices provided to parents by a board in Alabama that had no impact on their full and effective participation in the IEP process caused no harm.[34] In each of these cases, the courts agreed that insofar as the procedural errors did not result in substantive deprivations, they were insufficient to render otherwise appropriate IEPs invalid.

IEP Conferences

IEP conferences provide parents with the best opportunity to participate in the development of appropriate educational programs for their children. At these meetings, team members review evaluation results, develop IEPs, and make placement decisions. Prior to these conferences, parents may have attended meetings to discuss the needs of their children and may have provided information about their youngsters. These earlier meetings aside, most decisions about the future education of students are made at IEP conferences.

As an initial matter, school officials must take steps to ensure that at least one of a student's parents is present at IEP conferences.[35] Further, while officials are required to notify parents about meetings at which the IEPs or placements of their children are to be discussed, this does not mean that they must be notified each and every time school personnel confer. In one such case, the Fifth Circuit affirmed that officials from Texas were not required to notify a child's parents every time one of his teachers discussed his progress with an administrator.[36]

> Parental participation is meaningless if parents do not understand the proceedings of IEP conferences. School officials should therefore take the necessary steps to ensure that parents understand what is taking place at IEP meetings.

Parental participation is meaningless if parents do not understand the proceedings of IEP conferences. School officials should therefore take the necessary steps to ensure that parents understand what is taking place at IEP meetings. For example, the Second Circuit affirmed the relevant part of an earlier order directing school officials in New York to provide sign language interpreters so that parents who were hearing impaired could participate in meetings and conferences that were important to the education of their non–hearing-impaired children.[37] Even though neither of the children in this dispute needed special education services, and the case was resolved under Section 504 of the Rehabilitation Act,[38] the legal principles are applicable for IEP meetings.

In helping parents to understand IEP meetings and other proceedings, educators may have to go the proverbial "extra mile." In two separate cases, the federal trial court in Connecticut concurred that parents had the right to tape-record IEP conferences. In the first suit, the court pointed out that insofar as the child's mother had limited English proficiency, her request to tape-record the proceedings so that she could better understand and follow them was reasonable.[39] In the second case, the court allowed the child's mother to tape-record the proceedings because she could not take notes due to a disabling hand injury.[40] Both courts agreed that insofar as the IDEA's intent of parental participation meant more than mere presence at IEP conferences, allowing parents to make tape recordings afforded them the opportunities to become active and meaningful participants.

School board officials may also have the right to make records of IEP proceedings. The First Circuit affirmed that educators in New Hampshire had the right to employ a court reporter at an administrative hearing in order to secure a verbatim record of the proceedings.[41] Although the nature of an administrative hearing is different from that of an IEP conference, in some situations the need for a verbatim record may exist. In situations such as this, courts are likely to grant boards the right to create verbatim transcripts of meetings.

As indicated, procedural errors can create serious problems for school boards since they may cause courts to enter judgments in favor of parents in disagreements involving IEPs. Yet, as a case from the Sixth Circuit indicated, parents may give up some of their rights by failing to participate in the IEP process.[42] Parents from Ohio challenged the adequacy of an IEP because all of the required participants were not present at the IEP conference, but then rejected the board's offer to convene a properly constituted session. The court remarked that the parents relinquished their right to a procedurally correct IEP conference by rejecting the board's offer to schedule such a session.

IEP Revisions

From time to time, along with conducting annual and triennial reviews, school officials may need to alter IEPs due to changing circumstances within educational environments or changes in student needs. Minor adjustments not resulting in changes in student placements are of little consequence.

If changes substantially alter IEPs or result in their not being implemented as written, then the IDEA's procedural protections are triggered. Parents must be notified of changes in the educational placements of their children and must be given opportunities to participate in making these modifications.[43] In reviewing IEPs, teams are expected to consider the lack of expected progress toward achieving students' annual goals, the results of reevaluation information provided to or about students by their parents, their anticipated needs, other matters,[44] and/or special factors.[45]

In addition, IEP meetings must include a child's regular education teacher.[46] Moreover, a change in the IDEA and its regulations permits changes to IEPs to be made by means of video conferences and conference calls.[47]

> Minor adjustments to IEPs that do not result in a change in student placement are of little consequence. Changes that alter IEPs substantially or result in their not being implemented as written trigger the IDEA's procedural protections.

The District of Columbia Circuit decided that the failure of school board officials to notify a surrogate parent of the curtailment of a student's instructional program constituted a denial of an appropriate education.[48] The student lived in a children's hospital and was transported to a board facility to receive educational services. The record reflected that educators discontinued the child's educational program for several months because medical problems prohibited his being transported. However, the court acknowledged that officials did not provide alternative services and that his surrogate parent was never notified that educational services were no longer being provided. In another case, the Third Circuit affirmed that a board from New Jersey did not violate the IDEA when officials modified an IEP as a result of discussions that had taken place pursuant to a rejected IEP, even though they had not followed the normal IEP revision process.[49] The court agreed with the earlier order that school officials made the modifications in the spirit of compromise.

Noncustodial Parents

> Absent court orders to the contrary, the IDEA's parental rights apply to parents who do not have custody of their children due to divorce.

In today's world many students do not live with both parents. As discussed below in the section on privacy and student records, absent court orders to the contrary, the IDEA's parental rights apply to parents who do not have custody of their children due to divorce. In one such case, the Seventh Circuit ruled that a noncustodial father from Illinois had standing to sue a school board over his son's IEP.[50] Even though the divorce decree gave the custodial mother the right to make educational decisions, the court found that nothing in it stripped the noncustodial father of his parental interest in educational matters.

A case from Texas illustrates how judicial proceedings can alter parental rights. The court thought that a noncustodial father lacked standing to challenge his daughter's placement because a divorce decree awarded full authority for educational decision making to her mother.[51] Earlier, the Second Circuit affirmed that under Vermont law, a noncustodial mother lacked standing to demand a hearing under the IDEA over the appropriateness of her daughter's IEP evaluation.[52] The court posited that the mother lost the right to participate in her daughter's education in a divorce decree that awarded full custody of the child to her father, who opposed the hearing, on the basis that it was against his daughter's best interests. A case with similar circumstances, where a father secured the right to make educational decisions for his children, arose in Florida. The Eleventh Circuit affirmed that insofar as the noncustodial mother's legal relationship to her children was legally terminated, she was not a parent under state law. The court thus concluded that the mother lacked standing to bring suit under the IDEA.[53]

Another case from the Second Circuit illustrates the importance of state law and the content of orders contained in divorce decrees in determining a noncustodial parent's rights. The court, reiterating that state law controlled parental rights in divorce situations, certified, to New York's Court of Appeals for an opinion, the question of whether a noncustodial father retained rights when the divorce decree was silent regarding educational decisions.[54] The state's highest court ascertained that unless an order expressly permitted joint decision-making authority or designated particular authority with respect to a child's education, a noncustodial parent had no right to control such matters.[55] After receiving that guidance, the Second Circuit affirmed that a noncustodial father lacked standing to request a due process hearing to challenge the adequacy of his son's IEP.[56]

Adult Students

Many students continue to receive special education services after reaching their 18th birthdays. While these students assume rights of their own on reaching the age of majority, and most of the rights accorded to parents by the IDEA are transferred to the students, their parents do not lose their rights under the IDEA just because their children have reached this milestone.[57] Thus, parents are still entitled to notice as to what is taking place with regard to the education of their children even though all other rights associated with the IDEA are transferred to the students. Further, the IDEA requires states to establish procedures for parents or other appropriate individuals to represent the educational interests of students over the age of majority who lack the ability to provide informed consent.[58]

The Second Circuit reasoned that the IDEA's procedural safeguards apply to students between the ages of 18 and 21 even if they have not been declared incompetent.[59] School officials terminated special education services for a 20-year-old student from Connecticut with his consent but without notifying his mother. The court indicated that the termination of services without parental notification violated the IDEA because the mother was entitled to be informed of the change.

Students who are incarcerated in adult prisons are an important subset of children with disabilities whose rights are addressed in the IDEA. The statute provides that all rights accorded to parents under the IDEA transfer to children who are incarcerated in an adult or juvenile correctional facility.[60] Further, if students with disabilities are convicted as adults under state law and incarcerated in adult prisons, IEP teams may modify their IEPs or placements as long as state officials can demonstrate that they cannot otherwise accommodate bona fide security or compelling penological interests.[61] State law is important in this regard. For example, in a case from Florida, the Department of Corrections claimed that insofar as a 16-year-old student was incarcerated as an adult, he had the transferred right of majority. The trial court disagreed, clarifying that the rights of majority do not transfer until a child reaches the age of majority under state law.[62]

Student Records and Privacy

In 1974, a year before enacting the Education of All Handicapped Children Act (the original name of the IDEA), Congress passed the Family Educational Rights and Privacy Act (FERPA),[63] also known as the Buckley Amendment after its primary sponsor, then-Senator James Buckley of New York. FERPA, which clarifies the rights of students and their parents with regard to educational records, has two main goals: to grant parents and eligible students, meaning those over 18, access to their educational records and to limit the access of outsiders to these records. FERPA, along with the IDEA and its regulations, has a significant impact on the delivery of special education that applies with equal force to parents[64] and eligible students with disabilities. Insofar as parents, rather than special education students, typically exercise the right to access the records of their children, this discussion focuses on parental rights.

Records Covered

> FERPA covers "education records" containing personally identifiable information relating to students that are maintained by educational agencies or by persons acting on their behalf.

FERPA covers "education records" containing personally identifiable information relating to students that are maintained by educational agencies or by persons acting on their behalf.[65] Since education records may include information about more than one student, parents who review the records of their children can examine only those portions of group data specific to their own children.[66]

Two cases highlight the importance of safeguarding student records. In the first, the federal trial court in Connecticut wrote that school officials violated the privacy rights of parents by releasing their names and that of their son to a local newspaper following a due process hearing.[67] The Eighth Circuit, affirming that public policy favors protection of the privacy of minors where sensitive matters are concerned, upheld an order from a federal trial court in Missouri that judicial proceedings under the IDEA can be closed to the public.[68] The court pointed out that the IDEA restricts the release of information about students with disabilities without parental permission. In order to safeguard the information at issue while preventing the stigmatization of the student, the court declared that access to the courtroom could be restricted and the files sealed.

Another form of records that school systems preserve is so-called directory information, which includes each child's

> name, address, telephone listing, date and place of birth, major field of study, participation in officially recognized activities and sports, weight and height of members of athletic teams, degrees and awards received, and the most recent previous educational agency or institution attended by the student.[69]

Before school officials can release directory information about current students, they must provide the students' parents with notice of the categories of records that are designated as directory and afford parents a reasonable time to request that the material not be released without their consent.[70] Insofar as the disclosure provisions relating to directory information do not apply to former students, officials can release such data without obtaining any prior approvals.[71]

At the same time, FERPA requires school officials to notify parents of their annual right to inspect and review, request amendment of, and consent to disclosure of educational records as well as to file complaints with the federal Department of Education alleging failures to comply with the statute's dictates.[72] Typically, parents receive a single notice by a means that is reasonably likely to inform them of their rights, such as on school websites, in school newsletters, student handbooks, notes home, local access TV, e-mail, or some other method or combination of means designed to ensure that they receive notice.

The comprehensiveness of FERPA aside, four major exceptions mean that a variety of documents are not classified as educational records[73] subject to the act's mandatory disclosure provisions.

- First, records made by educational personnel that are in the sole possession of their makers and are not accessible by or revealed to other persons, except temporary substitutes, are not subject to release.[74]

- Second, records kept separately by law enforcement units of educational agencies that are used only for their own purposes cannot be accessed by third parties.[75]
- Third, records that are made in the ordinary course of events relating to individuals who work at, but who do not attend, educational institutions, and that refer exclusively to their capacity as employees and are not available for any other purpose are not subject to disclosure.[76]
- Fourth, records relating to students who are 18 years of age or older, or who attend postsecondary educational institutions, that are made by physicians, psychiatrists, psychologists, or other professionals or paraprofessionals for use in their treatment and are not available to others, except at the request of the students, cannot be released.[77]

Access Rights

As noted, pursuant to FERPA, parents have the right to inspect and review records containing personally identifiable information relating to the education of their children.[78] It is important to recognize that absent court orders or applicable state law, FERPA grants noncustodial parents the same right of access to educational records as custodial parents.[79] When court orders are in effect or if state laws prohibit disclosure to noncustodial parents, school officials would be wise to consider keeping files in two separate locations. Put another way, in order to avoid the risk of mistakenly granting access to noncustodial parents or their representatives, educators should place essentially blank files in the main set of student records directing individuals who need to see them to a second, more secure location. Along with access rights, FERPA requires school officials to provide parents with reasonable interpretations and explanations of information contained in the records of their children.[80]

Under FERPA, parental permission or consent is transferred to eligible students who reach their 18th birthday or who attend postsecondary institutions.[81] In an important exception relating to special education, school officials can take the age and types or severity of students' disabilities into account when considering whether to grant rights of access.[82] Other restrictions of interest are that postsecondary institutions do not have to permit students to inspect financial records in their files that include information about the resources of their parents[83] or letters of recommendation where they waived their rights of access,[84] typically by checking off such an item on a recommendation form. Further, school officials are not required to grant access to records pertaining to individuals who never were students at their institutions.[85]

> Third parties generally can access school records, other than directory information, only if parents or qualified students provide written consent.

Third parties generally can access school records, other than directory information, only if parents or qualified students provide written consent.[86] In order to assist in the smooth operation of schools, especially as officials in different systems interact with one another, FERPA contains eleven major exceptions where permission is not required before officials can review educational records.

- First, school employees with legitimate educational interests can access student records;[87] for example, at the end of a school year, or over a summer, a third grade teacher can read the records of second grade children who will be in her class in the fall in order to prepare classes and other lessons. However, the teacher would be unlikely to have a legitimate need to see the files of children entering fifth grade, because she would not be instructing or interacting with them in an official capacity.
- Second, officials representing schools to which students applied for admission can access their records as long as parents receive proper notice that the information has been sent to the receiving institutions.[88]
- Third, authorized representatives of the U.S. comptroller general, the secretary of the Department of Education, and state and local education officials who are authorized to do so by state law can view student records for law enforcement purposes.[89]
- Fourth, persons who are responsible for evaluating the eligibility of students for financial aid can review appropriate educational records.[90]
- Fifth, members of organizations conducting studies on behalf of educational agencies or institutions developing predictive tests or administering aid programs and improving instruction can view records as long as doing so does not lead to the release of personal information about students.[91]
- Sixth, individuals acting in the course of their duties for accrediting organizations can review student records.[92]
- Seventh, parents of dependent children can access student records pertaining to their own children.[93]
- Eighth, in emergency situations, persons who protect the health and safety of students or other persons can view records.[94]
- Ninth, written permission is not necessary if records are subpoenaed or otherwise sought via judicial orders, but the parents or qualified students must be notified in advance of compliance by school boards.[95] Even so, prior to ordering the release of information, courts weigh the need for access against the privacy interests of students.
- Tenth, when conducting program monitoring, evaluations, and performance measurements of agencies and institutions receiving federal funding for school lunch programs, the secretary of agriculture, authorized representatives, or contractors acting on behalf of the food and nutrition service can access records when the results are reported in an aggregate form that does not identify any individual.

Any data collected for this purpose must be protected such that it does not permit the personal identification of students and their parents by other than authorized representatives of the secretary. Further, personally identifiable data must be destroyed when the information is no longer needed.[96]

- Eleventh, caseworkers or other representatives of specified child welfare agencies who have a right to access case plans for children in their care can access the education records or the personally identifiable information contained in such records. Caseworkers may not disclose information except to individuals or entities engaged in addressing the education needs of the students and are authorized to receive such disclosures, consistent with applicable law protecting the confidentiality of the education records of the students.[97]

FERPA adds that its provisions do not prohibit education officials from disclosing information concerning registered sex offenders who are required to register by federal law. Of course, in any of these situations, education officials cannot release or quote any personally identifiable information relating to students without parental consent.

A third party seeking disclosure of student records must have written consent from parents or qualified students specifying the record(s) to be released, the reason(s) for the proposed release, and to whom the information is to be given.[98] FERPA further specifies that parents or qualified students have the right to receive copies of the materials to be released.[99] In addition, school officials must keep records of all individuals or groups, except exempted parties, who request or obtain access to student records.[100] These records must not only explain the legitimate interests of those who were granted access to the educational files but must also be kept with the records of the student in question.[101]

Educational agencies that maintain student records must comply with requests for review without unnecessary delay. More specifically, unless parents or qualified students agree otherwise, officials must grant them access no later than 45 days after receiving their requests.[102] Needless to say, nothing prohibits school officials from granting parental requests for access to student records more quickly. Agencies that receive requests for access to records cannot charge fees to search for or to retrieve student records.[103] Once materials are located, officials can charge parents or qualified students for copies as long as a payment does not effectively prevent them from exercising their rights to inspect and review the educational records at issue.[104]

Amending Records

Parents or qualified students who disagree with the content of educational records can ask school officials to amend the disputed information.

Parents or qualified students who disagree with the content of the educational records can ask school officials to amend the disputed information.[105] If officials refuse to grant requests to amend records within a reasonable time,[106] parents or qualified students are entitled to hearings at which hearing officers evaluate whether the challenged material is accurate and appropriately contained within the disputed educational records.[107] Hearing officers must both conduct hearings and render decisions within a reasonable time.[108] If hearing officers are convinced that contested material is inaccurate or misleading, or if it otherwise violates the rights of students to privacy, school officials must amend the contested material accordingly and inform qualified students or their parents in writing that this has been done.[109] In contrast, if hearing officers are satisfied that the materials in educational records are not inaccurate or misleading, or do not otherwise violate students' privacy rights, the records need not be removed or amended.[110] Parents or qualified students who remain concerned over the content of the educational records at issue, even after hearing officers decide that they are acceptable, can add statements explaining their objections to the records. These statements must be kept with the contested information for as long as the records are kept on file.[111]

Destruction of Records

The number of records in the files of students who are in special education placements can multiply rapidly. Accordingly, it should not be surprising that the IDEA's regulations discuss the destruction of information that is no longer needed. Although neither the IDEA nor its regulations define the term, the latter indicate that records can be destroyed when they are no longer needed to provide children with services.[112] This could include, but is not limited to, outdated IEPs and test protocols. The regulation adds that parents or qualified students must be advised that records are going to be destroyed and that school officials can save, without any time limitation, records including students' names, addresses, phone numbers, grades, attendance records, classes attended, and grade levels completed along with the years they were completed.[113]

Enforcement

If parents or qualified students are denied the opportunity to review the records they seek or if information is released impermissibly (as in the case of students who are over the age of 18 in postsecondary institutions), the education officials who denied appropriate access or granted inappropriate access can be charged with violating FERPA, thereby triggering its enforcement provisions. As the Supreme Court ruled in *Gonzaga University v. Doe*,[114] admittedly a case from higher education, an aggrieved party must file a written complaint detailing the specifics of an alleged violation with the federal Department of Education's Family Policy Compliance Office (FPCO).[115]

Complaints must be filed within 180 days of either alleged violations or the dates when claimants knew or reasonably should have known about violations.[116] When the FPCO receives complaints, its staff must notify officials at the educational institution in writing, detailing the substance of the alleged violations and asking them to respond before considering whether to proceed with investigations.[117] If, after investigations[118] are completed, the FPCO staff agrees that violations occurred, the Department of Education can withhold future payments under its programs, issue orders to compel compliance, or ultimately terminate an institution's eligibility to receive federal funding if officials refuse to comply within a reasonable time,[119] a draconian solution that has yet to occur.

In the only other Supreme Court case involving FERPA in a K–12 context, *Owasso Independent School District v. Falvo*,[120] the Court held that insofar as "peer grading," whereby teachers permit students to grade the papers of classmates, does not turn the papers into educational records covered by FERPA, a school board in Oklahoma did not violate the law by permitting teachers to use the practice over the objection of a mother whose children attended schools in the district.[121] The Court explained that student papers do not become educational records within the meaning of FERPA until such time as they are entered into the grade books of teachers.

FREQUENTLY ASKED QUESTIONS

Q: What rights do noncustodial parents have in the IEP process?

A: Absent court orders or state law to the contrary, noncustodial parents retain all of the rights of custodial parents. This is true even if noncustodial parents do not live within a school district's boundaries. Thus, noncustodial parents have the right to challenge proposed IEPs. However, as the answer to this question is very much affected by state law, school administrators must consult the requirements of state law. For example, state law may specify how noncustodial parents are to be notified of IEP meetings and may require custodial parents to be notified whenever noncustodial parents request information.

Q: Do parents lose all of their rights under the IDEA when their children reach the age of majority?

A: Although most of the rights accorded to parents under the IDEA transfer to the students when they reach the age of majority, school boards must continue to provide notice to the parents as well as the students. In other words, parents

(Continued)

(Continued)

must be kept informed. Further, states are required to establish procedures for appointing parents or other responsible individuals to represent the interests of students who have reached the age of majority but lack the ability to provide informed consent. State law may also dictate who can represent children over the age of majority who have been declared legally incompetent.

Q: If parents or qualified students disagree with material in disputed school records, can they insist that it be removed?

A: No. Parents or qualified students are entitled to proceedings at which hearing officers can consider whether the challenged materials are inaccurate and/or inappropriate for school records. If hearing officers decide in favor of parents or qualified students, the records must be amended. Conversely, if hearing officers agree with school officials that the materials are accurate and appropriately placed in the records, the parents or qualified students may add statements to the files explaining their objections; these statements must be preserved for as long as the records are maintained

Q. I was told that I cannot look at the records of former students to see how they are doing. As a teacher at their school, am I not entitled to see their records?

A. No. Under FERPA only school personnel who have legitimate educational reasons to access student records may do so. Although their desire to see the records may be well intentioned, teachers usually do not have a need to know what is contained in the records of former students. A desire to follow students to see how they are doing is not a sufficient reason to access their records. There are exceptions to when teachers may look at records of former students, but these exist only when educators have legitimate reasons for viewing the files. For instance, when teachers are asked to write recommendations for former students, they may consult students' records for information needed to write these letters.

Recommendations

The IDEA and its regulations provide students with disabilities and their parents with specific procedural rights. Those rights are included in the statute because Congress intended parents to be equal partners with school officials in the development of appropriate educational programs for their children. The Supreme Court reasoned that in enacting the IDEA, Congress was well aware that school boards had all too often denied students with disabilities an appropriate education, without consulting their parents.[122] In order to remedy situations relating to children with disabilities, Congress emphasized the importance and necessity of parental participation throughout the IDEA. To this end, school officials should

- Periodically review all notices to parents to make sure that they are up-to-date and comply with current federal and state laws.
- Guarantee parental input into the evaluation and placement process through frequent communication with parents even if this requires home visits.
- Ensure parental participation in the IEP development process by making reasonable attempts to schedule IEP meetings at times that are convenient for parents and investigate alternative means for parental attendance at IEP meetings, such as telephone or video conferencing, when parents cannot attend in person.
- Listen to, discuss, and give due consideration to all parental concerns and suggestions.
- Provide parents with interpreters for IEP meetings and any progress conferences if their primary mode of communication is not English.
- Allow parents to tape-record IEP meetings if doing so will assist them in participating in the process.
- Consistent with state law, remind noncustodial parents of their rights with respect to the IEP process. Transfer rights given to parents by the IDEA to students when they reach the age of majority but continue to provide notice to parents; notify parents when rights are being transferred.
- Take all necessary steps to protect the privacy of special education students.
- Be diligent in ensuring that parents are afforded all of the rights and protections that they are guaranteed by the IDEA.
- Provide hearings for parents or qualified students who object to the contents of educational records.
- Amend records that are shown to be inaccurate or misleading.
- Allow parents or qualified students to include statements in the records explaining their concerns when records are not amended.

Endnotes

1. 20 U.S.C. §§ 1400–1482 (2012). The IDEA's regulations can be found at Assistance to the States for the Education of Children with Disabilities, 34 C.F.R. §§ 300.1–300.818 (2013).
2. 20 U.S.C. § 1400(c)(5)(B).
3. 20 U.S.C. § 1415(b)(1).
4. 20 U.S.C. § 1402(23).
5. Orange County Department of Education v. California Department of Education, 668 F.3d 1052 at 1061 (9th Cir. 2011), *citing* Cal. Educ. Code § 48200.

More recently, in an unpublished decision that same court held that a responsible adult appointed by a California state court to make educational decisions was a parent within the meaning of state law. Irvine Unified School District v. California Department of Education, 506 F. App'x 548 (9th Cir. 2013).

6. Russo, C. J., & Osborne, A. G. (2007). Parental rights in special education: The ongoing debate in the US. *Education Law Journal, 8*(4), 245–254.

7. Deal v. Hamilton County Board of Education, 392 F.3d 840 (6th Cir. 2004), *rehearing and rehearing en banc denied* (6th Cir. 2005).

8. White *ex rel.* White v. Ascension Parish School Board, 343 F.3d 373 (5th Cir. 2003).

9. Osborne, A. G. (1993). Parental rights under the IDEA. *Education Law Reporter, 80,* 771–777.

10. Winkelman *ex rel.* Winkelman v. Parma City School District, 550 U.S. 516 (2007). For a commentary on this case, see Russo, C. J. (2007). The rights of non-attorney parents under the IDEA: *Winkelman v. Parma City School District. Education Law Reporter, 221,* 1–19.

11. 20 U.S.C. § 1415(d)(1)(A); 34 C.F.R. § 300.504(a).

12. 20 U.S.C. § 1415(d)(1)(A); 34 C.F.R. § 300.504(a).

13. 20 U.S.C. § 1415(d)(B); 34 C.F.R. § 300.504(b).

14. Kroot v. District of Columbia, 800 F. Supp. 977 (D.D.C. 1992).

15. 34 C.F.R. § 300.503(b).

16. Max M. v. Thompson, 566 F. Supp. 1330 (N.D. Ill. 1983).

17. Hall v. Vance County Board of Education, 774 F.2d 629 (4th Cir. 1985), *citing* Board of Education of the Hendrick Hudson Central School District v. Rowley, 458 U.S. 176 (1982).

18. C.H. v. Cape Henlopen School District, 606 F.3d 59 (3d Cir. 2010).

19. N.L. *ex rel.* Mrs. C. v. Knox County Schools, 315 F.3d 688 (6th Cir. 2003).

20. Smith v. Squillacote, 800 F. Supp. 993 (D.D.C. 1992).

21. Magyar v. Tucson Unified School District, 956 F. Supp. 1423 (D. Ariz. 1997).

22. Smith v. Henson, 786 F. Supp. 43 (D.D.C. 1992).

23. El Paso Independent School District v. Richard R., 567 F. Supp. 2d 918 (W.D. Tex. 2008).

24. Carnwath v. Board of Education of Anne Arundel County, 33 F. Supp. 2d 431 (D. Md. 1998).

25. 20 U.S.C. § 1414(a)(1)(D)(i).

26. 20 U.S.C. § 1414(a)(1)(D)(ii)(I).

27. M.L. *ex rel.* A.L. v. El Paso Independent School District, 610 F. Supp. 2d 582 (W.D. Tex. 2009), *affirmed* 369 F. App'x 573 (5th Cir. 2010).

28. 20 U.S.C. § 1414(a)(1)(D)(ii)(II).

29. Durkee v. Livonia Central School District, 487 F. Supp. 2d 313 (W.D.N.Y. 2007).

30. 458 U.S. 176 (1982).

31. Board of Education of the County of Caball v. Dienelt, 843 F.2d 813 (4th Cir. 1988).

32. Thomas v. Cincinnati Board of Education, 918 F.2d 618 (6th Cir. 1990).

33. Hiller v. Board of Education of Brunswick Central School District, 743 F. Supp. 958 (N.D.N.Y. 1990).

34. Doe v. Alabama State Department of Education, 915 F.2d 651 (11th Cir. 1990).

35. 34 C.F.R. § 300.322(a).

36. Buser v. Corpus Christi Independent School District, 51 F.3d 490 (5th Cir. 1995).
37. Rothschild v. Grottenthaler, 907 F.2d 286 (2d Cir. 1990).
38. Rehabilitation Act of 1973, Section 504, 29 U.S.C. § 794.
39. E.H. and H.H. v. Tirozzi, 735 F. Supp. 53 (D. Conn. 1990).
40. V.W. and R.W. v. Favolise, 131 F.R.D. 654 (D. Conn. 1990).
41. Caroline T. v. Hudson School District, 915 F.2d 752 (1st Cir. 1990).
42. Cordrey v. Euckert, 917 F.2d 1460 (6th Cir. 1990).
43. 20 U.S.C. § 1415(d)(4)(A)(ii); 34 C.F.R. § 300.503(a)(2).
44. 34 C.F.R. § 300.503(b)(1)(ii).
45. 34 C.F.R. § 300.503(b)(2).
46. 34 C.F.R. § 300.503(b)(3).
47. 20 U.S.C. § 1414(d)(7)(f); 34 C.F.R. §§ 300.322(c), 300.328.
48. Abney v. District of Columbia, 849 F.2d 1491 (D.C. Cir. 1988).
49. Fuhrmann v. East Hanover Board of Education, 993 F.2d 1031 (3d Cir. 1993).
50. Navin v. Park Ridge School District, 270 F.3d 1147 (7th Cir. 2001).
51. Schares v. Katy Independent School District, 252 F. Supp. 2d 364 (S.D. Tex. 2003).
52. Taylor v. Vermont Department of Education, 313 F.3d 768 (2d Cir. 2002).
53. Driessen v. Lockman, 518 F. App'x 809 (11th Cir. 2013).
54. Fuentes v. Board of Education of the City of New York, 540 F.3d 145 (2d Cir. 2008); *certified question accepted*, 866 N.Y.S.2d 602 (N.Y. 2008); *cert. denied*, 555 U.S. 1190 (2009).
55. Fuentes v. Board of Education of the City of New York, 879 N.Y.S.2d 818 (N.Y. 2009) *certified question answered*.
56. Fuentes v. Board of Education of the City of New York, 569 F.3d 46 (2d Cir. 2009) *answer to certified question conformed to.*
57. 20 U.S.C. § 1415(m)(1).
58. 20 U.S.C. § 1415(m)(2).
59. Mrs. C. v. Wheaton, 916 F.2d 69 (2d Cir. 1990).
60. 20 U.S.C. § 1415(m)(1)(D).
61. 20 U.S.C. § 1414(d)(7)(B).
62. Paul Y. by Kathy Y. v. Singletary, 979 F. Supp. 1422 (S.D. Fla. 1997).
63. 20 U.S.C. § 1232g (2012).
64. 20 U.S.C. § 1232(g); 34 C.F.R. § 99.4.
65. 20 U.S.C. § 1232g(a)(4)(A).
66. 20 U.S.C. § 1232g(a)(1)(A).
67. Sean R. v. Board of Education of the Town of Woodbridge, 794 F. Supp. 467 (D. Conn. 1992).
68. Webster Groves School District v. Pulitzer Publishing Co., 898 F.2d 1371 (8th Cir. 1990).
69. 20 U.S.C. § 1232g(a)(5)(A).
70. 20 U.S.C. § 1232g(a)(5)(B); 34 C.F.R. § 99.37.
71. 34 C.F.R. § 99.37(b).
72. 34 C.F.R. §§ 99.7, 300.612.
73. 34 C.F.R. § 99.3(b).
74. 20 U.S.C. § 1232g(a)(4)(B)(1).
75. 20 U.S.C. § 1232g(a)(4)(B)(2).
76. 20 U.S.C. § 1232g(a)(4)(B)(3).

77. 20 U.S.C. § 1232g(a)(4)(B)(4).
78. 20 U.S.C. § 1232g(a)(1)(A); 34 C.F.R. § 300.613.
79. 34 C.F.R. § 99.4.
80. 34 C.F.R. § 99.10(c).
81. 20 U.S.C. § 1232g(d); 34 C.F.R. § 300.625(b).
82. 34 C.F.R. §§ 300.574, 300.625(a).
83. 20 U.S.C. § 1232g(a)(1)(B); 34 C.F.R. § 99.12(b)(1).
84. 20 U.S.C. § 1232g(a)(1)(C); 34 C.F.R. § 99.37(b)(2)(3).
85. 20 U.S.C. § 1232g(a)(6).
86. 20 U.S.C. §§ 1232g(b)(1), 1232g(b)(2)(A).
87. 20 U.S.C. § 1232g(b)(1)(A).
88. 20 U.S.C. § 1232g(b)(1)(B).
89. 20 U.S.C. § 1232g(b)(1)(C)(E).
90. 20 U.S.C. § 1232g(b)(1)(D).
91. 20 U.S.C. § 1232g(b)(1)(F).
92. 20 U.S.C. § 1232g(b)(1)(G).
93. 20 U.S.C. § 1232g(b)(1)(H).
94. 20 U.S.C. § 1232g(b)(1)(I).
95. 20 U.S.C. §§ 1232g(b)(1)(J), 1232g(b)(2)(B).
96. 20 U.S.C. § 1232g(b)(1)(K).
97. 20 U.S.C. § 1232g(b)(1)(L).
98. 34 C.F.R. § 99.30.
99. 20 U.S.C. § 1232g(b)(2)(A).
100. 20 U.S.C. § 1232g(b)(4)(A).
101. 20 U.S.C. § 1232g(b)(4)(A); 34 C.F.R. § 300.614.
102. 20 U.S.C. § 1232g(a)(1)(A); 34 C.F.R. § 99.10(b).
103. 34 C.F.R. §§ 99.11(b), 300.614(b).
104. 34 C.F.R. §§ 99.11(a), 300.614(a).
105. 34 C.F.R. §§ 99.20(a), 300.618(a).
106. 34 C.F.R. §§ 99.20(b)(c), 300.618(b)–(c).
107. 34 C.F.R. §§ 99.21, 300.619.
108. 34 C.F.R. § 99.22.
109. 34 C.F.R. §§ 99.21(b)(1), 300.620(a).
110. 34 C.F.R. §§ 99.21(b)(2), 300.620(b).
111. 34 C.F.R. §§ 99.21(c), 300.620(c).
112. 34 C.F.R. § 300.624(a).
113. 34 C.F.R. § 300.624(b).
114. 536 U.S. 273 (2002).
115. 34 C.F.R. § 99.63.
116. 34 C.F.R. § 99.64.
117. 34 C.F.R. § 99.65.
118. 34 C.F.R. § 99.66.
119. 34 C.F.R. § 99.67.
120. 534 U.S. 426 (2002).
121. Russo, C. J., & Mawdsley, R. D. (2002). *Owasso Independent School District v. Falvo*: The Supreme Court upholds peer-grading. *School Business Affairs*, *68*(5), 34–36.
122. Honig v. Doe, 484 U.S. 305 (1988).

Due Process Procedures for Evaluation, Development of IEPs, and Placement

Key Concepts in This Chapter

- Requirements for Student Evaluation and Assessment
- Process of Developing IEPs
- IDEA's Status Quo Provision

The Individuals with Disabilities Education Act (IDEA)[1] is unique in providing an elaborate system of procedural due process safeguards to ensure that students with disabilities are properly identified, evaluated, and placed according to its dictates.[2] The IDEA's safeguards are designed to make parents and/or guardians equal partners with school officials in the education of their children. Never before has the law afforded parents such explicit rights to protect the education of their children.

117

The IDEA requires school officials to work with parents to develop individualized education programs (IEPs) for all children in need of special education and related services.[3] In fact, the IDEA's regulations add that states, through local school boards or other agencies and officials, must provide parents of students with disabilities with opportunities to participate in the development of IEPs for their young.[4]

Prior to the passage of the IDEA, school personnel typically made placement decisions for students with disabilities without considering either their wishes or those of their parents. Unfortunately, allowing school personnel to make unilateral placement decisions for students with disabilities, especially those who were difficult to educate, led to the exclusion of significant numbers of these children from many school activities.

The IDEA and its regulations ensure that school officials cannot act without parental knowledge or informed parental consent prior to conducting evaluations[5] or making initial placements.[6] Moreover, the IDEA specifies that parental consent for initial evaluations cannot be treated as consent for placements and receipt of special education and related services.[7] The IDEA also directs educators to provide parents with prior written notice whenever they propose or refuse to initiate changes after making original placements.[8]

> The importance of procedural compliance cannot be overemphasized because the Supreme Court ruled *in Board of Education of the Hendrick Hudson Central School District v. Rowley* that an educational program is not appropriate unless it is developed according to the IDEA's procedures.

This chapter examines the IDEA's due process mechanisms relating to the identification, evaluation, and placement of students with disabilities. The importance of procedural compliance cannot be overemphasized because the Supreme Court ruled in *Board of Education of the Hendrick Hudson Central School District v. Rowley*[9] that an educational program is not appropriate unless it is developed according to the IDEA's procedures.

Evaluation Procedures

The IDEA, in an approach that makes it different from other education-related laws, places an affirmative obligation on states, through local school boards and their officials, to establish procedures to ensure that all children with disabilities are properly identified and evaluated to determine whether they are entitled to receive special education and related services.[10] This means that officials must conduct full initial evaluations before providing students with special education and related services.[11]

Once students are identified as being in need of special education and related services, their IEPs must be reviewed at least annually[12] and reevaluated at least once every three years unless their parents and local school officials agree that re-evaluations are unnecessary.[13]

Due to ongoing difficulties with regard to the overrepresentation of minority students,[14] the current version of the IDEA includes a provision addressing the status of children based on race and ethnicity that is worth reviewing before turning to the substance of the law's evaluation procedures. The IDEA requires states and local school board officials to develop policies and procedures to prevent the overidentification or disproportionate representation by race and ethnicity of children with disabilities.[15] In addition, this provision obligates educators to record the number of students from minority groups who are in special education classes and to provide early intervention services for children in groups deemed to be overrepresented.

In a related provision, the IDEA directs educators to examine data, including information disaggregated by race and ethnicity, to consider whether there are significant discrepancies in the rate of long-term suspensions and expulsions of student with disabilities.[16] The IDEA further mandates that officials review, and if appropriate, revise, policies, procedures, and practices related to the implementation of IEPs. At the same time, the IDEA obligates educators to use positive behavioral interventions and supports as well as procedural safeguards to ensure their compliance with the law[17] in avoiding this problem.

According to the IDEA, school officials must complete evaluations of students suspected of having disabilities within 60 days of when they receive informed parental consent or within the parameters of state guidelines if states establish their own rules.[18] Depending on how state laws are worded, education officials may be required to conduct evaluations over summer vacation periods if necessary to complete them within the prescribed time limits. For instance, a federal trial court in Maryland, where state law required evaluations to be completed within 45 calendar days of referrals, reasoned that board officials violated a student's rights by not conducting an evaluation within the appropriate time frame.[19] The record indicated that the child's mother requested an evaluation in May but officials informed her that they could not complete it during the summer.

The IDEA's 60-day rule does not apply if "the parent of a child repeatedly fails or refuses to produce the child for the evaluation."[20] Even if parents refuse to respond to requests to provide consent for initial evaluations or to services, educational officials may still continue with evaluations as long as they follow the procedures identified in the IDEA.[21] In another clarification, a regulation specifies that generalized screenings employed by educators for instructional purposes, such as at the beginning of terms to evaluate the ability of students in classes, cannot be considered evaluations for special education and related services.[22]

In conducting evaluations, school officials must "use a variety of assessment tools and strategies to gather relevant functional, developmental, and academic information, including information provided by the parent,"[23] examining students "in all areas of suspected disability"[24] that may assist in determining whether they are eligible for IDEA services. Put another way, since the evaluation process needs to be individualized and multidisciplinary, no single procedure can be the sole criterion for determining eligibility or placement.[25] More specifically, all testing and evaluation materials and procedures must be

> selected and administered so as not to be discriminatory on a racial or cultural basis; are provided and administered in the language and form most likely to yield accurate information on what the child knows and can do academically, developmentally, and functionally, unless it is not feasible to so provide or administer; are used for purposes for which the assessments or measures are valid and reliable; are administered by trained and knowledgeable personnel; and are administered in accordance with any instructions provided by the producer of such assessments.[26]

If parents are dissatisfied with the results of school board assessments, they have the right to seek independent evaluations of their children at public expense.[27] However, parents are not entitled to publicly paid independent evaluations simply because they wish second opinions or desire more information. In order to obtain independent evaluations at public expense, parents must disagree with and challenge the appropriateness of board assessments.[28] Boards can challenge independent evaluations via due process hearings in attempting to demonstrate that their own evaluations met the IDEA's requirements. If educational officials succeed in proving that their evaluations were proper, boards do not have to pay for independent evaluations.[29] Courts order boards to reimburse parents for independent evaluations when the parents can prove that disputed evaluations were inappropriate and their independent evaluations were appropriate.[30]

If due process hearing officers agree that school board evaluations are appropriate, parents retain the right to independent evaluations but not at public expense.[31] School officials may ask parents why they are seeking independent evaluations but cannot require them to provide explanations; in addition, the IDEA forbids educators from unreasonably delaying either providing evaluations at public expense or filing requests for due process hearings to defend their public evaluations.[32] Although parents do not need to notify educational officials that they are seeking independent evaluations, their failure to provide prior notice could jeopardize claims for reimbursement if doing so prevents board representatives from requesting due process hearings in seeking to prove that their evaluations were proper.[33] If parents request independent evaluations, the onus is on educational officials to ask for hearings to demonstrate that board evaluations were appropriate or that the parental independent evaluations were inappropriate in order to avoid paying for independent evaluations.[34] Ultimately, parents are entitled to public payment for only one independent evaluation.[35]

When parents obtain independent evaluations at their own expense, school officials must take them into consideration as long as they meet district assessment criteria.[36] Requiring school officials to consider the results of independent evaluations does not mean that they must adopt the recommendations of independent evaluators.[37]

In a dispute over an independent evaluation, the First Circuit affirmed that requiring school officials to consider the content of outside assessments did not mean that an IEP team from New Hampshire had to engage in a substantive discussion of its findings.[38] In a case from Connecticut, the Second Circuit explained that the plain meaning of the word *consider* is to reflect on or think about with care, but does not require a board to comply with independent evaluators' recommendations.[39] Similarly, the Eighth Circuit was satisfied that an IEP team from Minnesota met its obligation to consider an independent evaluation because it incorporated many of the recommendations offered by the evaluator into the final IEP.[40] These cases reveal that school officials meet the IDEA's requirement to consider independent evaluations as long as they review the results of such assessments at IEP conferences. Once independent evaluations are completed, either party may present the results of parentally initiated evaluations at due process hearings over the placement of children.[41]

IEPs can be invalidated if they are not based on proper evaluations of children. Assessments must address all areas of suspected disabilities.

The importance of the evaluation process is reflected in the fact that hearing officers and courts can invalidate IEPs if they are not based on proper evaluations. The federal trial court in New Jersey held that a proposed IEP for a child who was deaf was inappropriate because school personnel failed to follow proper evaluation procedures.[42] The court noted that the board's evaluation team based its placement decision on simple observations. The court pointed out that educators acted improperly since they did not use validated instruments to measure the child's aptitude, and the procedures that they used tended to be biased against students with hearing impairments. The court also acknowledged that board officials did not include an expert on the education of students with hearing impairments on the evaluation team. Subsequently, in a case from Washington, the Ninth Circuit interpreted the IDEA as requiring evaluations to be completed by multidisciplinary teams including at least one person with knowledge in the suspected area of disability.[43] Moreover, the Tenth Circuit affirmed that an evaluation by a multidisciplinary team from Kansas that included assessments in all areas of suspected disability met the IDEA's requirements.[44]

In an early case involving the education of students with emotional problems causing acting out and aggressive behavior, a federal trial court in New York declared that their being placed in special education was improperly based on vague criteria that tended to discriminate against minorities.[45] The court observed that once the students were placed, they were not re-evaluated as mandated by state and federal law. In seeking to remedy the situation, the parties implemented a court-approved nondiscriminatory assessment procedure.

School personnel are not required to leave their districts in order to evaluate students whose parents unilaterally place their children in out-of-state facilities. Where parents in Michigan enrolled their son in an out-of-state residential school without their board's knowledge or consent, a federal trial court maintained that officials had the right to evaluate the student, whose parents requested that it pay tuition for the out-of-state residential school. Also, the court made it clear that officials were not required to leave the state to evaluate the child.[46] More recently, the Seventh Circuit affirmed that school personnel were not required to leave Illinois to evaluate a student.[47]

As noted, the IDEA requires board officials to evaluate students before they can be initially placed in special education[48] and re-evaluate them at least once every three years, unless their parents and educators agree that re-evaluations are unnecessary.[49] When dealing with disputes of this nature, the Fifth[50] and Seventh[51] Circuits agreed that board officials may insist on evaluating students using their own personnel rather than be forced to rely on outside professionals. In the case from the Fifth Circuit, when the parents, acting on recommendations from the child's physician, refused to allow board officials in Texas to evaluate the student but provided third-party evaluations, officials responded that the evaluations did not meet state criteria. Reversing an earlier judgment in favor of the parents, the court agreed with board officials that the third-party evaluations were inappropriate.

Conversely, as reflected by a case from the nation's capitol, local board officials may not be able to insist on conducting their own assessments if doing so duplicates tests administered by outside evaluators.[52] This means that educators may rely on outside evaluations or tests conducted by personnel from other school systems as long as the information is still relevant.[53]

Figure 5.1 summarizes the steps in the evaluation and placement process.

Figure 5.1   Steps in the Evaluation and Placement Process

- Teachers, counselors, principals, parents, or other knowledgeable persons such as pediatricians or dentists can refer students who are suspected of having disabilities and being in need of special education.
- School officials notify parents or guardians in writing or other mode of communication that their children have been referred; this notice must also include the reasons for the referral.
- School officials request consent to conduct evaluations in writing.
- After obtaining consent, educators schedule and complete evaluations by multidisciplinary teams. Students must be assessed in all areas of suspected disabilities.
- School officials convene a meeting to discuss the results of the evaluation; make a determination as to whether students need special education and related services; and, if students are found to have a need, develop IEPs.
- IEP teams, including the parents or guardians of students with disabilities, develop IEPs. The parents or guardians may accept or reject proposed IEPs, formulate alternative IEPs, or postpone decisions while seeking independent evaluations of their children.
- If parents or guardians accept IEPs, the plans must be implemented immediately.
- If parents or guardians reject IEPs, the IDEA's dispute resolution procedures become operative. IEPs are then implemented on resolution of the dispute(s).
- School officials must ensure that all IEPs are reviewed annually and students are re-evaluated at least every three years.

Developing Individualized Education Programs

The IDEA defines IEPs as written statements for each child with disabilities that are developed, reviewed, and revised in accordance with its dictates. IEPs must contain seven major elements:

- Statements about students' current levels of academic achievement and functional performances[54]
- Measurable annual goals for children, including academic and functional goals[55]
- Descriptions of how officials plan to measure students' progress toward meeting their annual goals and when such periodic reports are to be provided, as well as statements of special education and related services along with supplementary aids and services, based on peer-reviewed research to the extent practicable[56]
- Statements specifying the special education, related services, and supplementary aids and services that children will receive[57]
- Explanations of the extent to which children are excluded from participating in regular classes with peers who are not disabled[58]

- Information detailing individual appropriate accommodations that are necessary to measure the academic achievement and functional performance of students on state and district assessments[59]
- The projected date of initiation and duration of special education services that children are to receive[60]

In addition, when the IEPs that are to be in effect for students who reach the age of 16 are developed, plans must include an eighth element:

- a statement of appropriate, measurable postsecondary education goals, to be updated annually, and transition services; this also requires that at least one year before children reach the age of majority, they must be provided with notice of the rights that will transfer to them (such as rights associated with their educational records) on reaching the age of majority.[61]

IEPs must be developed at meetings including a wide variety of people. IEP teams must include the parents of children with disabilities; at least one of a student's regular education teachers if the student is in, or will be participating in, regular education; at least one special education teacher or, if appropriate, one special education provider; a representative of the school system who is qualified to provide or supervise the delivery of special education and knowledgeable about general education, the school system's resources, and evaluation procedures (typically this is a director of special education or an assistant superintendent for students); a professional who can interpret the instructional implications of evaluation results; others, at the discretion of parents or school officials, who are knowledgeable or have special expertise concerning the student(s) at issue; and, when appropriate, the children.[62]

Litigation has reached mixed results about the composition of IEP teams. Courts generally invalidate IEPs when the exclusion of required members interferes with parental participation or causes inadequacies in IEPs.[63] The Ninth Circuit held that the failure of school officials in Washington to include a regular education teacher on a child's IEP team constituted a significant violation of the IDEA since the student was going to spend time in a regular education setting.[64] In this respect, in another case that same court acknowledged that boards have some discretion in selecting the regular education teachers who sit on teams.[65] The important criteria are that the teachers selected for IEP teams should have knowledge of the students and program options. In like manner, a federal trial court in New York was of the opinion that a board failed to comply with the IDEA's procedural requirements when it did not include a representative, either by telephone or in person, from its recommended therapeutic placement for a student at the child's IEP meeting.[66]

On the other hand, courts overlook the fact that IEP teams had missing members if their absence did not result in the denial of FAPEs.[67] The Fourth

Circuit affirmed that it was unnecessary for a school board from North Carolina to have a regular education teacher at an IEP meeting since the student was not being considered for a placement in such a setting.[68] In like manner, the federal trial court in Kansas ruled that a board did not violate the IDEA by excluding a regular education teacher from a child's IEP team because he was not going to spend any time in a general education setting.[69] Although the IDEA requires the presence of the special education providers on IEP teams, in a case from New York the Second Circuit maintained that not having a special educator who taught the student at an IEP meeting was a harmless error since a certified special education teacher was present.[70]

IEP meetings must take place within 30 calendar days of findings that children require special education and related services.[71] School boards are required to take steps to ensure the participation of at least one of a student's parents at IEP meetings.[72] If students attend private schools, then representatives of the private schools should be present at IEP conferences.[73]

> Parental input into the IEP process cannot be minimized. One of the IDEA's unique features is that it specifically provides for parental participation. . . . Parents cannot simply be given token opportunities for participation. Rather, their input into the IEP process has to be genuine.

Parental input into the IEP process cannot be minimized. One of the IDEA's unique features is that it specifically provides for parental participation. It should go without saying that the failure of school boards to include parents on IEP teams is a serious procedural violation of the IDEA.[74] Parents cannot simply be given token opportunities for participation. Rather, their input into the IEP process must be genuine.

The Ninth Circuit affirmed the invalidation of an IEP that was developed by school officials in Montana without input from a student's parents and his teacher at his private school.[75] The court explained that procedural violations that infringe on the parents' opportunity to participate in the formulation of IEPs result in the denial of a FAPE. The court later echoed that opinion in a case from Hawaii, holding that a child was denied a FAPE when the IEP team met without his father.[76] The parent was unable to attend because of illness but school officials, concerned that the deadline for revising the child's IEP was approaching, decided to hold the meeting anyway. Similarly, the federal trial court in the District of Columbia reasoned that the failure of board officials to attend an IEP meeting that took place at a private school in which a student was enrolled rendered their proposed placement invalid.[77]

Informal contacts between parents and school officials do not fully meet the IDEA's parental participation requirements. An appellate court in

Pennsylvania observed that impromptu meetings between a student's mother and school officials did not satisfy the IDEA's requirement of affording her the opportunity to participate in the development of her daughter's IEP.[78]

According to the Eighth Circuit, though, school officials in Missouri could not be faulted when parents refused to participate in discussions about placement options.[79] The Ninth Circuit reached a like outcome in agreeing that the Hawaii Department of Education did not violate the IDEA by conducting an IEP meeting without a mother who failed to respond to multiple attempts to schedule meetings or contact school personnel to reschedule the sessions.[80] Also, the Fifth Circuit affirmed that school personnel in Texas did not deny a mother the full opportunity to participate in the development of her child's IEP when they terminated IEP meetings early due to her behavior and scheduled follow-up meetings.[81] In contrast, the Ninth Circuit held that school officials in Hawaii denied a child a FAPE by holding an IEP meeting even though the child's father stated that he could not attend due to illness and asked that it be rescheduled.[82]

A federal trial court in Michigan explained that school board officials are required to ensure, if possible, that the teachers of special education students participate in IEP meetings before drastic changes in placements can occur.[83] The court indicated that simply inviting teachers to attend IEP meetings did not fulfill that duty since special education teachers had to be active participants. Yet, a federal trial court in Tennessee declared that the failure of a child's teacher to attend an IEP meeting was harmless since persons knowledgeable about the student were present.[84] In a similar case, the federal trial court in Maryland noted that a board's failure to include representatives from the treatment center a student attended in an IEP conference was not a serious procedural violation because data that were obtained from the treatment center were used in developing the child's IEP.[85] The Sixth Circuit affirmed that inasmuch as a board in Michigan included persons knowledgeable about placement options on an IEP team, it was not required to include an expert in the parents' preferred methodology.[86] Even so, failure to include a knowledgeable school board representative on an IEP team can be fatal to a recommended program if the omission has the effect of denying parents the opportunity to discuss available resources for their children.[87]

IEPs do not have to be written perfectly in order to survive judicial scrutiny. Courts generally allow some flaws in IEPs as long as they do not compromise the appropriateness of educational programming for students. Courts are ordinarily more forgiving if the missing information was available or provided in another form. For example, in a case from Tennessee, the Sixth Circuit affirmed that an IEP was appropriate that did not specifically contain current levels of performance or the objective criteria for evaluating progress, because the disputed information was known to all concerned.[88] The court was unwilling to exalt form over substance, declaring that the emphasis on procedural safeguards referred to the process by which the IEP was developed, not the myriad technical items that should have been included in the written document. Further, the federal trial court in Delaware recognized that even though an IEP had flaws, they did not rise to the level of a violation of the IDEA because they did not hamper the parents' opportunity to participate in its development.[89]

On the other hand, courts have nullified IEPs for missing important elements. For example, a federal trial court in California invalidated an IEP that failed to address all areas of a student's disabilities and that did not contain a statement of the specific services to be provided.[90] The court thought that an IEP with those defects would have compromised the integrity of the student's educational program. Also, a federal trial court in New York commented that an IEP was insufficient, containing vague information that did not establish a student's needs with precision.[91] The same court later wrote that an IEP was procedurally defective because it contained goals that were not tailored to a student's unique needs and abilities, generic objectives, and incomplete evaluation measures.[92]

IEPs containing all of the required elements, including specific information, pass judicial muster. By way of illustration, in two cases from Kansas, with the Tenth Circuit affirming both judgments, the federal trial court observed that IEPs including specific statements of students' present levels of functioning, annual goals adequately describing their anticipated educational performances, measurable short-term objectives, and criteria for measuring students' progress met all federal and state requirements.[93] Along the same lines, a federal trial court in Michigan accepted the adequacy of an IEP containing a series of tables covering each academic subject and including short-term objectives, performance criteria, evaluation procedures, and schedules for evaluation.[94] In spite of parental contentions to the contrary, other courts agreed that IEPs containing all of the required elements were not defective.[95]

An overriding theme of the IDEA is that IEPs and educational programs for students with disabilities must be individualized. Put another way, IEPs should be based on the unique characteristics of individual children, taking into consideration their strengths and weaknesses. Courts agree that IEPs that are not individualized are inappropriate. For instance, a federal court in Alabama invalidated an IEP as inappropriate because it lacked academic objectives and methods of evaluation addressing the student's unique needs and abilities.[96] Another federal trial court, in Maryland, criticized an IEP for failing to specifically address a child's needs because it was assembled using portions of IEPs that were developed for other students.[97]

Another major doctrine of the IDEA is that the placements must be rooted in the IEPs of students, not the other way around. In other words, educators must develop placements to fit the unique, individual needs of students rather than fit the children into available programs. Courts have invalidated the practice of writing IEPs based on what placements offer, as opposed to the specific needs of children. The Fourth Circuit affirmed that school officials in Virginia violated the IDEA when they chose to place a student in a county facility and then wrote an IEP to carry out this decision.[98] Moreover, the federal trial court in Connecticut concluded that board officials violated the IDEA when they proposed a placement without first evaluating a child or writing an IEP.[99] Also, a federal trial court in New York posited that school officials who placed a student in a program before they had an IEP in effect violated the IDEA.[100] Conversely, the First Circuit affirmed that an IEP team from New Hampshire who considered various options along a continuum from least to most restrictive did not finalize a student's placement prior to formulating his IEP.[101]

Disputes over whether school officials made placement decisions in advance notwithstanding, nothing in the IDEA prevents educators from presenting draft IEPs at conferences for the purpose of discussion. The federal trial court in Rhode Island declared that presenting parents with a completed IEP at a conference was not an indication that they were denied a meaningful opportunity to participate in its development.[102] Subsequently, in a case from New Hampshire, the First Circuit affirmed that it is acceptable for one person to draft an IEP as long as the parents and other members of an IEP team have the opportunity to provide input into its contents.[103] Similarly, the Eighth Circuit agreed that nothing in the IDEA or its regulations prohibited school personnel in Missouri from coming to an IEP meeting with tentative recommendations.[104] In another dispute, the Third Circuit affirmed that a draft IEP developed by a team from New Jersey did not violate the IDEA's parental participation requirement in light of evidence that the parents made suggestions for changes, some of which were incorporated into its final version.[105] The Ninth Circuit added that school officials from Washington did not violate the IDEA by conducting a preparatory meeting prior to an IEP conference since they did not make decisions at the preparatory meeting and the parents actively participated in the actual IEP meeting.[106]

Courts frown on attempts by school officials to develop IEPs beforehand and force them on parents without meaningful discussion of the educational needs of their children, but they do allow educators to prepare for IEP meetings. For instance, the Sixth Circuit ruled that educators from Tennessee could not predetermine a child's placement in an IEP since doing so prevented his parents from having a meaningful opportunity to participate in its development.[107] More recently, the federal trial court in New Jersey decreed that an IEP team predetermined a child's IEP, citing evidence that school personnel had come to definitive conclusions without parental input, failed to discuss parents' suggestions, and even failed to listen to parents' concerns.[108]

On the other hand, in an appeal from New York, the Second Circuit explained that the IDEA does not prohibit school officials from considering possible placement options prior to an IEP meeting, but rather, allows them to engage in preparatory activities to develop a proposal or respond to parental requests.[109] In the same way, a federal trial court in Virginia was of the opinion that while school officials must come to IEP conferences with open minds, this did not mean that they had to arrive with blank minds.[110] The court emphasized that even though board officials cannot finalize placement decisions before IEP conferences, they should give thought to them prior to the meetings. However, the court made it clear that board representatives must remain receptive to all parental concerns.

School board officials sometimes develop interim IEPs for students in order to cover short periods of time while preparing permanent IEPs. This may occur so that children can be placed in special education programs while undergoing evaluations or to cover the short periods of time during which teams prepare permanent IEPs. A federal trial court in Alabama asserted that the IDEA does not contain provisions for interim IEPs.[111] The court pointed out that boards are required to convene meetings to develop IEPs prior to the beginning of each school year, even if this means gathering over the summer. The federal trial court in Maryland insisted that board personnel must meet during summer months, if necessary, to develop IEPs within 30 days of determining that students need special education and related services.[112] Conversely, the federal trial court in Delaware refused to impose liability on a board for not having an IEP in place at the beginning of a school year since the child's parents were responsible for the delay.[113]

An exception may exist to the general rule when students move from one district to another and the board in the latter is unable to implement their existing IEPs immediately. Under these circumstances, a court may allow a temporary placement until the new board can develop a permanent IEP.[114] The IDEA distinguishes between students who transfer within states and those who move in from other jurisdictions. When students transfer within states, receiving boards must provide services that are comparable to those in students' previous IEPs until such time as school officials either adopt the previous IEPs or develop new IEPs.[115] On the other hand, when students transfer to districts in other states, the new boards must provide services comparable to those in the previous IEPs until such time as officials decide whether it is necessary to conduct evaluations and develop new IEPs.[116] Although the difference is slight, this provision recognizes that students who were eligible for services in one state may not necessarily be eligible in another due to differing state standards.

IEPs for students with disabilities must be reviewed and revised, if necessary, at least annually.[117] IEP teams should provide reviews and revisions more frequently if they are needed. Procedures for reviewing and amending IEPs generally are similar to those for developing initial IEPs. All of the IDEA's regulations' procedural and notification rights apply to meetings convened to review and possibly revise IEPs.[118] Naturally, parents must be given opportunities to provide input into the revision process, just as with initial IEPs.

IEPs should be reviewed if parents express any dissatisfaction with the educational programs of their children. To this end, the federal trial court in the District of Columbia was of the view that a mother's request for a due process hearing put her school board on notice that she was dissatisfied with her daughter's placement status and that officials were obligated to review and possibly revise the child's IEP.[119] In a case reaching the opposite result, the First Circuit affirmed that school personnel in Massachusetts had no obligation to review and revise an IEP for a student whose parents unilaterally placed him in a private school.[120]

There is a limit to the number of times school boards must review the IEPs of children. The federal trial court in Connecticut decreed that school officials were justified in refusing to conduct another IEP team meeting after they convened a large number of meetings in the previous six months at which all of the issues raised by the child's guardian had already been discussed and investigated.[121]

New IEPs should generally be developed if the placements of children are to change. Yet, this step is not always necessary. The Ninth Circuit acknowledged that school board officials from Washington were not required to write a new IEP for a student who was being transferred temporarily to an off-campus special education program for disciplinary reasons.[122] The court observed that the student's IEP could have been fully implemented in the new setting.

Change in Placement

Once students with disabilities are evaluated, school officials may not change their placements unless their parents have been notified in writing of planned actions and have been afforded opportunities to contest the proposed modifications.[123] In addition, the IDEA dictates that while administrative hearings or judicial proceedings are pending, a "child shall remain in the then current placement" unless the parents and school board agree otherwise.[124] This section of the IDEA, known as the "status quo" or "stay put" provision, has been subject to a great deal of litigation.

Then-Current Placement

Generally, the settings students are actually in when actions arise are considered to be their "then-current" or pendant placements. In a dispute that arose in Ohio, the Sixth Circuit defined a then-current placement as the operative placement functioning when a dispute arises.[125] The court noted that a proposed placement that never was implemented simply did not qualify as the status quo setting.

On occasion, school officials may make placements that are intended to be temporary. In such situations, officials are obliged to make their intentions clear or the courts are apt to consider those placements as the then-current placements.[126] Three cases involving the District of Columbia public schools illustrate this point. In one dispute, educators at a private facility developed an IEP for a student calling for a transfer to a residential school. The board agreed to the new placement, but a year later officials notified the student's parents that they saw no need for continued placement there and would no longer assume financial responsibility for the placement. The federal trial court decided that the residential school was the student's then-current placement because the board assumed responsibility for it and had given no indication at the time that it intended to do so for one year only.[127] In another case, the same court indicated that any limitation on a placement must be spelled out clearly and described in a settlement agreement.[128] Based on the mutual consent of school officials and the child's parents, the student was placed in a private school pending resolution of a placement dispute. The board argued that the private school was an interim placement only, but the court reasoned that it was the then-current placement since its interim status had not been articulated clearly. Similarly, the District of Columbia Circuit Court held that a private school placement ceased to be the then-current placement at the end of an academic year because a hearing officer's order stated clearly that it was to be for one year only.[129]

The Second Circuit pointed out that a private school placement that a hearing officer ordered a board in New York to fund for one year only was not the then-current placement.[130] Conversely, a federal trial court in New York, after uncovering no evidence that school officials limited funding for a private school placement to one school year, stipulated that the private school was the child's pendant, or current, placement.[131] In a case from Maine, the First Circuit, acknowledging that a private school placement was never intended to be more than temporary and that a settlement agreement specified that it would terminate at the end of the academic year, decreed that a public school placement was the student's then-current placement.[132]

Parentally made unilateral placements can be then-current placements if school boards fail to propose appropriate programs in a timely fashion. In such a case, the federal trial court for the District of Columbia was of the opinion that where educational officials failed to propose a program for a student by the deadline established by a hearing officer, his parents were justified in placing him in a private school.[133] The court was thus satisfied that this was the child's current educational placement.

If parents unilaterally remove their children from programs, those settings do not cease to be the then-current placements. For example, the Eighth Circuit maintained that the public school placement of a student from Minnesota whose parents removed him from school was the status quo.[134] The parents enrolled their child in another school system, but one month later they reenrolled him in his former district. The court rejected the mother's attempt to reenroll her son as a regular, rather than special, education student. The court observed that a one-month term as a regular education student in another district did not negate the child's special education history. Further, a federal trial court in Illinois wrote that the stay put provision does not apply to students whose parents unilaterally place them in private schools.[135] Figure 5.2 details actions that educators must take when changing the placement of students with disabilities.

Placement Pending Appeals

In an early dispute about placements pending appeals arising in Massachusetts, the First Circuit held that Congress did not intend to freeze an arguably inappropriate placement for the length of time it takes for review proceedings to culminate.[136] Consequently, parents can be reimbursed for the cost of tuition in private schools as long as courts agree that these are the then-current placements.[137]

A question arises as to when parents or school officials are entitled to make changes in the placements of students with disabilities pursuant to the orders of hearing officers or judges. Some courts agree that changes in placement can occur once administrative orders are issued, even if they are being appealed. In such a case, the Ninth Circuit ruled that once a state educational agency agreed that a parentally chosen placement was correct,

Figure 5.2   Changing the Placement of a Student With Disabilities

- Prior to changing the placement of students with disabilities, school officials must provide their parents or guardians with written notice of the proposed changes. Notice should include
  - Explanations of the IDEA's due process safeguards.
  - Descriptions of the proposed change or other options considered, with an explanation of why other options were rejected.
  - Explanations of all assessments used in making a determination.
  - Descriptions of other relevant factors used in making determinations.

  Notice must be written in a language understood by the general public and in the parents' or guardians' native language or other mode of communication. If necessary, notice can be provided orally. Notice should be provided within a reasonable time prior to the proposed change in placement.
- If parents or guardians object to proposed changes in placements, they are entitled to due process hearings.
- Until disputes are finally resolved, students are to remain in their then-current educational placements, unless their parents or guardians and school officials agree otherwise or judges or hearing officers order changes in placement. (Note: Exceptions exist for dangerous students. See Chapter 6 for explanations.)

it became the then-current placement under the IDEA, and a school board in California was required to keep it in effect pending judicial review.[138] The federal trial court in Massachusetts thought that if a state agency, such as the Bureau of Special Education Appeals, and the student's parent agreed on a placement, the school committee's approval was not required to make a change in placement.[139] In another case, a federal trial court in New York remarked that a board was not relieved of its obligation to fund an alternative school placement until final administrative review procedures were completed.[140] At the same time, the court was of the view that the board was financially responsible only until the date the final judgment was handed down, not until the end of the school year. It is important to keep in mind that board officials are required to review and, if necessary, revise IEPs even while appealing stay put orders.[141]

The IDEA calls for agreements by either states or local school boards and parents to effectuate changes in placements during the pendency of review proceedings. The Supreme Court, in dicta in *Burlington School Committee v. Department of Education of the Commonwealth of Massachusetts (Burlington),*[142] posited that a state-level hearing order in favor of the parents' chosen placement seems to constitute agreement by the state to a change in placement. Citing *Burlington,* in a case from New York, the Second Circuit ruled that a reimbursement order predicated on a finding that a proposed IEP is inappropriate constitutes a change in a student's current educational placement.[143] Other courts have followed this analysis in concurring that orders of state level hearing officers constitute changes in placements.[144]

As is explained more fully in Chapter 7, states have the option of establishing either one- or two-tiered administrative hearing systems.[145] In one-tiered systems, the sole hearing is conducted by the state. In two-tiered systems, initial hearings take place locally, and appeals are conducted by the state. There is some judicial agreement that in two-tiered systems, orders at the appellate level favorable to parents constitute agreements by the states.[146] In such a case, a federal trial court in New York suggested that an adjudication by either a state hearing officer in a one-tiered system or a state reviewing officer in a two-tiered system constituted an agreement by the state under the IDEA's stay put provision.[147] Previously, the Fifth Circuit affirmed that insofar as a review panel's reversal of an order from a hearing officer that had been in favor of a Louisiana school board's proposed placement constituted an agreement between the state and parents, a residential facility was the pendant placement during all proceedings.[148]

On the other hand, according to the District of Columbia Circuit and the Third Circuit the IDEA's status quo provision requires that student placements remain the same until all administrative hearings and trial court actions are completed. The District of Columbia court noted that the IDEA did not entitle a student to remain in a private school at public expense pending review by an appeals court; the hearing officer and federal trial court agreed that the IEPs offered by the school board were appropriate.[149] The Third Circuit agreed that a school board was required to maintain a student's private school placement until the completion of trial proceedings.[150] In a separate action in the same dispute that was not appealed, a federal trial court in Pennsylvania denied an injunction to require the board to continue funding the private school placement pending an appeal to the Third Circuit.[151] The court was of the opinion that providing status quo protection during the pendency of its own review ensured that school officials could not unilaterally move the child without federal review, but imposing status quo during federal appeals could yield absurd results by forcing boards to pay tuition even while multiple levels of review agreed that offered IEPs were appropriate. Conversely, the Ninth Circuit decreed that a board in California had to continue funding an in-home intervention program while an appeal of a trial court order was pending.[152]

Courts also consider special circumstances in rendering equitable orders. For example, the federal trial court for the District of Columbia declared that the school board was required to fund a private school placement during the pendency of a parental appeal of a hearing officer's order.[153] The court added that insofar as it would have been inappropriate, insensitive, and indefensible for it to have called for a change in placement one semester before the student completed his schooling, the board had to pay for the cost of his remaining in the private school until graduation, even though a hearing officer contended that the board's proposed change in placement was appropriate. In an analogous situation, a federal trial court in New York pointed out that the status quo provision prohibited a school board from permitting a student to graduate from high school during the pendency of administrative appeals because doing so would have terminated his rights to additional educational services.[154]

Pursuant to the IDEA's status quo provision, during the pendency of appeals over students who are seeking initial admissions to public schools and until all appeals are completed, children are to be placed in public school programs.[155] However, since the IDEA does not clarify whether these placements should be in general education classrooms or special education programs, litigation has ensued. In a case where parents and school officials agreed that a child's pendant placement was no longer appropriate but the parties could not agree on a new program, a federal trial court in Wisconsin ordered its immediate termination in favor of the board's proposal.[156] Even though the parent challenged the proposed IEP, the court ruled that it would provide a FAPE and ordered the immediate termination of the placement that all agreed was not proper.

Students whose school boards have yet to place them are not protected by the status quo provision. In a case on point, a federal trial court in Illinois explained that the IDEA's status quo provision did not apply to a student who was unilaterally placed by his parents before their school board had the opportunity to make a recommendation regarding his education.[157] The court wrote that while the status quo provision was designed to prevent interruptions in programming for students, it was not intended to protect children who were awaiting placements. By the same token, the Ninth Circuit pointed out that a private placement unilaterally chosen by parents in California before a school board developed an IEP failed to qualify as a current educational placement because there had not been a ruling regarding the appropriateness of that placement.[158]

Courts reach mixed results in situations where children are making transitions to school-aged programs from early intervention programs offered to infants and toddlers[159] under individual family service plans (IFSPs). The Eleventh Circuit affirmed that students from Florida who were transitioning from early intervention to preschool programs were essentially applying for initial admission to a public school.[160] As such, the court determined that the students were not entitled to continue receiving the services in their IFSPs pursuant to the status quo provision. A federal trial court in New York ruled that the IDEA did not require that a child whose parents were applying for initial admission to the public schools receive the same level of services provided by her early intervention program under her IFSP.[161] Conversely, the Third Circuit directed a board in Pennsylvania to continue the services in a child's IFSP until a dispute over her preschool IEP was settled.[162] Noting that Congress envisioned a smooth transition from early intervention programs to school-aged programs, the court wrote that the IDEA anticipates and condones the interchangeability of an IFSP and an IEP during the transition to preschool.

Change in Program Location

Courts agree that the general rule of the IDEA is that the term *change in placement* refers to changes that affect the form of educational instruction provided, not the location where it takes place. For various reasons, such as school closings, boards sometimes must move special education programs from one building to another. Courts share the perspective that transfers of entire classes or programs do not constitute changes in placement triggering the IDEA's due process procedures.[163]

When the physical locations of programs are moved from one place to another, the educational programming for children must remain substantially the same. For instance, the Fourth Circuit interpreted the IDEA's use of the term *educational placement* as referring to the services that children receive, not necessarily the location where they are provided.[164] Thus the court affirmed that to the extent that a child's new setting, in the least restrictive environment, duplicated the educational program in his original placement, albeit in a different location, school officials in Virginia satisfied the IDEA's stay put provision.

As illustrated by a case from New York, the elimination of a major component of a program can be sufficient cause to trigger the IDEA's due process mechanism. A federal trial court decreed that the elimination of the summer component of what had been a year-round residential program was of such critical magnitude that it constituted a change in a child's placement.[165] In another case, a federal trial court in Pennsylvania nullified the proposed transfer of two students from one program to another that involved a change in the method of instruction.[166] The court indicated that insofar as the students were making progress in their program, any changes had to be considered with caution.

When a transfer involves moving a single student, it may not be considered a change in placement if the new program is almost identical to the former one. The District of Columbia Circuit rejected the claim of a surrogate parent that moving a student with profound disabilities from a private to a government operated hospital was a change in placement.[167] The court specified that the claim failed because the surrogate parent was unable to demonstrate that the shift constituted a fundamental change in or the elimination of a basic element in the child's IEP. Subsequently, in a case from Louisiana, the Fifth Circuit adopted a similar rationale in expressing the view that a transfer from one school building to another was not a change in placement because the student's IEP was fully implemented following the move.[168] One year later, the Fifth Circuit approved a Texas magistrate judge's transfer of a student from one location to another on the basis that this did not alter her IEP.[169]

The failure of school officials to implement IEPs completely following changes of location can constitute changes in placements. In such a situation, the District of Columbia Circuit maintained that school board officials violated the IDEA's change in placement provisions when they failed to notify a student's surrogate parent that his educational program had been curtailed on account of his medical condition.[170] The court observed that even though the student's medical condition prevented him from being able to be transported to his special education program, school officials were still obligated to make attempts to provide him with services, albeit alternate services.

Changes in locations that render overall programs more restrictive for students generally constitute changes in placements. Even so, this issue is far from settled, particularly when transfers are made for disciplinary purposes. In one such dispute, a federal trial court in Louisiana treated a student's being moved from a self-contained special education class to an off-campus alternative program as a change in placement because the new setting would have deprived him of contact with peers who did not have disabilities.[171] On the other hand, a federal trial court in North Carolina refused to interpret a student's reassignment to a management school as a change in placement because the new setting provided the same curriculum and services that he received in his former program.[172]

In a series of judgments, the federal trial court in the District of Columbia decreed that the school board's failure to pay private school tuition on a timely basis violated the IDEA because it created the very real threat that the students would be removed from the schools.[173] According to the court, such an action would have violated the IDEA's prohibition against unilateral changes in placements.

Graduation Is a Change in Placement

As noted, major modifications to student IEPs amount to changes in placements. Moreover, courts agree that graduation is a change in placement because it terminates all educational services for students. In an illustrative case, the Supreme Judicial Court of Massachusetts ruled that the failure to provide parents with formal written notice that their son was to graduate violated the IDEA and a commonwealth statute.[174] Using a similar rationale, a federal trial court in New York treated graduation as analogous to an expulsion since it resulted in a student's total exclusion from his educational placement.[175]

Adjustments to IEPs

Generally, modifications to IEPs constitute changes in placement, but minor adjustments are allowable. As could be expected, this distinction is often subject to differing perspectives. The Third Circuit reasoned that the important element in evaluating whether a change in placement has occurred is whether a change is likely to affect a student's learning in some significant way.[176] The court viewed a minor change in the transportation arrangements for a student in Pennsylvania as not being a change in placement but warned that under some circumstances transportation could have a major impact on a child's learning. Two years later, the federal trial court in Massachusetts echoed the Third Circuit's analysis that a child's learning experience must be affected in some significant way when it decided that an adjustment to an IEP that was more superficial than substantive was not a change in placement.[177] The federal trial court in Maryland also treated minor modifications in a student's schedule that did not alter the goals and objectives in his IEP or the amount of special education time as not constituting a change in placement.[178]

Services Not in IEPs

School boards sometimes provide students with disabilities with auxiliary services that are not called for in their IEPs. If services are not being provided under the terms of IEPs, they can be changed without providing parents with the IDEA's due process safeguards. In such a case, the Ninth Circuit held that insofar as a tutoring program that was not provided as part of an IEP for a student in Washington was not a special education service, a change in tutors was not a change in placement.[179] Ironically, the record documented that officials provided tutoring after the student's parents rejected the board's offer to afford the child special education services. Similarly, the Sixth Circuit affirmed that board officials in Ohio did not violate the IDEA's stay put provision when they refused to leave a student in an extended school year program that was not included in his IEP.[180]

The IDEA's change in placement procedures are inapplicable to placements not made pursuant to its provisions. In other words, if state agencies make residential placements for social purposes, the IDEA's change in placement requirements cannot be invoked if officials attempt to transfer students to other facilities or otherwise remove them from residential facilities.[181] The IDEA's change in placement procedures apply only to services specified in IEPs. Accordingly, a service provider cannot invoke the IDEA's change in placement provision in license revocation proceedings.[182]

Programs That Are No Longer Appropriate

A special problem regarding the IDEA's status quo provision exists when it is no longer appropriate for students to remain in programs they have attended. This may occur for a variety of reasons: Schools may close, private schools can lose their state approval, programs can be found to be lacking in quality, students may age out of their current programs, or programs may no longer be able to serve particular children. Typically, in these situations courts approve placements in similar facilities. Once again, and as reflected in the following cases, the key element is that new programs must be able to implement student IEPs fully to pass muster under the status quo provision.

In New York, a federal trial court refused to treat students' transfers from a private school that was found to be lacking to more suitable facilities as a change in placement.[183] The court recognized that the board terminated its contract with the private school after an audit disclosed problems with its operations, including mismanagement of funds and serious educational deficiencies. A year later, in a second case from New York, the Second Circuit affirmed, but slightly modified, an order in favor of a student and his parents, declaring that their board had to leave him in a facility that had lost its state approval until such time as officials were able to offer an appropriate alternative.[184]

The Sixth Circuit affirmed that the transfer of students from a closed treatment facility in Kentucky to dissimilar alternate facilities was a change in placement.[185] At the same time, the court acknowledged that insofar as the closing occurred for financial reasons, the IDEA's procedural safeguards did not apply. The court added that the students could contest their new placements through the IDEA's administrative hearing process. In another case where a private school closed, the federal trial court for the District of Columbia upheld a hearing officer's order for the school board to fund a placement at another private school.[186] When the private school closed, the board offered the student a placement in a public school but failed to execute a complete IEP. The facts revealed that when school officials failed to present the child's parents with an IEP by the start of the next school year, they unilaterally enrolled their son in another private school. When a special education charter school in Texas closed and its students were enrolled in new schools, a federal trial court denied relief under the

IDEA's status quo provision because their parents failed to prove that the IEPs of the children would have been modified in their new placements.[187]

In two separate cases the District of Columbia Circuit posited that when officials in private schools determine that they can no longer serve students, school boards are obligated to locate and fund similar programs.[188] In the latter case, even though the private school placement was no longer available, the court allowed the board to make an interim placement in a public school program that was not inherently dissimilar until officials offered a final placement. Consistent with these cases, the federal trial court in the District of Columbia ordered the board to find similar placement alternatives to fulfill the requirements of student IEPs when their pendant placements were no longer available.[189]

A school board in New Hampshire proposed a placement in a public high school for a student who was too old to continue at the private residential school he attended at public expense. The federal trial court was convinced that insofar as such a transfer would have fundamentally altered the student's educational program, it was a change in placement.[190] The court concluded that the private school selected by the parents would have provided an experience substantially similar to the one in their son's former placement.

As the Seventh Circuit reasoned, educational methodologies that are appropriate in one environment may not always be effective in another. Therefore, the court maintained that flexibility is required when determining the status quo for students moving from one level to another, such as from a middle to a high school.[191] In remanding the case for further proceedings, the panel instructed a trial court in Illinois to consider whether specified methodologies were part of a student's IEP or simply chosen by the child's teachers.

Altering the Length of a School Year

In today's economic climate it is not unusual for school boards to institute cost-saving measures such as employee furloughs as a means of reducing budgets. Such a practice may not be problematic under the IDEA as long as it impacts all students equally. In the midst of a fiscal crisis, the State of Hawaii chose to close its schools on 17 Fridays during a school year. As part of that measure, the state negotiated an agreement with its teachers to implement the furloughs. Clearly, special education students could not have attended school on those Fridays. Yet, the Ninth Circuit agreed that closing school on the designated Fridays, thereby shortening the school year, did not constitute a change in placement under the IDEA.[192] The court insisted that Congress did not intend for the IDEA to apply to systemwide administrative decisions that affected all public schools and all students. Thus, the court believed that Hawaii's across-the-board reduction in school days did not conflict with Congressional intent of protecting students with disabilities from being singled out. Further, the court commented that to apply the IDEA's status quo provision in such a situation would have essentially given parents veto power over the state's authority regarding the management of its schools.[193]

Annual Reviews and Reevaluations

As reviewed earlier, the IDEA requires school officials to review the IEPs of students with disabilities at least annually[194] and to conduct re-evaluations at least once every three years, unless they and parents agree that re-evaluations are unnecessary.[195] Nonetheless, parents retain the right to request reevaluations more frequently than every three years.[196] Accordingly, hearing officers and courts cannot order school boards to maintain given placements for longer than one year. Of course, each year's IEP is subject to the IDEA's due process requirements. The federal trial court for the District of Columbia denied a parental request to prohibit the board from changing a private school placement for two years.[197] The court stated that board officials had to be free during that time frame to consider whether the private school was still appropriate.

At least one federal court, in Michigan,[198] ordered a school board to update evaluations before making significant changes in placements. Board officials proposed a change in placement for students with hearing impairments from a state school for the deaf to a program within the public schools. Since this change would have fundamentally altered the educational programs of the students, the court decided that the reevaluations were warranted. Yet, in another case the Tenth Circuit made it clear that even though graduation is generally considered to be a change in placement, a reevaluation was not required before a student's services were discontinued due to his graduation.[199] Where a student in Oklahoma asked for a due process hearing but the process was not completed until after he graduated, he alleged that he was denied services. The court affirmed that the student was not entitled to a hearing, because after graduation he was no longer protected by the IDEA.

FREQUENTLY ASKED QUESTIONS

Q: What are the required components of IEPs?

A: According to the IDEA, IEPs must contain

- Statements of the current level of academic achievement and functional performance of students
- Measurable annual goals for students, including academic and functional goals
- Descriptions of how officials plan to measure students' progress toward meeting their annual goals, as well as of when periodic reports on this progress are to be provided

- Statements of the special education and related services, as well as supplementary aids and services, that students are to receive, based on peer-reviewed research to the extent practicable
- Explanations of the extent, if any, to which students are not going to participate in regular classes with peers who are not disabled
- Statements of the individual appropriate accommodations necessary to measure the academic achievement and functional performance of students on state and district assessments
- Projected dates of initiation and duration of special education services that students are to receive

In addition, starting no later than when the first IEP is written that is to be in effect for students who reach the age of 16,

- Statements of appropriate measurable postsecondary education goals, to be updated annually, and transition services

At least one year before students reach the age of majority,

- Statements that they have been informed of their rights, if any, that will transfer at the age of majority (20 U.S.C. § 1414(d))

Q: If students are promoted from one level to another, such as elementary to middle school, does this constitute a change in placement?

A: No. These are not changes as long as new programs provide substantially the same educational benefits as the previous ones did. Although the IDEA permits minor adjustments reflecting changes to the new levels, the amounts and types of services must remain the same.

Q: Are school boards required to implement the findings and recommendations of independent evaluators?

A: No. The IDEA directs school boards to consider the findings and recommendations of independent evaluators but does not require them to adopt the recommendations. IEP teams can satisfy the requirement to consider these results by reading and discussing the reports of independent evaluators at IEP meetings with parents.

Q: Must school officials review IEPs each and every time a parent requests *a* review?

A: No. While school officials must address parental concerns and dissatisfaction with IEPs, once they have dealt with issues, they are not required to review them repeatedly every time parents voice concerns.

(Continued)

(Continued)

Q: Is it always necessary for all required members of IEP teams to be at each and every IEP team meeting?

A: No. The IDEA does allow for some team members to not be physically present at IEP conferences if parents agree that their presence is not essential and they provide written reports. Also, courts have overlooked improperly constituted IEP teams when school board officials have shown that the absence of some members did not have an effect on the final outcome and did not cause a denial of a FAPE or infringe on the parents' rights to fully participate in the process. This noted, board officials should always endeavor to make sure that all required members of IEP teams are present at all meetings. If a specific member is unable to attend for good cause (such as illness) board officials should provide appropriate substitutes or reschedule meetings.

Recommendations

The IDEA and its regulations establish specific criteria for school board officials to follow in locating, identifying, evaluating, and serving students with disabilities. As discussed more fully in the next chapter, the IDEA grants students and their parents specific procedural rights in this process to ensure that they are equal partners. The following recommendations were gleaned from the numerous cases interpreting the IDEA and its regulations regarding the procedures IEP teams must follow in evaluating students and developing IEPs to provide them with FAPEs. Since individual jurisdictions may afford students and their parents additional rights, they should also consult state laws and regulations.

School officials should

- Make sure to complete fair assessments of students with disabilities.
- Guarantee parental input into evaluation and placement processes.
- Ensure that testing and evaluation materials as well as procedures are selected and administered in a manner that is not racially or culturally biased.
- Include assessments in all areas of suspected disability in the multidisciplinary evaluation.
- Consult state laws and regulations for timelines for completing evaluations and making placements.
- Develop and implement policies and procedures to avoid the overidentification or disproportionate representation based on race and ethnicity of students with disabilities.

- Carefully review and discuss the results of independent evaluations, keeping in mind that educators do not have to adopt all findings of independent evaluators.
- Avoid the use of boilerplate text in IEPs; IEPs that are not individually tailored to meet the unique needs of students run the risk of being invalidated.
- Ensure that at least one person who is knowledgeable of placement options participates as a member of IEP teams.
- Be diligent in ensuring that IEPs contain all required elements, particularly students' current levels of functioning, annual goals and measurable short-term objectives, clearly stated performance criteria, evaluation procedures, and schedules for evaluation.
- Come to IEP meetings with proposals and even draft IEPs, but ensure that parents have input into the IEP process.
- Ensure that student placements are based on IEPs and that IEPs are not written to fit placements.
- State in unequivocal terms in IEPs that placements are intended to be only temporary if this is the case.
- Ensure that board representatives attend IEP meetings convened in private schools for students who attend private schools at public expense.
- Check with state officials to determine whether their states have been approved for pilot three-year IEPs.
- Consider taking steps to reduce paperwork, regardless of whether state officials choose to participate in the pilot national program.
- Implement the IDEA's procedural safeguards before making substantial changes to the IEPs or placements of students.
- Schedule review meetings if parents express dissatisfaction with IEPs or the progress of their children.
- Notify parents any time school board officials propose to act on placements of or refusals to initiate actions for students with disabilities.
- Make changes in placement only when parents agree to them or they are ordered by hearing officers or courts, keeping in mind that unilateral changes in placement cannot be made while appeals are pending.
- Ensure that IEPs can be fully implemented in new locations if changes in location for the delivery of services are required.
- Locate new programs that are substantially similar to current programs and that can implement student IEPs if the current program of students closes or becomes unavailable.
- When students move from one level to the next in a school system, make sure that their programs at the new level are as close as possible to their previous programs.

Endnotes

1. 20 U.S.C. §§ 1400–1982 (2012). The IDEA's regulations can be found at Assistance to the States for the Education of Children with Disabilities, 34 C.F.R. §§ 300.1–300.818 (2013).
2. 20 U.S.C. § 1415.
3. 20 U.S.C. § 1414(d).
4. 34 C.F.R. §§ 300.320–328.
5. 20 U.S.C. § 1414 (a)(1)(d)(i)(I).
6. 34 C.F.R. § 300.300(a)(1).
7. 20 U.S.C. § 1414 (a)(1)(d)(i)(II).
8. 20 U.S.C. § 1415(b)(3).
9. 458 U.S. 176 (1982).
10. 20 U.S.C. § 1212(a)(3)(A).
11. 20 U.S.C. § 1414(a)(1)(A).
12. 20 U.S.C. § 1414(d)(4).
13. 20 U.S.C. § 1414(a)(2).
14. Russo C. J., & Talbert-Johnson, C. (1997). The overrepresentation of African American children in special education: The resegregation of educational programming? *Education and Urban Society, 29*(2), 136–148.
15. 20 U.S.C. §§ 1412(a)(24), 1418 (d)(1)(A)(B).
16. 20 U.S.C. §§ 1412 (a)(22)(A), 1418(d)(1)(C).
17. 20 U.S.C. § 1412(a)(22)(B).
18. 20 U.S.C. §§ 1414(a)(1)(C)(i)(I), 1414(a)(1)(D)(i)(I)); 34 C.F.R. 300.301(c)(1). *See* Integrated Design and Electronics Academy Public Charter School v. McKinley *ex rel.* K.M., 570 F. Supp. 2d 28 (D.D.C. 2008).
19. Gerstmyer v. Howard County Public Schools, 850 F. Supp. 361 (D. Md. 1994).
20. 20 U.S.C. § 1414(a)(1)(C)(ii)(II).
21. 20 U.S.C. § 1414(a)(1)(D)(ii)(I)–(II).
22. 34 C.F.R. § 300.303.
23. 20 U.S.C. § 1414(b)(2)(A).
24. 20 U.S.C. § 1414(b)(3)(B). *See also* K.I. *ex rel.* Jennie I. v. Montgomery Public Schools, 805 F. Supp. 2d 1283 (M.D. Ala. 2011) (finding that insofar as board officials failed to conduct a cognitive evaluation or occupational therapy evaluation, the child's IEP was inadequate); D.B. v. Bedford County School Board, 708 F. Supp. 2d 564 (W.D. Va. 2010) (declaring that officials neglected to test a student for learning disabilities even though evidence suggested that he had a disorder that met the IDEA's definition). *But see* D.R. *ex rel.* Etsuko R. v. Department of Education, State of Hawai'i, 827 F. Supp. 2d 1161 (D. Haw. 2011) (refusing to impose liability on the Department of Education for failing to evaluate a student in all areas because his mother neglected to share relevant information with his IEP team).
25. 34 C.F.R. § 300.304(b)(2).
26. 20 U.S.C. § 1414(b)(3)(A)(i)–(v).
27. 20 U.S.C. § 1415(b)(1); 34 C.F.R. § 300.502(b)(1)–(2).
28. *See, e.g.,* Lauren W. *ex rel.* Jean W. v. DeFlaminis, 480 F.3d 259 (3d Cir. 2007). *See also* G.J. *ex rel.* E.J. and L.J. v. Muscogee County School District, 668 F.3d 1258 (11th Cir. 2012) (affirming that parents who never consented to a re-evaluation had no right to obtain one at public expense); P.P. *ex rel.* Michael P. v. West Chester Area School District, 585 F.3d 727 (3d Cir. 2009)

(affirming that parents were not entitled to reimbursement for an independent evaluation because they were not challenging a school board's evaluation); R.L. *ex rel.* Mr. L. v. Plainville Board of Education, 363 F. Supp. 2d 222 (D. Conn. 2005) (explaining that parents were not entitled to reimbursement for an independent evaluation since they agreed that an initial review was comprehensive and sought a second assessment merely to have another source of information).

29. Council Rock School District v. Bolick, 462 F. App'x 212 (3d Cir. 2012); Evanston Community Consolidated School Dist. Number 65 v. Michael M., 356 F.3d 798 (7th Cir. 2004); Hudson v. Wilson, 828 F.2d 1059 (4th Cir. 1987).

30. *See, e.g.,* Phillip C. *ex rel.* A.C. v. Jefferson County Board of Education, 701 F.3d 691 (11th Cir. 2012); Breanne C. v. Southern York County School Board, 732 F. Supp. 2d 474 (M.D. Pa. 2010).

31. 34 C.F.R. § 300.502(b)(3).

32. 34 C.F.R. § 300.502(b)(4).

33. Warren G. v. Cumberland County School District, 190 F.3d 80 (3d Cir. 1999); Raymond S. v. Ramirez, 918 F. Supp. 1280 (N.D. Iowa 1996). *But see* P.R. and B.R. v. Woodmore Local School District, 256 F. App'x 751 (6th Cir. 2007) (affirming that parents who did not give school board officials prior notice that they were seeking an independent evaluation, thus depriving the school board of the opportunity to initiate a due process hearing to show that its evaluation was appropriate, were not entitled to reimbursement).

34. Evans v. District No. 17, Douglas County, 841 F.2d 824 (8th Cir. 1988).

35. 34 C.F.R. § 300.502(b)(5). *See also* Board of Education of Murphysboro Community Unit School District No. 186 v. Illinois State Board of Education, 41 F.3d 1162 (7th Cir. 1994).

36. 34 C.F.R. § 300.502(b)(1).

37. 34 C.F.R. § 300.502(c)(1). *See, e.g.,* James and Lee Anne D. *ex rel.* Sarah D. v. Board of Education of Aptakisic-Tripp Community Consolidated School District No. 102, 642 F. Supp. 2d 804 (N.D. Ill. 2009) (holding that the IDEA's requirement does not obligate an IEP team to implement recommendations from an independent evaluation or even engage in a substantive discussion of its findings).

38. G.D. v. Westmoreland School District, 930 F.2d 942 (1st Cir. 1991). *See also* T.S. v. Ridgefield Board of Education, 808 F. Supp. 926 (D. Conn. 1992), *affirmed sub nom.* T.S. v. Board of Education of the Town of Ridgefield, 10 F.3d 87 (2d Cir. 1993) (affirming that the IDEA does not require school officials to accept the recommendations of independent evaluations or that these assessments be accorded any particular weight).

39. T.S. v. Board of Education of the Town of Ridgefield, 10 F.3d 87 (2d Cir. 1993).

40. K.E. *ex rel.* K.E. and T.E. v. Independent School District No. 15, 647 F.3d 795 (8th Cir. 2011).

41. 34 C.F.R. § 300.502(c)(2).

42. Bonadonna v. Cooperman, 619 F. Supp. 401 (D.N.J. 1985).

43. Seattle School District No. 1 v. B.S., 82 F.3d 1493 (9th Cir. 1996).

44. Logue v. Shawnee Mission Public School Unified School District No. 512, 959 F. Supp. 1338 (D. Kan. 1997), *affirmed* 153 F.3d 727 (10th Cir. 1998) (mem.).

45. Lora v. Board of Education of the City of New York, 456 F. Supp. 1211 (E.D.N.Y. 1978), *affirmed in part* 623 F.2d 248 (2d Cir. 1980), *final order* 587 F. Supp. 1572 (E.D.N.Y. 1984).

46. Lenhoff v. Farmington Public Schools, 680 F. Supp. 921 (E.D. Mich. 1988).
47. Patricia P. v. Board of Education of Oak Park and River Forest High School District No. 200, 8 F. Supp. 2d 801 (N.D. Ill. 1998), *affirmed* 203 F.3d 462 (7th Cir. 2000).
48. 20 U.S.C. § 1414(d)(4).
49. 20 U.S.C. § 1414(a)(2).
50. Andress v. Cleveland Independent School District, 64 F.3d 176 (5th Cir. 1995).
51. Patricia P. v. Board of Education of Oak Park and River Forest High School District No. 200, 8 F. Supp. 2d 801 (N.D. Ill. 1998), *affirmed* 203 F.3d 462 (7th Cir. 2000); Johnson v. Duneland School Corporation, 92 F.3d 554 (7th Cir. 1996).
52. Holland v. District of Columbia, 71 F.3d 417 (D.C. Cir. 1995).
53. Pitchford *ex rel.* M. v. Salem-Keizer School District No. 24J, 155 F. Supp. 2d 1213 (D. Or. 2001); Poolaw v. Bishop, 67 F.3d 830 (9th Cir. 1995).
54. 20 U.S.C. § 1414(d)(1)(A)(i)(I).
55. 20 U.S.C. § 1414(d)(1)(A)(i)(II).
56. 20 U.S.C. § 1414(d)(1)(A)(i)(III).
57. 20 U.S.C. § 1414(d)(1)(A)(i)(IV).
58. 20 U.S.C. § 1414(d)(1)(A)(i)(V).
59. 20 U.S.C. § 1414(d)(1)(A)(i)(VI).
60. 20 U.S.C. § 1414(d)(1)(A)(i)(VII).
61. 20 U.S.C. § 1414(d)(1)(A)(i)(VIII).
62. 34 C.F.R. § 300.321(a).
63. *See, e.g.,* S.H. *ex rel.* A.H. v. Plano Independent School District, 487 F. App'x 850 (5th Cir. 2012).
64. M.L. v. Federal Way School District, 394 F.3d 634 (9th Cir. 2005), *cert. denied,* 545 U.S. 1128 (2005), *on remand* 401 F. Supp. 2d 1158 (W.D. Wash. 2005) (awarding attorney fees).
65. R.B. *ex rel.* F.B. v. Napa Valley Unified School District, 496 F.3d 932 (9th Cir. 2007).
66. Werner v. Clarksville Central School District, 363 F. Supp. 2d 656 (S.D.N.Y. 2005).
67. The IDEA's regulations allow a required member to be excused from a meeting, with parental consent, if that person's presence is not necessary, or the individual submits written input into the development of the IEP. 34 C.F.R. § 300.321(e).
68. Cone v. Randolph County Schools, 103 F. App'x 731 (4th Cir. 2004), *cert. denied,* 543 U.S. 1124 (2005).
69. Johnson *ex rel.* Johnson v. Olathe District Schools Unified School District. No. 233, Special Services Division, 316 F. Supp. 2d 960 (D. Kan. 2003).
70. A.H. *ex rel.* J.H. v. Department of Education of City of New York, 394 F. App'x 718 (2d Cir. 2010).
71. 34 C.F.R. § 300.323(c)(1).
72. 34 C.F.R. § 300.322(a).
73. 34 C.F.R. § 300.325.
74. *See, e.g.,* Drobnicki v. Poway Unified School District, 358 F. App'x 788 (9th Cir. 2009) (declaring that proceeding with an IEP meeting instead of rescheduling it when parents notified school officials that they could not attend violated the IDEA); J.N. v. District of Columbia, 677 F. Supp. 2d 314 (D.D.C. 2010) (decreeing that failing to include a mother in an IEP meeting resulted in denying her son a FAPE).

75. W.G. and B.G. v. Board of Trustees of Target Range School District No. 23, Missoula, Montana, 789 F. Supp. 1070 (D. Mont. 1991), *affirmed* 960 F.2d 1479 (9th Cir. 1992).

76. Doug C. *ex rel.* Spencer C. v. Hawaii Department of Education, 720 F.3d 1038 (9th Cir. 2013).

77. Smith v. Henson, 786 F. Supp. 43 (D.D.C. 1992).

78. Big Beaver Falls Area School District v. Jackson, 615 A.2d 910 (Pa. Commw. Ct. 1992).

79. Blackmon v. Springfield R-XII School District, 198 F.3d 648 (8th Cir. 1999).

80. K.D. *ex rel.* C.L. v. Department of Education, State of Hawaii, 665 F. Supp. 2d 1110 (9th Cir. 2011).

81. R.P. *ex rel.* R.P. and C.P. v. Alamo Heights Independent School District, 703 F.3d 801 (5th Cir. 2012).

82. Doug C. *ex rel.* Spencer C. v. Hawaii Department of Education, 720 F.3d 1038 (9th Cir. 2013).

83. Brimmer v. Traverse City Area Public Schools, 872 F. Supp. 447 (W.D. Mich. 1994).

84. Daugherty v. Hamilton County Schools, 21 F. Supp. 2d 765 (E.D. Tenn. 1998).

85. Briley v. Board of Education of Baltimore County, 87 F. Supp. 2d 441 (D. Md. 1999).

86. Dong v. Board of Education of the Rochester Community Schools, 197 F.3d 793 (6th Cir. 1999).

87. Pitchford *ex rel.* M. v. Salem-Keizer School District No. 24J, 155 F. Supp. 2d 1213 (D. Or. 2001).

88. Doe v. Defendant I, 898 F.2d 1186 (6th Cir. 1990).

89. Coale v. State Department of Education, 162 F. Supp. 2d 316 (D. Del. 2001).

90. Russell v. Jefferson, 609 F. Supp. 605 (N.D. Cal. 1985).

91. Evans v. Board of Education of the Rhinebeck Central School District, 921 F. Supp. 1184, 930 F. Supp. 83 (S.D.N.Y. 1996).

92. M.H. and E.K. *ex rel.* P.H. v. New York City Department of Education, 712 F. Supp. 2d 125 (S.D.N.Y. 2010), *affirmed* 685 F.3d 217 (2012).

93. Logue v. Shawnee Mission Public School Unified School District No. 512, 959 F. Supp. 1338 (D. Kan. 1997), *affirmed* 153 F.3d 727 (10th Cir. 1998) (mem.); O'Toole v. Olathe District Schools Unified School District No. 233, 963 F. Supp. 1000 (D. Kan. 1997), *affirmed* 144 F.3d 692 (10th Cir. 1998).

94. Kuszewski v. Chippewa Valley Schools, 131 F. Supp. 2d 926 (E.D. Mich. 2001).

95. *See, e.g.,* Risinsky v. Green Bay Area School District, 667 F. Supp. 2d 964 (E.D. Wis. 2009); French v. Omaha Public Schools, 766 F. Supp. 765 (D. Neb. 1991).

96. Chris D. v. Montgomery County Board of Education, 753 F. Supp. 922 (M.D. Ala. 1990).

97. Gerstmyer v. Howard County Public Schools, 850 F. Supp. 361 (D. Md. 1994).

98. Spielberg v. Henrico County Public Schools, 853 F.2d 256 (4th Cir. 1988).

99. P.J. v. State of Connecticut Board of Education, 788 F. Supp. 673 (D. Conn. 1992).

100. Evans v. Board of Education of the Rhinebeck Central School District, 921 F. Supp. 1184, 930 F. Supp. 83 (S.D.N.Y. 1996).

101. G.D. v. Westmoreland School District, 930 F.2d 942 (1st Cir. 1991).

102. Scituate School Committee v. Robert B., 620 F. Supp. 1224 (D.R.I. 1985), *affirmed* 795 F.2d 77 (1st Cir. 1986) (mem.).

103. Hampton School Dist. v. Dobrowolski, 976 F.2d 48 (1st Cir. 1992).

104. Blackmon v. Springfield R-XII School District, 198 F.3d 648 (8th Cir. 1999).
105. Fuhrmann v. East Hanover Board of Education, 993 F.2d 1031 (3d Cir. 1993). *Also see* Tracy v. Beaufort County Board of Education, 335 F. Supp. 2d 675 (D.S.C. 2004).
106. J.L., M.L., K.L. v. Mercer Island School District, 592 F.3d 938 (9th Cir. 2010).
107. Deal v. Hamilton County Board of Education, 392 F.3d 840 (6th Cir. 2004), *rehearing and rehearing en banc denied* (No. 03-5396) (6th Cir. 2005).
108. D.B. and L.B. *ex rel.* H.B. v. Gloucester Township School District, 751 F. Supp. 2d 764 (D.N.J. 2010), *affirmed* 489 F. App'x 564 (3d Cir. 2012).
109. T.P. and S.P. *ex rel.* S.P. v. Mamaroneck Union Free School District, 554 F.3d 247 (2d Cir. 2009).
110. Doyle v. Arlington County School Board, 806 F. Supp. 1253 (E.D. Va. 1992). *See also* Board of Education of Township High School District No. 211 v. Ross, 468 F.3d 267 (7th Cir. 2007) (affirming that while school personnel prepared for an IEP meeting, this did not mean that their decisions were predetermined); Nack *ex rel.* Nack v. Orange City School District, 454 F.3d 604 (6th Cir. 2006) (affirming that although school personnel conducted discussions prior to an IEP meeting and drafted portions of the IEP, there was no evidence that they predetermined it).
111. Myles S. v. Montgomery County Board of Education, 824 F. Supp. 1549 (M.D. Ala. 1993).
112. Gerstmyer v. Howard County Public Schools, 850 F. Supp. 361 (D. Md. 1994).
113. C.H. v. Cape Henlopen School District, 566 F. Supp. 2d 352 (D. Del. 2008). *See also* Doe v. Hampden-Wilbraham Regional School District, 715 F. Supp. 2d 185 (D. Mass. 2010) (finding that insofar as parents were responsible for delays in developing an IEP, their son was not entitled to a new one).
114. Ms. S. *ex rel.* G. v. Vashon Island School District, 337 F.3d 1115 (9th Cir. 2003).
115. 20 U.S.C. § 1414(d)(2)(C)(i)(I).
116. 20 U.S.C. § 1414(d)(2)(C)(i)(II).
117. 20 U.S.C. § 1414(d)(4)(A)(i). The 2004 IDEA amendments allowed up to 15 states to pilot comprehensive multiyear IEPs that do not exceed three years and coincide with natural transition points, 20 U.S.C. § 1414(d)(5)(A). IEP teams in states piloting multiyear IEPs do not need to revise them annually unless revisions are required due to changing circumstances or parents request annual revisions.
118. 34 C.F.R. § 300.324(b).
119. Edwards-White v. District of Columbia, 785 F. Supp. 1022 (D.D.C. 1992).
120. Amann v. Stow School System, 982 F.2d 644 (1st Cir. 1992).
121. Lillbask *ex rel.* Mauclaire v. Sergi, 117 F. Supp. 2d 182 (D. Conn. 2000).
122. Clyde K. v. Puyallup School District No. 3, 35 F.3d 1396 (9th Cir. 1994).
123. 20 U.S.C. § 1415(b)(3)(A).
124. 20 U.S.C. § 1415(j).
125. Thomas v. Cincinnati Board of Education, 918 F.2d 618 (6th Cir. 1990).
126. Mehfoud, K. S., & Osborne, A. G. (1998). Making a successful interim placement under the IDEA. *Education Law Reporter, 124,* 7–12.
127. Jacobson v. District of Columbia Board of Education, 564 F. Supp. 166 (D.D.C. 1983).

128. Saleh v. District of Columbia, 660 F. Supp. 212 (D.D.C. 1987). *See also* K.D. *ex rel.* C.L. v. Department of Education, State of Hawaii, 665 F.3d 1110 (9th Cir. 2011) (affirming that a settlement agreement never placed a child in a private school but only that the board agreed to pay his tuition for one year).

129. Leonard v. McKenzie, 869 F.2d 1558 (D.C. Cir. 1989).

130. Zvi D. v. Ambach, 520 F. Supp. 196 (E.D.N.Y. 1981), *affirmed* 694 F.2d 904 (2d Cir. 1982).

131. Evans v. Board of Education of the Rhinebeck Central School District, 921 F. Supp. 1184, 930 F. Supp. 83 (S.D.N.Y. 1996).

132. Verhoeven v. Brunswick School Committee, 207 F.3d 1 (1st Cir. 1999).

133. Cochran v. District of Columbia, 660 F. Supp. 314 (D.D.C. 1987).

134. Digre v. Roseville Schools Independent School District No. 623, 841 F.2d 245 (8th Cir. 1988).

135. Joshua B. v. New Trier Township High School District 203, 770 F. Supp. 431 (N.D. Ill. 1991).

136. Doe v. Brookline School Committee, 722 F.2d 910 (1st Cir. 1983).

137. Spilsbury v. District of Columbia, 307 F. Supp. 22 (D.D.C. 2004), 377 F. Supp. 2d 1 (D.D.C. 2005).

138. Clovis Unified School District v. California Office of Administrative Hearings, 903 F.2d 635 (9th Cir. 1990). *See also* Department of Education, State of Hawaii v. M.F., 840 F. Supp. 2d 1214 (D. Haw. 2011) (noting that a private school became a child's status quo placement on the date a hearing officer identified it as an appropriate placement).

139. Grace B. v. Lexington School Committee, 762 F. Supp. 416 (D. Mass. 1991).

140. Board of Education of the City of New York v. Ambach, 612 F. Supp. 230 (E.D.N.Y. 1985).

141. Anchorage School District v. M.P., 689 F.3d 283 (9th Cir. 2012.

142. 471 U.S. 359 (1985).

143. Board of Education of the Pawling Central School District v. Schutz, 290 F.3d 476 (2d Cir. 2002).

144. *See, e.g.,* Board of Education of Montgomery County v. Brett Y., 959 F. Supp. 705 (D. Md. 1997); L.B. *ex rel.* Benjamin v. Greater Clark County Schools, 458 F. Supp. 2d 845 (S.D. Ind. 2006); Arlington Central School District v. L.P. *ex rel.* Mr. & Mrs. J.H., 421 F. Supp. 2d 692 (S.D.N.Y. 2006); Escambia County Board of Education v. Benton, 358 F. Supp. 2d 1112 (S.D. Ala. 2005).

145. 20 U.S.C. § 1415(f)–(g).

146. *See, e.g.,* Winkelman v. Ohio Department of Education, 616 F. Supp. 2d 714 (N.D. Ohio 2008).

147. Murphy v. Arlington Central School District Board of Education, 86 F. Supp. 2d 354 (S.D.N.Y. 2000).

148. St. Tammany Parish School Board v. State of Louisiana, 142 F.3d 776 (5th Cir. 1998).

149. Anderson v. District of Columbia, 877 F.2d 1018 (D.C. Cir. 1989).

150. J.E. *ex rel.* J.E. and A.E. v. Boyertown Area School District, 452 F App'x 172 (3d Cir. 2011).

151. J.E. v. Boyertown Area School District, 807 F. Supp. 2d 236 (E.D. Pa. 2011).

152. Joshua A. *ex rel.* Jorge A. v. Rocklin Unified School District, 559 F.3d 1036 (9th Cir. 2009).

153. Holmes v. District of Columbia, 680 F. Supp. 40 (D.D.C. 1988).

154. Cronin v. Board of Education of East Ramapo Central School District, 689 F. Supp. 197 (S.D.N.Y. 1988).

155. 20 U.S.C. § 1415(j).

156. Tammy S. v. Reedsburg School District, 302 F. Supp. 2d 959 (W.D. Wis. 2003).

157. Joshua B. v. New Trier Township High School District 203, 770 F. Supp. 431 (N.D. Ill. 1991).

158. L.M. *ex rel.* Sam M. v. Capistrano Unified School District, 556 F.3d 900 (9th Cir. 2009).

159. Part C of the IDEA, 20 U.S.C. §§ 1431–1444, provides grants to states to offer early intervention services to children with disabilities below the age of 3 and their families.

160. D.P. and L.P. *ex rel.* E.P. v. School Board of Broward County, 483 F.3d 725 (11th Cir. 2005).

161. M.M. and H.M. *ex rel.* A.M. v. New York City Department of Education, 583 F. Supp. 2d 498 (S.D.N.Y. 2008)

162. Pardini v. Allegheny Intermediate Unit, 420 F.3d 181 (3d Cir. 2005).

163. Middlebrook v. School District of the County of Knox, Tennessee, 805 F. Supp. 534 (E.D. Tenn. 1991); Concerned Parents and Citizens for the Continuing Education at Malcolm X. v. New York City Board of Education, 629 F.2d 751 (2d Cir. 1980).

164. A.W. *ex rel.* Wilson v. Fairfax County School Board, 372 F.3d 674 (4th Cir. 2004).

165. Gebhardt v. Ambach, EHLR 554:130 (W.D.N.Y. 1982).

166. Visco v. School District of Pittsburgh, 684 F. Supp. 1310 (W.D. Pa. 1988).

167. Lunceford v. District of Columbia Board of Education, 745 F.2d 1577 (D.C. Cir. 1984).

168. Weil v. Board of Elementary and Secondary Education, 931 F.2d 1069 (5th Cir. 1991).

169. Sherri A.D. v. Kirby, 975 F.2d 193 (5th Cir. 1992). *See also* Veazey v. Ascension Parish School Board, 121 F. App'x 552 (5th Cir. 2005).

170. Abney v. District of Columbia, 849 F.2d 1491 (D.C. Cir. 1988).

171. Jonathan G. v. Caddo Parish School Board, 875 F. Supp. 352 (W.D. La. 1994).

172. Glen III v. Charlotte-Mecklenburg School Board of Education, 903 F. Supp. 918 (W.D.N.C. 1995).

173. Petties v. District of Columbia, 881 F. Supp. 63, 888 F. Supp. 165, 894 F. Supp. 465, 897 F. Supp. 626 (D.D.C. 1995).

174. Stock v. Massachusetts Hospital School, 467 N.E.2d 448 (Mass. 1984).

175. Cronin v. Board of Education of East Ramapo Central School District, 689 F. Supp. 197 (S.D.N.Y. 1988).

176. DeLeon v. Susquehanna Community School District, 747 F.2d 149 (3d Cir. 1984). *See also* J.R. and K.R. v. Mars Area School District, 318 F. App'x 113 (3d Cir. 2009).

177. Brookline School Committee v. Golden, 628 F. Supp. 113 (D. Mass. 1986).

178. Cavanagh v. Grasmick, 75 F. Supp. 2d 446 (D. Md. 1999).

179. Gregory K. v. Longview School District, 811 F.2d 1307 (9th Cir. 1987).

180. Cordrey v. Euckert, 917 F.2d 1460 (6th Cir. 1990).

181. Corbett v. Regional Center for the East Bay, Inc., 676 F. Supp. 964 (N.D. Cal. 1988).

182. Corbett v. Regional Center for the East Bay, Inc., 699 F. Supp. 230 (N.D. Cal. 1988).

183. Dima v. Macchiarola, 513 F. Supp. 565 (E.D.N.Y. 1981).

184. Vander Malle v. Ambach, 673 F.2d 49 (2d Cir. 1982).

185. Tilton v. Jefferson County Board of Education, 705 F.2d 800 (6th Cir. 1983).

186. Block v. District of Columbia, 748 F. Supp. 891 (D.D.C. 1990).

187. Comb v. Benji's Special Education Academy, 745 F. Supp. 2d 755 (S.D. Tex. 2010).

188. Knight v. District of Columbia, 877 F.2d 1025 (D.D.C. 1989); McKenzie v. Smith, 771 F.2d 1527 (D.C. Cir. 1985).

189. Lester v. District of Columbia, 394 F. Supp. 2d 60 (D.D.C. 2005), 439 F. Supp. 2d 93 (D.D.C. 2006).

190. Henry v. School Administrative Unit #29, 70 F. Supp. 2d 52 (D.N.H. 1999).

191. John M. v. Board of Education of Evanston Township High School District, 502 F.3d 708 (7th Cir. 2007).

192. N.D. v. Hawaii Department of Education, 600 F.3d 1104 (9th Cir. 2010).

193. Osborne, A. G., & Russo, C. J. (2011). Teacher furloughs and the IDEA: An emerging issue? *School Business Affairs*, *77*(2), 34–36. Osborne, A.G. (2010). System-wide teacher furloughs and school shut downs do not violate the IDEA's status quo provision. *School Law Reporter*, *52*(8), 161–163.

194. 20 U.S.C. § 1414(d)(4).

195. 20 U.S.C. § 1414(a)(2).

196. 20 U.S.C. § 1414(a)(2)(A)(ii).

197. Kattan v. District of Columbia, 691 F. Supp. 1539 (D.D.C. 1988).

198. Brimmer v. Traverse City Area Public Schools, 872 F. Supp. 447 (W.D. Mich. 1994).

199. T.S. v. Independent School District No. 54, 265 F.3d 1090 (10th Cir. 2001).

Student Discipline

As originally enacted, the Individuals with Disabilities Education Act (IDEA)[1] did not mention discipline. Even so, many of the IDEA's provisions had implications that could have been applied to situations involving the disciplining of students with disabilities. Early litigation recognized that students with disabilities had additional due process rights when faced with such disciplinary sanctions as expulsions or long-term suspensions because such penalties could have denied them the free appropriate public educations (FAPEs) to which they were entitled under the IDEA.[2]

When Congress approved the most comprehensive amendments to the IDEA to date in 1997, it included provisions governing the disciplinary process applicable to students with disabilities for the first time. Consistent with their ordinary manner of doing business, Congress and the Federal Department of Education refined and reorganized these provisions as part of the 2004 IDEA amendments[3] and their regulations, respectively.[4]

As complex as the IDEA's disciplinary requirements are, this chapter explains that it is possible to extract guiding principles from the statutes, regulations, and numerous cases dealing with the rights of students with disabilities who are subject to discipline.[5]

This chapter details the requirements for administering disciplinary penalties to students with disabilities. In order to provide readers with an understanding of how and why many of the current disciplinary provisions of the IDEA came into being, the chapter begins with a historical overview of the case law that developed before the enactment of the IDEA's 1997 amendments. Now that much of the pre-1997 litigation is incorporated into the IDEA, this review of the early case law provides insight into how the law and regulations should be interpreted. The next sections cover the requirements of the current statute and recent litigation. The chapter ends with recommendations for practice.[6]

Pre-1997 Case Law

The IDEA, as originally written, contained no provisions directly addressing the discipline of students with disabilities. Yet, courts were often asked to resolve disputes arising out of disciplinary situations involving students with disabilities such that a large body of case law emerged. The IDEA now contains detailed disciplinary provisions. Consequently, since the IDEA incorporates much of earlier case law, a review of this litigation is instructive since it provides the necessary background for understanding the current version of the statute as well as its regulations.

Early Decisions

In *Stuart v. Nappi,*[7] school officials in Connecticut unsuccessfully tried to expel a student with disabilities who was involved in schoolwide disturbances. The student's attorney requested a due process hearing under the IDEA while obtaining an order from the federal trial court to prevent educators from conducting an expulsion hearing. Ruling in favor of the student, the court held that insofar as an expulsion was a change in placement that was inconsistent with the IDEA's procedures, school officials should have provided her and her parents with written prior notice before attempting to modify her educational placement.[8] The court added that educational officials could temporarily suspend disruptive students or change their placements to more restrictive settings by complying with the IDEA's procedures.

A year later, a federal trial court in Indiana, in *Doe v. Koger,*[9] overturned the expulsion of a student with a mild intellectual disability. The court noted that school officials could not expel students whose disruptive conduct was caused by their disabilities. The court pointed out that students with disabilities could be expelled when there was no relationship between their misconduct and their disabilities, a perspective that became known as the manifestation of the disability doctrine. Further, the court reasoned that disruptive special education students could be transferred to more restrictive settings as long as school officials followed the proper change in placement procedures.

The Fifth Circuit broadened the manifestation of the disability doctrine in *S-1 v. Turlington* (*Turlington*)[10] after one of an array of students in Florida who were expelled for acts of misconduct requested a manifestation hearing. The superintendent responded that because the student was not classified as emotionally disturbed, the misconduct was not a manifestation of his disability. In overturning the expulsion, the court found that a manifestation determination must be made by a specialized and knowledgeable group of persons. The court explained that even with expulsions, school officials could not completely cease serving students with disabilities, even in situations where there was no relationship between their misconduct and disability, and they were properly expelled by following the IDEA's procedures.

A case from the Fourth Circuit, affirming an earlier order from Virginia, illustrates that it is not necessarily difficult to establish connections between student disabilities and acts of misconduct. In *School Board of the County of Prince William v. Malone*[11] a student with a learning disability was involved in drug transactions. After a committee of special educators was satisfied that there was no causal relationship between the student's disability and his involvement in the drug transactions, he was expelled. On judicial review, a federal trial court decided that a relationship did, in fact, exist, because the student's learning disability caused him to have a poor self-image, which, in turn, led him to seek peer approval by becoming involved in the drug transactions. The court rejected the expulsion as improper because the student's learning disability prevented him from understanding the long-term consequences of his actions.

The early cases permitted school officials to exclude students with disabilities who posed dangers to themselves and/or others as long as educators followed proper procedures. For example, in *Jackson v. Franklin County School Board*,[12] the Fifth Circuit affirmed an order supporting a school board in Mississippi's exclusion of a student who was diagnosed as having a psychosexual disorder. Although a youth court committed the student to a state hospital for treatment, educational officials refused to admit him when he tried to return to school following his release from the hospital. The court agreed with the recommendation of educators that the student be placed in a private facility because of the danger that he presented to others.

Supreme Court Decision

In 1988 the Supreme Court handed down its first, and only, opinion involving discipline under the IDEA in *Honig v. Doe* (*Honig*),[13] a dispute concerning two special education students identified as John Doe and Jack Smith. Doe, who was emotionally disturbed with aggressive tendencies, attended a developmental center for children with disabilities. Soon after Doe was placed in the center, he assaulted a peer and broke a school window. Doe was initially suspended for five days, but was later placed on an indefinite suspension pending an expulsion hearing. Doe's lawyer unsuccessfully asked school officials to cancel the expulsion hearing and to reconvene a meeting of his individualized education program (IEP) team. Judicial review began after school board representatives ignored the attorney's request. A federal trial court eventually cancelled the expulsion hearing, ordered Doe's readmission to school, and prevented educators from excluding him while officials sought to place him in an alternative setting.

Smith was also emotionally disturbed and displayed aggressive tendencies. Educators placed Smith in a special education program within a regular school on a trial basis. After he committed a number of acts of misconduct, school authorities reduced Smith's program to a half-day schedule. Although his grandparents agreed to this reduction, they were not advised of their rights or options regarding Smith's IEP. Following an incident wherein he made sexual comments to female students, Smith was suspended for five days and school officials recommended his expulsion. Officials continued Smith's suspension pending resolution of expulsion proceedings. When Smith's attorney objected to the expulsion hearing, board officials canceled it and offered either to restore the half-day program or provide him with home tutoring. Smith's grandparents chose the home tutoring option.

> In the IDEA, Congress sought to strip school officials of their *unilateral* authority to exclude students with disabilities for disciplinary infractions, particularly children who were emotionally disturbed.

In the litigation initiated by Doe and Smith, now known as *Honig v. Doe*, a federal trial court in California, the Ninth Circuit, and the Supreme Court[14] agreed that students with disabilities could not be expelled for misbehavior that was related to their disabilities. The Supreme Court acknowledged that in enacting the IDEA, Congress intended to limit the authority of school officials to exclude students with disabilities, even for disciplinary purposes:

> We think it clear, however, that Congress very much meant to strip schools of the *unilateral* authority they had traditionally employed to exclude disabled students, particularly emotionally disturbed students, from school. In so doing, Congress did not leave school administrators powerless to deal with dangerous students; it did, however, deny school officials their former right to "self help," and directed that in the future the removal of disabled students could be accomplished only with the permission of the parents or, as a last resort, the courts.[15]

The Supreme Court did not leave school officials without recourse, as the Justices added that officials could suspend students with disabilities for up to 10 days if they posed immediate threats to the safety of others. The Court suggested that during the 10-day "cooling off" period, school officials should seek to reach agreements with parents for alternate placements for their children. In the event that parents adamantly refused to consent to changes in placements, the Court pointed out that officials could seek judicial aid. Under such circumstances the Court observed that educators were not required to exhaust administrative remedies prior to seeking judicial relief if they could show that administrative review would have been futile or inadequate. The Justices maintained that in appropriate cases the judiciary could temporarily prevent students who were dangerous from attending school.

At the same time, the Supreme Court added that officials could impose normal, non-placement-changing procedures such as, "the use of study carrels, time outs, detention, or the restriction of privileges."[16] The Court concluded by pointing out that the IDEA created a presumption in favor of students' current educational placements that school officials could overcome only by showing that preserving the status quo was substantially likely to result in injuries to those children and/or others.

Post-*Honig* Litigation

Since *Honig* cleared up many, but by no means all, issues regarding the discipline of special education students, litigation continued. *Honig* specified that students with disabilities could not be expelled for misbehavior that was related to their disabilities. Moreover, *Honig* suggested that educators could employ ordinary disciplinary sanctions that did not cause changes in placements, such as short-term suspensions of up to 10 school days.

In 1989 the Tenth Circuit affirmed that short-term disciplinary measures were not changes in placements under the IDEA.[17] The dispute began when the parents of two students from Kansas with histories of academic and behavior problems objected to the use of in-school suspensions and time-outs. The court commented that while these short-term measures did not amount to changes in placements, since they were matters relating to the education of the students, they were subject to the IDEA's administrative due process procedures.

By sanctioning suspensions of up to 10 school days in *Honig*, the Supreme Court envisioned a "cooling off" period to afford school officials and parents time to work together to devise other placements for students if they were needed. Unfortunately, educators and parents do not always agree generally, and sometimes cannot agree specifically on other options during the 10-day suspension periods. When parents and educators fail to agree, disputes are subject to the often lengthy administrative and judicial process.

Honig did give school officials the ability to seek injunctions to remove students with disabilities who are dangerous or who create serious disruptions to the educational process while administrative and judicial proceedings are pending. In such situations, the burden is on school officials to demonstrate that students are truly dangerous and that removal from their then-current educational placements is the only feasible option.

In the face of disruptive behavior by children with disabilities, school boards began filing suits seeking *Honig* injunctions to remove students who were dangerous. In Virginia, a commonwealth court granted an injunction against a 12-year-old student who was involved in fights, struck and yelled obscenities at school officials, and had to be restrained by the police on multiple occasions.[18]

A year later another commonwealth court in Virginia enjoined a student who set a fire in a school locker, among other infractions, from returning to class.[19] Similarly, a federal trial court in Illinois issued an injunction barring a student who violently struck other children and threatened to kill students and staff.[20] Finally, a state court in New York declared that educational officials met their burden of showing that a student, who ran out of the school waving an iron bar while threatening to kill someone, was likely to endanger other children if he returned to school.[21]

Courts also ordered alternative placements when granting *Honig* injunctions. A federal trial court in Texas prohibited a student who assaulted classmates and teachers, destroyed school property, used profanity, and threatened to kill himself and others from attending general education classes.[22] Moreover, the court decreed that pending the completion of the administrative review process, the student could either attend a behavioral class recommended by school officials or receive home tutoring.

In a case from New York, a federal trial court directed school officials to place a student in a special education class pending completion of a due process hearing.[23] The student frequently exhibited aggressive behavior such as punching other children, sticking a pencil in another student's ear, throwing his shoes at staff, hitting faculty, tipping over desks, and throwing chairs. In like fashion, a federal trial court in Florida granted an injunction allowing school board officials to transfer a student who had been involved in 43 instances of aggressive behavior to a special education center.[24]

Not all school board officials succeeded in securing *Honig* injunctions. A federal trial court in Missouri refused to allow the removal of a child who made numerous threats to peers and school officials, repeatedly exploded in anger, and threw furniture.[25] Although he injured a peer during one of these outbursts and teachers testified that they were afraid of him, the court did not think that this was enough to establish that serious personal injury was likely to occur if he remained in his current placement. In another dispute, a federal trial court in Pennsylvania refused to issue an injunction, asserting that school officials failed to show that they had taken every reasonable measure to mitigate the danger that the student at issue posed.[26]

The Eighth Circuit provided school officials with practical guidance on the removal of students with disabilities from their then-current educational settings in *Light v. Parkway C-2 School District.*[27] The court allowed the removal of a student from Missouri with mental disabilities, who exhibited a steady stream of aggressive and disruptive behaviors, from her then-current special education placement, on the basis that children whose misbehaviors flowed directly from their disabilities were subject to removal if they posed substantial risks of injuries to themselves or others. In addition to showing that this student presented such a danger, the court acknowledged that officials had to demonstrate that they made reasonable efforts to accommodate her disabilities so as to minimize the likelihood that she would injure herself or others. The court emphasized that only a showing of the likelihood of injury was required and that serious harm need not be inflicted before children could be considered likely to cause injury. The court further specified that injury is not defined solely as an infliction that draws blood or sends a victim to an emergency room but includes bruises, bites, and poked eyes.

Another issue that emerged in the years after *Honig* was whether students who were not yet identified as students with disabilities were entitled to the IDEA's protections if they claimed to be eligible. In a case where there was a disagreement over whether a student was qualified for IDEA services, education officials sought his expulsion for bringing a gun to school. In *Hacienda La Puente Unified School District of Los Angeles v. Honig,*[28] the Ninth Circuit interpreted *Honig* as requiring educational officials to provide all students with disabilities, regardless of whether they were previously identified as such, with the IDEA's procedural protections. The panel thus affirmed a hearing officer's order, and a trial court's refusal to hear the dispute, that the student be readmitted to school because educators violated his IDEA rights.

Along the same line, in *M.P. ex rel. D.P. v. Governing Board of the Grossmont Union High School District,*[29] a federal trial court in California held that the IDEA's procedural safeguards must be applied regardless of whether a student was previously diagnosed as having a disability. The court was of the opinion that a student who did not have a disability could attempt to be labeled as having one solely to gain the benefits of the IDEA, but remarked that the IDEA did not address this possibility. On the other hand, a federal trial court in Virginia decided that a student who was suspended for a weapons violation was not entitled to the protections of the IDEA because the question of her disability arose well after the infraction.[30] As is addressed later in this chapter, Congress specifically addressed this issue in the 2004 IDEA amendments.

A related issue is whether former special education students who were not receiving services when they committed their disciplinary infractions were entitled to the IDEA's protections. In one case, where a student was removed from special education at his mother's request because he no longer wished to receive special education, a federal trial court in Wisconsin answered in the affirmative. School officials removed the student from a special education class for the emotionally disturbed at his mother's request but against his teacher's recommendation. In *Steldt v. School Board of the Riverdale School District*,[31] the student was expelled for a series of acts including assaults on peers and school personnel. The court, noting that the mother's request to remove her son from special education did not change his status as being in need of special education, insisted that he was entitled to the IDEA's protections.

Another related issue is how school officials should treat students who were evaluated but not classified as having disabilities. As with most disputes, the answer is based on the unique facts of each case. In one case, a school's IEP team was convinced that a student from Illinois did not require special education, but his mother contested its recommendation. The Seventh Circuit maintained that the student was not entitled to an injunction barring his expulsion while administrative proceedings were pending.[32] The court refused the student's request where school officials lacked either knowledge or reasonable suspicion on which to decide that he had a disability, since not one single individual, teacher, guardian, parent, or educator had proposed or suggested that he may have needed special education. In a case such as this, the court wrote that educators needed to employ a flexible approach when applying the IDEA's stay put provision and should not apply it automatically to every student who was referred for a placement in special education.

In *Honig*, the Supreme Court held that special education students could be suspended for up to 10 days. Unfortunately, the Court failed to indicate whether the 10-day limit was consecutive or cumulative. In a case from Washington, the Ninth Circuit, in *Parents of Student W. v. Puyallup School District*,[33] interpreted *Honig* as rejecting the proposition that the 10-day limit referred to 10 total days. The court determined that the school board's suspension guidelines, wherein each exclusion triggered an evaluation to consider whether a student was receiving a FAPE, were lawful. On the other hand, in *Manchester School District v. Charles M.F.*,[34] the federal trial court in New Hampshire decreed that cumulative suspensions totaling more than 10 days constituted a pattern of exclusion that resulted in changes of placement.

In *Turlington*,[35] discussed earlier, the Fifth Circuit ruled that even when special education students were properly expelled by following all of the IDEA's due process procedures, the law did not authorize a complete cessation of services. According to *Turlington*, school boards must still provide special education and related services to students with disabilities who have been expelled for disciplinary infractions.

This issue arose again in Virginia in 1992 when commonwealth officials submitted their three-year plan for special education to the U.S. Department of Education. The plan included a regulation declaring that students with disabilities could be disciplined in the same manner as those without disabilities if there was no causal relationship between their misconduct and their disabilities. The U.S. Department of Education responded by notifying officials in Virginia that they could not discontinue educational services to special education students who had been expelled, even if the discipline resulted from behavior unrelated to their disabilities. When officials left the regulation unchanged, the ensuing dispute eventually ended up in the courts.

Following years of litigation, the Fourth Circuit, in *Commonwealth of Virginia Department of Education v. Riley* (*Riley*),[36] reasoned that the IDEA did not require local school boards to discipline students with disabilities differently from those without disabilities when their misconduct was unrelated to their disabilities. The court found that the IDEA only requires officials to provide students with disabilities with access to a FAPE that as with any right, could be forfeited by conduct antithetical to the right itself. The court concluded that board officials were not required to provide educational services to students with disabilities who forfeited their rights to a FAPE by willfully engaging in conduct so serious as to warrant the ultimate penalty of expulsion.

Later in the same year that the Fourth Circuit resolved *Riley*, the Seventh Circuit reached a similar outcome in *Doe v. Board of Education of Oak Park & River Forest High School District 200* (*Oak Park*).[37] When school officials in Illinois expelled a student for possessing a pipe and a small amount of marijuana, the board's evaluation team was unconvinced that there was a causal relationship between his disability and misconduct. Under the circumstances, a federal trial court observed that the board was not required to provide the student with alternative educational services during the expulsion period. The Seventh Circuit agreed, declaring that the IDEA was not intended to shield special education students from the usual consequences of misconduct when their misbehavior was unrelated to their disabilities.

Riley and *Oak Park* can be contrasted with the order of a federal trial court in Arizona. In *Magyar v. Tucson Unified School District*,[38] school officials expelled a student with a learning disability after he gave an assault-style knife to a peer. In ordering the student's reinstatement the court interpreted the IDEA as requiring school officials to provide all students with disabilities with a FAPE. The court thought that insofar as the use of the word *all* in the IDEA was clear and unequivocal, it did not include an exception for misbehaving students. Again, as discussed in the next section on the 1997 and 2004 IDEA amendments, the IDEA now includes language declaring that special education services must continue during expulsions.

Figure 6.1 summarizes the procedural steps required in disciplining a student with disabilities.

Figure 6.1   Procedural Steps and Timelines in the Disciplinary Process

When students with disabilities misbehave, educators should take the following steps (time limitations are in brackets):

- Take whatever measures are necessary to restore order and maintain discipline (immediately).
- Suspend students (for up to 10 school days) by following normal procedures.
- Conduct functional behavioral assessments (FBAs) and develop behavioral intervention plans (BIPs) if these are not already in place; review the FBAs and BIPs if they are in place (within 10 school days).
- If expulsion is under consideration, complete manifestation determination meetings (within 10 school days), keeping in mind that
  - If officials determine that student misbehaviors were manifestations of their disabilities, the children may not be expelled but may be moved to more restrictive placements by following the IDEA's change in placement procedures.
  - If officials decide that there is no relationship between student disabilities and misconduct, the children may be expelled, but they must continue to receive special education services during the expulsion period.
- If student misconduct involved weapons, drugs, or the infliction of serious bodily injuries, consider placing offenders in interim alternative educational settings (for up to 45 school days).
- Seek hearing officer or judicial orders to change the placements (immediately) if the students are not expelled or moved to interim alternative educational settings and school personnel are of the opinion that maintaining their then-current placements is likely to result in injuries to the students with disabilities and/or others.
- At the end of expulsion periods or interim alternative placements, either return students to their former settings or develop new ones by following the IDEA's change in placement procedures.

The 1997 and 2004 IDEA Amendments

Against this backdrop of litigation, combined with pressure from advocates for both school boards and students with disabilities, Congress added disciplinary provisions to the IDEA in 1997. These amendments implemented the most far-reaching changes to the IDEA since its initial enactment in 1975. Some of these provisions simply codified existing case law, others clarified gray areas, and some resolved judicial differences of opinion. Since the 1997 amendments did not settle all issues, litigation continued.[39] When Congress amended the IDEA again in 2004, it further refined the disciplinary provisions. The cumulative result of these two amendments is that the IDEA now includes comprehensive guidelines dealing with disciplining students with disabilities.[40] Consequently, litigation in this area has decreased.

Authority of School Personnel

The IDEA outlines the authority and obligations of school officials in disciplining students with disabilities. The current disciplinary language provides educators with more guidance than in the past. Still, questions do arise that lead to litigation.

Case-by-Case Determination

Recognizing that disciplinary infractions may present school officials with unique situations, Congress inserted a clause into the 2004 version of the IDEA affording education personnel flexibility. The IDEA explicitly permits educators to consider unique circumstances on case-by-case bases when evaluating whether changes in placement are necessary for students with disabilities who violate school rules.[41]

Suspensions and Placements in Interim Alternative Educational Settings

The IDEA clearly permits educational officials to remove students with disabilities who violate school rules to appropriate interim alternative settings or other placements or suspend them for up to 10 school days.[42] Even so, educators can implement such measures only to the extent that they use similar punishments when disciplining students who do not have disabilities. In addition, students may be removed to interim alternative educational settings for up to 45 school days under specified circumstances, without regard for whether their misbehaviors are manifestations of their disabilities.[43]

Short-Term Suspensions

> The IDEA now affords school personnel the explicit authority to suspend special education students for not more than 10 school days as long as similar sanctions apply to students in regular education.

The IDEA now affords school personnel the explicit authority to suspend special education students for not more than 10 school days as long as similar sanctions apply to students in regular education.[44] Under these circumstances, educators must conduct functional behavioral assessments of students if they have not already been completed; in addition, officials must address the misconduct of students so that it does not recur.[45] In such a case, the federal trial court in the District of Columbia thought that charter school officials violated the IDEA by failing to conduct a functional behavioral assessment and develop a behavioral intervention plan for a student who had multiple suspensions.[46] The court also insisted that charter school officials were obligated to provide the student with an alternative placement after his 10th day of suspension.

In a related matter, the IDEA's regulations specify that a series of removals of students with disabilities resulting in a pattern of exclusions cumulating to more than 10 school days may be considered changes in placements.[47] Pursuant to the regulation, in evaluating whether changes in placements occurred, decision makers must consider such factors as the length of each removal, the total amount of time that students are removed, and the proximity of the exclusions to one another.[48] The regulation adds that if students are suspended for misbehavior substantially similar to past misbehavior that was determined to be a manifestation of their disabilities, changes in placements occurred.[49] On the other hand, the Eighth Circuit acknowledged that school board officials in Minnesota were justified in repeatedly suspending a student for misbehaviors that endangered herself, peers, and staff, since her parents rejected offers to transfer her to a more appropriate setting.[50]

Suspensions for separate, but dissimilar, acts of misconduct may exceed 10 cumulative days in one school year.[51] School board officials are not required to continue special education services for students who are removed for up to 10 cumulative days unless educational services are routinely provided to students without disabilities under similar circumstances.[52] If subsequent suspensions exceed 10 cumulative school days in one year, however, services must begin again after the 10th day.[53] State laws may impose further restrictions on the length and number of suspensions.

Transfers to Other Settings for Disciplinary Reasons

The IDEA allows school officials to act unilaterally in placing students with disabilities in interim alternative educational settings for up to 45 school days for weapons and knowing drug violations. In an important clarification, this provision specifies that this period is for 45 school days, not calendar days.[54] Specifically, the IDEA and its regulations authorize school officials to transfer students to alternative settings if they carry or possess weapons at school, on school premises, or at school functions;[55] knowingly possess, use, sell, or solicit drugs under those same circumstances;[56] or inflict serious bodily injury on other persons at school, on school premises, or at school functions.[57] In such instances, IEP teams must identify interim alternative settings for students.[58] Further, in a case from South Dakota, the Eighth Circuit explained that making interim alternative placements under the IDEA does not require hearings, such as those typically provided prior to expulsion, since they are not the equivalent of long-term suspensions.[59]

The IDEA obligates school officials to conduct functional behavioral assessments and to implement behavioral intervention plans for students who are placed in interim alternative settings.[60] If parents disagree with the placements in the interim alternative settings and request hearings, students must remain in these placements pending the outcome of hearings or until the expiration of the 45-day period.[61] After the expiration of the 45-day period, students are entitled to return to their former placements even if hearings regarding school board proposals to change their placements are still pending.[62]

Weapons, Alcohol, and Drugs. School officials have the explicit authority to transfer students with disabilities to appropriate interim alternative placements for up to 45 school days for having weapons, knowingly possessing drugs, or presenting serious risks of injuries to others. This provision applies when a student

(i) carries or possesses a weapon to or at school, on school premises, or to or at a school function under the jurisdiction of a State or local educational agency;

(ii) knowingly possesses or uses illegal drugs, or sells or solicits the sale of a controlled substance, while at school, on school premises, or at a school function under the jurisdiction of a State or local educational agency; or

(iii) has inflicted serious bodily injury upon another person while at school, on school premises, or at a school function under the jurisdiction of a State or local educational agency.[63]

School officials have the explicit authority to transfer students with disabilities to appropriate interim alternative placements for up to 45 school days for having weapons, knowingly possessing drugs, or presenting serious risks of injuries to others.

The IDEA defines weapons and illegal drugs by referring to other federal legislation.[64] In this regard, the IDEA expanded the definition of a dangerous weapon beyond the previous definition enunciated in the Gun-Free Schools Act. Under this definition, what can be considered a dangerous weapon includes other instruments, devices, materials, and substances capable of inflicting harm in addition to firearms, but does not include small pocket knives.[65] The IDEA defines an illegal drug as a controlled substance, but excludes controlled substances that may be legally prescribed by physicians.[66] The Controlled Substances Act,[67] which is too lengthy to review here, sets forth the full categorization of controlled substances.

Infliction of Serious Bodily Injury. The IDEA allows educators to remove students with disabilities to interim alternative settings for inflicting serious bodily injuries.[68] The IDEA defines serious bodily injury by referencing another section of the United States Code, the official compilation of federal statutes.[69]

> The IDEA allows educators to remove students with disabilities to interim alternative settings for inflicting serious bodily injuries.

Serious bodily injury, a provision which has been subject to scant litigation, involves a substantial risk of death, extreme physical pain, protracted and obvious disfigurement, or protracted loss or impairment of the function of a bodily member, organ, or mental faculty.[70] Serious bodily injury may be contrasted with bodily injury, which generally involves only cuts, abrasions, bruises, burns, or other temporary injuries.[71]

Other Infractions. The IDEA permits school officials to remove students with disabilities from inclusive settings, moving them to interim alternative placements for infractions other than those specifically listed in its provisions.[72] When exercising this case-by-case authority, school officials are likely to be faced with parental challenges. Prior case law indicates that courts are likely to uphold the steps taken by educational officials as long as they can reasonably justify their actions.

As illustrated by a pre-2004 case from Texas, one such circumstance when educational officials might seek to remove a student with disabilities from school could be an act of sexual harassment. In *Randy M. v. Texas City ISD*,[73] officials recommended the transfer of a special education student to an alternative education program for the remainder of a school year after he, in consort with a peer, ripped the pants off a female student. Prior to making this recommendation, the child's IEP team determined that his misconduct was not a manifestation of his disability. When the student's parents sought to prevent the transfer, a federal trial court refused their request, expressing its view that the disciplinary actions of the school officials were entirely appropriate under the circumstances. The court explained that officials were justified in taking stern and aggressive remedial action when faced with such conduct.

Another circumstance that can lead to the removal of students with disabilities is behavior that may not necessarily have caused serious bodily injury but that if repeated, has the potential to do so. In such a case, an appellate court in New York approved the removal of a child who hit classmates and teachers, acknowledging that educators had shown that allowing the student to return to school was likely to result in injury to himself or others.[74]

Functional Behavioral Assessments and Behavioral Intervention Plans

The IDEA requires school personnel to conduct functional behavioral assessments (FBAs) and implement behavioral intervention plans (BIPs) under specified circumstances if they are not already in place, or to review such assessments and plans if they have been implemented for students with disabilities. In other words, officials must perform FBAs and implement BIPs whenever students with disabilities are removed from their then-current placements for disciplinary reasons for more than 10 school days.[75] Educators must also execute FBAs and BIPs, if they have not already been done, if they decide that student misbehaviors are not manifestations of their disabilities.[76]

> The IDEA requires school personnel to conduct functional behavioral assessments and implement behavioral intervention plans, if they are not already in place, or review such assessments and plans if they have been implemented for students with disabilities.

Even though it calls for their creation, neither the IDEA nor its regulations provide much guidance as to what should be included in FBAs or BIPs. Interestingly, in the wake of congressional action in adding disciplinary provisions to the IDEA, while overall litigation regarding discipline has decreased, many disputes have arisen involving questions about FBAs and BIPs.

In a dispute over a BIP that arose in Illinois, the Seventh Circuit held that absent substantive requirements for its content, the challenged plan could not have fallen short of criteria that did not exist.[77] Further, the Eighth Circuit, in a case from Minnesota, went so far as to comment that a BIP does not need to be written;[78] the court's position notwithstanding, school officials would be well advised that the safest course of action is to put both FBAs and BIPs in writing.

The lack of substantive criteria for FBAs and BIPs aside, this does not mean their development is unimportant. As shown below, courts not only often consider FBAs and BIPs when reviewing the overall appropriateness of proposed IEPs but also have been asked to evaluate whether students required FBAs or BIPS in given circumstances.

For the most part, courts defer to the expertise of hearing officers when reviewing administrative orders in evaluating whether FBAs and BIPs were reasonable in light of the evidence. In rejecting a school board's contention that an FBA and BIP were not needed for a child with autism, since the behaviors at issue were related to the child's disability, a federal trial court in Alabama upheld a hearing officer's adjudication that school board officials denied the child a FAPE.[79]

On the other hand, the Second Circuit agreed with a state review officer from New York that the failure of officials to conduct an FBA for a child with autism did not deprive him of a FAPE because his IEP adequately addressed his behavior.[80] In a later case from New York with a similar outcome, the Second Circuit explained that a failure of educational personnel to conduct an FBA does not render an IEP inadequate as long as the IEP adequately identifies a student's behavioral impediments and implements strategies to address that behavior.[81]

Also, a federal trial court in Virginia decided that board officials violated the IDEA by not conducting an FBA and developing a BIP for a special education student who had been suspended on multiple occasions.[82] The court agreed with a hearing officer that educators overlooked clear signs of the student's disability in failing to evaluate his suspected disability fully. By the same token, the federal trial court in the nation's capital was convinced that board officials should have conducted an FBA and developed a BIP for a student whose teachers noted that his misbehavior impacted his classroom functioning and that his behavior had declined.[83] The failure to do so, the court observed, denied the student a FAPE because his behavioral problems seriously affected his academic performance.

The Ninth Circuit affirmed that a BIP was unnecessary for a student from California whose behavior problems were neither severe nor caused harm or presented a serious threat of harm to persons or property.[84] Similarly, in New York, a federal trial court and the Second Circuit agreed with a hearing officer that an FBA was not required where a child's mother, teacher, and therapists reported that her interfering behaviors were diminished and well under control.[85]

Expulsions

The IDEA permits educators to expel students with disabilities as long as the misbehaviors giving rise to violations of school rules were not manifestations of their disabilities. Again, though, under these circumstances expulsions must be treated in the same manner and for the same duration as they would have been for students who did not have disabilities.[86]

Provision of Special Education Services During Expulsions

The IDEA makes it clear that special education services must continue during expulsions of students with disabilities.

The IDEA makes it clear that special education services must continue during expulsions.[87] This provision comports with the position previously taken by the U.S. Department of Education, effectively reversing judicial orders to the contrary.[88] The addition of this section to the IDEA ended a controversy that existed among the federal circuits prior to the enactment of the 1997 amendments.

Manifestation Doctrine

> When school officials contemplate the expulsions of children in special education placements, the IDEA requires educators first to evaluate whether student misbehaviors are manifestations of their disabilities.

As noted earlier in this chapter, the courts have long recognized that expulsions of students in special education settings constitute changes in placements. Expelling students for misconducts that were manifestations of their disabilities, the courts reasoned, would have been the equivalent of punishing children for behavior over which they had no control. In addition, the courts agree that expulsions would have resulted in denying students the FAPEs they were entitled to under federal law.

When school officials contemplate the expulsions of children in special education placements, the IDEA requires educators first to evaluate whether student misbehaviors are manifestations of their disabilities. If officials agree that there is no connection between student disabilities and their misconduct, they may be expelled.[89] Since it is highly likely that parents will challenge the expulsions of their children, it is imperative for school officials to follow proper procedures when making manifestation determinations.

Personnel Making the Manifestation Determination

It is up to school officials, parents, and relevant members of IEP teams to judge whether forms of student misconduct are manifestations of their disabilities.[90] Members of manifestation review committees should have personal knowledge of the students involved and of special education as well as an understanding of the characteristics of the disabilities of the children. The IDEA's regulations specify that parents of children with disabilities along with regular and special education teachers, a school board representative who is qualified to provide or supervise special education, a person qualified to interpret evaluation data, and the students (if appropriate) should be included in meetings at which IEPs are developed, reviewed, or revised.[91] Other qualified persons, such as current teachers or guidance counselors, may be called in to provide additional information.[92]

Parents must be invited to attend meetings where manifestation determinations are to be made about their children since the IDEA's regulations afford them the right to attend meetings in which the educational placements of their young are discussed.[93] Since manifestation determinations affect student placements, parents have the right to attend the meetings at which they are made.

Timeline

Manifestation determinations should be made immediately after but no later than 10 days following decisions to remove students from their then-current educational placements for more than 10 days.[94] Even so, the federal trial court in Maine pointed out that a delay in conducting a manifestation hearing was of no consequence where the parents were given the opportunity to participate and the delay did not affect its outcome.[95] The court observed that the board's special education director made multiple unsuccessful attempts to contact the parents in seeking to schedule the hearing within the 10-day time period.

Manifestation as Defined in the IDEA

Prior to 1997 the IDEA did not include a precise definition of the term *manifestation*. The current version of the IDEA, refined by the 2004 amendments, specifies that misconduct should be considered to be manifestations of students' disabilities if the behaviors were caused by or had a direct and substantial relationship to their disabilities or if it was the direct result of failures to implement their IEPs.[96] Earlier case law can provide some guidance on how this new language can be interpreted.

The language presently included in the IDEA's definition of manifestation (see Figure 6.2) is similar to the wording that the Ninth Circuit used in *Doe v. Maher*, the case that on appeal, became known as *Honig v. Doe*.[97] The court acknowledged that manifestation of the disability refers to "conduct that is caused by, or has a direct and substantial relationship to" the student's disability.[98] The court offered further clarification in explaining that disabilities must significantly impair students' behavioral controls, but their definition does not embrace conduct that "bears only an attenuated relationship" to children's disabilities.[99]

Figure 6.2   Definition of Manifestation

The IDEA defines *manifestation* as conduct that was caused by or had a direct and substantial relationship to students' disabilities, or conduct that was the direct result of the schools' failure to implement students' IEPs.[100]

In a judgment handed down before the 2004 amendments and the current definition of manifestation became effective, a federal trial court in New York overturned a finding that a student's misconduct was not a manifestation of his disability. Although it is a pre-2004 amendment opinion, this case illustrates one way that a disability may be deemed to have a direct relationship to a student's misconduct. When the student was disciplined after an altercation with a schoolmate, he claimed that his actions were in response to taunting from the other child about his being in a special education placement. The court was thus satisfied that the student's disability was directly involved in the ensuing altercation for which he was disciplined.[101] While the Second Circuit overturned this judgment on other grounds, the trial court's decision remains instructive because the panel agreed that the manifestation determination was erroneous.

In another pre-2004 amendment case, the Fourth Circuit upheld a school board in Virginia's manifestation determination where a child coerced a peer into putting a threatening note in the computer file of a third student. The court was convinced that the student was aware of the consequences of sending the threatening note, and even anticipated them by enlisting the services of another child. Uncovering nothing in the student's records indicating his inability to manage his emotional problems, the court agreed that his misconduct was not a manifestation of his disability.[102] More recently, a federal trial court in Virginia upheld an IEP team's determination that a student's misconduct was not a manifestation of his disability.[103] The court ruled that evidence supported the IEP team's determination, since the student, along with peers, shot paintballs at his school and vehicles parked on school property. Moreover, the student suggested the idea, offered to drive, stashed the paintball gun in his car, and engaged in the activity three times stretching for hours.

Decisions Manifestation Teams Must Make

Along with evaluating whether misconduct was caused by or had a direct and substantial relationship to student disabilities, manifestation review committees must consider whether behavior was due to IEPs that were not properly implemented. Interestingly, the IDEA requires manifestation review committees to find manifestations when misbehavior is the "direct result of the local educational agency's failure to implement the IEP,"[104] but does not describe an inappropriate IEP as a basis for finding a manifestation. In a case dealing with this situation, a federal trial court in Virginia wrote that even where it is clear that school officials failed to meet their obligations under the IDEA and deprived a child of a FAPE, the team was not required to find a manifestation.[105] The court held that insofar as the student's inappropriate IEP was implemented as written, his behavior could not have been attributed to the failure to implement an IEP. This could lead to the absurd result that even if the denial of a FAPE is the direct cause of misbehavior, offending students can still be expelled. In other words, officials may be able to expel students even when disciplinary infractions result from the officials' own failures.

If manifestation review committees decide that the misconduct of students either involves manifestations of their disabilities or results from inappropriate placements or IEPs, children may not be expelled or suspended for more than 10 days and school officials must reconsider their then-current placements. Also, school officials can consider making appropriate nonpunitive changes in placements such as the use of time-out rooms and study carrels,[106] which can be implemented subject to the IDEA's procedural safeguards and least restrictive environment provisions. Students may be suspended for more than 10 days, or expelled, if their misconduct is not caused by their disabilities or does not result from inappropriate IEPs or placements.

Consideration of the Student's Disability Classification

Manifestation determinations must be individualized. Blanket judgments based on the characteristics generally exhibited by others with the same disability are not allowed. Therefore, manifestation review committees must consider whether disabilities, as they impact students, are related to specific types of misconduct. An important consideration here is the severity of student disabilities.[107] Manifestation review committees should also evaluate whether students have previously unidentified disabilities that could have caused their wrongdoings.[108] Further, manifestation determinations must refer to specific incidents since generalizations cannot be the key factor. In other words, manifestation review committees must consider whether the disabilities exhibited by students could have caused the specific misconduct giving rise to their proposed expulsions.

Consideration of Causes Other Than Disability

Manifestation review committees must consider other factors that could have caused student misbehaviors.[109] When multiple factors, of which a disability is one, contribute to misbehavior, as long as manifestation review committees can establish connections between the disabilities and misconduct, students cannot be expelled.

Reevaluation Requirement

If evaluation data are not up to date, school officials should conduct reevaluations.[110] Even though the IDEA requires educational officials to conduct reevaluations every three years, reevaluations are warranted earlier if the circumstances surrounding students change. One circumstance that could require an earlier evaluation is a sudden change in the behavior of students. At least one court ruled that reevaluations are required whenever IEP teams are contemplating significant changes in placements.[111] Reevaluations should include psychological assessments designed specifically to elicit data relative to the behavior that led to the disciplinary action. If the professionals who conducted the most recent assessments are not part of the groups making manifestation determinations, they should be consulted regarding the specific incidents in question. If available evaluation data are more than one year old, school officials should make sure that reevaluations are completed before convening manifestation determination meetings.

Making Decisions

According to the IDEA and its regulations, teams making manifestation determinations must consider all relevant information, including evaluative and diagnostic results and observations of children.[112] After manifestation review committees study the relevant information, members should proceed as they would in making other identifications, classifications, or placements. Manifestation review committees must thus exercise sound professional judgment. Members of manifestation review committees must rely on their professional knowledge, knowledge of the students, and understanding of the circumstances that led to the misconduct in making these critical judgments.

Appeals

As are any matters related to the special education programs of students, manifestation determinations are subject to the IDEA's administrative appeals process. The statute dictates that when dealing with manifestation determinations, officials must expedite hearings, meaning that they must occur within 20 school days of the date on which they were requested; decisions must be rendered within 10 days of hearings.[113] If parents contest manifestation determinations, school officials must postpone any long-term suspensions or expulsions until hearings have been completed, even though students may remain in interim alternative educational settings.[114]

Authority of Hearing Officers

The IDEA affords hearing officers the authority to change student placements.[115] Essentially, when hearing appeals, officers have two options: They may either return students to the placements from which they were removed or mandate their being placed in interim alternative settings. If hearing officers choose the latter option, placements may not be for more than 45 school days.

Placement Pending Appeals

When parents challenge the placement decisions of school boards, the IDEA requires officials to permit students to remain in their then-current placements pending the outcome of the hearings.[116] As stated above, an exception exists when parents challenge board actions that would place children in interim alternative settings for disciplinary reasons. The IDEA declares that while such appeals are pending, students are to remain in interim alternative settings until hearing officers render judgments or the 45-day limit has expired.[117] In these circumstances, hearings must take place within 20 days and decisions must be rendered within another 10 days.[118]

> Hearing officers have the authority to order changes in placement to appropriate interim alternative educational settings for periods of up to 45 days. This change does not prohibit school officials from seeking injunctive relief to bar students from attending school.

Injunctions to Allow School Boards to Exclude Dangerous Students

In *Honig* the Supreme Court granted school officials the authority to seek injunctions to exclude dangerous students with disabilities from regular education environments. Hearing officers now have the authority to order changes in placement to appropriate interim alternative educational settings for periods of up to 45 days, when school officials can demonstrate that keeping students in their then-current placements is substantially likely to result in injuries to the students at issue and/or others.[119] Still, this change does not prohibit school officials from seeking injunctive relief to bar students from attending school.

In a case that was litigated prior to the most recent changes in the IDEA and its regulations, a federal trial court in Alabama acknowledged that the IDEA allows school boards to pursue orders from hearing officers but does not require their doing so prior to seeking injunctions.[120] The court ruled that the expedited hearing provision in the amended IDEA is permissive; the exhaustion of administrative remedies is not required if boards choose to seek *Honig* injunctions.

An appellate court in New York, in like fashion, affirmed an injunction allowing school board officials to exclude a student, placing him on homebound instruction after he committed acts of misconduct, including hitting peers and teachers.[121] The court agreed that the evidence presented by educators clearly demonstrated that allowing the student to return to school was substantially likely to result in injury to himself and/or others.

Rights of Students Not Yet Identified as Having Disabilities

The IDEA and its regulations require school board officials to extend the statute's protections to students who have not been determined to be eligible for special education, if educators knew that children had disabilities before the misbehavior occurred.[122] The IDEA and its regulations also outline the circumstances under which educators are considered to have knowledge that students have disabilities. Factors giving rise to educator knowledge that students have disabilities are written expressed concern from parents that their children may require special education or requests for evaluations, prior behavioral and academic performance of students, and expressed concern from teachers about the performance of students.[123] If school officials conducted evaluations but did not think that students had disabilities, then boards are not considered as having knowledge of disabilities under these provisions. Further, if parents refused permission for evaluations or declined offered special education services, school officials are not deemed to have knowledge of student disabilities.[124]

If school board officials lack prior knowledge that students have disabilities, children may be disciplined in the same manner as peers who do not have disabilities.[125] Moreover, requests for evaluations made during a time period in which officials impose disciplinary sanctions must be conducted in an expedited manner.[126] However, unlike guidelines for conducting expedited hearings, neither the IDEA nor its regulations establish time periods within which these evaluations must be completed. Until these evaluations are completed, students must remain in the educational placements selected by school officials, which can be suspensions or expulsions without the receipt of educational services.[127] If, following the evaluations, school officials remain convinced that students do have disabilities, the children are entitled to special education and related services.[128]

In *Colvin v. Lowndes County, Mississippi, School District*,[129] a federal trial court held that parents had not shown that their son had a disability even though they requested that he be evaluated. The court did observe that school officials violated the IDEA by failing to provide some assessment procedure to evaluate whether the student had a disability.

In contrast, the federal trial court in Connecticut, in *J.C. v. Regional School District No. 10*,[130] decided that a student whose parents expressed concern over his poor performance and requested evaluations was entitled to the protections of the IDEA when faced with expulsion. The student was evaluated, but school officials did not believe that he was entitled to an IEP because their evaluation did not indicate that he had disabilities. When the student again faced expulsion, he was reevaluated at his parents' request; this time the school board agreed that the student had disabilities and was eligible for special education. Similarly, the federal trial court in Massachusetts overturned the expulsion of a student who failed all of her courses. Prior to conducting the student's expulsion hearing, educational

officials evaluated her and agreed that she did not have disabilities, leading her attorney to request a due process hearing to contest that outcome.
The court noted that the evaluation team's finding that the student failed
to qualify as having disabilities was not final and was subject to the pending hearing. The court reasoned that if the evaluation team's decision was
overturned by a hearing officer, the student could sufficiently state a claim
that school officials should have known that she had disabilities, entitling
her to the protections of the IDEA.[131]

Effect of the IDEA on the Juvenile
Court and Law Enforcement Authorities

The IDEA maintains that nothing in its provisions can be interpreted
as prohibiting school officials from reporting crimes committed by special
education students to the proper authorities or to impede law enforcement
and judicial authorities carrying out their responsibilities.[132] Further, if
school officials do report crimes, the IDEA requires them to furnish the
special education and disciplinary records of students to the appropriate
authorities.

In a case from Massachusetts, an appellate panel emphasized that a
juvenile court proceeding did not constitute a change in placement under
the IDEA even though it took place as a consequence of misconduct that
occurred at school.[133] The court, in upholding the student's adjudication as
a delinquent for possession of marijuana in school, pointed out that the
IDEA clearly authorized educational officials to report criminal activities
to the proper authorities.

Judicial proceedings may trigger the IDEA's change in placement provisions. In such a case, school officials in New York unsuccessfully initiated proceedings to have an eight-year-old student declared to be a person
in need of services due to his tardiness, absenteeism, and misconduct. In
dismissing the request in favor of the student, the court held that before
initiating their action, which would have changed his placement, school
officials failed to review his IEP to consider whether additional interventions had been warranted.[134]

FREQUENTLY ASKED QUESTIONS

Q: Does the IDEA create a dual system of discipline?

A: No. The IDEA does not prevent school officials from disciplining students
with disabilities. The IDEA does provide for additional procedural protections
to ensure that students with disabilities are not disciplined for behavior over
which they have no control and that the disciplinary process cannot be used
to circumvent the obligations of educators to provide special education and
related services.

Q: Is the 10-day limit on a suspension consecutive or cumulative?

A: Unless state law dictates otherwise, this limit refers to 10 consecutive days. However, a series of suspensions totaling more than 10 days in a school year may constitute a pattern of exclusion that could be considered the equivalent of an expulsion. Factors to be considered in evaluating whether multiple suspensions constitute a pattern of exclusion include the length of each suspension, the proximity of suspensions to each other, and the total amount of time the student has been excluded from school.

Q: Can the parents of students who have not been identified as having disabilities thwart the disciplinary process by claiming that their children have disabilities and requesting evaluations?

A: School officials are required to provide the IDEA's protections to students who were previously not identified as having disabilities if the educators either knew, or should have known, that the children had disabilities. Factors that officials should consider in this regard include prior parental concerns that children might require special education, requests for evaluations, behavioral and academic performances, and expressed concerns by teachers about the performance of students. If parents refused to submit their children to evaluations or to accept offered services, school officials are not required to provide the IDEA's protections in disciplinary situations. Unfortunately, the IDEA's processes can be abused and may be used to slow down the disciplinary process, but cannot be used by students who do not have disabilities to avoid disciplinary sanctions.

Q: Does the IDEA prevent school officials from referring misbehaving students to law enforcement authorities?

A: No. The IDEA specifically states that nothing in its provisions can be interpreted as prohibiting school officials from reporting crimes or impeding law enforcement or judicial authorities from carrying out their duties. Thus, when special education students are reported for suspicion of having committed crimes, school officials must furnish their special education and disciplinary records to the proper authorities.

Q: What do school officials need to do to obtain injunctions or orders from hearing officers in order to prevent dangerous students from attending school?

A: School officials must show that maintaining students in their then-current placements is likely to result in injuries to themselves and/or others. Further, officials must demonstrate that they have taken reasonable steps to control the behavior of students and that less restrictive alternatives are not feasible. For this purpose, thorough documentation of the history of student misconduct and the response of school officials is a must.

Recommendations

The IDEA makes it clear that students with disabilities are subject to the disciplinary process when they misbehave. Yet, to the extent that the IDEA entitles students with disabilities to a FAPE, additional due process may be required if disciplinary actions can result in substantial losses of educational opportunities. Perhaps no area of special education law is more contentious than the imposition of disciplinary sanctions on students with disabilities.[135]

The IDEA, its regulations, and case law strike an appropriate balance. School officials may take disciplinary actions against students with disabilities by following the IDEA's procedures. This balance allows educators to discipline misbehaving students while removing the possibility that they can be deprived of educational opportunities for behavior stemming from their disabilities. The recommendations below have been developed from the IDEA, its regulations, and case law. Even so, readers should also consult state law in this area since many jurisdictions impose additional requirements when educators discipline students with disabilities.

School officials should

- Impose normal minor disciplinary sanctions such as detentions or time-outs by following their usual procedures.
- Follow their usual procedures when suspending students with disabilities for periods of up to 10 school days.
- Immediately initiate the IDEA's due process protections whenever disciplinary sanctions may involve expulsions or transfers to other educational settings such as alternative schools.
- Determine whether acts of misconduct are manifestations of students' disabilities.
- Render manifestation determinations within 10 school days of deciding to change student placements.
- Ensure that manifestation determinations are made by school personnel, including professionals from students' IEP teams, in conjunction with children's parents.
- Make sure that parents are invited to participate in manifestation determination meetings and are notified of their rights.
- Ensure that the teams making manifestation determinations examine whether the misconduct in question either was caused by or had a direct and substantial relationship to students' disabilities.
- Make sure that the teams making manifestation determinations consider whether student IEPs were properly implemented.
- Ensure that evaluation data are current and conduct reevaluations if they are not.

- Provide special education services during expulsion periods for students who have been properly expelled pursuant to the terms of the IDEA.
- Propose new placements if IEP teams determine that the then-current placements of students did not meet their needs, especially since this may have been a contributing factor in their misbehaviors.
- Provide expedited hearings to parents who disagree with the results of manifestation determinations.
- Immediately remove students who are charged with having weapons or knowingly possessing drugs on school property or at school functions by following the normal suspension procedures.
- Place students who are charged with the possession of weapons or who knowingly have drugs on school property or at school functions in interim alternative settings for 45-day periods following their initial 10-day suspensions.
- Consider whether students who caused serious bodily harm should be removed to interim alternative settings for 45-day periods.
- Ensure that alternative settings allow students to progress in general education curricula and permit the delivery of their special education services.
- Seek judicial or hearing officer orders to remove students whose presence in school could cause a danger to themselves and/or others or could substantially interrupt the education process.
- Be prepared to show that they did everything possible to mitigate the danger or chance of disruption and that there is no less restrictive alternative than removal when seeking injunctions to exclude students from their educational programs.
- Conduct functional behavioral assessments and develop behavioral intervention plans as part of the annual IEP process for students with disabilities who have histories of misbehavior.
- Review functional behavioral assessments and behavioral intervention plans when students are faced with serious disciplinary action, or when manifestation determinations are scheduled.
- Include the following elements in functional behavioral assessments: observations of students, documenting aspects of their behavior; analysis of the situations that trigger misbehavior; review of the effectiveness of previous interventions; medical, psychological, and social data that could affect behavior; and any other information that could provide insight into the behaviors.
- Include the following elements in behavioral intervention plans: strategies for dealing with student behaviors at the time they surface, long-term plans for preventing future occurrences, supportive services that can be provided to the students to help them to deal with situations that tend to precipitate the unwanted

behaviors, expected behaviors, descriptions of inappropriate behaviors, and statements of the positive and negative consequences for (mis)behaviors.

- Afford the IDEA's protections to students who have not been identified as having disabilities but who may, in fact, have disabilities.
- Provide special education and disciplinary records of students to the appropriate authorities if school personnel report crimes in which students were involved.
- Carefully and completely document student misbehaviors as well as official actions taken in response to such misbehavior.
- Develop and implement policies and procedures designed to ensure that the rate of long-term suspensions and expulsions of students with disabilities does not evidence significant discrepancies based on race and ethnicity.

Endnotes

1. 20 U.S.C. §§ 1400–1482 (2006). The IDEA's regulations can be found at Assistance to the States for the Education of Children with Disabilities, 34 C.F.R. §§ 300.1–300.818 (2006).
2. Russo, C. J., & Osborne, A. G. (2012). Disciplining students with disabilities: An American perspective. *International Journal of Law and Education, 17,* 63–73.
3. 20 U.S.C. § 1415(k).
4. 34 C.F.R. §§ 530–537.
5. Dayton, J. (2002). Special education discipline law. *Education Law Reporter, 163,* 17–35.
6. For a more comprehensive treatment of this topic, *see* Osborne, A. G., & Russo, C. J. (2009). *Discipline in special education.* Thousand Oaks, CA: Corwin.
7. 443 F. Supp. 1235 (D. Conn. 1978).
8. 20 U.S.C. § 1415(b)(3).
9. 480 F. Supp. 225 (N.D. Ind. 1979).
10. 635 F.2d 342 (5th Cir. 1981).
11. 762 F.2d 1210 (4th Cir. 1985).
12. 765 F.2d 535 (5th Cir. 1985).
13. 484 U.S. 305 (1988).
14. Doe v. Maher, 793 F.2d 1470 (9th Cir. 1986), *affirmed* Honig v. Doe, 484 U.S. 305 (1988).
15. Honig v. Doe, 484 U.S. 305, 323–324 (1988).
16. *Id.* at 325.
17. Hayes v. Unified School District No. 377, 877 F.2d 809 (10th Cir. 1989).
18. School Board of the County of Prince William v. Wills, 16 EHLR 1109 (Va. Cir. Ct. 1989).
19. School Board of the County of Stafford v. Farley, 16 EHLR 1119 (Va. Cir. Ct. 1990).

20. Board of Education of Township High School District v. Kurtz-Imig, 16 EHLR 17 (N.D. Ill. 1989).
21. East Islip Union Free School District v. Andersen, 615 N.Y.S.2d 852 (N.Y. Sup. Ct. 1994).
22. Texas City Independent School District v. Jorstad, 752 F. Supp. 231 (S.D. Tex. 1990).
23. Binghamton City School District v. Borgna, 17 EHLR 677 (N.D.N.Y. 1991).
24. School Board of Pinellas County v. J.M. by L.M., 957 F. Supp. 1252 (M.D. Fla. 1997).
25. Clinton County R-III School District v. C.J.K., 896 F. Supp. 948 (W.D. Mo. 1995).
26. School District of Philadelphia v. Stephan M. and Theresa M., 1997 WL 89113 (E.D. Pa. 1997).
27. 41 F.3d 1223 (8th Cir. 1994).
28. 976 F.2d 487 (9th Cir. 1992).
29. 858 F. Supp. 1044 (S.D. Cal. 1994).
30. Doe v. Manning, 1994 WL 99052, 21 IDELR 357 (W.D. Va. 1994).
31. 885 F. Supp. 1192 (W.D. Wis. 1995).
32. Rodiriecus L. v. Waukegan School District No. 60, 90 F.3d 249 (7th Cir. 1996).
33. 31 F.3d 1489 (9th Cir. 1994).
34. 1994 WL 485754, 21 IDELR 732 (D.N.H. 1994).
35. 635 F.2d 342 (5th Cir. 1981).
36. 106 F.3d 559 (4th Cir. 1997).
37. 115 F.3d 1273 (7th Cir. 1997).
38. 958 F. Supp. 1423 (D. Ariz. 1997).
39. Daniel, P. T. K. (2001). Discipline and the IDEA reauthorization: The need to resolve inconsistencies. *Education Law Reporter*, *142*, 591–607.
40. Osborne, A. G., & Russo, C. J. (2009). Update on the disciplinary provisions of the 1997 and 2004 IDEA amendments. *Education Law Reporter*, *244*, 915–922. Reprinted in *ELA Notes*, *45*(2), 8–11 (2010).
41. 20 U.S.C. § 1415(k)(1)(A); 34 C.F.R. § 300.530(a).
42. 20 U.S.C. § 1415(k)(1)(B); 34 C.F.R. § 300.530(b).
43. 20 U.S.C. § 1415(k)(1)(G); 34 C.F.R. § 300.530(g).
44. 20 U.S.C. § 1415(k)(1)(B); 34 C.F.R. § 300.530(b).
45. 20 U.S.C. § 1415(k)(1)(D)(ii); 34 C.F.R. § 300.530(d)(ii).
46. Shelton v. Maya Angelou Public Charter School, 578 F. Supp. 2d 83 (D.D.C. 2008).
47. 34 C.F.R. § 300.536(a)(2)(i).
48. 34 C.F.R. § 300.536(a)(2)(iii).
49. 34 C.F.R. § 300.536(a)(2).
50. M.M. *ex rel.* L.R. v. Special School District No. 1, 512 F.3d 455 (8th Cir. 2008).
51. 34 C.F.R. § 300.530(b)(1).
52. 34 C.F.R. § 300.530(d)(3).
53. 34 C.F.R. § 300.530(b)(2).
54. *Id.*
55. 20 U.S.C. § 1415(k)(1)(G)(i); 34 C.F.R. § 300.530(g)(1).
56. 20 U.S.C. § 1415(k)(1)(G)(ii); 34 C.F.R. § 300.530(g)(2).
57. 20 U.S.C. § 1415(k)(1)(G)(iii); 34 C.F.R. § 300.530(g)(3).

58. 20 U.S.C. § 1415(k)(2). *See* Couture v. Board of Education of Albuquerque Public Schools, 535 F.3d 1243 (10th Cir. 2008) (deciding that use of time-outs, as called for in a student's IEP, did not violate his Fourth Amendment rights); School Board of the City of Norfolk v. Brown, 769 F. Supp. 2d 928 (E.D. Va. 2010) (holding that a board's placing a child in an interim alternative setting violated the IDEA since the statute vests the IEP team with that decision). *See also* Mawdsley, R. D., & Osborne, A. G. (2011). Restraint of students in schools. *Education Law Reporter, 268*, 1–8. Reprinted in *ELA Notes, 47*(1), 18–22 (2012).

59. Doe v. Todd County School District, 625 F.3d 459 (8th Cir. 2010).

60. 20 U.S.C. § 1415(k)(1)(D)(ii); 34 C.F.R. § 300.530(d)(ii).

61. 20 U.S.C. § 1415(k)(4); 34 C.F.R. § 300.533.

62. 20 U.S.C. § 1415(k)(4)(A).

63. 20 U.S.C. § 1415(k)(1)(G)(i)–(ii); 34 C.F.R. §§ 300.530(g)(1)–(2).

64. 20 U.S.C. § 1415(k)(7)(A)–(B); 34 C.F.R. § 300.530(i).

65. 18 U.S.C. § 930(g)(2).

66. 20 U.S.C. § 1415(k)(7)(B); 34 C.F.R. § 300.530(i)(1).

67. Controlled Substances Act, 21 U.S.C. § 812 (1999).

68. 20 U.S.C. § 1415(k)(1)(G)(iii); 34 C.F.R. § 300.530(g)(3).

69. 20 U.S.C. § 1415(k)(7)(C); 34 C.F.R. § 300.530(i)(3).

70. 18 U.S.C. § 1365(h)(3).

71. 18 U.S.C. § 1365(h)(4).

72. 20 U.S.C. § 1415(k)(1)(A); 34 C.F.R. § 300.530(a).

73. 93 F. Supp. 2d 1310 (S.D. Tex. 2000).

74. Roslyn Union Free School District v. Geffrey W., 740 N.Y.S.2d 451 (N.Y. App. Div. 2002).

75. 20 U.S.C. § 1415(k)(1)(D)(ii); 34 C.F.R. § 300.530(d)(1)(ii).

76. 20 U.S.C. § 1415(k)(1)(F)(i); 34 C.F.R. § 300.530(f)(1).

77. Alex R. v. Forrestville Valley Community Unit School District, 319 F.3d 446 (7th Cir. 2004).

78. School Board of Independent School District No. 11 v. Renollett, 440 F.3d 1007 (8th Cir. 2006).

79. Escambria County Board of Education v. Benton, 406 F. Supp. 2d 1248 (S.D. Ala. 2005).

80. A.C. and M.C. *ex rel.* M.C. v. Board of Education of Chappaqua Central School District, 553 F.3d 165 (2d Cir. 2009).

81. M.W. *ex rel.* S.W. and E.W. v. New York City Department of Education, 725 F.3d 131 (2d Cir. 2013).

82. School Board of the City of Norfolk v. Brown, 769 F. Supp. 2d 928 (E.D. Va. 2010).

83. Long v. District of Columbia, 780 F. Supp. 2d 49 (D.D.C. 2011).

84. Rodriguez v. San Mateo Union High School District, 357 F. App'x 752 (9th Cir. 2009).

85. P.K. and T.K. *ex rel.* S.K. v. New York City Department of Education, 819 F. Supp. 2d 90 (E.D.N.Y. 2011), *affirmed* 526 F. App'x 135 (2d Cir. 2013) (table). *See also* F.B. and E.B. *ex rel.* L.B. v. New York City Department of Education, 923 F. Supp. 2d 570 (S.D.N.Y. 2013) (ruling that an FBA and BIP were not necessary since the child's behaviors did not interfere with his instruction);

J.A. and E.A. *ex rel.* M.A. v. East Ramapo Central School District, 603 F. Supp. 2d 684 (S.D.N.Y. 2009) (declaring that an FBA was unnecessary since none of the child's evaluation reports suggested that one be completed).

86. 20 U.S.C. § 1415(k)(1)(C); 34 C.F.R. § 300.530(c).
87. 20 U.S.C. §§ 1412(a)(1)(A), 1415(k)(1)(D)(i); 34 C.F.R. § 300.530(d)(1)(i).
88. Doe v. Board of Education of Oak Park & River Forest High School District 200, 115 F.3d 1273 (7th Cir. 1997); Commonwealth of Virginia Department of Education v. Riley, 106 F.3d 559 (4th Cir. 1997).
89. 20 U.S.C. § 1415(k)(1)(C); 34 C.F.R. § 300.530(c).
90. 20 U.S.C. § 1415(k)(1)(E); 34 C.F.R. § 300.530(e).
91. 34 C.F.R. § 300.321(a).
92. 34 C.F.R. § 300.321(a)(6).
93. 34 C.F.R. §§ 300.321–300.322.
94. 20 U.S.C. § 1415(k)(1)(E)(i); 34 C.F.R. § 300.530(e)(1).
95. Farrin v. Maine School Administrative District No. 59, 165 F. Supp. 2d 37 (D. Me. 2001).
96. 20 U.S.C. § 1451(k)(1)(E); 34 C.F.R. § 300.530(e)(1).
97. Doe v. Maher, 793 F.2d 1470 (9th Cir. 1986), *affirmed* Honig v. Doe, 484 U.S. 305 (1988).
98. *Id.* Doe v. Maher at 1480–1481, note 8.
99. *Id.*
100. 20 U.S.C. § 1415(k)(1)(E)(i).
101. Coleman v. Newburgh Enlarged City School District, 319 F. Supp. 2d 446 (S.D.N.Y. 2004), *reversed on other grounds* 503 F.3d 198 (2d Cir. 2007).
102. AW *ex rel.* Wilson v. Fairfax County School Board, 372 F.3d 674 (4th Cir. 2004).
103. Fitzgerald v. Fairfax County School Board, 556 F. Supp. 2d 543 (E.D. Va. 2008).
104. 20 U.S.C. § 1415(k)(1)(E)(i)(II). *See also* 34 C.F.R. § 300.530(e)(ii).
105. School Board of the City of Norfolk v. Brown, 769 F. Supp. 2d 928 (E.D. Va. 2010).
106. Honig v. Doe, 484 U.S. 305 (1988).
107. Elk Grove Unified School District, 16 EHLR 622 (SEA Cal. 1989).
108. Modesto City Schools, 21 IDELR 685 (SEA Cal. 1994).
109. Elk Grove Unified School District, 16 EHLR 622 (SEA Cal. 1989).
110. In re Child with Disabilities, 16 EHLR 207 (SEA Cal. 1989).
111. Brimmer v. Traverse City Area Public Schools, 872 F. Supp. 447 (W.D. Mich. 1994).
112. 20 U.S.C. § 1415(k)(1)(E)(i); 34 C.F.R. § 300.530(e)(1).
113. 20 U.S.C. § 1415(k)(4)(B); 34 C.F.R. § 300.532(c).
114. 20 U.S.C. § 1415(k)(4)(A); 34 C.F.R. § 300.533.
115. 20 U.S.C. § 1415(k)(3)(B); 34 C.F.R. § 300.532(b)(2)(ii).
116. 20 U.S.C. § 1415(j).
117. 20 U.S.C. § 1415(k)(4)(A); 34 C.F.R. § 300.533.
118. 20 U.S.C. § 1415(k)(4)(B); 34 C.F.R. § 300.532(c).
119. 20 U.S.C. § 1415(k)(3)(B)(ii); 34 C.F.R. § 300.532(b)(2)(ii).
120. Gadsden City Board of Education v. B.P., 3 F. Supp. 2d 1299 (N.D. Ala. 1998).
121. Roslyn Union Free School District v. Geffrey W., 740 N.Y.S.2d 451 (N.Y. App. Div. 2002).

122. 20 U.S.C. § 1415(k)(5); 34 C.F.R. § 300.534.

123. 20 U.S.C. § 1415(k)(5)(B); 34 C.F.R. § 300.534(b).

124. 20 U.S.C. § 1415(k)(5)(C); 34 C.F.R. § 300.534(c).

125. 20 U.S.C. § 1415(k)(5)(D)(i); 34 C.F.R. § 300.534(d)(1).

126. 20 U.S.C. § 1415(k)(5)(D)(ii); 34 C.F.R. § 300.534(d)(2).

127. 34 C.F.R. § 300.534(d)(2)(ii).

128. 34 C.F.R. § 300.534(d)(2)(iii).

129. 114 F. Supp. 2d 504 (N.D. Miss. 1999).

130. 115 F. Supp. 2d 297 (D. Conn. 2000), *reversed on other grounds* 278 F.3d 119 (2d Cir. 2002).

131. S.W. and Joanne W. v. Holbrook Public Schools, 221 F. Supp. 2d 222 (D. Mass. 2002).

132. 20 U.S.C. § 1415(k)(6); 34 C.F.R. § 300.535.

133. Commonwealth v. Nathaniel N., 764 N.E.2d 883 (Mass. App. Ct. 2002).

134. In re Doe, 753 N.Y.S.2d 656 (N.Y. Fam. Ct. 2002).

135. Russo, C. J., & Osborne, A. G. (2012). Disciplining students with disabilities: An ongoing challenge. *School Business Affairs, 78*(2), 33–36.

Dispute Resolution

Key Concepts in This Chapter

- Mediation and Resolution Sessions
- Administrative Due Process Hearings
- Judicial Review and Court Proceedings
- Statutes of Limitations
- Cases Decided Under Other Statutes

As discussed throughout this book, the Individuals with Disabilities Education Act (IDEA)[1] is designed to afford parents and school officials opportunities to work together to develop individualized educational programs (IEPs) for students with disabilities. Yet, in recognizing that parents and educators may not agree in all situations, Congress included dispute resolution provisions in the IDEA.[2]

Parents of students with disabilities may request mediation[3] or due process hearings[4] if they disagree with the actions of school board officials regarding proposed IEPs or the provision of a free appropriate public education (FAPE) for their children. After having exhausted administrative remedies, parents may request judicial review in federal or state courts.[5] Courts can waive the exhaustion requirement only when it clearly is futile to pursue additional administrative remedies.[6] Students must remain in their then-current, or pendant, placements while administrative or judicial actions are pending unless school officials and parents agree to other arrangements,[7] hearing officers order changes,[8] or judicial decrees call for new placements.[9]

> In *Board of Education of the Hendrick Hudson Central School District v. Rowley*, the Supreme Court cautioned judges not "to substitute their own notions of sound educational policy for those of the authorities which they review" (p. 206).

The IDEA empowers the judiciary to review the records of administrative proceedings, hear additional evidence, and "grant such relief as the court determines is appropriate"[10] based on the preponderance of the evidence standard.[11] Still, in *Board of Education of the Hendrick Hudson Central School District v. Rowley*, the Supreme Court cautioned judges not "to substitute their own notions of sound educational policy for those of the authorities which they review."[12]

Mediation

In order to provide parents with an alternative dispute mechanism to remedy their complaints in disputes over the placements of their children, the IDEA[13] and its regulations direct states and school officials to offer mediation, at public expense,[14] as an option when due process hearings may be possible. To date, these provisions have been subject to little litigation.

The IDEA specifies that mediation must be voluntary on the part of the parties; cannot be used to deny or delay parental rights to due process hearings or to deny any other rights under the IDEA; and must be conducted by trained, qualified, impartial mediators[15] whose names are on state-maintained lists of qualified mediators in special education.[16]

Mediators can neither be employees of states, school boards, or other agencies that provide direct services to students who are subject to the mediation process nor can they have personal or professional conflicts of interest.[17] Individuals who otherwise qualify as mediators are not considered employees of states or boards solely by virtue of being paid to serve as mediators.[18]

Mediation sessions must be scheduled in a timely manner in locations convenient to the parties.[19] Agreements that the parties reach as a result of mediation must be formalized in writing.[20] Discussions occurring during mediation must be kept confidential and cannot be used as evidence in subsequent due process hearings or civil proceedings; the parties may also be required to sign confidentiality pledges prior to the commencement of such processes.[21] Further, a regulatory subsection makes it clear that the results of mediation agreements can be enforced in federal or state courts.[22]

Insofar as the mediation process is voluntary, if parents choose not to participate in such sessions, states may establish procedures allowing them to meet at convenient times and locations with disinterested third parties who are under contract with parent training and information centers, community parent resource centers, or appropriate alternative dispute resolution entities to encourage the use of, and explain the benefits of, the process.[23]

Resolution Sessions

The IDEA[24] requires school board officials to convene meetings between parents and relevant members of the IEP teams of their children[25] within 15 days of parental requests for due process hearings in an attempt to resolve placement disputes.[26] If educators do not convene requested resolution sessions within 15 days, parents can seek the intervention of hearing officers to begin this process.[27] In such a case, the federal trial court in Delaware did not render a school board liable for failing to schedule a resolution session within the required 15-day period because the delay was not its fault.[28]

Resolution sessions must include a school board representative with decision-making authority on its behalf[29] but may not include board attorneys unless parents are also accompanied by counsel.[30] However, if school officials are unable to get parents to participate in resolution sessions within a 30-day period, and can document their reasonable efforts to secure parental participation, hearing officers can dismiss the parents' complaints.[31] The parties need not attend resolution sessions if they agree, in writing, to waive their meetings or agree to mediation.[32] An order of the federal trial court in the District of Columbia emphasizes that parties can forego resolution sessions only by mutual consent.[33] Parents cannot insist that boards bypass this step if officials are willing to conduct resolution meetings.

If parties do not resolve their disputes within 30 days, they should schedule due process hearings[34] at which evidence from resolution sessions can be introduced.[35] If the parties do resolve their differences at resolution sessions, they must execute and sign legally binding settlement agreements.[36] Settlement agreements are enforceable in state or federal courts, but either party may void such agreements within three business days.[37]

Due Process Hearings

Pursuant to the IDEA, parents have the right to request due process hearings on any matters concerning the delivery of a FAPE to their children, including identification, evaluation, and placement.[38] School board officials may ask for hearings if parents refuse to consent to evaluations[39] and must provide parents with proper notice of their rights when school personnel make requests to evaluate their children.[40] Of course, as noted, while administrative or judicial actions are pending, students must remain in their then-current placements unless parents and school officials agree to other settings,[41] hearing officers order changes,[42] or judicial decrees mandate changes in placements.[43]

Parents have the option of choosing whether to have their children present at hearings[44] and whether hearings should be open to the public.[45] If officials cannot identify parents, their whereabouts cannot be discovered, or children are wards of the state, they have the authority to appoint surrogate parents to safeguard the educational interests of children.[46] Surrogate parents are authorized to represent children in all matters related to the receipt of FAPEs,[47] including requesting hearings. The IDEA's regulations explain that the appointing agency must ensure that surrogate parents are not employees of school boards or state educational agencies, cannot have personal or professional conflicts of interest with regard to the interest of the children involved, and have the knowledge and skill to act in this capacity.[48] State laws and regulations govern other qualifications for surrogate parents.

Parties filing due process complaints must forward copies of them to their state education agencies.[49] Complaints must include the names and addresses of the children, their schools, and, if children are homeless, available contact information. In addition, complaints must include descriptions of the nature of the problems relating to the proposed or refused initiations or changes in the placements of the children, including facts relating to the problems and proposed resolutions to the extent known and available to the parties.[50]

One of the IDEA's regulations indicates that due process hearings cannot take place until one of the parties, or its attorney, files a sufficient complaint.[51] Complaints are to be deemed sufficient unless the parties receiving them notify the hearing officer and the other party in writing, within 15 days of receipt of the complaints, that they are insufficient.[52] Within five days of receipt of such responses, hearing officers must evaluate whether complaints are sufficient on their face and must immediately notify the parties of their decisions.[53]

Parties may amend due process complaints only if the opposing parties consent in writing and are given the opportunity to resolve the underlying disputes through resolution sessions, or if hearing officers grant permission to make the changes no later than five days before hearings begin.[54] If parties file amended complaints, the timelines for the resolution sessions to resolve the dispute begin anew.[55]

Assuming, as is almost always the case, that parents requested due process hearings, school officials must respond within 10 days of receiving complaints. Responses must include explanations of why officials proposed or refused to take the actions raised in the complaints; a description of other options that IEP teams considered and the reasons why they were rejected; a description of each evaluation procedure, assessment, record, or report they relied on as the basis for the proposed or refused actions; and a description of the other factors that were relevant to the proposed or refused actions. The regulations add that responses cannot be interpreted as precluding board officials from asserting, if appropriate, that parental due process complaints are insufficient.[56]

Depending on the law in given jurisdictions, either state-level or local school boards may conduct due process hearings.[57] If local boards conduct initial hearings, either party may initiate state-level appeals.[58] States are free to establish either one- or two-tiered administrative due process mechanisms. While procedures vary from one state to the next, most jurisdictions have created two-tiered systems that begin with hearings in front of individual hearing officers and provide for appeals to review panels. In two-tiered systems, both procedures cannot be at the state level.[59]

In jurisdictions with two-tiered administrative hearing systems, some courts agreed that appeals heard by the head of state educational agencies failed to meet the IDEA's impartiality requirements. For example, the Third Circuit ruled that Pennsylvania's Secretary of Education was not an impartial third party decision maker.[60] Earlier, the same court maintained that employees of the Delaware Department of Public Instruction were forbidden to serve as state-level review officers.[61] Similarly, courts in New York agreed that the state commissioner of education lacked impartiality.[62] Yet, a state court in New York decided that review officers who were appointed to oversee adjudications of local hearing officers were impartial even though they were subordinate to the commissioner.[63]

The IDEA mandates that parties must request hearings within two years of the date they knew or should have known of the action forming the basis of their complaint.[64] At the same time, if state laws create other limitation periods, they prevail.[65] Moreover, the federal timeline is to be stayed if parents can show that school officials misrepresented that they resolved the problems or if they withheld pertinent information from parents.[66] Once final administrative orders are rendered, parties have 90 days to appeal to state or federal courts.[67]

Subject Matter of Hearings

Parents can request due process hearings on matters relating to the education of their children with disabilities.[68] For instance, parents have the right to ask for hearings if school officials refuse to assess whether their children have disabilities,[69] if they disagree with findings or recommendation offered by school officials,[70] or if they are dissatisfied with the content or implementation of the IEPs of their children.[71] In a novel defense, a school board in California claimed that parents lacked an entitlement to a due process hearing because officials had not refused to provide services, but rather had ignored their daughter's disabilities. The Ninth Circuit was not convinced, emphasizing that parents may raise complaints with respect to matters relating to the identification, evaluation, or educational placement of their children.[72] State laws and regulations may provide parents with additional rights over the content and structure of due process hearings.

School officials may, but are not required to, request due process hearings to pursue initial evaluations, if appropriate, when parents fail or refuse to respond to requests to provide consent for initial evaluations, except to the extent that requesting hearings for this purpose would be inconsistent with state laws relating to parental consent.[73] If officials choose not to pursue evaluations under the circumstances, parents may not accuse them of violating their duties under the IDEA.[74] School officials can request hearings if parents refuse to consent to evaluations,[75] but not if parents refuse to consent to the provision of services for their children.[76]

Another circumstance under which parents can request due process hearings is after the eligibility of their children to receive special education expires because students may be entitled to compensatory educational services if courts agree that they were denied a FAPE. In a case of this type, the Supreme Court of Ohio reasoned that a student was entitled to a hearing even though the request for it was submitted one day before his eligibility for special education services expired under state law.[77] The record reflected that board officials objected to the hearing, since the student was no longer eligible for services. Reversing in favor of the student, the court disagreed, reasoning that insofar as it was possible to award compensatory services to children who were denied an appropriate education, he was entitled to the hearing.

Parties requesting IDEA due process hearings are precluded from raising issues that were not included in the complaints that they filed to initiate the proceedings, unless the other parties agree otherwise.[78]

Impartiality of Hearing Officers

Hearing officers, typically selected pursuant to provisions in state law,[79] must be impartial, meaning that they cannot be employees of the states or boards involved in the education of the children whose cases appear before them or have personal or professional interests in these students.[80] Individuals who otherwise qualify as hearing officers are not considered employees of states or local boards solely by virtue of being paid to serve in this capacity.[81] State education agencies are required to keep lists of qualified hearing officers along with descriptions of their qualifications.[82]

Hearing officers who are employed by other school boards are not automatically rendered ineligible or regarded as biased. In a representative challenge to the impartiality of a hearing officer from Utah, the Tenth Circuit reiterated the rule that an officer's being employed by another board did not violate the IDEA's prohibition against working for the system involved in a hearing.[83] Moreover, the court confirmed that a hearing officer must not have any personal or professional interest that would conflict with his or her objectivity.

The fact that hearing officers may have personal relationships with individuals who have interests in cases they hear, by itself, does not establish bias. Parents in New York unsuccessfully challenged the impartiality of a state review officer based on his domestic situation. A federal trial court was satisfied that there was no evidence of bias even though the hearing officer cohabited with an employee of the state education agency who had some involvement in special education matters.[84] Further, the court was unconvinced that statistical evidence indicating that the officer entered adjudications in favor of school boards in a majority of cases was sufficient to establish bias.[85] By the same token, in a case arising in Pennsylvania, the Third Circuit affirmed that a hearing officer who was a former coworker of the school board's attorney and a current coworker of that attorney's wife was not biased.[86] Similarly, the federal trial court in Hawaii found that a hearing officer's having formerly served as a deputy state attorney general and having been a coworker of the attorney representing the education department at the hearing did not give the appearance of bias.[87]

Authority of Hearing Officers

In due process hearings, hearing officers must sort out what took place and apply the law to the facts in a manner similar to that of trial court judges. Like judges, hearing officers are empowered to issue orders, grant equitable relief regarding the provision of a FAPE for students with disabilities, and have immunity for their official acts.[88]

There are limitations on the power of hearing officers. Hearing officers generally lack the authority to mandate remedies when broad policies or procedures that affect a large number of students are challenged or to address matters of law because they are not empowered to consider the constitutionality of statutes or regulations. Rather, the power of hearing officers is limited to the facts of the disputes at hand. For example, the Ninth Circuit noted that a hearing officer in Oregon lacked the power to address the legislature's failure to appropriate sufficient funds for special education programs.[89] Along the same line, a federal trial court in Indiana declared that a hearing officer did not have the authority to rule on the legality of a state-required application review process for students who needed residential placements or to provide a remedy.[90] In addition, the IDEA limits the awarding of attorney fees to prevailing parents in special education disputes to the discretion of federal courts.[91]

Training of Hearing Officers

As noted, the IDEA and its regulations require hearing officers to be impartial and have no personal or professional interest in the outcome of the disputes before them.[92] However, since these provisions do not contain specific language regarding the other qualifications of hearing officers, these criteria are left up to the states to establish. In one of the few cases on point, the federal trial court in Connecticut decided that the failure of state officials to train hearing officers was not a violation of the IDEA.[93]

Burden of Proof

Since the IDEA and its regulations are silent as to which party bears the burden of proof in due process hearings, such determinations were historically based on state laws or judicial discretion, leading to a great deal of disagreement, and inconsistency, over this important question. In 2005 the Supreme Court resolved the controversy over who had the burden of proof in *Schaffer v. Weast* (*Schaffer*).[94] In conceding that arguments could be made on both sides of the issue, the Court saw no reason to depart from the usual rule that the party seeking relief bears the burden of persuasion. In IDEA cases, this is generally the parents.[95] The issue was important because the assignment of the burden of proof can well determine the final outcome in close cases.[96] Under the Court's rationale, parents who challenge proposed IEPs must demonstrate that the plans are deficient unless state laws provide otherwise.[97] Citing *Schaffer*, the Ninth Circuit affirmed that parents from Oregon, as the party objecting to a proposed IEP, bore the burden of proof at an administrative hearing.[98]

Exhaustion of Administrative Remedies

> The IDEA requires parties to exhaust administrative remedies before filing suit unless it clearly is futile to do so.

Based on Congressional desire for reasonably quick resolution of disputes over the placements of students with disabilities, the IDEA requires parties to exhaust administrative remedies before filing suits unless it clearly is futile to do so.[99] Exhaustion of administrative remedies may be excused if school officials either deny parental requests for due process hearings or frustrate parental attempts to challenge the results of hearings,[100] or if it is impossible for parents to obtain adequate relief through hearings.[101]

Exhaustion is not required to enforce final administrative orders, except that these cases must be filed under the Civil Rights Act of 1871, Section 1983 (Section 1983),[102] a statute that is discussed later in this chapter. Put another way, as reviewed in the next section, because parties may not file suit until administrative appeals are pursued, courts refuse to address issues that were not subject to complete exhaustion.[103]

Exhaustion Required

Courts have long refused to hear special education cases where the parties bringing suit have not exhausted administrative remedies.[104] Exhaustion is required for a variety of reasons. By way of illustration, since judges consider themselves generalists when reviewing the educational needs of students with disabilities and hearing officers are more experienced in these matters,[105] jurists want to be able to review complete records that have been developed by professionals with competence in this complex area of the law. In one dispute from New York, where a student sought damages over a board's alleged failure to provide IDEA services, the Second Circuit determined that this did not entitle her to sidestep the exhaustion requirement, because the real problem was the lack of specificity in her IEP rather than the board's failure to comply with its content.[106]

Most courts treat class action suits, wherein one person or a small group of individuals files a case on behalf of a larger group of similarly aggrieved individuals challenging policies and/or procedures with widespread application, as being subject to the exhaustion requirements.[107] One court went so far as to declare that all members of a class had to exhaust administrative remedies prior to bringing suit.[108] Other courts have pointed out that filing representative claims served the purposes of exhaustion.[109]

The Tenth Circuit, in a case from Colorado, asserted that the issue of whether a state's policies denied students with disabilities a FAPE entailed a factually intensive inquiry into the circumstances of their cases and was the type of issue the administrative process was designed to address.[110] A federal trial court in Indiana reached a different result in ruling that plaintiffs representing a class need not exhaust administrative remedies because class action administrative hearings are not permitted.[111]

Insofar as litigants must exhaust administrative remedies, parties cannot file suit based on issues that have not already been addressed at due process hearings. In this regard, the Second Circuit was of the opinion that a student's attorney could not claim on his request for compensatory education that a school board in Connecticut committed procedural violations since the issue had not been raised at a due process hearing.[112] A federal court in New York also explained that parents could not raise the issue of the appropriateness of an evaluation facility because they failed to challenge the hearing officer's recommendation on the issue in the presence of a state-level review officer.[113]

Parties must exhaust administrative remedies when claims are made under statutes other than the IDEA,[114] when classroom procedures are challenged,[115] or when seeking enforcement of administrative orders if state regulations provide for this through the administrative process.[116] Courts have been insistent that parents cannot circumvent the IDEA's process by raising claims under statutes such as Section 504 of the Rehabilitation

Act (Section 504)[117] that could be resolved via an IDEA administrative hearing. For instance, a federal trial court in Ohio decreed that parents could not avoid the exhaustion requirement by stating claims under Section 504 or Section 1983 if the claims were actionable under the IDEA.[118]

Exhaustion Not Required

Courts generally agree that parents are not required to exhaust administrative remedies under a variety of circumstances.[119] For example, suits in which parents seek damages for common law torts are generally not subject to the IDEA's exhaustion requirement, even when they arise in a special education situation.[120]

Courts excuse parents from exhausting administrative remedies when they can show that school board officials effectively prevented them from exercising their rights by not providing them with obligatory due process. In the first of three cases on point, the Ninth Circuit agreed that parents from Oregon were able to skip a due process hearing when their complaint was that they were denied access to that process.[121] In the second, the federal trial court in Arizona indicated that exhaustion would have been futile where a parent claimed that she was denied meaningful access to the IDEA's due process procedures.[122] In the final case, a federal trial court in New York excused parents from the exhaustion requirement because school board officials failed to provide notice of their procedural rights.[123]

Parties may also not be required to exhaust administrative remedies when complaints allege systemic failures. In a case from New York, the Second Circuit acknowledged that a school board's alleged failure to prepare and implement IEPs, notify parents of meetings, provide parents with required progress reports, perform timely evaluations, provide adequate procedural safeguards, carry out their required responsibilities in a timely fashion, and offer appropriate training for staff members were systemic failures that could not be remedied through the administrative hearing process.[124]

Challenges to school board policies that could violate the IDEA may not be subject to the administrative process.[125] As such, the Ninth Circuit was convinced that a claim that the school day for specified special education students in California was shorter than for regular education pupils was not subject to the exhaustion requirement because it had nothing to do with individual IEPs.[126] The federal trial court in the District of Columbia was satisfied that parents who filed a class action suit alleging that school board officials failed to discharge their child find obligations did not need to first seek a hearing on the matter because the claim challenged policies, patterns, and practices causing a systemic failure to comply with the IDEA.[127]

Courts have considered exhaustion to be futile when hearing officers lacked authority to grant the requested relief. The Eighth Circuit affirmed that parents seeking an order to prevent the closing of a state-operated school for students with hearing impairments in South Dakota were excused from exhausting administrative remedies since they could not obtain adequate relief through that process.[128] The Second Circuit observed that a father's complaint about the method by which hearing officers were selected in New York was not subject to exhaustion since a sole hearing officer lacked the authority to alter the procedure.[129] Federal trial courts in New York agreed that exhaustion was unnecessary in two cases: In the first, where parents sought to have their son placed in a school that was not on the state's list of approved placements, the court rejected exhaustion as unnecessary because the hearing officer could not order a student to attend classes in an unapproved facility.[130] In the second, the court viewed exhaustion as unnecessary because parents were challenging an adjudication of officials of the state education department who rejected their specific request and who also declined to make an exception to general procedures.[131]

Previous sections of this chapter discussed cases wherein courts subjected class action suits to the exhaustion of remedies requirement. Yet, since courts agree, exhaustion may not be necessary in class action suits where the claims of plaintiffs are systemic in nature and hearing officers would not have the authority to order relief. In such a case, the Second Circuit remarked that exhaustion was not required when a hearing officer in New York could not order a systemwide change to correct the alleged wrongs.[132]

Exhaustion may be unnecessary in emergency situations if it would cause severe or irreparable harms to students.[133] Nevertheless, in a case from New Jersey, the Third Circuit specified that insofar as mere allegations of irreparable harm are insufficient to excuse exhaustion, a plaintiff must present actual evidence to support such a claim.[134] The Ninth Circuit affirmed that parents who were seeking an injunction to prevent the Hawaii Department of Education from shortening the school year were excused from the exhaustion requirement since the administrative process could not remedy the alleged harm to the affected students.[135]

When litigation involves issues that are purely legal, rather than factual, exhaustion may not be required.[136] Similarly, exhaustion may not be necessary if state officials persistently fail to render expeditious orders regarding the educational placements of students.[137]

Courts may not allow parents to circumvent the exhaustion requirement by filing suits under other statutes, but courts do not necessarily insist on exhaustion when parents' claims are noneducational.[138] In a case resolved by an en banc panel, the Ninth Circuit decided that a mother from Washington who sought general damages for her child's suffering, along with punitive damages, was not required to exhaust administrative remedies.[139] The court reasoned that the IDEA's exhaustion requirement is not jurisdictional, but rather, is a mechanism for claims processing that defendants may offer as an affirmative defense. Thus, the court determined that the IDEA's exhaustion provision applies only in cases where the relief sought by a plaintiff in the pleadings is available under the IDEA. Non-IDEA claims in which parties are not seeking relief under the IDEA are excused from the exhaustion requirement even if they allege injuries that could conceivably have been redressed by the IDEA. The court stated that the IDEA requires exhaustion of remedies only when the civil action brought under other statutes seeks relief that is also available under the IDEA. In such a situation the court observed that parents and students must exhaust the remedies available under the IDEA before seeking the same relief under other laws.

The Ninth Circuit asserted that the IDEA requires exhaustion in three situations: when plaintiffs seek IDEA remedies or their functional equivalents, when plaintiffs seek prospective injunctive relief to alter IEPs or the educational placement of students with disabilities, and when plaintiffs seek to enforce rights arising as a result of denials of FAPEs, whether pled as IDEA claims or other charges that rely on the denial of FAPEs to provide the bases for causes of action. According to the court, if the measure of a plaintiff's damages is the cost of counseling, tutoring, or private schooling, relief that is available under the IDEA, then the IDEA requires exhaustion. In other words, to the extent that a request for monetary damages functions as a substitute for relief under the IDEA, a plaintiff cannot escape the exhaustion requirement simply by limiting the request for relief to damages. However, to the extent that a plaintiff has laid out a plausible claim for damages unrelated to the deprivation of a FAPE, the IDEA does not require the plaintiff to exhaust administrative remedies before seeking damages in court.

Finally, courts have refused to apply the exhaustion requirement when students do not need special education. To this end, courts agree that parents do not have to exhaust administrative remedies in cases under Section 504 if their children are not receiving services under the IDEA, even if their children are impaired.[140]

Rights of Parties to a Hearing

Parties involved in due process hearings have the right to be accompanied and advised by counsel with special knowledge concerning the education of students with disabilities.[141] In a key point, the Supreme Court of Delaware held that the IDEA does not authorize nonattorneys to represent parents at hearings.[142] Consequently, the court affirmed an order forbidding nonattorneys with special knowledge and training with respect to the problems of students with disabilities to represent parents at due process hearings.

Insofar as due process hearings are quasi-judicial proceedings, the parties may present evidence, compel the attendance of witnesses, and cross-examine witnesses during hearings.[143] The parties can prohibit the introduction of evidence that is not disclosed at least five business days prior to hearings.[144] At the same time, the parties have the right to obtain a written verbatim record of the hearing, or, at the option of the parents, an audio recording of what was said, as well as findings of fact and decisions.[145]

In a procedural matter, the federal trial court in New Jersey observed that a mother who was indigent, and could not afford to pay for a written transcript of a hearing, was entitled to receive one at public expense so that she could challenge the resulting order.[146] The court contended that a copy of the transcript of the lengthy and complex hearing was an essential tool for the mother's effective and efficient review of its outcome. In a slightly different case, the First Circuit ruled that educational officials could provide either a written transcript or an electronic record of the administrative hearings to indigent parents.[147]

Pursuant to the IDEA, hearing officers must render final decisions within 45 days of requests for hearings.[148] Even so, hearing officers can grant requests from the parties for extensions or continuances.[149] The adjudications of hearing officers are final unless they are appealed.[150]

In jurisdictions with two-tiered due process hearing systems, officials must ensure that final decisions, based on the record, are reached within 30 days of requests for review.[151] At least one court decreed that the IDEA's finality requirement precludes a hearing officer from taking any action that interferes with rendering a final adjudicative order. The federal trial court in Delaware acknowledged that a hearing panel may not refer a case to some other body for review.[152] In this case, a hearing panel commented that a student was entitled to a residential placement but did not order the child to be moved to such a setting. Instead, the panel commented that a mechanism should have been established to evaluate options. The court concluded that referring the case for additional review did not comport with the IDEA's finality requirements, thereby undermining the concern for prompt resolution of placement disputes.

Once administrative review is complete, aggrieved parties may file suit in federal or state courts.[153] Aggrieved parties are generally considered to be the losing parties or the ones who did not obtain the relief sought. While prevailing parties are ordinarily not viewed as aggrieved, the federal trial court in Delaware permitted parents who won on the legal issues but did not obtain the relief they sought to be treated as the aggrieved party so that they could seek judicial review.[154]

Judicial Review

As reflected in Figure 7.1, and as mentioned earlier, under the IDEA, either party can appeal the results of due process hearings to federal or state courts once the party has exhausted administrative remedies. As important as this issue is, though, the IDEA is silent on whether cases must be submitted to juries. Insofar as due process hearings generate their own records, the courts generally do not conduct trials *de novo*. In other words, courts ordinarily do not repeat investigations that occurred administratively.

Rather, the courts examine the records of hearings and hear new or additional testimony when necessary before ruling. Due to the importance Congress placed on the administrative process, courts are required to give due weight to the results of due process hearings and overturn adjudication only when they are convinced that it was clearly erroneous.

Pro Se Parents

As a preliminary matter, while parents have the right to have attorneys represent them at trials and parents who are lawyers can represent themselves, the issue of attorney fees aside, questions have arisen over whether

Figure 7.1   Dispute Resolution Under the IDEA

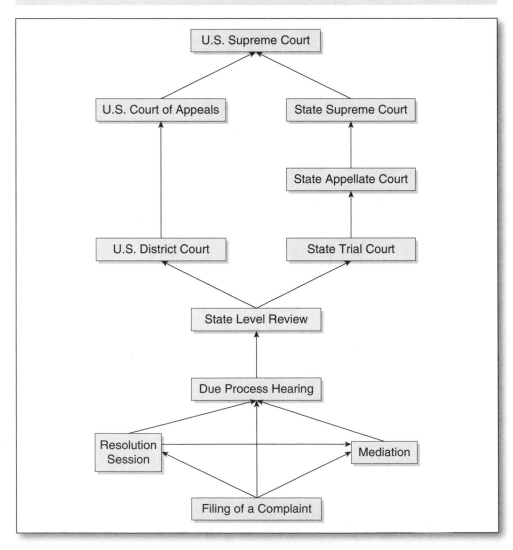

parents who are not attorneys can represent their children in judicial proceedings. Consistent with many other areas under the IDEA, the courts are split on the question of whether parents who are not attorneys can act as pro se plaintiffs, literally, "on behalf of the self," in disputes over the education of their children in IDEA actions.[155]

The Supreme Court, in *Winkelman ex rel. Winkelman v. Parma City School District* (*Winkelman*),[156] settled the controversy in 2007. *Winkelman* began when the parents of a student in Ohio who was autistic initiated a pro se action in a federal trial court seeking a FAPE for their son. After failing to gain the sought relief, the parents appealed, again in a pro se action. Relying on its own precedent[157] as well as an earlier case from the Third Circuit,[158] the Sixth Circuit held that the legislative purpose of the IDEA did not support the parents' right to proceed pro se.[159]

On further review in *Winkelman*, the Supreme Court reversed, noting that the parents enjoy enforceable rights during administrative hearings and it would be inconsistent with the statutory scheme to bar them from continuing to assert those rights in federal court. The Court found nothing in the IDEA's provisions to exclude parents who exercised their own rights from statutory protections the moment the administrative proceedings are over. The Court added that the IDEA does not bar parents from seeking to vindicate the rights accorded them once the time comes for a civil action, interpreting the statute's references to parental rights as meaning that rights are conveyed to parents as well as to their children. Through its text and structure, the Court interpreted the IDEA as creating an independent stake for parents in the procedures, with costs implicated by this process but also in the substantive decisions to be made.

In a dissent, Justice Scalia maintained that parents have the right to proceed pro se when seeking reimbursement for private school expenses or to redress violations of their own procedural rights under the IDEA, but not when they seek judicial declarations that the education of their children is substantially inadequate. In Scalia's view, the right to a FAPE belongs to the children who receive the education. Although parents have an interest in ensuring that their children receive proper educations, Scalia believed that there is a difference between an interest and a statutory right.

In *Winkelman* the Supreme Court indicated that parents could file suit pro se in federal court because their rights under the IDEA were coexistent with those of their children. Subsequently, two circuits agreed that where only the children's rights were at issue, the parents were barred from proceeding pro se. The Third Circuit, in a case from New Jersey, stated that *Winkelman* did not allow parents to pursue any statutory or common law claims on their children's behalf.[160] In a Second Circuit dispute from Vermont, the court acknowledged that parents have independent, enforceable rights under the IDEA, but insisted that insofar as the complaint in the present action named only their incompetent adult child as a petitioner and did not assert any claims on their own behalf, they could not represent her.[161]

The court explained that laymen cannot represent anyone other than themselves. It is important to note that insofar as both of these cases were unpublished, they are not binding precedent.

Standing

In order to file suit, parties bringing suit must have standing, or legitimate interests, in the issues litigated. Put another way, parties must be able to show that they were faced with threatened injuries or deprivations of rights. As most of the cases in this chapter, and book, reveal, the vast majority of cases litigated on behalf of students with disabilities are filed by their parents; moreover, surrogate parents can file suits to protect the rights of these children.[162] For example, the Second Circuit acknowledged that the father of a student with disabilities from New York had standing to sue over the methods by which hearing officers were selected.[163] The court added that insofar as the father had an enforceable right to an impartial hearing on behalf of his son, he had standing to challenge how hearing officers are selected.

Parents can lose their standing if they are no longer the legal guardians of their children. In such a case, the Fifth Circuit maintained that under Texas law, a child's managing conservator, not her father, had the authority to file suit on her behalf.[164] In another dispute, where a divorce decree granted a mother the sole custody of her daughter, a federal trial court in Pennsylvania concluded that the father did not have standing to sue.[165]

In a case seeking reimbursement for the partial depletion of health insurance benefits that were used to procure special education services, the Fourth Circuit agreed that a student from North Carolina had standing.[166] The court noted that insofar as using her insurance benefits to pay for special education diminished the student's resources because the policy capped her available benefits, she had a legitimate interest in the outcome of the litigation. The same court subsequently affirmed that a father from Virginia who sought reimbursement of placement expenses paid by his insurance did not have standing because a decrease in lifetime benefits would not have affected his child since she was no longer covered by the policy that paid the benefits.[167] In two separate actions, a federal trial court in Pennsylvania declared that an insurance company lacked standing under the IDEA when attempting to compel a board to provide services it had been paying for under health insurance policies.[168] The court dismissed the cases on the bases that only aggrieved parents or school boards had access to the IDEA's due process mechanism.

The IDEA permits school officials to ask for hearings if parents refuse to consent to evaluations.[169] Unfortunately, the courts do not agree on whether states can be aggrieved parties that challenge the results of due process hearings. In one such case, the Ninth Circuit decided that a board from California could file such a suit.[170] Similarly, the Seventh Circuit asserted that a nonprofit corporation in Indiana that operated a licensed child care facility had standing to advocate for the rights of students with disabilities placed in its custody.[171] The court wrote that the corporation had standing because the denial of the students' IDEA rights would have deprived it of money to which it otherwise would have been entitled. According to the court, the corporation was an aggrieved party in light of the outcome of a due process hearing.

On the other hand, the Third[172] and Eleventh[173] Circuits, in cases from New Jersey and Georgia, respectively, concurred that school boards lacked standing to seek to compel the state educational agency to provide special education services. The courts were convinced that the IDEA was designed to resolve disputes about particular IEPs and that nothing in it permits local boards to sue states to compel them to fulfill their statutory duties. Further, the Sixth[174] and Ninth[175] Circuits affirmed that school boards in Michigan and Washington, respectively, could not sue the state to challenge their compliance with the procedural provisions set out in the IDEA. In like fashion, federal trial courts in the District of Columbia,[176] Indiana,[177] and New York[178] agreed that local boards lacked standing to sue each other in disputes under the IDEA. In a series of cases, the federal trial court in the District of Columbia maintained that the board there could not be joined as a party in suits against charter schools.[179] Since charter schools in the District act as their own local education agencies, the court essentially found that the public school officials had no interest in the outcome of the cases.

The Second Circuit affirmed that parents in New York whose children attended an out-of-state facility had standing to sue the state's education department to prevent it from enforcing a regulation prohibiting the use of aversive interventions.[180] Insofar as the state in which the facility was located allowed the use of aversive interventions, the methodology the plaintiffs desired, the court was of the view that if the parents prevailed, their children could receive this form of treatment.

The Third Circuit affirmed that a former special education student from Pennsylvania could not bring suit under the IDEA alleging that she had been misidentified as a student with disabilities.[181] The court reasoned that claims could be brought under the IDEA only on behalf of "children with disabilities." Since the student claimed that she did not have, and had never had, disabilities, the court determined that she was excluded from the IDEA's protections.

Burden of Proof

The Supreme Court resolved who bears the burden of proof in challenging IEPs in due process hearings. Yet, the IDEA and its regulations remain silent on who bears the burden of proof in judicial disputes. As such, this is a question left for judicial discretion.[182] Insofar as the courts are unable to agree on who bears the burden of proof in judicial proceedings, two perspectives have emerged.

The First,[183] Fourth,[184] Fifth,[185] Sixth,[186] Seventh,[187] Tenth,[188] and Eleventh[189] Circuits agree that the party challenging an IEP or the result of a due process hearing bears the burden of proof. These courts generally concur that while the outcome of a due process hearing is entitled to a degree of judicial deference, the parties seeking to set aside administrative orders must demonstrate that the final results were inappropriate. In addition, the courts agreed that insofar as the IDEA creates a presumption in favor of then-current placements, the parties challenging student placements must prove that they were inappropriate.

Conversely, in judgments handed down prior to the Supreme Court's ruling in *Schaffer,* the burden of proof in administrative hearings has generally been on the parties challenging IEPs, but the Third Circuit[190] and a federal trial court in West Virginia[191] placed the burden of proof on school boards. These courts agreed that insofar as boards bear the ultimate responsibility for providing special education, they should have to prove that proposed IEPs are appropriate. The courts also recognized the advantage school officials have over parents in proceedings brought pursuant to the IDEA. However, it is important to note that the rationales in these cases may no longer be valid in light of *Schaffer*. For example, a federal trial court in Pennsylvania declared that the burden of proof should remain on the same party throughout the case.[192]

Since litigation may take more than a year, IEPs that are being challenged may have expired by the time courts act. In the meantime, the parties may have initiated challenges to more recently developed IEPs. In cases such as this, courts ordinarily treat the losing parties in disputes over original IEPs as bearing the burden of producing evidence of changed circumstances that rendered initial IEPs inappropriate.[193] When this happens, there is a presumption in favor of the placements that were ordered as a result of the first, disputed IEPs, unless parties can prove that the circumstances have changed.

Judicial Deference

In line with the Supreme Court's directive that judges should not substitute their views for those of school authorities,[194] most jurists defer to educators on matters dealing with appropriate instructional methodologies as long as school officials followed procedural requirements. The Fourth Circuit thus reiterated the widely accepted notion that neither it nor a trial court in Virginia should have disturbed an IEP simply because judges disagreed with its contents, since the judiciary owes deference to educators as long as IEPs meet the IDEA's basic requirements.[195] Due to its having found that school officials failed to follow proper procedures in developing the IEP, the court refused to grant deference to the hearing officer's order.

Most judges defer to educators on matters about appropriate methodology as long as procedural requirements are followed.

The Supreme Court[196] and other federal courts[197] agree that the IDEA's mandate requiring judges to review the records of due process hearings implies that their results must be given due weight. Still, it is unclear how much weight is due to these results. In *Board of Education of the Hendrick Hudson Central School District v. Rowley*,[198] the Court added that questions of methodology are for resolution by the states, clarifying that the judiciary should defer to hearing officers on questions of the substantive content of IEPs and instructional methodology.

In a case from Massachusetts, the First Circuit declared that a trial court must reach its own independent judgment based on the record of the due process hearing as supplemented at trials.[199] The court specified that while the amount of weight to be afforded the result of hearings is left to the discretion of trial courts, judges must consider the records carefully and endeavor to respond to administrative resolutions of all material issues. In another dispute, the First Circuit affirmed that a trial court in Maine did not err in failing to overlook or misconstrue evidence where its judgment was based on a supportable finding that an IEP was reasonably calculated to address a student's needs.[200]

In a related matter, federal trial courts in California[201] and New Jersey[202] rejected the notion that judges have broad power to overturn the orders of hearing officers. These courts shared the view that the IDEA's mandate for judicial review is not an open invitation for judges to substitute their views of sound educational policy for those of school officials. The Fourth Circuit, in a case from North Carolina, posited that a court is bound by an administrative record and additional evidence as produced at trial, but must act independently.[203] Even so, in a separate order, the same court noted that a trial court erred by not deferring to a hearing officer who conducted a proper hearing, resolved factual questions in the normal way, and complied with all federal and state requirements.[204] Conversely, in a case from Texas, the Fifth Circuit decided that jurists need not defer to hearing officers when judicial review reveals that officers erroneously assessed the facts or misapplied the law.[205]

The District of Columbia Circuit acknowledged that courts overturning the results of due process hearings must explain their grounds for doing so.[206] In addition, a trial court in the same jurisdiction pointed out that judges may reverse the orders of hearing officers only when the judges are satisfied that school officials have proved that the officers erred.[207] Moreover, the federal trial court in Massachusetts noted that while a hearing officer's order must be accorded some deference, it is not entitled to great deference on matters of law.[208]

In two-tiered due process hearing schemes, courts usually defer to final administrative orders.[209] Conversely, if review procedures are flawed, courts defer to initial adjudications.[210] In such a case, the Fourth Circuit reasoned that a hearing officer in Virginia's judgment should not have been accorded weight since he discredited a witness he had not seen or heard testify, while a local hearing officer relied on the credibility of the same witness.[211] On remand, a trial court considered the fact that all of the parents' witnesses had a record of testifying against the school board in evaluating the record of the due process hearing.[212] The Fourth Circuit again affirmed, but it did so without a written opinion.[213]

Admission of Additional Evidence

The IDEA permits courts to hear additional evidence at the request of one of the parties.[214] Still, courts can limit the amount and kind of extra evidence they are willing to admit, especially if it had not been introduced prior to judicial review.[215] In the first of two cases, the Eleventh Circuit affirmed that a trial court in Georgia had the discretion to refuse to receive and consider evidence that a school board wished to offer in addition to the record of a due process hearing.[216] However, the Sixth Circuit commented that a trial court in Tennessee erred in relying on additional evidence to address issues beyond those presented at a due process hearing over the appropriateness of a student's IEP.[217]

The First Circuit affirmed that a party seeking to admit additional evidence must justify its request.[218] Here, a trial court in Massachusetts refused to hear the testimony of witnesses for parents who could have testified at a due process hearing but whose testimony was deliberately withheld by their attorney. The panel determined that the trial court did not abuse its discretion in refusing to allow the witnesses to testify. In addition, a federal trial court in Illinois refused to admit evaluation materials that school officials had not previously submitted to the hearing officer.[219] Noting that withholding this information from the hearing officer severely undercut the role of the administrative hearing, the court thought that such action deprived the court of the hearing officer's expertise on the matter.

On the other hand, the Sixth Circuit expressed the view that a federal trial court in Tennessee was justified in admitting additional evaluation materials.[220] The court recognized that the parents had neither the opportunity nor the resources to procure additional evaluations before the due process hearing took place.

A party wishing to present additional evidence must make its intention to do so clearly known to a court. For instance, the Seventh Circuit judged that where neither party made an intention to submit additional evidence known, a federal trial court in Illinois was entitled to assume that they wished to have the case resolved on the basis of the administrative record.[221]

The Sixth Circuit affirmed that it was appropriate for a trial court in Tennessee to consider evidence that a hearing officer failed to review.[222]

The court stressed that the admission of additional evidence did not undercut the administrative process. In a similar case from Texas, the Fifth Circuit agreed that a trial court gave due weight to the result of a due process hearing but was free to take additional evidence into consideration.[223]

Due to the delay that often occurs between the time when placements are finalized and when judicial review is initiated, additional evidence may be available about how students progressed in the disputed settings. It is not clear whether courts should admit evidence that develops after officials make disputed placements. The Ninth Circuit ruled that a trial court in California had the discretion to admit additional evidence concerning relevant events occurring after an administrative hearing.[224] A federal trial court in Wisconsin also admitted evidence about a student's progress in a home-based program during the time between the hearing and court review.[225]

On the other hand, in a case from New Jersey, the Third Circuit affirmed that IEPs and placements should be reviewed from the perspective of the information that was available when initial actions occurred.[226] While the court conceded that events occurring after placements are made may be relevant, it refused to allow them to be substituted for threshold determinations of whether IEPs were reasonably calculated to confer FAPEs when they were written.

Mootness

Courts do not accept cases unless they present live controversies, meaning that the parties have real interests in their outcomes. To this end, courts have rejected cases as moot where they could not grant effective relief due to a student's graduation[227] or where relief would have served no purpose because a student moved.[228] However, if the controversies that initiated complaints are no longer alive, but remain capable of repetition, courts may still hear the cases. In such a dispute, the Supreme Court acknowledged that judges may adjudicate ongoing controversies and have jurisdiction if there is a reasonable likelihood that a party will again suffer the deprivation of the rights that initiated the suit.[229]

> Courts will not accept cases unless they present live controversies.

The Fifth Circuit declared a case moot after a school board in Mississippi agreed to provide a student with services.[230] Similarly, the federal trial court in New Hampshire rejected the notion that a case was moot where a school year ended and there was no reasonable expectation that the controversy would have recurred.[231] Subsequently, federal trial courts in Indiana[232] and Texas[233] dismissed claims as moot where students were no longer eligible to receive services because they reached the maximum eligibility age under state law. Once a student is removed from a disputed setting and receives a new placement, the placement issue is moot.[234] Moreover, cases are moot if the parties no longer retain interests in their outcome.[235]

In its only special education case involving mootness, albeit not as the main issue, *Honig v. Doe*,[236] the Supreme Court affirmed that a dispute was not moot for a 20-year-old student who was still eligible to receive services under the IDEA, where there was a reasonable expectation that he would again be subjected to the deprivation of rights complained about in the litigation. Other courts have refused to treat cases as moot where issues were capable of repetition, such as when a school year ended,[237] when the basic complaint still existed,[238] when the IEP on which the suit was brought was superseded by a new IEP,[239] and when parents enrolled their child in a private school.[240] One federal appellate court went so far as to assert that a case was not moot when parents approved an IEP because the school board's past failures to adhere to the IDEA enhanced the probability that future violations could occur.[241]

The Third Circuit, noting that a school board in New Jersey no longer responsible for educating a child must still be responsible for its past transgressions, observed that a child's move out of state did not moot his claims for compensatory education.[242] The Tenth Circuit was satisfied that even though a student from New Mexico left school and showed no desire to return, her suit for compensatory services was not moot.[243] The court explained that the student was not seeking prospective relief, but rather, had alleged an injury for which a remedy could be fashioned. In the same way the federal trial court in the District of Columbia asserted that a live controversy remained in a case where a mother withdrew her child from a charter school and enrolled him in a private school because she sought compensatory services to remedy a past harm.[244] In like manner, the First Circuit declared that parents' move from Massachusetts to Connecticut did not moot their claims for reimbursement and attorney fees.[245]

Exchange of Information

Attorneys in IDEA proceedings generally exchange information prior to trials. Principles of fairness in the IDEA dictate that one side cannot withhold information that is crucial to the other party's case because, just as in due process hearings, the goal is to have all possible evidence available to help measure the appropriateness of IEPs rather than to prevail in disputes just for the sake of winning. For example, the federal trial court for the District of Columbia held that the school board had to provide parents with information about private schools, the qualifications of the teachers in them, and the disabilities of the students attending them since these matters were not privileged.[246] At the same time, the court acknowledged that the board was not required to provide information about due process hearings and suits challenging other placements since the parents' attorney could obtain this material through normal legal research.

Res Judicata

Based on the principle of res judicata, courts cannot hear cases or render judgments on matters that they have already resolved. *Res judicata* stands for the proposition that a final judgment by a court of competent jurisdiction is conclusive and acts as an absolute bar to a subsequent action involving the same claim. By way of illustration, the Eleventh Circuit, in a case from Florida that was before it for the second time, affirmed that under res judicata, a trial court's order prior to the first appeal precluded additional consideration of the issues.[247] The federal trial court in the District of Columbia found that even though a mother masked her argument under a new legal theory, since all of her complaints ultimately relied on the same factual nucleus as an issue that had been resolved, her suit was barred by res judicata.[248]

Settlement Agreements

During the course of disputes, parents and school officials often negotiate settlement agreements designed effectively to end controversies. Settlement agreements are sometimes reached as a result of mediation that occurs before due process hearings have started or during litigation. When the parties agree to settlements during litigation, hearing officers or courts may either approve or reject them if they deem their terms to be contrary to public policy or existing law. In a representative case of this nature from Florida, the Eleventh Circuit reasoned that a trial court could vitiate a settlement agreement only if it violates public policy.[249] The panel believed that the high cost of a proposed resolution in a settlement agreement did not render the agreement void as it was not contrary to public policy and did not contravene any statutes. Thus, the court issued an order enforcing the provisions of the settlement agreement to provide housing for a student with disabilities.

In a case from New Jersey, the federal trial court noted that the existence of a settlement agreement negotiated by parents and school officials during a due process hearing did not bar it from hearing the case.[250] The court explained that despite the settlement agreement, school officials still had the duty to provide the student with a FAPE. The same court also offered that a settlement agreement reached through mediation formed a contract between the parties, but the court did not allow the board to avoid its responsibilities under the IDEA.[251] The court emphasized that there was a presumption that the services agreed to by the parties at the time that they entered into the agreement met the student's special education needs. In addition, the court pointed out that the parents had the right to question the terms of the agreement if there was a change in circumstances. On the other hand, in a case from Ohio the Sixth Circuit affirmed that a settlement agreement that unambiguously stated that all issues had been resolved precluded judicial review of its terms.[252]

Statutes of Limitations

Earlier versions of the IDEA did not contain a statute of limitations either for requesting due process hearings or filing suits after exhausting administrative remedies.[253] Consequently, in amending the IDEA in 2004, Congress included specific statutes of limitations governing the timelines for seeking such actions.

The IDEA and its regulations now require parties to request impartial due process hearings within two years of the date they knew or should have known about the actions that form the bases of their complaints.[254] Moreover, if states have explicit time limitations for requesting hearings, these limitations prevail.[255]

Limitations periods may be set aside if school boards specifically misrepresented that they resolved the problems forming the basis of complaints or if officials withheld information that they should have provided to parents.[256] After final administrative orders are rendered, parties have 90 days to file judicial appeals.[257] Again, if state laws provide otherwise, they prevail.[258]

Beginning and Waiving a Limitations Period

Pursuant to the IDEA, limitations periods for requesting administrative due process hearings begin when aggrieved parties either knew or should have known of the actions forming the bases of their complaints. This date is often established when parents reject offered IEPs. In other situations, such as when parents claim that earlier IEPs failed to provide FAPEs, courts must pinpoint dates on which the parents should have realized that they had reason for complaints.

Where a child was misdiagnosed and subsequently placed in an inappropriate program, a federal trial court in Georgia maintained, and the Eleventh Circuit agreed, that the statute of limitations did not begin to run until the correct diagnosis was established, because the parents did not know of the student's injury until that time.[259] In addition, the Second Circuit decided that a mother from New York should have known about alleged past denials of a FAPE when she first observed her daughter's improvement in a new program and an expert expressed the opinion that she had not received appropriate services.[260]

In three disputes where parents sought compensatory education services as remedies for the past failures of school boards to provide appropriate services, federal trial courts in Pennsylvania agreed that there is no limitations period on compensatory education claims.[261] In the earliest case the court explained that unlike reimbursement, which is a right that belongs to parents, compensatory education awards belong to children and their entitlement to such awards should not depend on the diligence of their parents.[262]

Limitations periods for seeking judicial review of administrative adjudications generally begin when final orders are released. Federal trial courts in the District of Columbia[263] and New Hampshire[264] clarified that the statute of limitations begins to run on the day decisions are released, not the day the aggrieved parties receive copies of them in the mail. Likewise, the federal trial court in Connecticut set the beginning of a limitations period on the date a final order was mailed.[265]

Conversely, the Seventh Circuit affirmed that where a prevailing parent sought to recover attorney fees from a school board in Illinois, the statute of limitations did not begin until after the expiration of the time when the school board could file an appeal of the hearing officer's adjudication.[266] The court added that the mother could neither have recovered attorney fees until administrative and judicial proceedings were finished nor have known that the board would not have appealed the administrative order until after the time period to do so expired. In cases not necessarily involving appeals of due process hearings, courts agree that the clock begins to run on the day that students reach the age of majority,[267] their eligibility for services ends,[268] or they graduate.[269]

Occasionally, difficulties ensue when parents are not fully aware of their procedural rights under the IDEA. A federal trial court in Illinois commented that a case filed after the statute of limitations expired was not untimely where parents were unaware of the limitations period and were not apprised of the deadline for challenging the results of a due process hearing.[270] The court interpreted the IDEA as requiring state officials to inform parents of the full range of available procedural avenues. In addition, the federal trial court in New Hampshire declared that a case filed after the statute of limitations expired was not time-barred since the hearing officer failed to inform the parents of how much time they had to file an appeal.[271]

Courts set aside limitations periods when school boards withhold information from parents or fail to notify them properly of their rights. For example, the federal trial court in New Jersey waived the limitations period because school personnel did not provide parents with written notice explaining their reasons for denying the parents' request for an evaluation.[272] Similarly, federal trial courts in California[273] and Texas[274] agreed that the failure of board officials to provide parents with procedural safeguards notices created an exception to the statute of limitations.

In other cases federal trial courts in the District of Columbia[275] and New Mexico[276] suspended the statute of limitations because board officials failed to inform the parents of the limitations period.

In a case from Pennsylvania, the Third Circuit affirmed that for the IDEA's exceptions to the statute of limitations to apply, school officials must know that their representations of a student's progress or disabilities are untrue or inconsistent with their own assessments.[277] The court wrote that in order to be excused from the limitations period, parents must show that school personnel intentionally misled them or knowingly deceived them regarding their children's status. Further, the court thought that parents must show that misrepresentations or withholding of information caused their failure to request hearings or file complaints in timely manners.

As illustrated by a case from Connecticut, limitations periods may be tolled, or suspended, for good reason. The federal trial court tolled the limitations period when a mother requested clarification of a hearing officer's order.[278] In like manner, the federal trial court in the District of Columbia tolled the limitations period where parents requested reconsideration of hearing officers' adjudication.[279]

The First Circuit permitted a suit that was filed after the statute of limitations expired to continue where the parental delay was not unreasonable because in the interim they attempted to resolve their differences with the school committee.[280] On remand, the federal trial court in New Hampshire found,[281] and the First Circuit affirmed,[282] that the case was not barred by the doctrine of laches, which applies when a party fails to assert a right, along with a lapse of time and other circumstances that put the other party at a disadvantage. The court conceded that school board officials failed to show that witnesses were unavailable or had failed memories. In a separate suit from Maine the First Circuit agreed that insofar as a parental delay in seeking reimbursement was unreasonable, it was barred by the doctrine of laches.[283] In a conceptually related dispute, the Eleventh Circuit was of the opinion that insofar as school officials from Florida never raised the issue of a suit's being time-barred, they waived the right to use the statute of limitations as a defense.[284]

Since the IDEA has not established a statute of limitations for requesting attorney fees, courts must set limitations periods based on analogous state statutes.[285] Therefore, limitations periods for seeking attorney fees vary from one jurisdiction to the next.

Cases Under Other Statutes

The IDEA is the primary, but not only, federal statute protecting the rights of students with disabilities. Parents can seek protection for the educational rights of their children with disabilities under other federal statutes and, in particular, under state laws thåt may provide greater protection than the IDEA.[286] To this end, the IDEA specifies that none of its provisions can be interpreted as restricting, or limiting, the rights, procedures, and remedies available under the Constitution, Title V of the Rehabilitation Act of 1973, or other federal statutes protecting the rights of students with disabilities.[287] The IDEA adds that before suits can be filed under one of these other laws, dissatisfied parties must exhaust all available administrative remedies.[288]

Most cases seeking relief under statutes other than the IDEA are filed pursuant to Section 1983 of the Civil Rights Act of 1871,[289] an expansive law used to enforce rights secured by federal law or the Constitution. A variety of courts have agreed that Section 1983 may be used to enforce the results of a due process hearing[290] or to remedy a deprivation of due process or other rights secured by the IDEA.[291] Yet, courts have made it clear that cases filed under Section 1983 must be predicated on more than re-allegations of claims presented under the IDEA,[292] that Section 1983 charges lack viability when adequate remedies exist under other laws,[293] and that Section 1983 cannot be used to expand the rights of students or remedies available under the IDEA.[294] For example, since damages are unavailable under the IDEA, courts have refused to allow parents to proceed with such claims under Section 1983.[295]

Pursuant to Section 1983, school officials acting under the color of state law, meaning that they acted as if they had the official authority to act as they did, may be liable for actions that have the effect of depriving students (or their parents) of rights secured by federal law. In such a case, a federal trial court in Indiana ruled that an attorney who was hired to represent a school board in a special education case could be sued under Section 1983.[296] The student's parents successfully claimed that the advice the attorney gave the board led officials to deprive their son of his IDEA rights.

Section 504 of the Rehabilitation Act of 1973 (Section 504)[297] prohibits discrimination against individuals with disabilities in programs receiving federal financial assistance. As might have been expected, parties frequently file suit alleging discrimination under Section 504 and the deprivation of rights under the IDEA. However, if disputes can be settled under the IDEA's provisions, courts do not turn to Section 504 for relief. A case from Pennsylvania is illustrative.[298] The parents of a student with physical disabilities requested a due process hearing after school officials refused to permit him to have his service dog accompany him to class unless he moved to a less restrictive placement. After a hearing officer maintained that the student could be educated in the less restrictive environment, his parents filed suit under Section 504 rather than challenge the hearing officer's order. In denying the parental claim, a federal trial court viewed the IDEA as the exclusive avenue through which they could bring equal protection claims on behalf of their son's right to a FAPE. If relief is unavailable under the IDEA, a case may proceed under Section 504.[299]

The bottom line is that if school officials comply with the IDEA, courts are generally satisfied that they will have met the dictates of Section 504.[300] In addition, at least one court declared that a party cannot rely on Section 504 to expand the rights available under the IDEA.[301] Students' rights under Section 504 are covered thoroughly in Chapter 9.

FREQUENTLY ASKED QUESTIONS

Q: What is the advantage of using the mediation process as opposed to proceeding directly to due process hearings?

A: Unfortunately, due process hearings can be very adversarial. Mediation, on the other hand, can be a nonadversarial process to help the parties to communicate more readily and resolve their dispute in a manner acceptable to both sides. The adversarial nature of due process hearings often causes permanent breakdowns in the relationships between parents or guardians and school officials. Conversely, mediation may help to maintain working relationships between parents or guardians and school officials.

Q: Since many special education disputes end up in court, why is it necessary to exhaust administrative remedies? Would disputes be settled faster if the parties could go directly to court?

A: Exhaustion has two primary purposes: First, exhaustion allows for fact-finding by hearing officers who are familiar with special education; second, exhaustion provides a factual record for judicial review. While the results of many hearings are appealed to the courts, the majority are not. The administrative process provides a fairly expedient means of settling disputes. If disputes are appealed, judicial review can be rendered more quickly because factual records exist and courts do not need to engage in fact-finding.

Q: If parents are not satisfied with the decisions of the IEP teams of their children, how long do they have to request due process hearings?

A: The IDEA contains a two-year statute of limitations for requesting hearings. The timeline begins on the date parents knew, or should have known, of the actions that are the bases of their complaints. The limitations period can be extended if school officials misrepresented or withheld critical information from parents that interfered with their ability to request hearings. If state laws have established different limitations periods, affording students greater protection, these prevail over the IDEA and its regulations.

Q: How long do the losing parties to administrative hearings have to file judicial appeals?

A: The losing parties to administrative hearings have 90 days to file appeals unless state law dictates otherwise. Insofar as statutes of limitations may vary considerably from state to state, it is important for school administrators to check state law in this regard.

Q: Which party bears the burden of proof in administrative hearings?

A: The Supreme Court held that the parties challenging IEPs bear the burden of proof. Since it is rare for school board officials to challenge their own IEPs, this effectively places the burden of proof on parents.

Q: Which party bears the burden of proof in court?

A: This varies by jurisdiction. Some courts have ruled that the parties bringing appeals bear the burden of proof, while others have decided that those challenging IEPs or the status quo have the burden of showing why they are inappropriate. Yet, based on state laws, other courts have reasoned that the burden is always on school boards to show that their proposed IEPs and placements are appropriate. It is important for school officials to be aware of where courts within their jurisdictions place the burden of proof.

Q: Can parents bypass the IDEA by filing suit under other statutes such as Section 504 or Section 1983?

A: The IDEA specifically states that none of its provisions can be interpreted as restricting or limiting the remedies available under the Constitution, Section 504, or other statutes protecting the rights of students with disabilities. Thus, parents or guardians may file suits under statutes other than the IDEA. Even so, courts have required parents or guardians to exhaust all administrative remedies under the IDEA if such remedies have the potential to provide appropriate relief for their complaints.

Recommendations

In light of the IDEA's extensive mechanism for dispute resolution, educators should

- Familiarize themselves with the dispute resolution provisions in both federal and state law. This is important because procedures vary from one jurisdiction to the next, especially, for example, when it comes to due process hearings, since even though the majority of jurisdictions provide two levels of review, others are restricted to one.

- Take formal steps to explain to parents all of their rights to challenge any aspect of the education of their children.
- Make sure to inform parents that they may request mediation, which remains optional, or due process hearings if disputes cannot be resolved.
- Notify parents of their obligation to exhaust administrative remedies unless it is clearly not feasible to do so.
- Pay careful attention, in consultation with their attorneys, to the date restrictions in the IDEA and state law with regard to initiating due process hearings and statutes of limitations, which vary significantly from one state to the next.
- When preparing for due process hearings, comply with the IDEA's requirement directing them to share all information with parents at least five days prior to the hearings.
- Keep careful records of all materials relating to student placements since this information is most useful in due process hearings and judicial proceedings.
- Remind parents that they may safeguard the rights of their children under other federal and state laws in addition to the IDEA.

Endnotes

1. 20 U.S.C. §§ 1400–1482 (2012). The IDEA's regulations can be found at Assistance to the States for the Education of Children with Disabilities, 34 C.F.R. §§ 300.1–300.818 (2013).
2. 20 U.S.C. § 1415.
3. 20 U.S.C. § 1415(e).
4. 20 U.S.C. § 1415(f).
5. 20 U.S.C. § 1415(i)(2)(A).
6. Honig v. Doe, 484 U.S. 305 (1988).
7. 20 U.S.C. § 1415(j).
8. 20 U.S.C. § 1415(k)(3)(B).
9. Honig v. Doe, 484 U.S. 305 (1988).
10. 20 U.S.C. § 1415(i)(2)(C)(iii).
11. 20 U.S.C. § 1415(i)(2)(C)(iii).
12. 458 U.S. 176, 206 (1982).
13. 20 U.S.C. § 1415(e)(1).
14. 20 U.S.C. § 1415(e)(2)(D).
15. 20 U.S.C. § 1415(e)(2)(A)(iii); 34 C.F.R. § 300.506(b)(1).
16. 20 U.S.C. § 1415(e)(2)(C).
17. 34 C.F.R. § 300.506(c)(1).
18. 34 C.F.R. § 300.506(c)(2).
19. 20 U.S.C. § 1415(e)(2)(E).
20. 20 U.S.C. § 1415(e)(2)(F).
21. 20 U.S.C. § 1415(e)(2)(G).

22. 34 C.F.R. § 300.506(b)(7). *See* J.M.C. and M.E.C. *ex rel.* E.G.C. v. Louisiana Board of Elementary and Secondary Education, 562 F. Supp. 2d 748 (M.D. La. 2008), 584 F. Supp. 2d 894 (M.D. La. 2008).

23. 20 U.S.C. § 1415(e)(2)(B).

24. Osborne, A. G.. & Russo, C. J. (2007). Resolution sessions under the IDEA: Are they mandatory? *Education Law Reporter, 218,* 7–12.

25. 34 C.F.R. § 300.510(a)(4).

26. 20 U.S.C. § 1415(f)(1)(B)(i); 34 C.F.R. § 300.510(a).

27. 34 C.F.R. § 300.510(b)(5).

28. J.D.G. v. Colonial School District, 748 F. Supp. 2d 362 (D. Del. 2010).

29. 34 C.F.R. § 300.510(a)(1)(i).

30. 34 C.F.R. § 300.510(a)(1)(ii).

31. 34 C.F.R. § 300.510(b)(4).

32. 34 C.F.R. § 300.510(a)(3).

33. Spencer v. District of Columbia, 416 F. Supp. 2d 5 (D.D.C. 2006). *See also* K.S. *ex rel.* P.S. v. Fremont Unified School District, 545 F. Supp. 2d 995 (N.D. Cal. 2008) (treating a hearing officer's sanctions against parent's attorney for walking out of a resolution session as warranted).

34. 20 U.S.C. § 1415(f)(1)(B)(ii); 34 C.F.R. § 300.510(b).

35. Friendship Edison Public Charter School v. Smith *ex rel.* L.S. 561 F. Supp. 2d 74 D.D.C. 2008).

36. 20 U.S.C. § 1415(f)(1)(B)(iii); 34 C.F.R. § 300.510(c).

37. 20 U.S.C. § 1415(f)(1)(B)(iv); 34 C.F.R. § 300.510(d). *See* J.M.C. and M.E.C. *ex rel.* E.G.C. v. Louisiana Board of Elementary and Secondary Education, 562 F. Supp. 2d 748 (M.D. La. 2008), 584 F. Supp. 2d 894 (M.D. La. 2008).

38. 20 U.S.C. § 1415(f).

39. 34 C.F.R. § 300.300(a)(3).

40. 34 C.F.R. § 300.503(a).

41. 20 U.S.C. § 1415(j).

42. 20 U.S.C. § 1415(k)(3)(B).

43. Honig v. Doe, 484 U.S. 305 (1988).

44. 34 C.F.R. § 300.512(c)(1).

45. 34 C.F.R. § 300.512(c)(2).

46. 20 U.S.C. § 1415(b); 34 C.F.R. § 300.30(a)(5).

47. 34 C.F.R. § 300.519(g).

48. 34 C.F.R. § 300.519(d)(2).

49. 34 C.F.R. § 300.508(a)(2).

50. 34 C.F.R. § 300.508(b).

51. 34 C.F.R. § 300.508(c).

52. 34 C.F.R. § 300.508(d)(1).

53. 34 C.F.R. § 300.508(d)(2).

54. 34 C.F.R. § 300.508(d)(3).

55. 34 C.F.R. § 300.508(d)(4).

56. 34 C.F.R. § 300.508(e).

57. 20 U.S.C. § 1415(f)(1)(A).

58. 20 U.S.C. § 1415(g).

59. Burr v. Ambach, 863 F.3d 1071 (2d Cir. 1988), *vacated sub nom.* Sobol v. Burr, 492 U.S. 902 (1989), *affirmed* 888 F.2d 258 (2d Cir. 1989), *cert. denied,* 494 U.S. 1005 (1990).

60. Muth v. Central Bucks School District, 839 F.2d 113 (3d Cir. 1988), *affirmed on other grounds sub nom.* Dellmuth v. Muth, 491 U.S. 223 (1989); Johnson v. Lancaster-Lebanon Intermediate Unit No. 13, Lancaster City School District, 757 F. Supp. 606 (E.D. Pa. 1991).

61. Grymes v. Madden, 672 F.2d 321 (3d Cir. 1982).

62. Burr v. Ambach, 863 F.3d 1071 (2d Cir. 1988), *vacated sub nom.* Sobol v. Burr, 492 U.S. 902 (1989), *affirmed* 888 F.2d 258 (2d Cir. 1989), *cert. denied*, 494 U.S. 1005 (1990); Louis M. v. Ambach, 714 F. Supp. 1276 (N.D.N.Y. 1989); Holmes v. Sobol, 690 F. Supp. 154 (W.D.N.Y. 1988); Antkowiak v. Ambach, 838 F.2d 635 (2d Cir. 1988).

63. Board of Education of the Baldwin Union Free School District v. Commissioner of Education, 610 N.Y.S.2d 426 (N.Y. Sup. Ct. 1994).

64. 20 U.S.C. § 1415(f)(3)(C).

65. 34 C.F.R. § 300.507(a)(2).

66. 20 U.S.C. § 1415(f)(3)(D).

67. 20 U.S.C. § 1415(i)(2)(B).

68. 20 U.S.C. § 1415(f)(1)(A).

69. Hacienda La Puente Unified School District of Los Angeles v. Honig, 976 F.2d 487 (9th Cir. 1992).

70. Dong v. Board of Education, 197 F.3d 793 (6th Cir. 1999).

71. Kuszewski v. Chippewa Valley Schools, 117 F. Supp. 646 (E.D. Mich. 2000).

72. Compton Unified School District v. Addison, 598 F.3d 1181 (9th Cir. 2010).

73. 34 C.F.R. § 300.300(a)(3)(i).

74. 34 C.F.R. § 300.300(a)(3)(ii).

75. 34 C.F.R. § 300.300(a)(3).

76. 34 C.F.R. § 300.300(b)(2).

77. Board of Education of Strongville City School District v. Theado, 566 N.E.2d 667 (Ohio 1991).

78. 20 U.S.C. § 1415(f)(3)(B); 34 C.F.R. § 300.511(d).

79. Cothern v. Mallory, 565 F. Supp. 701 (W.D. Mo.1983).

80. 20 U.S.C. § 1415(f)(3)(A); 34 C.F.R. § 300.511(c).

81. 34 C.F.R. § 300.511(c)(2).

82. 34 C.F.R. § 300.511(c)(3).

83. L.B. and J.B. *ex rel.* K.B. v. Nebo School District, 379 F.3d 966 (10th Cir. 2004).

84. W.T. and K.T. *ex rel.* J.T. v. Board of Education of the School District of New York City, 716 F. Supp. 2d 270 (S.D.N.Y. 2010).

85. *Also see* C.G. and L.G. *ex rel.* B.G. v. New York City Department of Education, 752 F. Supp. 2d 355 (S.D.N.Y. 2010) (rejecting statistical evidence of a state review officer's past bias as insufficient to sustain an argument against granting his orders due weight).

86. A.B. *ex rel.* Susan and Mark B. v. Montgomery County Intermediate Unit, 409 F. App'x 602 (3d Cir. 2011).

87. D.R. *ex rel.* Etsuko R. v. Department of Education, State of Hawai'i, 827 F. Supp. 2d 1161 (D. Haw. 2011).

88. Singletary v. Department of Health and Human Services, 848 F. Supp. 2d 588 (E.D.N.C. 2012); B.J.S. *ex rel.* N.S. v. State Education Department/University of New York, 699 F. Supp. 2d 586 (W.D.N.Y. 2010).

89. Kerr Center Parents Association v. Charles, 897 F.2d 1463 (9th Cir. 1990).

90. Bray v. Hobart City School Corporation, 818 F. Supp. 1226 (N.D. Ind. 1993).

91. 20 U.S.C. §1415(i)(3)(B).
92. 34 C.F.R. § 300.511(c).
93. Canton Board of Education v. N.B. and R.B., 343 F. Supp. 2d 123 (D. Conn. 2004).
94. 546 U.S. 49 (2005).
95. Osborne, A. G., & Russo, C. J. (2005). The burden of proof in special education hearings: *Schaffer v. Weast. Education Law Reporter, 200*, 1–12.
96. Wenkart, R. D. (2004). The burden of proof in IDEA due process hearings. *Education Law Reporter, 187*, 817–823.
97. Russo, C. J., & Osborne, A. G. (2006). The Supreme Court clarifies the burden of proof in special education due process hearings: *Schaffer ex rel. Schaffer v. Weast. Education Law Reporter, 208*, 705–717.
98. Van Duyn v. Baker School District, 502 F. Supp. 2d 811 (9th Cir. 2007). *See also,* M.M. *ex rel.* L.R. v. Special School District No. 1, 512 F.3d 455 (8th Cir. 2008) (declaring that the trial court erred by assigning the burden of proof to parents).
99. Honig v. Doe, 484 U.S. 305 (1988).
100. Independent School District No. 623 v. Digre, 893 F.2d 987 (8th Cir. 1990); Abney *ex rel.* Kantor v. District of Columbia, 849 F.2d 1491 (D.C. Cir. 1988).
101. Padilla v. School District No. 1, 233 F.3d 1268 (10th Cir. 2000).
102. Civil Rights Act of 1871, Section 1983, 42 U.S.C. § 1983 (2006).
103. T.S. v. Ridgefield Board of Education, 10 F.3d 87 (2d Cir. 1993).
104. *See, e.g.,* D.C. *ex rel.* S.K. v. Hamamoto, 97 F. App'x 736 (9th Cir. 2004); Doe v. Arizona Department of Education, 111 F.3d 678 (9th Cir. 1997); T.S. v. Ridgefield Board of Education, 10 F.3d 87 (2d Cir. 1993); Gardener v. School Board of Caddo Parish, 958 F.2d 108 (5th Cir. 1992); Christopher W. v. Portsmouth School Committee, 877 F.2d 1089 (1st Cir. 1989); Cox v. Jenkins, 878 F.2d 414 (D.C. Cir. 1989); Doe v. Smith, 879 F.2d 1340 (6th Cir. 1989); Riley v. Ambach, 668 F.2d 635 (2d Cir. 1981).
105. Crocker v. Tennessee Secondary Schools Athletic Association, 873 F.2d 933 (6th Cir. 1989), 980 F.2d 382 (6th Cir. 1992).
106. Polera v. Board of Education of the Newburgh Enlarged City School District, 288 F.3d 478 (2d Cir. 2002).
107. Hoeft v. Tucson Unified School District, 967 F.2d 1298 (9th Cir. 1992).
108. Jackson v. Fort Stanton Hospital and Training School, 757 F. Supp. 1243 (D.N.M. 1990).
109. Association for Community Living in Colorado v. Romer, 992 F.2d 1040 (10th Cir. 1993); Association for Retarded Citizens of Alabama v. Teague, 830 F.2d 158 (11th Cir. 1987).
110. Association for Community Living in Colorado v. Romer, 992 F.2d 1040 (10th Cir. 1993).
111. Evans v. Evans, 818 F. Supp. 1215 (N.D. Ind. 1993).
112. Garro v. State of Connecticut, 23 F.3d 734 (2d Cir. 1994).
113. Stellato v. Board of Education of the Ellenville Central School District, 842 F. Supp. 1512 (N.D.N.Y. 1994). *See also* Loch v. Board of Education of Edwardsville Community School District #7, 573 F. Supp. 2d 1072 (S.D. Ill. 2008) (barring parents from raising claims about the sufficiency of an evaluation since they failed to raise these allegations before a hearing); O'Dell v. Special School District of St. Louis County, 503 F. Supp. 2d 1206 (E.D. Mo. 2007) (parents could not raise a claim that an IEP team was improperly constituted because they had not raised the issue at the hearing).

114. *See, e.g.*, R.M., D.M., and B.M. v. Waukee Community School District, 589 F. Supp. 2d 1141 (S.D. Iowa 2008); Torrie v. Cwayna, 841 F. Supp. 1434 (W.D. Mich. 1994).

115. Hayes v. Unified School District No. 377, 877 F.2d 809 (10th Cir. 1989).

116. Norris v. Board of Education of Greenwood Community School Corporation, 797 F. Supp. 1452 (S.D. Ind. 1992).

117. 29 U.S.C. § 794 (2012).

118. Bishop v. Oakstone Academy, 477 F. Supp. 2d 876 (S.D. Ohio 2007). *See also* Baldessarre v. Monroe-Woodbury Central School District, 820 F. Supp. 2d 490 (S.D.N.Y. 2011), *affirmed* 496 F. App'x 131 (2d Cir. 2012) (affirming that parents were required to exhaust the IDEA's administrative remedies since relief was available via this process); G.J. *ex rel.* E.J. and L.J. v. Muscogee County School District, 704 F. Supp. 2d 1299 (M.D. Ga. 2010) (requiring exhaustion where parents sought relief that was available under the IDEA), *affirmed on other grounds*, 668 F.3d 1258 (11th Cir. 2012).

119. Clark, S. G. (2002). Administrative remedy under IDEA: Must it be exhausting? *Education Law Reporter, 163,* 1–15.

120. *See, e.g.,* Muskrat v. Deer Creek Public Schools, 715 F.3d 775 (10th Cir. 2013) (affirming that parents seeking damages for alleged physical abuse by school staff were not required to exhaust administrative remedies).

121. Kerr Center Parents Association v. Charles, 897 F.2d 1463 (9th Cir. 1990).

122. Begay v. Hodel, 730 F. Supp. 1001 (D. Ariz. 1990). *See also* Massey v. District of Columbia, 400 F. Supp. 2d 66 (D.D.C. 2005).

123. Dean *ex rel.* J.D.J. v. School District of Niagara Falls, 615 F. Supp. 2d 63 (W.D.N.Y. 2009).

124. J.S. *ex rel.* N.S. v. Attica Central Schools, 386 F.3d 107 (2d Cir. 2004).

125. *See, e.g.,* S.W. *ex rel.* J.W. v. Warren, 528 F. Supp. 2d 282 (S.D.N.Y. 2007) (a hearing officer lacked the authority to require changes in policies and procedures whose implementation resulted in systemic violations of the IDEA).

126. Christopher S. *ex rel.* Rita S. v. Stanislaus County Office of Education, 384 F.3d 1205 (9th Cir. 2004).

127. DL v. District of Columbia, 450 F. Supp. 2d 11 (D.D.C. 2006). *See also* Kalliope R. v. New York State Department of Education, 827 F. Supp. 2d 130 (E.D.N.Y. 2010) (parents challenging a policy on student-to-teacher ratios did not need to exhaust administrative remedies); L.M.P. *ex rel.* E.P. v. School Board of Broward County, 516 F. Supp. 2d 1294 (S.D. Fla. 2007) (treating exhaustion as futile where parents alleged that the board had a uniform policy of denying all requests for applied behavioral analysis).

128. Barron v. South Dakota Board of Regents, 655 F.3d 787 (8th Cir. 2011).

129. Heldman v. Sobol, 962 F.2d 148 (2d Cir. 1992).

130. Straube v. Florida Union Free School District, 801 F. Supp. 1164 (S.D.N.Y. 1992).

131. Vander Malle v. Ambach, 667 F. Supp. 1015 (S.D.N.Y. 1987).

132. J.G. v. Board of Education of the Rochester City School District, 830 F.2d 444 (2d Cir. 1987).

133. *See, e.g.,* R.B. v. Mastery Charter School, 762 F. Supp. 2d 745 (E.D. Pa. 2010) (excusing a mother who sought relief after charter school officials unilaterally disenrolled her daughter from exhausting the IDEA's administrative remedies because immediate interim relief was essential).

134. Komninos v. Upper Saddle River Board of Education, 13 F.3d 775 (3d Cir. 1994).

135. N.D. v. Hawaii Department of Education, 600 F.3d 1104 (9th Cir. 2010).

136. Lester H. v. Gilhool, 916 F.2d 865 (3d Cir. 1990).

137. Frutiger v. Hamilton Central School District, 928 F.2d 68 (2d Cir. 1991).

138. *See, e.g.,* Tristan *ex rel.* E.A.T. v. Socorro Independent School District, 902 F. Supp. 2d 870, 873 (W.D. Tex. 2012) (a damages claim for noneducational injuries was not subject to the exhaustion requirement); Sagan v. Sumner County Board of Education, 726 F. Supp. 2d 868 (M.D. Tenn. 2010), *dismissed in part, vacated in part and remanded on other grounds* 501 F. App'x 537 (6th Cir. 2012) (parents who alleged unlawful use of force and negligence by school officials were not subject to the IDEA's exhaustion requirement); Funez v. Guzman, 687 F. Supp. 2d 1214 (D. Or. 2009) (parents who requested monetary damages for their son's injuries were not required to exhaust administrative remedies); Lopez v. Metropolitan Government of Nashville and Davidson County, 646 F. Supp. 2d 891 (M.D. Tenn. 2009) (parents who sought redress for their child's injuries were not required to exhaust administrative remedies).

139. Payne v. Peninsula School District, 653 F.3d 863 (9th Cir. 2011).

140. *See, e.g.,* D.R. *ex rel.* Courtney R. v. Antelope Valley Union High School District, 746 F. Supp. 2d 1132 (C.D. Cal. 2010); M.G. v. Crisfield, 547 F. Supp. 2d 399 (D.N.J. 2008); Robertson v. Granite City Community Unit School District No. 9, 684 F. Supp. 1002 (S.D. Ill. 1988); Doe v. Belleville Public School District No. 118, 672 F. Supp. 342 (S.D. Ill. 1987).

141. 20 U.S.C. § 1415(h)(1).

142. In re Arons, 796 A.2d 867 (Del. 2000).

143. 20 U.S.C. § 1415(h)(1)(2).

144. 34 C.F.R. § 300.512(a)(3).

145. 20 U.S.C. § 1415(h)(3)–(4).

146. Militello v. Board of Education of the City of Union City, 803 F. Supp. 974 (D.N.J. 1992).

147. Edward B. v. Paul, 814 F.2d 52 (1st Cir. 1987). Subsequently, the IDEA was amended to give parents the option of receiving an electronic verbatim record. 20 U.S.C. § 1415(h)(3).

148. 34 C.F.R. § 300.515(a).

149. 34 C.F.R. § 300.515(c).

150. 20 U.S.C. § 1415(i)(1)(A).

151. 34 C.F.R. § 300.515(b).

152. Slack v. State of Delaware Department of Public Instruction, 826 F. Supp. 115 (D. Del. 1993).

153. 20 U.S.C. § 1415(i)(2)(A).

154. Slack v. State of Delaware Department of Public Instruction, 826 F. Supp. 115 (D. Del. 1993).

155. Russo, C. J. (2007). The rights of non-attorney parents under the IDEA: *Winkelman v. Parma City School District. Education Law Reporter, 221,* 1–19.

156. 550 U.S. 516 (2007).

157. Cavanaugh v. Cardinal Local School District, 409 F.3d 753 (6th Cir. 2005).

158. Collinsgru v. Palmyra Board of Education, 161 F.3d 225 (3d Cir. 1998).

159. Winkelman *ex rel.* Winkelman v. Parma City School District, 150 F. App'x 406 (6th Cir. 2005).

160. Woodruff v. Hamilton Township Public Schools, 305 F. App'x 833 (3d Cir. 2009).

161. KLA *ex rel.* B.L. v. Windham Southeast Supervisory Union, 348 F. App'x 604 (2d Cir. 2009).

162. 34 C.F.R. § 300.30(a)(5).

163. Heldman v. Sobol, 962 F.2d 148 (2d Cir. 1992).

164. Susan R.M. v. Northeast Independent School District, 818 F.2d 455 (5th Cir. 1987).

165. Carpenter v. Pennell School District Elementary Unit, 2002 WL 1832854 (E.D. Pa. 2002), *affirmed sub nom.* Carpenter v. Children and Youth Services, 64 F. App'x 850 (3d Cir. 2003) (table), *cert. denied*, 540 U.S. 819 (2003).

166. Shook v. Gaston County Board of Education, 882 F.2d 119 (4th Cir. 1989).

167. Emery v. Roanoke City School Board, 432 F.3d 294 (4th Cir. 2005).

168. Gehman v. Prudential Property and Casualty Insurance Company, 702 F. Supp. 1192 (E.D. Pa. 1989); Allstate Insurance Co. v. Bethlehem Area School District, 678 F. Supp. 1132 (E.D. Pa. 1987).

169. 34 C.F.R. § 300.300(a)(3).

170. Clovis Unified School District v. California Office of Administrative Hearings, 903 F.2d 635 (9th Cir. 1990).

171. Family & Children's Center v. School City of Mishawaka, 13 F.3d 1052 (7th Cir. 1994).

172. Lawrence Township Board of Education v. New Jersey, 417 F.3d 368 (3d Cir. 2005). *See also* Rancocas Valley Regional High School Board of Education v. M.R., 380 F. Supp. 2d 177 (D.N.J. 2005) (a board lacked standing to sue the state to compel it to pay a student's tuition).

173. Andrews v. Ledbetter, 880 F.2d 1287 (11th Cir. 1989).

174. Traverse Bay Area Intermediate School District v. Michigan Department of Education, 615 F.3d 622 (6th Cir. 2010).

175. Lake Washington School District No. 414 v. Office of Superintendent of Public Instruction, 634 F.3d 1065 (9th Cir. 2011).

176. Idea Public Charter School v. District of Columbia, 374 F. Supp. 2d 158 (D.D.C. 2005).

177. Metropolitan School District v. Buskirk, 950 F. Supp. 899 (S.D. Ind. 1997).

178. Board of Education of the Seneca Falls Central School District v. Board of Education of the Liverpool Central School District, 728 F. Supp. 910 (W.D.N.Y. 1990).

179. Friendship Edison Public Charter School v. Murphy, 448 F. Supp. 2d 166 (D.D.C. 2006); Friendship Edison Public Charter School v. Smith, 429 F. Supp. 2d 195 (D.D.C. 2006); Hyde Leadership Public Charter School v. Clark, 424 F. Supp. 2d 58 (D.D.C. 2006).

180. Bryant v. New York State Education Department, 692 F.3d 202 (2d Cir. 2012).

181. S.H. *ex rel.* Durrell v. Lower Merion School District, 2013 WL 4752015 (3d Cir. 22013).

182. Osborne, A. G. (2001). Proving that you have provided a FAPE under IDEA. *Education Law Reporter, 151*, 367–372.

183. Doe v. Brookline School Committee, 722 F.2d 910 (1st Cir. 1983).

184. Barnett v. Fairfax County School Board, 927 F.2d 146 (4th Cir. 1991), *cert. denied*, 502 U.S. 859 (1991).

185. Christopher M. v. Corpus Christi Independent School District, 933 F.2d 1285 (5th Cir. 1991).

186. Dong v. Board of Education, 197 F.3d 793 (6th Cir. 1999).
187. Board of Education of Community Consolidated School District v. Illinois State Board of Education, 938 F.2d 712 (7th Cir. 1991).
188. Johnson v. Independent School District No. 4, 921 F.2d 1022 (10th Cir. 1990), *cert. denied*, 500 U.S. 905 (1991).
189. Devine v. Indian River County School Board, 249 F.3d 1289 (11th Cir. 2001).
190. Oberti v. Board of Education of the Borough of Clementon School District, 995 F.2d 1204 (3d Cir. 1993).
191. Board of Education of County of Kanawha v. Michael M., 95 F. Supp. 2d 600 (S.D. W. Va. 2000).
192. Leighty *ex rel.* Leighty v. Lauren School District, 457 F. Supp. 2d 546 (W.D. Pa. 2006).
193. Town of Burlington v. Department of Education, Commonwealth of Massachusetts, 736 F.2d 773 (1st Cir. 1984), *affirmed on other grounds sub nom.* Burlington School Committee v. Department of Education of the Commonwealth of Massachusetts, 471 U.S. 359 (1985).
194. Board of Education of the Hendrick Hudson Central School District v. Rowley, 458 U.S. 176 (1982).
195. Tice v. Botetourt County School Board, 908 F.2d 1200 (4th Cir. 1990).
196. Board of Education of the Hendrick Hudson Central School District v. Rowley, 458 U.S. 176 (1982).
197. Kerkham v. Superintendent, District of Columbia Schools, 931 F.2d 84 (D.C. Cir. 1991); Briggs v. Board of Education of Connecticut, 882 F.2d 688 (2d Cir. 1989); Roncker v. Walter, 700 F.2d 1058 (6th Cir. 1983).
198. 458 U.S. 176 (1982).
199. Town of Burlington v. Department of Education, Commonwealth of Massachusetts, 736 F.2d 773 (1st Cir. 1984), *affirmed on other grounds sub nom.* Burlington School Committee v. Department of Education of the Commonwealth of Massachusetts, 471 U.S. 359 (1985).
200. Lenn v. Portland School Community, 998 F.2d 1083 (1st Cir. 1993).
201. Bertolucci v. San Carlos Elementary School District, 721 F. Supp. 1150 (N.D. Cal. 1989).
202. Woods v. New Jersey Department of Education, 796 F. Supp. 767 (D.N.J. 1992); 823 F. Supp. 254 (D.N.J. 1993).
203. Burke County Board of Education v. Denton, 895 F.2d 973 (4th Cir. 1990).
204. J.P. *ex rel.* Peterson v. County School Board of Hanover County, 516 F.3d 254 (4th Cir. 2008).
205. Teague Independent School District v. Todd D., 999 F.2d 127 (5th Cir. 1993).
206. Kerkham v. McKenzie, 862 F.2d 884 (D.C. Cir. 1988).
207. Block v. District of Columbia, 748 F. Supp. 891 (D.D.C. 1990).
208. Puffer v. Raynolds, 761 F. Supp. 838 (D. Mass. 1988).
209. Thomas v. Cincinnati Board of Education, 918 F.2d 618 (6th Cir. 1990); Karl v. Board of Education of the Genesco Central School District, 736 F.2d 873 (2d Cir. 1984).
210. Puffer v. Raynolds, 761 F. Supp. 838 (D. Mass. 1988).
211. Doyle v. Arlington County School Board, 953 F.2d 100 (4th Cir. 1991), *on remand* 806 F. Supp. 1253 (E.D. Va. 1992), *affirmed* 39 F.3d 1176 (4th Cir. 1994) (mem.).
212. 806 F. Supp. 2d (E.D. Va. 1992).
213. 39 F.3d 1176 (4th Cir. 1994) (mem.).

214. 20 U.S.C. § 1415(i)(2)(C)(ii).
215. Clark, S. G. (2005). Judicial review and the admission of "additional evidence" under the IDEIA: An unusual mixture of discretion and deference. *Education Law Reporter, 201*, 823–843.
216. Walker County School District v. Bennett, 203 F.3d 1293 (11th Cir. 2000).
217. Metropolitan Board of Public Education v. Guest, 193 F.3d 457 (6th Cir. 1999).
218. Roland M. v. Concord School Committee, 910 F.2d 983 (1st Cir. 1990), *cert. denied* 499 U.S. 912 (1991). *See also* I.M. *ex rel.* C.C. v. Northampton Public Schools, 858 F. Supp. 2d 132 (D. Mass. 2012) (parents could not submit evidence that was available at the time of an administrative hearing).
219. Board of Education of the Paxton-Buckley-Loda Unit School District No. 10 v. Jeff S., 184 F. Supp. 2d 790 (C.D. Ill. 2002).
220. Metropolitan Board of Public Education of the Metropolitan Government of Nashville and Davidson County v. Bellamy, 116 F. App'x 570 (6th Cir. 2004).
221. Hunger v. Leininger, 15 F.3d 664 (7th Cir. 1994), *cert. denied*, 513 U.S. 839 (1994).
222. Metropolitan Government of Nashville and Davidson County v. Cook, 915 F.2d 232 (6th Cir. 1990).
223. Teague Independent School District v. Todd D., 999 F.2d 127 (5th Cir. 1993).
224. Ojai Unified School District v. Jackson, 4 F.3d 1467 (9th Cir. 1993), *cert. denied*, 513 U.S. 825 (1994).
225. Konkel v. Elmbrook School District, 348 F. Supp. 2d 1018 (E.D. Wis. 2004).
226. Fuhrmann v. East Hanover Board of Education, 993 F.2d 1031 (3d Cir. 1993).
227. Moseley v. Board of Education of Albuquerque Public Schools, 483 F.3d 689 (10th Cir. 2007); Thomas R.W. v. Massachusetts Department of Education, 130 F.3d 477 (1st Cir. 1997); Doe v. Maher, 793 F.2d 1470 (9th Cir. 1986), *affirmed* Honig v. Doe, 484 U.S. 305 (1988); M.K. *ex rel.* Mrs. K. v. Sergi, 554 F. Supp. 2d 201 (D. Conn.2008).
228. Smith v. Special School District No. 1, 184 F.3d 764 (8th Cir. 1999).
229. Honig v. Doe, 484 U.S. 305 (1988).
230. Lee v. Biloxi School District, 963 F.2d 837 (5th Cir. 1992).
231. Greene v. Harrisville School District, 771 F. Supp. 1 (D.N.H. 1990).
232. Merrifield v. Lake Central School Corporation, 770 F. Supp. 468 (N.D. Ind. 1991).
233. McDowell v. Fort Bend Independent School District, 737 F. Supp. 386 (S.D. Tex. 1990).
234. Robbins v. Maine School Administrative District No. 56, 807 F. Supp. 11 (D. Me. 1992).
235. Stellato v. Board of Education of the Ellenville Central School District, 842 F. Supp. 1512 (N.D.N.Y. 1994).
236. 484 U.S. 305 (1988).
237. Jenkins v. Squillacote, 935 F.2d 303 (D.C. Cir. 1991).
238. Straube v. Florida Union Free School District, 801 F. Supp. 1164 (S.D.N.Y. 1992).
239. DeVries v. Spillane, 853 F.2d 264 (4th Cir. 1988).
240. Daniel R.R. v. State Board of Education, 874 F.2d 1036 (5th Cir. 1989).
241. Abney *ex rel.* Kantor v. District of Columbia, 849 F.2d 1491 (D.C. Cir. 1988).
242. D.F. *ex rel.* A.C. v. Collingswood Public Schools, 694 F.3d 488 (3d Cir. 2012).

243. Garcia v. Board of Education of Albuquerque Public Schools, 520 F.3d 1116 (10th Cir. 2008).

244. S.S. *ex rel.* Tamika Shank v. Howard Road Academy, 562 F. Supp. 2d 126 (D.D.C. 2008). *See also* Theodore v. Government of the District of Columbia, 655 F. Supp. 2d 136 (D.D.C. 2009) (refusing to bar claims for compensatory education based on the doctrine of mootness).

245. E.D. *ex rel.* Doe v. Newburyport Public Schools, 654 F.3d 140 (1st Cir. 2011).

246. Fagan v. District of Columbia, 136 F.R.D. 5 (D.D.C. 1991).

247. Jenkins v. State of Florida, 931 F.2d 1469 (11th Cir. 1991).

248. Theodore v. Government of the District of Columbia, 772 F. Supp. 2d 287 (D.D.C. 2011).

249. In re Smith, 926 F.2d 1027 (11th Cir. 1991).

250. Woods v. New Jersey Department of Education, 796 F. Supp. 767 (D.N.J. 1992); 823 F. Supp. 254 (D.N.J. 1993).

251. D.R. v. East Brunswick Board of Education, 838 F. Supp. 184 (D.N.J. 1993), *reversed on other grounds* 109 F.3d 896 (3d Cir. 1997).

252. Amy S. v. Danbury Local School District, 174 F. App'x 896 (6th Cir. 2006).

253. Osborne, A. G. (2004). Statutes of limitations for filing a lawsuit under the IDEA: A state by state analysis. *Education Law Reporter, 191*, 545–556. Zirkel, P. A., & Maher, P. J. (2003). The statute of limitations under the Individuals with Disabilities Education Act. *Education Law Reporter, 175*, 1–5. Osborne, A. G. (1996). Statutes of limitations for filing a lawsuit under the Individuals with Disabilities Education Act. *Education Law Reporter, 106*, 959–970.

254. 20 U.S.C. § 1415(f)(3)(C); 34 C.F.R. § 300.511(e).

255. *See, e.g.,* D.C. and A.C. v. Klein Independent School District, 711 F. Supp. 2d 739 (S.D. Tex. 2010) (applying Texas's one-year statute of limitations).

256. 20 U.S.C. § 1415(f)(3)(D); 34 C.F.R. § 300.511(f).

257. 20 U.S.C. § 1415(g)(2)(B); 34 C.F.R. § 300.516(b).

258. *See, e.g.,* Brennan v. Regional School District No. 1 Board of Education, 531 F. Supp. 2d 245 (D. Conn. 2008) (applying Connecticut's 45-day statute of limitations).

259. Draper v. Atlanta Independent School System, 480 F. Supp. 2d 1331 (N.D. Ga. 2007), *affirmed* 518 F.3d 1275 (11th Cir. 2008).

260. Samoza v. New York City Department of Education, 538 F.3d 106 (2d Cir. 2008).

261. Heather D. v. Northampton Area School District, 511 F. Supp. 2d 549 (E.D. Pa. 2007); A.A. *ex rel.* E.A. v. Exeter Township School District, 485 F. Supp. 2d 587 (E.D. Pa. 2007); Keystone Central School District v. R.E. *ex rel.* H.E., 438 F. Supp. 2d 519 (M.D. Pa. 2006).

262. Keystone Central School District v. R.E. *ex rel.* H.E., 438 F. Supp. 2d 519 (M.D. Pa. 2006).

263. J.S. v. District of Columbia, 533 F. Supp. 2d 160 (D.D.C. 2008); Smith v. District of Columbia, 496 F. Supp. 2d 125 (D.D.C. 2007); R.P. v. District of Columbia, 474 F. Supp. 2d 152 (D.D.C. 2007); Carruthers v. Ludlow Taylor Elementary Schools, 432 F. Supp. 2d 75 (D.D.C. 2006).

264. G.D. v. Westmoreland School District, 783 F. Supp. 1532 (D.N.H. 1992); I.D. v. Westmoreland School District, 788 F. Supp. 632 (D.N.H. 1991).

265. Brennan v. Regional School District No. 1 Board of Education, 531 F. Supp. 2d 245 (D. Conn. 2008).

266. McCartney C. v. Herrin Community Unit School District No. 4, 21 F.3d 173 (7th Cir. 1994).

267. Shook v. Gaston County Board of Education, 882 F.2d 119 (4th Cir. 1989).

268. Hall v. Knott County Board of Education, 941 F.2d 402 (6th Cir. 1991).

269. Richards v. Fairfax County School Board, 798 F. Supp. 338 (E.D. Va. 1992).

270. Board of Education of the City of Chicago v. Wolinsky, 842 F. Supp. 1080 (N.D. Ill. 1993).

271. Hebert v. Manchester, New Hampshire, School District, 833 F. Supp. 80 (D.N.H. 1993).

272. D.G. v. Somerset Hills School District, 559 F. Supp. 2d 484 (D.N.J. 2008).

273. Ravenswood City School District v. J.S., 870 F. Supp. 2d 780 (N.D. Cal. 2012).

274. El Paso Independent School District v. Richard R., 567 F. Supp. 2d 918 (W.D. Tex. 2008).

275. Abraham v. District of Columbia, 338 F. Supp. 2d 113 (D.D.C. 2004).

276. Chavez *ex rel.* E.C. v. Española Public Schools, 795 F. Supp. 2d 1244 (D.N.M. 2011).

277. D.K. *ex rel.* Stephen K. v. Abington School District, 696 F.3d 233 (3d Cir. 2012).

278. R.M. *ex rel.* J.M. v. Vernon Board of Education, 208 F. Supp. 2d 216 (D. Conn. 2002).

279. Theodore v. Government of the District of Columbia, 655 F. Supp. 2d 136 (D.D.C. 2009); Stanton v. District of Columbia, 639 F. Supp. 2d 1 (D.D.C. 2009); R.S. v. District of Columbia, 292 F. Supp. 2d 23 (D.D.C. 2003).

280. Murphy v. Timberlane Regional School District, 973 F.2d 13 (1st Cir. 1992), *on remand*, 819 F. Supp. 1127 (D.N.H.1993), *affirmed* 22 F.3d 1186 (1st Cir. 1994), *cert. denied*, 513 U.S. 987 (1994).

281. *Id.*

282. *Id.*

283. School Union No. 37 v. Ms. C., 518 F.3d 31 (1st Cir. 2008).

284. J.S.K. v. Hendry County School Board, 941 F.2d 1563 (11th Cir. 1991).

285. Brandon E. v. Department of Education, State of Hawaii, 621 F. Supp. 2d 1013 (D. Haw. 2008) (applying a six-year catchall statute of limitations); Brown *ex rel.* P.L. v. Barbara Jordan P.C.S., 495 F. Supp. 2d 1 (D.D.C. 2007) (setting a three-year limitations period).

286. Geis v. Board of Education, 774 F.2d 575 (3d Cir. 1985).

287. 20 U.S.C. § 1415(1).

288. 20 U.S.C. § 1415(i)(A). *See also* Quackenbush v. Johnson City School District, 716 F.2d 141 (2d Cir. 1983).

289. Civil Rights Act of 1871, Section 1983, 42 U.S.C. § 1983 (2013).

290. Grace B. v. Lexington School Committee, 762 F. Supp. 416 (D. Mass. 1991); Reid v. Board of Education, Lincolnshire–Prairie View School District 103, 765 F. Supp. 965 (N.D. Ill. 1990); Robertson v. Granite City Community Unit School District No. 9, 684 F. Supp. 1002 (S.D. Ill. 1988).

291. Digre v. Roseville School Independent School District No. 623, 841 F.2d 245 (11th Cir. 1988); Mrs. W. v. Tirozzi, 706 F. Supp. 164 (D. Conn. 1989); Hiller v. Board of Education of the Brunswick Central School District, 674 F. Supp. 73 (N.D.N.Y. 1987), 687 F. Supp. 735 (N.D.N.Y. 1988).

292. Barnett v. Fairfax County School Board, 927 F.2d 146 (4th Cir. 1991), *cert. denied*, 502 U.S. 859 (1991). Osborne, A. G. (2008). Can Section 1983 be used to redress violations of the IDEA: An update. *Education Law Reporter, 230,* 453–467.

293. Fee v. Herndon, 900 F.2d 804 (5th Cir. 1990).

294. D.A. *ex rel.* L.A. v. Houston Independent School District, 629 F.3d 450 (5th Cir. 2010); A.W. v. Jersey City Public Schools, 486 F.3d 791 (3d Cir. 2007); Crocker v. Tennessee Secondary Schools Athletic Association, 873 F.2d 933 (6th Cir. 1989), 980 F.2d 382 (6th Cir. 1992); Hinson *ex rel.* N.H. v. Merritt Educational Center, 521 F. Supp. 2d 22 (D.D.C. 2007).

295. Blanchard v. Morton School District, 509 F.3d 934 (9th Cir. 2007); Diaz-Fonseca v. Commonwealth of Puerto Rico, 451 F.3d 13 (1st Cir. 2006).

296. Bray v. Hobart City School Corporation, 818 F. Supp. 1226 (N.D. Ind. 1993).

297. 29 U.S.C. §§ 792, 794 (2006).

298. Gaudiello v. Delaware County Intermediate Unit, 796 F. Supp. 849 (E.D. Pa. 1992).

299. University Interscholastic League v. Buchannan, 848 S.W.2d 298 (Tex. App. 1993).

300. Barnett v. Fairfax County School Board, 927 F.2d 146 (4th Cir. 1991), *cert. denied*, 502 U.S. 859 (1991); Cordrey v. Euckert, 917 F.2d 1460 (6th Cir. 1990); Doe v. Alabama State Department of Education, 915 F.2d 651 (11th Cir. 1990).

301. Carey v. Maine School Administrative District 17, 754 F. Supp. 906 (D. Me. 1990).

Remedies for Failure to Provide a Free Appropriate Public Education

Key Concepts in This Chapter

- Reimbursement for Privately Obtained Services
- Compensatory Educational Services
- Reimbursement for Attorney Fees and Legal Costs
- Awards for Damages

I f school board officials fail to provide students with disabilities with the free appropriate public educations (FAPEs) to which they are entitled pursuant to the Individuals with Disabilities Education Act (IDEA),[1] the courts are empowered to review the records of administrative proceedings, hear additional evidence at the request of a party, and grant appropriate relief based on the preponderance of the evidence standard.[2] One form of relief that courts often award is reimbursement of tuition and other costs that parents incurred in unilaterally obtaining appropriate services for their children. Another type of relief, one that is available to parents who financially cannot obtain private services in advance, is compensatory educational services to make up for services that their children were denied. Under some circumstances, parents are also entitled to reimbursement for their legal expenses. Further, courts consistently agree that awards of punitive damages are unavailable under the IDEA and are reluctant to grant such relief pursuant to other statutes that are often used to enforce rights established to effectuate federal statutes such as Section 1983 of the Civil Rights Act of 1871 (Section 1983).[3]

A great deal of litigation has focused on remedies in special education, including key cases that made their way to the Supreme Court. Many of the existing remedies available to compensate parents for the failure of school officials to provide FAPEs to their children are based on case law. Nevertheless, in amending the IDEA, Congress provided additional guidance about the types of remedies available to students and parents and clarified the circumstances under which remedies may be granted in response to judicial interpretations of the IDEA. This chapter reviews the remedies available to parents and students, including those based on provisions in the IDEA and those emerging from case law.

This chapter begins with an overview of the most common judicial remedies: awards for tuition reimbursement and compensatory educational services. The next section of the chapter examines situations where parents received awards of attorney fees in disputes with their school boards as well as the rarer occurrence of boards being reimbursed for their legal costs before discussing the evolving law of damages. Like previous chapters in this book, this chapter ends with recommendations for practitioners.

Tuition Reimbursement

According to the IDEA, while administrative or judicial proceedings involving placement disputes are pending, students must remain in their then-current, or pendant, educational placements unless their parents and school board or state officials agree otherwise.[4] Due process proceedings under the IDEA can often take months or even years to complete. Parents who are concerned that the then-current placements of their children are inappropriate may not wish to have their children remain in those settings for the length of time it takes to reach final settlements. Parents in these situations frequently opt to remove their children from their then-current placements and enroll them in private facilities. Parents who prevail in their placement challenges can, under appropriate circumstances, be reimbursed for the tuition and other expenses associated with the private placements. While case law provided parents with this relief for many years, the IDEA and its regulations now explicitly authorize tuition reimbursement.[5]

Supreme Court Cases

The Supreme Court handed down three important judgments about reimbursement of tuition when parents unilaterally placed their children in private schools. In *Burlington School Committee v. Department of Education, Commonwealth of Massachusetts (Burlington)*[6] the Justices affirmed that the IDEA allowed reimbursements as long as the parentally chosen placements were determined to be the appropriate placements for their children. The Court ruled that when Congress empowered the judiciary to grant appropriate relief, it intended to include retroactive remedies. The Court reasoned that reimbursement merely requires school boards to pay the expenses that they would have been paying all along if officials had developed proper individualized education programs (IEPs) from the beginning. If reimbursement were unavailable, the Court explained, then the rights of students to FAPEs, those of their parents to participate fully in developing appropriate IEPs, and the IDEA's procedural safeguards would have been less than complete. Moreover, the Court maintained that a parental violation of the IDEA's status quo provision does not constitute a waiver of the right to tuition reimbursement. However, the Court cautioned parents who make unilateral placements that they do so at their own financial risk since they will not be reimbursed if school officials can show that their boards proposed, and had the capacity to implement, appropriate IEPs.

Eight years later, in a unanimous judgment, the Supreme Court, in *Florence County School District Four v. Carter (Carter)*,[7] affirmed that parentally chosen placements need not be in state-approved facilities in order for parents to obtain tuition reimbursement. In *Carter*, parents who were dissatisfied with the IEP that school officials in South Carolina developed for their daughter placed her in a private school that was not identified on the state-approved list of facilities. Eventually, a trial court found that insofar as the board's IEP was inadequate, it had to reimburse the parents for the cost of the private school placement. The Fourth Circuit affirmed, noting that the private school provided an educational program that met the Supreme Court's standard of appropriateness as enunciated in *Board of Education of the Hendrick Hudson Central School District v. Rowley (Rowley)*,[8] even though it was not state-approved and failed to comply fully with the IDEA. The Fourth Circuit observed that when the board defaulted on its obligations under the IDEA, reimbursement for the placement at a facility that was not state-approved was not forbidden as long as the educational program provided there met the *Rowley* standard. The Supreme Court agreed, emphasizing that the IDEA is designed to ensure that all students with disabilities receive educations that are both appropriate and free. The Justices added that barring reimbursement under the circumstances in *Carter* would have defeated the IDEA's statutory purposes.

In the third case, *Forest Grove School District v. T.A. (Forest Grove)*,[9] the Supreme Court was asked to address whether the IDEA permitted tuition reimbursement for unilateral private school placements if students never received special education services in public schools.[10] The parents of the student at the center of the case, who reached the eleventh grade without having ever received special education services, removed their son from his local high school and enrolled him in a private residential school, partly in response to his use of marijuana and personality changes. A hearing officer awarded reimbursement for the private placement in finding that the student had disabilities and was eligible for special education. Subsequently, the federal trial court in Oregon held that the parents were statutorily ineligible for reimbursement under the IDEA.[11] The Ninth Circuit, in turn, reversed on the basis that interpreting the IDEA as categorically prohibiting reimbursement to parents of students who have not yet received special education and related services from public schools ran contrary to the statute's express purpose of ensuring that all children with disabilities had rights to FAPEs.

On appeal, the Supreme Court affirmed that when a child requires special education services, a school board's failure to propose an IEP is at least as serious a violation of the IDEA as its not having provided a FAPE. Further, the Justices thought that denying reimbursement would also have been at odds with the general remedial purpose of the IDEA and its amendments, since this conflicted with the statute's child find requirements. The Court pointed out that it would have been strange that the IDEA provided a remedy when board officials offer students inadequate special education but left parents without relief in the more egregious situation in which educators unreasonably denied students access to services altogether.

Reimbursement Ordered Under
Burlington, *Carter*, and *Forest Grove*

> Tuition reimbursement is frequently awarded when parents can show that school officials failed to offer appropriate IEPs but their own chosen facilities did provide their children with appropriate educational programs.

Courts may deny parental requests for tuition reimbursement awards if they are convinced that school officials offered, and had the capacity to implement, appropriate IEPs.[12] Yet, courts refuse to approve reimbursement awards when parents make unilateral placements primarily for non-educational reasons.[13] Even so, courts grant reimbursement awards to cover the medical, social, and emotional needs of children when they are not segregable from the children's educational needs.[14] Once courts agree that proposed IEPs are appropriate, they do not need to examine the appropriateness of the parents' chosen placements. Yet, courts frequently award tuition reimbursement when parents can show that officials failed to offer appropriate IEPs but their chosen facilities did provide their children with appropriate educational programs.

Parents' Chosen Placements Must Be Appropriate, Not Perfect

Burlington illustrates that parents can be reimbursed for private school costs when their chosen placements provide FAPEs and those of board officials are inappropriate. Recognizing that parents are not experts in selecting educational placements, courts do not expect them to make the exact required placements. Rather, as long as hearing officers or courts are satisfied that parentally chosen placements are more appropriate than those proposed by school officials, the judiciary generally awards reimbursement, even when the chosen facilities are not identical to those finally judged to be appropriate. The courts reach these outcomes in acknowledging that when parents make unilateral placements, they may not have as many options available to them as do boards. Consequently, the courts do not expect parents to make exactly the same appropriate placement decisions that educators might have made. Not surprisingly, courts agree that reimbursement is still an available remedy under these circumstances. For example, in a case from California the Ninth Circuit affirmed a reimbursement award even though the parentally chosen facility did not satisfy all of a student's needs.[15]

On the other hand, courts do not approve full reimbursement awards under all circumstances. In these cases, courts have denied full reimbursement requests when parentally chosen placements went well beyond what was required in IEPs and were more costly than necessary.[16] Still, this does not mean that courts always deny or reduce reimbursement awards simply because private placements provide benefits beyond those required by the IDEA and student IEPs.[17] In such circumstances, courts make case-by-case determinations in balancing the equities in fashioning reimbursement awards. In doing so, courts consider the other options parents had in choosing private facilities.

The amount of advice and counsel that school board officials provide to parents who seek to make unilateral placements may influence the extent of reimbursement awards. The Eleventh Circuit agreed that a residential placement was required for an autistic child, but was troubled by the fact that his parents, who lived in Georgia, selected a facility located in Tokyo, Japan.[18] The court affirmed that the parents were entitled to some reimbursement, but it was not convinced that a placement so far from home was necessary. Other courts denied full reimbursement to parents who chose residential placements when private day schools were sufficient to provide their children with FAPEs.[19] Under these conditions, courts generally award reimbursement for students' educational expenses at schools but not the costs of room and board.

Courts have denied parental requests for tuition reimbursement for unilaterally obtained placements if they are not appropriate, even when school officials fail to offer appropriate IEPs. For example, the federal trial court in Connecticut declared that a school board's IEP did not provide a FAPE because school personnel committed errors in the IEP process. Even so, the court denied a request for reimbursement because the parents' chosen placement was inappropriate since the school was not staffed by professionals who could deliver the services the child needed.[20] Similarly, the Second Circuit rejected a reimbursement request as unwarranted where a hearing officer in New York commented that although a board's proposed placement was inappropriate, so, too, was the setting the parents sought.[21] In this respect, and in view of the IDEA's least restrictive environment mandate, in some circumstances courts may deny reimbursements when they deem parentally chosen facilities to be overly restrictive.[22]

At the same time, courts can order reimbursements for parents under *Carter* if their chosen facilities can deliver FAPEs, regardless of the certification levels of the institutions or their staff. In a case from California, the Ninth Circuit affirmed a reimbursement award to the parents of a student with autism who unilaterally enrolled him in a private clinic that was not certified to provide special education services.[23] The court acknowledged that school board officials failed to offer an appropriate placement and that the student received educational benefit from his placement at the private clinic. Likewise, the Third Circuit affirmed that parents from Pennsylvania could be reimbursed for a private school whose teachers were not certified to provide special education since their daughter received a FAPE and made progress while there.[24] Also, in a case from New York, the Second Circuit affirmed that parents, who enrolled their son in a program that lacked staff members who were certificated, were entitled to reimbursement because the program still offered the child a FAPE.[25] The court concluded that the promise of the IDEA would have been defeated if reimbursement were barred since the parentally chosen providers were not certified, and the reason the service was not offered by the state was due to a shortage of qualified providers.

The Third Circuit affirmed an award of monetary damages to compensate a mother for the time she spent providing services to her preschool-age daughter. After the mother requested, but was denied, the addition of Lovaas therapy to her program, she received training to provide it herself and offered the services to her child. A commonwealth court posited that insofar as the child's program was inadequate, it had to remand the dispute to a hearing officer in Pennsylvania to consider an appropriate remedy. A hearing officer awarded reimbursement to compensate the mother for the time she spent providing therapy to her daughter. The Third Circuit agreed with the award because the services the mother provided were appropriate, while the county's denial of programming violated the IDEA.[26]

The School Board Must Be Given the Opportunity to Act

In *Burlington* the Supreme Court decided that parents who violated the status quo provision did not waive their right to reimbursement. Yet, in post-*Burlington* cases courts agreed that parents waived this right when they made unilateral placements before giving school board officials the opportunities to address their concerns. To this end, parents must notify officials that they are dissatisfied with the IEPs of their children in order to afford educators the opportunity to take appropriate corrective actions. This case law is now incorporated into the IDEA and its regulations.[27]

According to the IDEA and its regulations, the cost of reimbursement may be reduced or denied under four circumstances:

- First, costs can be reduced or denied if, at the most recent IEP team meetings that parents attended prior to removing their children from public schools, they did not inform their teams that they were rejecting the proposed placements; this notice must include statements of parental concerns and their intent to enroll their children in private schools at public expense.[28]
- Second, costs can be reduced or denied if parents fail to provide school officials with written notice of their intent to remove their children from public schools at least 10 business days (including holidays that occur on business days) prior to doing so.[29]
- Third, costs can be reduced or denied if, before parents removed their children from public schools, educators informed the parents of their intent to evaluate the students, including statements of the purpose of the evaluations that were appropriate and reasonable, but the parents did not make their children available for evaluation.[30]
- Fourth, costs can be reduced or denied if courts find parental actions to have been unreasonable.[31]

A case from Nebraska, although resolved before the 2004 provisions were incorporated into the IDEA, is illustrative. The Eighth Circuit ascertained that parents were not entitled to reimbursement because they failed to give school officials the opportunity to make changes to their daughter's IEP.[32] The student regressed, and school officials wanted to meet to discuss the situation, but the student's parents unilaterally changed her placement before the session could occur. The court asserted that insofar as there was no indication that the educators would have refused to change the student's program, the board was entitled to have the opportunity to modify her IEP and placement. The court stated that school officials must be put on notice that parents disagree with the educational programs of their children and must be given opportunities to modify placements voluntarily before parents are justified in taking unilateral actions. Ten years later, the same court denied reimbursement to parents who, without discussing the matter with educational personnel regarding possible accommodations to meet their child's needs, removed him from school after one day in the eighth grade.[33]

Courts frequently deny reimbursement when parents act unilaterally before giving school officials opportunities to intervene. Generally, courts reason that equity prevents these awards from accruing prior to when school officials had opportunities to evaluate students and make placement recommendations.[34] Parents may also forfeit their right to tuition reimbursement if they fail to cooperate with school officials in the evaluation process.[35]

As noted, the IDEA obligates parents to provide education officials with written notification of their intent to enroll their children in private schools at public expense if they hope to obtain reimbursement awards. Parents who fail to challenge the IEPs of their children and provide school officials with the written notice required by the IDEA prior to making unilateral placements have been denied reimbursements.[36]

Reimbursement May Be Granted When School Officials Commit Procedural Errors

The fact that school officials devised appropriate educational programs for students is not sufficient to preclude reimbursement awards. IEP teams must spell out appropriate placements in properly executed IEPs. Procedural errors are sufficient grounds for awarding reimbursement for unilateral placements because, under *Rowley*, an educational placement is inappropriate if it is not contained in a properly executed IEP. For instance, the Third Circuit ruled that reimbursement was warranted when a school board in Pennsylvania proposed an appropriate program but the IEP was not developed within prescribed timelines.[37] School officials then proposed a placement that was later deemed appropriate but failed to write an IEP for it. Similarly, the Fourth Circuit affirmed a reimbursement award in deciding that board officials failed to provide an appropriate education for a child.[38] A trial court in West Virginia had held that the board's IEP was inappropriate due to procedural defects where school officials failed to conduct annual reviews and involve the parents in the IEP process.

As indicated, school boards must be given opportunities to evaluate students and propose appropriate placements. This means that school boards may be liable for tuition reimbursement if officials do not properly evaluate children. In one such instance, the Fourth Circuit affirmed that parents were justified in making a unilateral placement when school officials in Virginia failed to propose an appropriate placement due to an improper evaluation of the child.[39] The court maintained that the parents did not waive their right to reimbursement when they removed their child from the public schools before school personnel conducted additional assessments and proposed a final IEP.

The IDEA requires parents to provide school personnel notice of their intent to place their children in private facilities in order to qualify for reimbursements. Even so, as reflected by a case from Maryland, parental failure to notify school personnel may be excused if board officials did not follow proper procedures. The federal trial court was of the view that parents could not be denied reimbursement because they failed to notify officials of their intent where educators failed to afford them notice of procedural requirements as mandated by state law and the IDEA.[40]

As illustrated by a case from Ohio, an improperly written IEP can provide the basis for a reimbursement award. The Sixth Circuit, noting that flaws in an IEP were not harmless technical errors, awarded reimbursement to parents who rejected an IEP that failed to provide an objective means to measure progress and did not adequately explain the services that their daughter would receive.[41] Along the same lines, the Second Circuit approved a reimbursement award to parents who enrolled their daughter in a private school after board officials in New York proposed a Section 504 accommodation plan instead of an IEP.[42] The trial court had specified that the student qualified for special education because she had emotional disabilities. Moreover, the Sixth Circuit affirmed a reimbursement award to parents from Tennessee in concluding that school board officials denied a FAPE to their son when the board determined his placement based on his disability classification rather than his individual needs.[43]

According to the Fourth Circuit, procedural errors must actually interfere with the provision of a FAPE before parents are entitled to reimbursement awards. At issue was a dispute that arose when the parents sought summer services but school officials in Maryland failed to give their request proper consideration. The court treated this as a harmless error because the evidence revealed that the student was not entitled to summer services.[44]

Parental Delays or Failure to Cooperate May Affect Reimbursement Awards

As a federal trial court in New York pointed out, the IDEA does not prevent parents from being reimbursed for tuition costs even if they cause delays in the hearing process.[45] The court indicated that the parents could still be reimbursed because their choice of a private school was the appropriate placement. The parents sought reimbursement, but school officials argued that insofar as the parents caused delays in the proceedings, they should not be reimbursed for the period of each of the delays. The court disagreed, stating that the board was responsible for the private school tuition for the entire time period regardless of whether there were delays in the proceedings.

In contrast, other courts have interpreted the IDEA as denying parental requests for reimbursement when the parents engaged in unreasonable delays in requesting hearings. In a case from New Jersey the Third Circuit observed that parents waived their right to reimbursement if they did not initiate review proceedings within a reasonable period of time.[46] The parents waited two years before filing their claim, and the court thought that waiting this amount of time without a mitigating excuse was unreasonable. Echoing this rationale, five years later the same court affirmed in relevant part that parents who enrolled their children, gifted students who had learning disabilities, in a private school, but waited 16 months before requesting tuition reimbursement, were precluded from recovering the costs for the time period prior to their request for a hearing.[47] It is also worth noting that state statutes of limitations may impose further limits on the time frames within which parents may file reimbursement claims.

As exemplified by recent litigation, parental actions frustrating the attempts of school board officials to develop IEPs may result in reductions or losses of reimbursement awards. The First Circuit affirmed that parents from Maine who withdrew from an IEP meeting were not entitled to reimbursement because their actions obstructed the IEP process.[48] The court agreed that had the parents cooperated, school personnel would have developed an appropriate IEP. The Third Circuit insisted that parents from Delaware who delayed the continuation of an IEP meeting and cancelled scheduled evaluations of their son, substantially precluding any possibility that school officials could develop an IEP within an appropriate time frame, were not entitled to reimbursement.[49] Courts in New Jersey[50] and Wisconsin[51] denied reimbursement requests from parents who refused to allow public school personnel to evaluate their children before enrolling them in private settings. In essence the courts agreed that educators could not develop IEPs in these cases due to the parents' failure to cooperate.

Reimbursement for Related Services

> In addition to tuition, courts consistently award reimbursement for the costs of related services. The criteria for reimbursement of related services are the same as for tuition expenses: Parents must demonstrate that the services were required for students to receive FAPEs.

Along with tuition, courts consistently award reimbursement for the costs of related services. The criteria for reimbursement of related services are the same as for tuition: Parents must demonstrate that the services were required for students to receive FAPEs. In most cases, related services are provided at private schools in conjunction with special education services. Courts often award reimbursement for the costs of privately obtained related services when board officials fail to provide needed services along with public special education placements.

Courts frequently grant reimbursement awards for the costs of psycho-therapy or counseling services.[52] In some cases the courts ordered thera-peutic services for students who were placed in private schools or psychiatric facilities due to emotional difficulties. In others, parents obtained counseling services privately to supplement the services the students received in public school settings. Regardless of the setting where stu-dents receive special education services, parents seeking reimbursement awards must show that their children would not benefit from special edu-cation without psychotherapy or counseling.

School board officials must provide transportation, when needed, because students cannot benefit from special education services if they are unable to get to where the services are being offered. Boards must even provide students who attend private schools at public expense with appropriate transportation. Frequently, tuition reimbursement awards include compensation for other necessary costs such as transportation. Even when tuition reimbursement is not an issue, it may be awarded to parents when board officials fail to provide appropriate transportation. In such a case, the First Circuit permitted a father from Rhode Island to be reimbursed for driving his son, who had physical disabilities, to school himself after school personnel failed to make appropriate arrangements.[53] In another case, a trial court in New York directed a board to reimburse a care provider for costs associated with transporting a student to an educa-tional facility for children with physical disabilities.[54] The award included reimbursement for hiring a babysitter to watch other children while the caretaker transported the child to the center. A trial court in South Dakota awarded reimbursement for transportation for a student who moved into the district with an IEP calling for door-to-door transportation.[55] The suit arose after the child's mother challenged the board's denial of her request for special transportation for her daughter. While a hearing officer upheld the action of school officials, the court explained that the board was required to honor the terms of the previous IEP until such time as they could review it and develop a new plan for the child.

Courts award reimbursement for a variety of related services such as occupational therapy[56] and speech therapy.[57] The Ninth Circuit awarded reimbursement for the cost of lodging for a student from California and his mother that was required because the facility he attended was not within daily commuting distance of the family's residence.[58]

The Hearing Officer May Grant Reimbursement Awards

As reviewed, the courts have granted parental requests for reimburse-ment. Even so, parents do not necessarily have to seek judicial review in order to obtain these awards. Hearing officers have the authority to grant reimbursement awards along with other forms of appropriate equi-table relief. For example, a federal trial court in North Carolina ruled that reimbursement was included in the IDEA's provision that a hearing may be conducted on any matter relating to a FAPE.[59] The court also believed that Congress did not intend to give courts any greater equity power than hearing officers. In that respect, the IDEA and its regulations grant hearing officers the authority to confer reimbursement awards.[60]

Compensatory Educational Services

Courts can grant awards of compensatory educational services when school board officials fail to provide appropriate educational placements for children and their parents lack the financial means to obtain alternate services.[61] Absent judicial relief, some parents must allow their children to remain in inappropriate settings while administrative hearings are pending. Consequently, children may lose years of appropriate educational services during the often lengthy appeals process. Generally, courts grant awards of compensatory services during times when students would otherwise have been ineligible for services. In most cases involving awards of compensatory services, the courts apply the *Burlington* rationale in evaluating whether they are warranted.[62]

> Courts can grant awards of compensatory educational services when school board officials fail to provide appropriate educational placements for children and their parents lack the financial means to obtain alternate services. Generally, courts grant awards of compensatory services during time periods when students would otherwise have been ineligible for services.

Compensatory Services Granted

The courts agree that they have the authority to award compensatory services because Congress empowered them to fashion appropriate remedies to cure deprivations of rights secured by the IDEA. Courts agree that compensatory services, like reimbursement, merely compensate students and their parents for the inappropriate educations they received while placement issues were in dispute or school officials failed to act properly. The theory behind compensatory educational services awards is that appropriate remedies are not limited to those parents who can afford to provide their children with alternate educational placements while litigation is pending.[63] Although the time periods vary based on the facts of every situation, courts frequently award compensatory services for periods equal to the time students were denied services.[64] Courts may even grant awards of compensatory services after students have passed the ceiling age for eligibility under the IDEA.[65]

A case from Alabama illustrates the similarity between awards of tuition reimbursement and compensatory services. The Eleventh Circuit affirmed that an award of compensatory educational services was similar to one for tuition reimbursement because it was necessary to preserve the student's right to a FAPE.[66] The court decided that without compensatory services awards, the rights of students under the IDEA would depend on the ability of their parents to obtain services privately when due process hearings were pending. The Eighth Circuit reached a like outcome in finding that compensatory educational services were available to the father of a student with disabilities in Missouri who could not afford to provide appropriate services himself during a lengthy court battle.[67] In granting the award of compensatory education, the court added that Congress did not intend for the entitlements of special education students to FAPEs to rest on the ability of their parents to pay for the costs of their placements in advance. A third court agreed that if compensatory services were unavailable, parents would have earned Pyrrhic victories because the rights of their children to a FAPE would have been illusory.[68]

Courts may grant students awards of compensatory services even after they earn valid high school diplomas. After discovering that educational officials failed to follow proper procedures, the federal trial court in Massachusetts awarded such services to a student who earned a high school diploma.[69] The court reasoned that the student's having earned a diploma failed to demonstrate that she had no need for required special education services. Rather, the court treated the student's having earned her diploma as evidence that she succeeded despite the shortcomings of her educational program. A federal trial court in New York also wrote that a student who graduated was entitled to compensatory educational services while attending college, but not in the form of tuition.[70] The federal trial court in the District of Columbia maintained that even though a child was no longer eligible for IDEA services because she had earned a high school diploma, she retained her right to compensatory education.[71]

Compensatory services awards accrue from the point that school board officials knew, or should have known, that the IEPs of students were inadequate.[72] Generally, courts grant awards of compensatory services based on reasonable projections of what is needed to place students in the positions they would have been in but for the past deprivation of services.[73] As the District of Columbia Circuit found, such awards should be reasonably calculated to provide the educational benefits that likely would have accrued from the special education services the board should have provided in the first place.[74] A trial court in the nation's capital ordered the reevaluation of a student so that officials could better understand his educational abilities and needs.[75] The court subsequently determined that the child required individualized tutoring designed to allow him to progress the equivalent of 1.5 grade levels.[76]

Compensatory services awards may take on many forms. In some situations courts simply order amounts of services equivalent to those which the students were denied. For example, federal trial courts in Pennsylvania based awards on the number of hours of special education services the children lost.[77] In another case the Eleventh Circuit ordered a school board in Georgia to provide additional years of placement in a private school.[78] In a case from California, the Ninth Circuit affirmed compensatory services in the form of training for a child's teachers so that they could better meet his needs.[79]

Hearing officers have the power to grant awards of compensatory educational services. As they do with the power to grant tuition reimbursement, courts recognize that hearing officers may fashion appropriate relief, which sometimes requires awards of compensatory services.[80]

Compensatory Services Denied

Like tuition reimbursement, compensatory services are available only when parents can demonstrate that their children were denied the FAPEs mandated by the IDEA.[81] Nevertheless, a federal trial court in Tennessee denied an award of compensatory education in positing that although the homebound program that the student received was inappropriate, at that time neither school officials nor the parents were aware of the existence of an appropriate program.[82] Insofar as school officials had not taken any actions that resulted in the denial of a FAPE to the student, the court did not think that the board had to provide compensatory services.

The Third Circuit pointed out that compensatory services are warranted only when parents can demonstrate that their children underwent prolonged or gross deprivations of the right to a FAPE.[83] Absent such evidence, the court denied an award of compensatory services where an administrative appeals panel in Pennsylvania ordered additional services included in a student's IEP. In like fashion, the Eighth Circuit affirmed that a student was not entitled to compensatory services absent a showing of egregious circumstances or culpable conduct on the part of school board officials from South Dakota.[84] A student's not having regressed as a result of his school board's failure to provide an appropriate program in a timely fashion caused a trial court in New York, in an order affirmed by the Second Circuit, to deny compensatory services.[85] In addition, a school board's timely action to correct deficiencies in a student's IEP led the federal trial court in New Jersey to deny a parental request for compensatory services.[86]

Failure to take advantage of offered services may be the basis for denial of an award of compensatory services. In such a case the Ninth Circuit uncovered evidence that educational officials in Washington offered parents extra tutoring and summer school for their child, but they rejected the proposal.[87] The court thus denied the parents' request for compensatory services. In a conceptually related case, the federal trial court in Minnesota denied compensatory speech therapy services where parents withdrew their son from his educational program and rejected the services that school officials offered.[88]

As reviewed in the previous section, while some courts ordered school boards to provide compensatory services even after students earned high school diplomas, not all agree. A federal trial court in Oregon decreed that a student who graduated from high school with a standard diploma demonstrated that he was not lacking in any areas due to the denial of a FAPE.[89] In like manner, the federal trial court in the District of Columbia did not think that a board needed to provide compensatory services for a student who graduated even though officials in his charter school failed to provide him with mandated special education services during an expulsion period.[90]

Attorney Fees and Costs

The IDEA contains one of the most comprehensive mechanisms that Congress ever created for dispute resolution. Litigation is expensive, and many parents, after succeeding in their disputes with school boards, believe that they should be reimbursed for their costs in securing the rights of their children. These parents sense that they achieve nugatory victories if they prevail in showing that school board officials failed to provide the FAPE their children were entitled to receive under the IDEA, but are left with large legal bills. Initially, most courts viewed awards of attorney fees as awards for damages.[91]

> Litigation is expensive, and many parents, after succeeding in their disputes with school boards, believe that they should be reimbursed for their costs in securing the rights of their children. Many parents sense that they achieve nugatory victories if they prevail in showing that school board officials failed to provide the FAPE their children were entitled to receive under the IDEA but are left with large legal bills.

In 1984 the Supreme Court ruled in *Smith v. Robinson*[92] that recovery of the cost of attorney fees was unavailable under the IDEA. Congress responded by amending the IDEA in 1986 with the Handicapped Children's Protection Act (HCPA).[93] The HCPA allows courts to provide awards of reasonable attorney fees to parents who prevail against school boards in actions or proceedings brought pursuant to the IDEA. Awards must be based on the prevailing rates in the communities in which the cases arose. Courts have the authority to judge what constitutes a reasonable amount of time spent preparing and arguing cases in terms of the issues litigated. Attorney fee awards may include reimbursement for expenses such as photocopying and faxing[94] but not for expert witnesses, a topic discussed in more detail later in this chapter. Further, courts can award parents fees for successfully litigating fee petitions.[95]

Awards may be limited if school boards made settlement offers more than 10 days before proceedings began that were equal to or more favorable than the final relief the parents obtained.[96] Fee awards also may be reduced if courts believe that parents unreasonably protracted disputes, the hourly rates of attorneys were excessive, or the time lawyers spent and legal services furnished were excessive in light of the issues litigated.[97] Courts may award attorney fees for representation at administrative and judicial hearings but not at IEP meetings unless sessions were convened as a result of administrative or judicial orders.[98] The IDEA specifically prohibits awards of attorney fees for resolution sessions.[99]

Hearing officers cannot grant awards of attorney fees since this authority is reserved for the courts.[100] Yet, parents do not necessarily have to go to court to recover their legal expenses. Parents and their lawyers can negotiate with school boards for payments of their legal expenses. If parents successfully initiate legal claims to recover attorney fees, they may recover their costs in filing the fee petitions as well.[101] Parents do not need to exhaust administrative remedies prior to filing fee petitions since hearing officers cannot award attorney fees.[102]

Since the implementation of the HCPA there has been a flood of litigation over attorney fees. Much of this litigation is fairly routine where courts are asked to settle disputes over hourly rates or the number of hours billed by attorneys. The following sections address issues of general applicability rather than those that are case specific.[103]

When Parents Prevail

One of the most often litigated issues under the IDEA is whether parents were actually the prevailing parties in litigation. While on its face the issue seems fairly straightforward, unfortunately it is not. Most special education disputes involve multiple issues and parents may have had only partial success. Courts generally define prevailing parents as those who succeeded on most of the issues that were litigated.[104] Even so, when parents have not prevailed on all issues, some courts have granted partial awards.

Full Awards

Parents are entitled to full reimbursement when they obtain all elements of the relief they sought.[105] For the most part, courts grant full awards when parents prevail on the major issues in the litigation even if they did not succeed on some minor points. In most cases, the work performed litigating minor issues is inseparable from that of contesting major issues, is insignificant compared to that required by the major issues, and/or is performed in conjunction with the work completed for major issues.[106] Courts ordinarily agree that parents are the prevailing parties when they acquire the primary relief they sought or prevail on significant issues in their suits.[107]

Parents may receive full reimbursement of their legal expenses even when they do not prevail on all issues. Typically, courts make full awards if the time spent litigating the various issues cannot be easily apportioned on an issue-by-issue basis. In such a case, the Sixth Circuit awarded attorney fees to parents from Tennessee who did not receive the residential placement they requested but succeeded in obtaining additional services.[108] In other cases, courts have permitted parents to receive full fee awards because the matters before administrative hearings were intertwined and could not have been viewed as a series of separate claims, and the parents received most of what they requested.[109] In a case from West Virginia, the Fourth Circuit affirmed that even when parents lose on the most central issue, they are still a prevailing party if they receive enforceable judgments on other issues.[110]

Partial Awards

Courts grant partial awards of attorney fees when parents do not prevail on the most significant issue in the litigation but succeed on some of the contested matters.[111] In addition, parents may receive only partial awards when they prevail on some of their claims and the issues litigated are distinct enough so that the work done on each can be separated from the work done on all of the others.[112] As the Ninth Circuit explained in a case from California, not awarding fees for unsuccessful claims will help deter the submission of multiple, nonmeritorious claims.[113] Requested fee awards have been reduced for other reasons such as where a court determined that a requested hourly rate or the number of hours billed was excessive,[114] was not satisfied with the documentation supporting an attorney's requested rate,[115] treated the time sheets submitted by an attorney as faulty,[116] or viewed an attorney's conduct as unprofessional or contentious.[117]

As reflected by a variety of cases, courts can adjust requested fee awards. In Indiana, a federal trial court reduced a requested fee amount because the parents' counsel unnecessarily protracted the proceedings.[118] A federal trial court in Kentucky decided that an attorney who was unfamiliar with special education laws could not bill for the time and research expended in getting up to speed with the statutes.[119] Also, a federal trial court in Wisconsin subtracted time an attorney spent communicating with the press about the case.[120]

Courts do not always reduce awards by evaluating the number of hours spent litigating each issue and lowering awards by the amount of fees charged for unsuccessfully litigating specified issues. Sometimes awards are adjusted in proportion to the parents' overall success and failure in the litigation. When, for instance, federal trial courts in Connecticut[121] and New Jersey[122] had difficulty apportioning legal costs issue by issue, they simply reduced the requested fee awards by 40% and 50%, respectively, because the parents had not achieved their primary objective even though they succeeded on other significant questions.

When Parents Do Not Prevail

Parents cannot recover their legal expenses when school boards are the prevailing parties.[123] It almost goes without saying that parents who fail to succeed on any of their claims do not achieve prevailing party status.[124] As discussed in the previous section, parents may receive limited reimbursements if they prevail on at least some of their claims. Parents are not entitled to attorney fees if their legal relationship with their school boards remains unaltered as a result of the litigation, even if they received minor victories through their legal actions.[125] Parents are also denied the status of prevailing parties if the changes that occur are not a direct result of the litigation but are brought about by other factors such as private settlement agreements.[126]

As noted, courts sometimes grant parents partial reimbursement of their legal expenses if they obtain some, but not all, of the relief they sought. If the relief that parents obtained is insignificant, courts may not grant even partial awards. In an illustrative case, the Seventh Circuit affirmed the denial of a request for attorney fees, even though the parents obtained an order from a hearing officer in Illinois conferring benefits on their daughter, on the ground that the ultimate outcome of the dispute negated the value of those benefits.[127] A federal trial court in Wisconsin denied a fee request in writing that the relief the parents obtained was minimal in light of their overall objectives.[128]

Courts may deny fee awards if they deem that parents unnecessarily protracted proceedings[129] or that the issues about which they complained could have been resolved without resort to administrative or judicial review.[130] Parents may not receive fee awards if they request administrative hearings before school officials have had opportunities to develop appropriate IEPs.[131] In one case, the federal trial court in the District of Columbia denied fees where a hearing officer ordered the board there to pay for an independent evaluation but the parents never followed through on obtaining such an assessment.[132] That same court denied fees in another case[133] and reduced attorneys' rates to those of paralegals in two others where the lawyers were not licensed in the District.[134]

In a case with a twist, homeschooling parents who did so for religious reasons were successful in litigation initiated by their school board to compel an evaluation of the child. Yet, a federal trial court in New York contended that the parents were not entitled to attorney fees because reimbursement is available only to parents of children with disabilities.[135] The court wrote that even though the parents succeeded in preventing the board from evaluating their child, since the student was not classified as one with a disability, they could not be treated as the prevailing under the IDEA because it was inapplicable in this dispute.

Catalyst Theory

In the past courts awarded attorney fees based on the catalyst theory, even if administrative hearings or judicial actions never took place.[136] Under the catalyst theory, courts can award fees if suits, or even threats of litigation, motivate change in the behavior of defendants, causing the termination of proceedings. However, this has changed such that the catalyst theory is no longer a viable argument for obtaining fee awards.[137]

In a nonschool case, *Buckhannon Board & Care Home v. West Virginia Department of Health and Human Resources (Buckhannon)*,[138] the Supreme Court rejected the catalyst theory in deciding that in order to qualify as a prevailing party, a claimant must prevail before the courts in a judgment on the merits or through a consent decree.[139] Subsequently, circuit courts denied fee requests rooted in the rationale in *Buckhannon*, explaining that the high Court's opinion governed claims filed pursuant to the IDEA.[140]

Fees for Administrative Hearings

The IDEA provides for the recovery of attorney fees by parents who prevail in "any action or proceeding" brought under its procedural safeguards section.[141] The meaning of the phrase "any action or proceeding" has been in dispute. Many school boards have claimed that it refers only to judicial actions and that attorney fees are not recoverable for work performed at the administrative hearing level. After some controversy, it is now well settled that attorney fees are available for representation at administrative hearings even if disputes are settled without judicial intervention. It is equally well settled that parents can file suit solely for the purpose of recovering legal expenses.[142]

The District of Columbia Circuit resolved the leading, and most controversial, case on the topic in 1990.[143] Initially, a divided three-judge panel decreed that congressional language in the HCPA/IDEA provided for awards of attorney fees only in cases where the losing parties in administrative actions appealed to the courts and prevailed in the judicial actions.[144] According to the court, fees could not be awarded to parents who prevailed at the administrative level and brought judicial action only to obtain attorney fees. While this opinion was contrary to the majority of cases from the other circuits, the court granted a rehearing en banc.[145]

On further review, the en banc panel vacated the earlier judgment, declaring that attorney fees were available for administrative proceedings. The court concluded that Congressional use of the phrase "any action or proceeding" meant to authorize fees for parents who prevailed in civil actions or administrative proceedings. The court added that the legislative history of the HCPA/IDEA supported its interpretation. Later courts unanimously agreed that parents who prevailed at the administrative level could recover their legal expenses.[146]

Settlement Offers

School boards can lessen their liability for fees by attempting to reach settlements with parents before beginning administrative hearings. One section of the HCPA/IDEA provides that fees are unavailable for legal representation that occurs after school boards make written settlement offers if the final relief obtained by the parents is not more favorable to them than the settlement offers. Settlement offers must be made at least 10 days before the scheduled start of due process hearings.[147]

In order to avoid paying fee awards, school board settlement offers must be deemed to be equal to or better than the final relief obtained by the parents. Settlement offers do not need to be identical to final administrative orders in order to stop the time clocks of attorneys from ticking. Parents are not entitled to awards of attorney fees when the final relief they obtain is substantially similar to the last offers they receive from school boards[148] or is less favorable than those offers.[149] For example, the federal trial court in Massachusetts denied a fee request in acknowledging that a hearing officer's order essentially adopted the school committee's settlement offer.[150] On the other hand, parents can be reimbursed for their legal costs when they win more favorable terms than their school boards offer.[151]

Courts may be called on to consider whether settlement offers were, in fact, more favorable than the final results obtained through administrative hearings. In such a case, a federal trial court in Illinois rejected a school board's claim of a more favorable settlement offer because the hearing officer granted relief for items that were not included in the settlement offer.[152] The court rejected the board's claims in pointing out that the parents addressed all of these matters with the requisite level of specificity. Similarly, another federal trial court in Illinois was convinced that a settlement offer was not more favorable than the relief parents finally obtained because the agreement failed to specify where the student would be placed and did not provide compensatory services.[153]

Prior to *Buckhannon* courts awarded attorney fees for legal work completed up to the time of settlement offers, even when hearings were canceled because parents accepted settlement offers.[154] In the wake of *Buckhannon*, though, courts routinely denied fees when the parties reached settlement agreements before completing administrative hearings.[155] At the same time, attorney fees may be awarded for settlement agreements if hearing officers or courts sanction the agreements in some way. Courts agree that incorporating settlement agreements into orders or reading them into the record confer on them the judicial imprimatur that *Buckhannon* required.[156] In a case from Pennsylvania, the Third Circuit upheld a denial of fees, maintaining that private settlement agreements must be judicially sanctioned to confer prevailing party status for fee-shifting purposes and that the parties themselves cannot create judicial imprimatur by stipulation in their settlement agreements.[157]

Fees to Attorneys From Public Agencies

Many parents use attorneys from public advocacy agencies in special education litigation because these attorneys provide low-cost or free legal services via sliding scale fee arrangements. It is well settled that if parents who are represented by public agency attorneys prevail in special education actions, their attorneys are entitled to reimbursement at the prevailing rate in their communities even when it is higher than what the agencies otherwise would have charged.[158]

Fees to Lay Advocates and Pro Se Parents

During the early stages of disputes parents frequently rely on the services of lay advocates to advise and represent them in meetings with school boards.[159] Although the services of lay advocates may be beneficial in resolving disputes, because they are not attorneys, these individuals may not be reimbursed for legal representation.[160] If advocates work in conjunction with attorneys, it is possible that they may be reimbursed for their services as part of the attorneys' costs.[161] Even so, representation solely by lay advocates is not reimbursable.[162]

Most courts agree that parents who represent themselves or their children may not be compensated under the HCPA even if they are members of the bar.[163] Yet, a federal trial court in Georgia decreed that nothing in the language of the IDEA prohibits awards of fees to attorney-parents.[164] The Ninth Circuit, while agreeing that pro se parents from California were ineligible to receive attorney fees, stated that other nonparent relatives, such as the child's grandmother, may obtain fees.[165]

Costs of Expert Witnesses and Consultants

The HCPA/IDEA permits parents to recover other costs, along with attorney fees, in bringing special education suits.[166] Still, in the past courts disagreed over whether parents could recover the costs of expert witness fees. A variety of federal courts concurred that parents may include the costs of expert witnesses in their requests for attorney fees awards, reasoning that these expenses were often a necessary part of administrative hearings.[167] Other courts flatly denied reimbursement requests for expert witness fees.[168]

As is often the case, the Supreme Court intervened to resolve the split between the Circuits and to ensure a more uniform interpretation of the IDEA. In *Arlington Central School District v. Murphy* (*Arlington*),[169] the Court, reversing the Second Circuit's earlier order to the contrary,[170] interpreted the IDEA as not permitting parents to be reimbursed for the services of expert witnesses or consultants who assisted them in their disputes with school boards. Although recognizing that this created the anomalous situation whereby parents who prevailed in their disputes with their school boards could recover attorney fees, but not expenses to cover the costs associated with expert witnesses or consultants who helped them to win their cases, the Justices concluded that insofar as Congress was aware of this fact but refused to modify the IDEA accordingly, there was no reason to rewrite the statute. In fact, Congress has yet to act on making such a modification.[171]

Courts have followed *Arlington* in unanimously agreeing that fees for educational consultants and expert witnesses are not recoverable.[172] One practical result of *Arlington* is that school boards should be able to save money by eliminating costs that they might otherwise have had to incur for expert witnesses and consultants.

In a novel, albeit unsuccessful, strategy an expert witness included a clause in her contract to compel parents to seek reimbursement for her services. When the parents did not do so, the witness filed suit against them and their attorney for breach of contract. An appellate court in New York affirmed that insofar as the parents would have been unsuccessful in light of *Arlington*, enforcement of the contract was barred by the doctrine of frustration of purpose.[173]

Fees for Representation in Complaint Resolution Procedures

The IDEA's regulations require states to adopt procedures for resolving complaints filed by organizations or individuals regarding violations of the IDEA.[174] Whether fees are available for representation in filing complaints through the IDEA's complaint resolution procedures is unsettled. The Ninth Circuit[175] and the federal trial court in Vermont[176] agreed that fees may be awarded for representation in filing complaints under a state's or the IDEA's complaint resolution procedures. Conversely, the federal trial court in Minnesota denied a fee award for an attorney who filed a complaint on behalf of a student with disabilities.[177] The court ascertained that the filing of a complaint was not an action or proceeding for purposes of recovering attorney fees under Section 1415. In a case from New York, the Second Circuit affirmed that inasmuch as complaint resolution proceedings are not civil actions or due process hearings, they are not covered by the IDEA's attorney fees provision.[178]

Fees for Representation at IEP Meetings

The IDEA specifically prohibits reimbursement of attorney fees for attendance at IEP meetings unless these sessions were convened as a result of administrative or judicial actions.[179] Courts have consistently denied fees for representation at IEP meetings.[180] At least one court did allow reimbursement for the time an attorney spent scheduling an IEP meeting when that effort was the direct result of a court order.[181]

Awards to School Boards

The HCPA/IDEA allows prevailing parents to recover legal expenses. Yet, when this modification to the IDEA was first enacted, it did not afford school boards the right to seek reimbursement for their legal expenses if they succeeded in litigation. Using their general powers of equity, courts sometimes, albeit reluctantly, awarded attorney fees to school boards when parental claims were frivolous or for unnecessarily prolonged litigation. The First Circuit, for example, held that a school committee in New Hampshire was entitled to reimbursement of legal expenses under Appellate Rule 38[182] in finding that the parents' suit was "completely devoid of merit and plagued by unnecessary delay."[183] The court commented that the parents engaged in tactics throughout the proceedings that led to undue delays and also failed to cooperate in negotiations to settle the dispute. In another case, a federal trial court in New York denied a prevailing school board's request for attorney fees based on the claim that the parents brought the action in bad faith.[184] The court was convinced that both parties proceeded in good faith and should bear their own costs.

The 2004 IDEA amendments added a provision that now allows school boards to seek reimbursement of their legal expenses when parents file complaints that are determined to be frivolous, unreasonable, or without foundation or when the litigation was continued after it clearly became frivolous, unreasonable, or without foundation.[185] Boards may also obtain awards when parental suits are filed for improper purposes, cause unnecessary delays, or needlessly increase the costs of litigation.[186] Under these provisions, awards are to be levied against the parents' attorney, not the parents themselves.

As an initial matter, in order to collect fees, school boards must be the prevailing party.[187] Even so, as emphasized by the Ninth Circuit in a case from Arizona, the fact that parental arguments are unsuccessful does not automatically make them frivolous, entitling boards to fees.[188] While it is still rare, courts have awarded fees to boards. In one case the Fifth Circuit affirmed an award to a board in Texas on the ground that the parents' attorney stonewalled efforts to end the case by continuing to litigate claims for unnecessary services and advising his client to not accept the board's offers.[189] The federal trial court in the District of Columbia awarded fees to officials of a charter school in declaring that even though a mother lacked a factual basis for her complaints, she continued to pursue them after they became frivolous.[190] On the other hand, a federal trial court in Texas denied fees in positing that the school board, not the parents, was responsible for protracted litigation.[191]

At the same time, school boards may not continue litigation that is clearly frivolous, unreasonable, or without foundation or engage in any tactics that unnecessarily prolong litigation or otherwise abuse the process. Under the Federal Rules of Civil Procedure, a federal trial court in California issued sanctions against a board and its attorney for raising frivolous objections, making misstatements, and mischaracterizing facts.[192]

Damages

The term *damages,* by its broad definition, typically refers to monetary relief awarded to compensate aggrieved parties for losses.[193] The term, as used in this chapter, is defined in a narrower context. Here the term *damages* refers to monetary awards granted to persons who were injured by the actions of others or for punitive purposes.[194] For the purposes of this chapter, compensatory awards, such as reimbursements for tuition and other out-of-pocket expenses, are not treated as damages awards. In the context of special education, courts, especially in recent years, have treated punitive damages as a separate entity from compensation for lost services.

Failure to Provide an Appropriate Education

> Courts historically agreed that damages were not available under the IDEA unless school board officials flagrantly failed to comply with the act's procedural requirements.

Courts historically agreed that damages were not available under the IDEA unless school board officials flagrantly failed to comply with the act's procedural requirements.[195] The Seventh Circuit, in a case where parents from Wisconsin actually sought tuition reimbursement, insisted that monetary awards were unavailable under the IDEA unless exceptional circumstances existed such as when officials acted in bad faith by egregiously disregarding the IDEA's procedural provisions.[196] While this case involved an award of tuition reimbursement, other courts either cited it or used analogous rationales in rejecting damages as unavailable under the IDEA.[197]

The Supreme Court specifically struck down the Seventh Circuit's treatment of reimbursement as a damages award in *Burlington School Committee v. Department of Education, Commonwealth of Massachusetts.*[198] This judgment notwithstanding, the legal principle that a damages award was unavailable unless school boards acted in bad faith survived for years with some courts indicating that damages awards were theoretically possible under specified circumstances[199] Even so, most courts agree, as the Eleventh Circuit stated, that the purpose of the IDEA is to provide qualified students with FAPEs and not provide tort-like relief.[200] Thus, although early judicial opinions on point left the door open for damages when the conduct of school officials was egregious, recent cases have closed that door.

In an early case from Texas the Fifth Circuit asserted that insofar as damages awards are inconsistent with the goals of the IDEA, appropriate relief does not include punitive damages when school officials act in good faith.[201] Similarly, in a case from Virginia, the Fourth Circuit affirmed that damages are unavailable unless parents can demonstrate that educators acted in bad faith or committed intentional acts of discrimination.[202] A trial court in New York decided that while damages were allowed for bad faith or egregious failures to comply with the IDEA, they were not warranted when officials made good faith efforts to provide appropriate placements but committed misjudgments.[203]

The Fourth Circuit has since ruled that awards of compensatory and punitive damages are inconsistent with the IDEA's structure.[204] Explaining that a claim brought by a student from Virginia, alleging that the deprivation of a FAPE was indistinguishable from the all-but-nonjusticiable tort of educational malpractice, the court emphasized that such damages were simply inconsistent with the IDEA's intent. The Third,[205] Ninth,[206] and Tenth[207] Circuits agreed with this rationale, noting that compensatory and punitive damages are unavailable under the IDEA.

Trial courts have rejected claims for monetary damages under the IDEA. By way of illustration, federal trial courts in Michigan agreed that when placements ordered by school boards are inappropriate, judicial authority to fashion appropriate remedies does not include damages, even when school officials acted in bad faith.[208] Similarly, courts in Arkansas,[209] Iowa,[210] New Jersey,[211] Pennsylvania,[212] and Wisconsin[213] agreed with the weight of authority in rejecting claims for monetary damages under the IDEA. In like manner, in a case that arose in New York, the Second Circuit maintained that a damages award not only would have been inconsistent with the IDEA's goals but would have undercut its carefully structured procedure for administrative remedies.[214] Echoing this sentiment, in a case from Puerto Rico, the First Circuit affirmed that the primary purpose of the IDEA is to ensure a FAPE, not provide a mechanism for compensating personal injury.[215]

Section 1983

Section 1983 of the Civil Rights Act of 1871[216] provides for punitive damages designed to punish and discourage individuals who deprive others of rights, privileges, and immunities secured by the Constitution and laws of the United States. Some courts left open the possibility that Section 1983 could be used as a back door to gain damages awards for violations of the IDEA.[217] Again, as with damages awards under the IDEA itself, more recent cases have closed this door.

Some courts initially allowed Section 1983 suits to be brought to enforce the rights identified in the IDEA.[218] However, the weight of authority now precludes using Section 1983 for this purpose.[219] In an appeal from Virginia, the Fourth Circuit affirmed that the IDEA did not permit plaintiffs to sue under Section 1983 for an IDEA violation, which is statutory in nature.[220] The court reasoned that the IDEA failed to express unambiguous Congressional intent to permit IDEA violations to be remedied by Section 1983. The Tenth Circuit agreed with the Fourth Circuit that the IDEA may not provide the basis for Section 1983 claims.[221] The latter court pointed out that insofar as parents from Colorado could not recover damages under the IDEA, they lacked the ability to pursue damages awards under Section 1983 for violations of the IDEA. In a case from Puerto Rico, the First Circuit, agreeing with this line of thinking, observed that Section 1983 cannot be used to escape the strictures on damages under the IDEA.[222] Likewise, a federal trial court in California remarked that parents cannot bypass the procedural and remedial scheme of the IDEA by repackaging their claim as one under Section 1983 so that a jury may award damages.[223]

The Third Circuit, following guidelines established by the Supreme Court in a noneducation case, *City of Rancho Palos Verdes v. Abrams*,[224] effectively abrogated an earlier order to the contrary[225] in acknowledging that Congress did not intend for Section 1983 to remedy violations of the IDEA.[226] In an appeal from the federal trial court in New Jersey, the Third Circuit expressed the view that insofar as the IDEA included a judicial remedy for violations of rights relating to the identification, evaluation, or educational placement of a student, or for violations of rights related to the provision of a FAPE, Congress did not intend to leave open a more expansive remedy under Section 1983. The Fifth Circuit, reviewing a case from Texas, agreed that the comprehensive enforcement scheme of the IDEA justifies the assumption that it is meant to be exclusive and that nothing in the statute indicates Congressional intent for Section 1983 to be used in addition to the IDEA's carefully calibrated mechanism to prevent or remedy violations.[227]

This still leaves open the question of whether parents can use Section 1983 when they allege that school officials acted in bad faith and egregiously violated their procedural rights under the IDEA. For example, could parents sue under Section 1983 in a situation where they claim school officials intentionally disregarded their clearly established IDEA rights? In fairly recent opinions the federal trial court in the District of

Columbia recognized that parents may seek redress under Section 1983 if they can successfully allege facts implying that a school board has a custom or practice that was the moving force behind alleged IDEA violations, that exceptional circumstances existed, or that the normal remedies offered under the IDEA are inadequate to compensate children for the harm allegedly suffered.[228] In spite of the Third Circuit's sweeping pronouncement in the case discussed above, in a later dispute from Pennsylvania the court affirmed that parents were not entitled to damages under Section 1983 since there was no evidence that school officials intentionally violated their procedural rights or exhibited reckless or gross negligence.[229]

Torts

Tort remedies are intended to compensate individuals for injuries resulting from the unreasonable conduct of others. Torts are civil wrongs, typically other than breaches of contracts, committed against someone's person or property. Torts may result from either intentional or unintentional acts. In order to receive damages awards, litigants must prove negligence on the part of the person or persons who allegedly committed the torts. Awards may be granted to compensate for actual losses and, much less frequently, for punitive purposes.[230] In the realm of special education in particular, because the nature of their disabilities may increase the likelihood of injury to special education students, school officials may have to adopt a heightened standard of care.[231]

State courts in California, Louisiana, and Michigan addressed a variety of issues dealing with negligence. The court in California thought that tort damages were unavailable under the IDEA for a claim that a student was denied a FAPE, deciding that the appropriate remedy for a denial of services would have been an award of compensatory educational services.[232] Similarly, a court in Michigan asserted that damages for negligence were not recoverable under the IDEA for a school board's failure to evaluate a student properly.[233] The court was unconvinced that Congress intended for the IDEA to serve as a vehicle for a private cause of action for damages. The court in Louisiana specified that school boards are unlikely to be liable for injuries sustained by students who have been mainstreamed as long as their placements were reasonable.[234]

In related matters, the Sixth Circuit affirmed that the IDEA does not create a right to recover damages for a student's loss of earning power attributed to the failure of school officials to provide the student with a FAPE.[235] Here, a student from Kentucky sued to recover lost wages allegedly resulting from the insufficient education that he received. The same court later remarked that a student could not receive a damages award for the emotional injury allegedly suffered when he was wrongfully barred from participating in sports.[236]

FREQUENTLY ASKED QUESTIONS

Q: Under what circumstances may parents be reimbursed for unilaterally enrolling their children in private schools?

A: Parents must first notify school board officials, in writing, of their dissatisfaction with the current placements of their children and of their intent to enroll the children in private schools. If hearing officers or courts later agree with parents that the IEPs offered by school officials failed to provide the students with FAPEs, and the parentally chosen placements are judged to be appropriate, the parents can be reimbursed. Reimbursement is available even if parentally chosen facilities are not state approved.

Q: Why can school boards be ordered to provide compensatory educational services?

A: The theory behind compensatory education awards is that they are similar to tuition reimbursement awards. In each case, awards are designed to right wrongs and put injured parties in the position that they would have been in but for the harm they experienced. Reimbursement compensates parents for providing appropriate educational services when their school boards fail to do so. Compensatory education awards provide students with the appropriate education services that were denied; the awards are meant to make up for the lost services. Courts often grant compensatory education awards in cases where parents were unable to provide the appropriate services themselves.

Q: Many frivolous cases are filed. Can school boards recover their legal costs when parents file frivolous claims?

A: A provision of the IDEA allows courts to award attorney fees to school boards when complaints are deemed to be frivolous, unreasonable, or without foundation or when the litigation was continued after it became frivolous, unreasonable, or without foundation. Courts can also grant awards if the parents filed complaints for improper purposes, caused unnecessary delays, or needlessly increased the cost of litigation. Interestingly, the IDEA specifies that the fees are to be assessed against the parents' attorneys, not the parents themselves.

Q: Can school boards be assessed punitive damages?

A: In spite of recent litigation on this topic, this is an area of special education law that is still unsettled. Almost all courts now agree that punitive damages are unavailable under the IDEA. The vast weight of authority also suggests that parents cannot use Section 1983 as a vehicle to obtain damages for school boards' failures to provide FAPEs. What remains open is whether parents can sue for damages under Section 1983 when school board officials egregiously violated the parents' procedural rights under the IDEA. Even so, it is unlikely that courts would assess damages unless it can be shown that school officials acted in bad faith or intentionally discriminated against students with disabilities.

Q: Why should school officials make every effort to reach settlement agreements with the parents?

A: Litigation can be expensive, not only in terms of legal fees, but also in terms of time, resources, and aggravation. Litigation, because of its adversarial nature, may also bring about an irreparable breakdown in the relationship between the parents or guardians and school officials. Reaching settlement agreements prior to litigation often can salvage these relationships. Recently, courts have denied attorney fees to parents who resolved their complaints via settlement agreements. It may be much more cost effective for school officials to compromise, and reach settlements, than to continue litigation.

Recommendations

Courts are empowered to grant appropriate relief when school boards fail to provide children with FAPEs as mandated by the IDEA. Under most circumstances, the appropriate judicial relief is ordering school officials to provide FAPEs in the future. However, in many cases parents and children sought compensation for the past failure of educators to provide the services that students were entitled to receive under the IDEA. The courts have used their traditional equity powers to provide students with disabilities with compensation for lost services and their parents' out-of-pocket expenses.

Following a great deal of legal controversy, the courts and Congress provided guidelines for the types of compensation that may be provided to parents when school officials fail to meet their obligations under the IDEA. The following recommendations are based on the IDEA and the many cases in which courts awarded compensation to parents. Although this is an area governed more by federal than state law, as always, readers should consult state as well as federal statutes and regulations.

School officials should

- Take immediate actions to review student IEPs and placements when parents notify them of their dissatisfaction.
- Immediately correct deficiencies identified in IEPs.
- Attempt to settle placement disputes with parents as quickly as possible, thereby reducing potential retroactive tuition reimbursement or compensatory education awards.
- Provide information about possible private school placements when parents express their intent to make unilateral changes in their children's placements.

- Be prepared to show that the IEPs and placements proposed by school officials meet the requirements for FAPEs.
- Be ready to demonstrate that school board officials followed the IDEA's procedural requirements developing IEPs and making placement recommendations.
- Be able to show that parents were notified of their procedural rights at regular junctures throughout the evaluation and placement process.
- Be willing to compromise and consider alternative dispute resolution procedures.
- Make written settlement offers to parents throughout litigation; recall that offers later determined to be equal to or better than the final relief obtained by parents can reduce attorney fees awards.
- Agree to pay legal expenses when it is clear that parents were the prevailing parties in special education disputes, since additional legal actions over attorney fees can only incur additional costs for school boards.
- Always proceed in good faith, carefully following the IDEA's procedures.

Endnotes

1. 20 U.S.C. §§ 1400–1482 (2012). The IDEA's regulations can be found at Assistance to the States for the Education of Children with Disabilities, 34 C.F.R. §§ 300.1–300.818 (2013).
2. 20 U.S.C. § 1415(i)(2); 34 C.F.R. § 300.516(c)(3).
3. Civil Rights Act of 1871, Section 1983, 42 U.S.C. § 1983 (2012).
4. 20 U.S.C. § 1415(j); 34 C.F.R. § 300.518(a).
5. 20 U.S.C. § 1412(a)(10)(C)(ii); 34 C.F.R. § 300.148.
6. 471 U.S. 359 (1985).
7. 510 U.S. 7 (1993).
8. 458 U.S. 176 (1982).
9. 557 U.S. 230 (2009).
10. For background information, *see* Oluwole, J. O. (2010). *Forest Grove School District v. T.A.: The Supreme Court, tuition reimbursement and prior receipt of special education services under the IDEA. Education Law Reporter, 255,* 505–523. Mawdsley, R. D. (2009). The Supreme Court's reassessment of parental unilateral placement under the IDEA: *Forest Grove School District v. T.A. Education Law Reporter, 251,* 1–18. Osborne, A. G., & Russo, C. J. (2009). *Forest Grove School District v. T.A.*: The reimbursement rights of parents who unilaterally place their children with disabilities in private schools without having had them receive special education from public agencies. *Education Law Reporter, 250,* 1–17.
11. *Citing* 20 U.S.C. § 1412(a)(10)(C)(ii).
12. *See, e.g.,* T.B. *ex rel.* W.B. v. St. Joseph School District, 677 F.3d 844 (8th Cir. 2012); P.P. *ex rel.* Michael P. v. West Chester Area School District, 585 F.3d 727 (2d Cir. 2009).

13. *See, e.g.,* Munir v. Pottsville Area School District, 723 F.3d 423 (3d Cir. 2013); Ashland School District v. Parents of Student E.H., 587 F.3d 1175 (9th Cir. 2009); L.G. and K.G. v. School Board of Palm Beach County, 512 F. Supp. 2d 1240 (S.D. Fla. 2007).

14. Jefferson County School District v. Elizabeth E. *ex rel.* Roxanne B., 798 F. Supp. 2d 1177 (D. Colo. 2011).

15. C.B. *ex rel.* Baquerizo v. Garden Grove Unified School District, 635 F.3d 1155 (9th Cir. 2011).

16. *See, e.g.,* Alamo Heights Independent School District v. State Board of Education, 790 F.2d 1153 (5th Cir. 1986).

17. *See, e.g.,* Jennifer D. *ex rel.* Travis D. v. New York City Department of Education, 550 F. Supp. 2d 420 (S.D.N.Y. 2008).

18. Drew P. v. Clarke County School District, 676 F. Supp. 1559 (M.D. Ga. 1987), *affirmed,* 877 F.2d 927 (11th Cir. 1989).

19. Board of Education of Oak Park & River Forest High School District No. 200 v. Illinois State Board of Education, 21 F. Supp. 2d 862 (N.D. Ill. 1988), *vacated and remanded on other grounds sub nom.* Board of Education of Oak Park & River Forest High School District No. 200 v. Kelly E., 207 F.3d 931 (7th Cir. 2000); Lascari v. Board of Education of the Ramapo Indian Hills Regional High School District, 560 A.2d 1180 (N.J. 1989).

20. P.J. v. State of Connecticut Board of Education, 788 F. Supp. 673 (D. Conn. 1992). *See also* J.G. and R.G. *ex rel.* N.G. v. Kiryas Joel Union Free School District, 777 F. Supp. 2d 606 (S.D.N.Y. 2011) (denying parental reimbursement for a unilateral placement in a sectarian school that lacked the capacity to educate children with disabilities); Covington v. Yuba City Unified School District, 780 F. Supp. 2d 1014 (E.D. Cal. 2011) (rejecting a request for parental reimbursement for a placement in a sectarian school that lacked licensed special education teachers, had a curriculum that did not meet state standards, and had no one on staff trained to provide needed interventions).

21. M.S. *ex rel.* S.S. v. Board of Education of the City School District of the City of Yonkers, 231 F.3d 96 (2d Cir. 2000). *See also* Gagliardo v. Arlington Central School District, 489 F.3d 105 (2d Cir. 2007); Matrejek v. Brewster Central School District, 471 F. Supp. 2d 415 (S.D.N.Y. 2007), *affirmed,* 293 F. App'x 20 (2d Cir. 2008).

22. *See, e.g.,* Schreiber v. East Ramapo Central School District, 700 F. Supp. 2d 529 (S.D.N.Y. 2010). *But see* C.B. *ex rel.* B.B. and C.B. v. Special School District No. 1, Minneapolis, 636 F.3d 981 (8th Cir. 2011) (ruling that a private placement need not satisfy the IDEA's least restrictive environment provision in order to be proper).

23. Union School District v. Smith, 15 F.3d 1519 (9th Cir. 1994).

24. Lauren W. *ex rel.* Jean W. v. DeFlaminis, 480 F.3d 259 (3d Cir. 2007). *See also* N.G. v. District of Columbia, 556 F. Supp. 2d 11 (D.D.C. 2008); Gerstmyer v. Howard County Public Schools, 850 F. Supp. 361 (D. Md. 1994).

25. Still v. DeBuono, 101 F.3d 888 (2d Cir. 1996).

26. Bucks County Department of Mental Health/Mental Retardation v. Commonwealth of Pennsylvania, 379 F.3d 61 (3d Cir. 2004).

27. 20 U.S.C. § 1412(a)(10)(C)(iii); 34 C.F.R. § 300.148(d).

28. 20 U.S.C. § 1412(a)(10)(C)(iii)(I)(aa); 34 C.F.R. § 300.148(d)(1)(i).

29. 20 U.S.C. § 1412(a)(10)(C)(iii)(I)(aa); 34 C.F.R. § 300.148(d)(1)(i).

30. 20 U.S.C. § 1412(a)(10)(C)(iii)(II); 34 C.F.R. § 300.148(d)(2).

31. 20 U.S.C. § 1412(a)(10)(C)(iii)(III); 34 C.F.R. § 300.148(d)(3).

32. Evans v. District No. 17 of Douglas County, 841 F.2d 824 (8th Cir. 1988).
33. Schoenfield v. Parkway School District, 138 F.3d 379 (8th Cir. 1998).
34. Tucker v. Calloway County Board of Education, 136 F.3d 495 (6th Cir. 1998); Johnson v. Metro Davidson County School System, 108 F. Supp. 2d 906 (M.D. Tenn. 2000); L.K. ex rel. J.H. v. Board of Education for Transylvania County, 113 F. Supp. 2d 856 (W.D.N.C. 2000); Ash v. Lake Oswego School District, 766 F. Supp. 852 (D. Or. 1991), *affirmed*, 980 F.2d 585 (9th Cir. 1992).
35. Patricia P. v. Board of Education of Oak Park and River Forest High School District No. 200, 203 F.3d 462 (7th Cir. 2000).
36. Ashland School District v. Parents of Student E.H., 587 F.3d 1175 (9th Cir. 2009); S.W. *ex rel.* M.W. v. New York City Department of Education, 646 F. Supp. 2d 346 (S.D.N.Y. 2009); Ms. M. *ex rel.* K.M. v. Portland School Committee, 360 F.3d 267 (1st Cir. 2004); Greenland School District v. Amy N., 358 F.3d 150 (1st Cir. 2004); Nein v. Greater Clark County School Corporation, 95 F. Supp. 2d 961 (S.D. Ind. 2000).
37. Muth v. Central Bucks School District, 839 F.2d 113 (3d Cir. 1988), *reversed and remanded on other grounds sub nom.* Dellmuth v. Muth, 491 U.S. 223 (1989).
38. Board of Education of the County of Cabell v. Dienelt, 843 F.2d 813 (4th Cir. 1988).
39. Hudson v. Wilson, 828 F.2d 1059 (4th Cir. 1987).
40. Mayo v. Baltimore City Public Schools, 40 F. Supp. 2d 331 (D. Md. 1999).
41. Cleveland Heights–University Heights City School District v. Boss, 144 F.3d 391 (6th Cir. 1998).
42. Muller v. Committee on Special Education of the East Islip Union Free School District, 145 F.3d 95 (2d Cir. 1998).
43. Deal *ex rel.* Deal v. Hamilton County Department of Education, 392 F.3d 840 (6th Cir. 2004), 258 F. App'x 863 (6th Cir. 2008).
44. DiBuo v. Board of Education of Worcester County, 309 F.3d 184 (4th Cir. 2002).
45. Eugene B. v. Great Neck Union Free School District, 635 F. Supp. 753 (E.D.N.Y. 1986).
46. Bernardsville Board of Education v. J.H., 42 F.3d 149 (3d Cir. 1994).
47. Warren G. v. Cumberland County School District, 190 F.3d 80 (3d Cir. 1999).
48. C.G. *ex rel.* A.S. v. Five Town Community School District, 513 F.3d 279 (1st Cir. 2008). *See also* Glendale Unified School District v. Almasi, 122 F. Supp. 2d 1093 (C.D. Cal. 2000).
49. C.H. v. Cape Henlopen School District, 606 F.3d 59 (3d Cir. 2010).
50. M.S. and D.S. v. Mullica Township Board of Education, 485 F. Supp. 2d 555 (D.N.J. 2007).
51. Suzawith v. Green Bay Area School District, 132 F. Supp. 2d 718 (D. Wis. 2000).
52. *See, e.g.*, Babb v. Knox County School System, 965 F.2d 104 (6th Cir. 1992); Tice v. Botetourt County School District, 908 F.2d 1200 (4th Cir. 1990); Gary A. v. New Trier High School District No. 203, 796 F.2d 940 (7th Cir. 1986); Straube v. Florida Union Free School District, 778 F. Supp. 774 (S.D.N.Y. 1991), 801 F. Supp. 1164 (S.D.N.Y. 1992); Vander Malle v. Ambach, 667 F. Supp. 1015 (S.D.N.Y. 1987); Doe v. Anrig, 651 F. Supp. 424 (D. Mass. 1987); Max M. v. Thompson, 566 F. Supp. 1330 (N.D. Ill. 1983), 592 F. Supp. 1437 (N.D. Ill. 1984), *sub nom.* Max M. v. Illinois State Board of Education, 629 F. Supp. 1504 (N.D. Ill. 1986).
53. Hurry v. Jones, 734 F.2d 879 (1st Cir. 1984).
54. Taylor v. Board of Education of Copake–Taconic Hills Central School District, 649 F. Supp. 1253 (N.D.N.Y. 1986).

55. Malehorn v. Hill City School District, 987 F. Supp. 772 (D.S.D. 1997).

56. Rapid City School District v. Vahle, 922 F.2d 476 (8th Cir. 1990).

57. Johnson v. Lancaster-Lebanon Intermediate Unit 13, Lancaster City School District, 757 F. Supp. 606 (E.D. Pa. 1991).

58. Union School District v. Smith, 15 F.3d 1519 (9th Cir. 1994).

59. S-1 v. Spangler, 650 F. Supp. 1427 (M.D.N.C. 1986), *vacated and remanded due to mootness* 832 F.2d 294 (4th Cir. 1987), *on remand* (unpublished opinion), *affirmed sub nom.*, S-1 v. State Board of Education, 6 F.3d 160 (4th Cir. 1993), *rehearing en banc*, *reversed* 21 F.3d 49 (4th Cir. 1994).

60. 20 U.S.C. § 1412(a)(10)(C)(ii); 34 C.F.R. § 300.148.

61. Osborne, A. G., & Russo, C. J. (2009). Compensatory services and students with disabilities. *School Business Affairs, 75*(6), 34–36.

62. Zirkel, P. A., & Hennessy, M. K. (2001). Compensatory educational services in special education cases: An update. *Education Law Reporter, 150*, 311–332.

63. Murphy v. Timberlane Regional School District, 973 F.2d 13 (1st Cir. 1992), *on remand* 819 F. Supp. 1127 (D.N.H. 1993), *affirmed,* 22 F.3d 1186 (1st Cir. 1994), *contempt finding,* 855 F. Supp. 498 (D.N.H. 1994); Todd D. v. Andrews, 933 F.2d 1576 (11th Cir. 1991); Lester H. v. Gilhool, 916 F.2d 865 (3d Cir. 1990); Manchester School District v. Christopher B., 807 F. Supp. 860 (D.N.H. 1992); White v. State of California, 240 Cal. Rptr. 732 (Cal. Ct. App. 1987).

64. Manchester School District v. Christopher B., 807 F. Supp. 860 (D.N.H. 1992); Valerie J. v. Derry Cooperative School District, 771 F. Supp. 483 (D.N.H. 1991); Big Beaver Falls Area School District v. Jackson, 624 A.2d 806 (Pa. Commw. Ct. 1993).

65. Pihl v. Massachusetts Department of Education, 9 F.3d 184 (1st Cir. 1993); State of West Virginia *ex rel.* Justice v. Board of Education of the County of Monongalia, 539 S.E.2d 777 (W.Va. 2000).

66. Jefferson County Board of Education v. Breen, 853 F.2d 853 (11th Cir. 1988).

67. Miener v. Missouri, 800 F.2d 749 (8th Cir. 1986).

68. Cremeans v. Fairland Local School District Board of Education, 633 N.E.2d 570 (Ohio Ct. App. 1993).

69. Puffer v. Raynolds, 761 F. Supp. 838 (D. Mass. 1988).

70. Straube v. Florida Union Free School District, 778 F. Supp. 774 (S.D.N.Y. 1991), 801 F. Supp. 1164 (S.D.N.Y. 1992).

71. Brooks v. District of Columbia, 841 F. Supp. 2d 253 (D.D.C. 2012).

72. Ridgewood Board of Education v. N.E., 172 F.3d 238 (3d Cir. 1999); M.C. *ex rel.* J.C. v. Central Regional School District, 81 F.3d 389 (3d Cir. 1996).

73. Draper v. Atlanta Independent School System, 518 F.3d 1275 (11th Cir. 2008).

74. Reid v. District of Columbia, 401 F.3d 516 (D.C. Cir. 2005).

75. Friendship Edison Public Charter School v. Nesbitt, 583 F. Supp. 2d 169 (D.D.C. 2008).

76. Friendship Edison Public Charter School v. Nesbitt, 669 F. Supp. 2d 80 (D.D.C. 2009). *See also* Cousins v. District of Columbia, 880 F. Supp. 2d 142 (D.D.C. 2012) (awarding compensatory services based on experts' estimates regarding the nature and quantity of what was required to make up for the lost educational benefit).

77. Breanne C. v. Southern York County School District, 732 F. Supp. 2d 474 (M.D. Pa. 2010); Heather D. v. Northampton Area School District, 511 F. Supp. 2d 549 (E.D. Pa. 2007); Keystone Central School District v. E.E. *ex rel.* H.E. 438 F. Supp. 2d 519 (M.D. Pa. 2006).

78. Draper v. Atlanta Independent School System, 518 F.3d 1275 (11th Cir. 2008).

79. Park v. Anaheim Union High School District, 464 F.3d 1025 (9th Cir. 2006).

80. Cocores v. Portsmouth, New Hampshire School District, 779 F. Supp. 203 (D.N.H. 1991); Big Beaver Falls Area School District v. Jackson, 624 A.2d 806 (Pa. Commw. Ct. 1993).

81. P.P. *ex rel.* Michael P. v. West Chester Area School District, 585 F.3d 727 (3d Cir. 2009); Garro v. State of Connecticut, 23 F.3d 734 (2d Cir. 1994); Timms v. Metropolitan School District, 718 F.2d 212 (7th Cir. 1983), *amended* 722 F.2d 1310 (7th Cir. 1983); Gregory-Rivas v. District of Columbia, 577 F. Supp. 2d 4 (D.D.C. 2008).

82. Brown v. Wilson County School District, 747 F. Supp. 436 (M.D. Tenn. 1990).

83. Carlisle Area School District v. Scott P., 62 F.3d 520 (3d Cir. 1995).

84. Yankton School District v. Schramm, 900 F. Supp. 1182 (D.S.D. 1995), *affirmed*, 93 F.3d 1369 (8th Cir. 1996).

85. Wenger v. Canastota Central School District, 979 F. Supp. 147 (N.D.N.Y. 1997), *affirmed*, 146 F.3d 123 (2d Cir. 1998).

86. D.B. v. Ocean Township Board of Education, 985 F. Supp. 457 (D.N.J. 1997).

87. Parents of Student W. v. Puyallup School District No. 3, 31 F.3d 1489 (9th Cir. 1994).

88. Moubry v. Independent School District No. 696, 951 F. Supp. 867 (D. Minn. 1996).

89. G.R. *ex rel.* Russell v. Dallas School District No. 2, 823 F. Supp. 2d 1120 (D. Or. 2011).

90. Fisher v. Friendship Edison Charter School, 857 F. Supp. 2d 64 (D.D.C. 2012).

91. *See, e.g.*, Diamond v. McKenzie, 602 F. Supp. 632 (D.D.C. 1985).

92. 468 U.S. 992 (1984).

93. Now codified at 20 U.S.C. § 1415(i)(3).

94. Johnson v. District of Columbia, 850 F. Supp. 2d 74 (D.D.C. 2012).

95. Wright v. District of Columbia, 883 F. Supp. 2d 132 (D.D.C. 2012).

96. 20 U.S.C. § 1415(i)(3)(D)(I).

97. *See, e.g.*, Field v. Haddonfield Board of Education, 769 F. Supp. 1313 (D.N.J. 1991).

98. 20 U.S.C. § 1415(i)(3)(D)(ii); 34 C.F.R. § 300.517(c)(2)(ii).

99. 20 U.S.C. § 1415(i)(3)(D)(iii).

100. Mathern v. Campbell County Children's Center, 674 F. Supp. 816 (D. Wyo. 1987).

101. Angela L. v. Pasadena Independent School District, 918 F.2d 1188 (5th Cir. 1990).

102. J.G. v. Board of Education of the Rochester City School District, 648 F. Supp. 1452 (W.D.N.Y. 1986), *affirmed*, 830 F.2d 444 (2d Cir. 1987); Sidney K. v. Ambach, 535 N.Y.S.2d 468 (N.Y. App. Div. 1988); Esther C. v. Ambach, 535 N.Y.S.2d 462 (N.Y. App. Div. 1988).

103. For commentaries on attorney fees, *see* Osborne, A. G., & Russo, C. J. (2012). The IDEA and attorney fees. *School Business Affairs, 78*(6), 33–37. Osborne, A. G. (2005). Update on attorneys' fees under the IDEA. *Education Law Reporter, 193*, 1–12.

104. *See, e.g.*, James S. *ex rel.* Thelma S. v. School District of Philadelphia, 559 F. Supp. 2d 600 (E.D. Pa. 2008).

105. *See, e.g.*, C.Z. *ex rel.* Ziemba v. Plainfield Community Unit School District, 680 F. Supp. 2d 950 (N.D. Ill. 2010).

106. *See, e.g.*, Phelan v. Bell, 8 F.3d 369 (6th Cir. 1993); Angela L. v. Pasadena Independent School District, 918 F.2d 1188 (5th Cir. 1990); E.S. and M.S. *ex rel.*

B.S. v. Katonah-Lewisboro School District, 796 F. Supp. 2d 421 (S.D.N.Y. 2011); Turton v. Crisp County School District, 688 F. Supp. 1535 (M.D. Ga. 1988).

107. Compton Unified School District v. Addison, 598 F.3d 1181 (9th Cir. 2010); Mitten v. Muscogee County District, 877 F.2d 932 (11th Cir. 1989); Doe v. Boston Public Schools, 550 F. Supp. 2d 170 (D. Mass. 2008); Dudley *ex rel.* W.J.W. v. Lower Merion School District, 768 F. Supp. 2d 779 (E.D. Pa. 2011).

108. Krichinsky v. Knox County Schools, 963 F.2d 847 (6th Cir. 1992).

109. Moore v. Crestwood Local School District, 804 F. Supp. 960 (N.D. Ohio 1992).

110. J.D. *ex rel.* Davis v. Kanawha County Board of Education, 571 F.3d 381 (4th Cir. 2009).

111. *See, e.g.,* Park v. Anaheim Union High School District, 464 F.3d 1025 (9th Cir. 2006). For a discussion of fees for partially successful plaintiffs, *see* Mawdsley, R. D. (2007). Attorney fees for partially successful IDEA claimants. *Education Law Reporter, 217,* 769–788.

112. *See, e.g.,* M.K. *ex rel.* Mrs. K. v. Sergi, 578 F. Supp. 2d 425 (D. Conn. 2008); Koswenda v. Flossmoor School District No. 161, 227 F. Supp. 2d 979 (N.D. Ill. 2002); Burr v. Sobol, 748 F. Supp. 97 (S.D.N.Y. 1990); Max M. v. Illinois State Board of Education, 684 F. Supp. 514 (N.D. Ill. 1988), *affirmed* 859 F.2d 1297 (7th Cir. 1988).

113. Aguirre v. Los Angeles Unified School District, 461 F.3d 1114 (9th Cir. 2006).

114. *See, e.g.,* Judah M. v. Board of Education of City of Chicago District 299, 798 F. Supp. 2d 942 (N.D. Ill. 2011); L.V. v. New York City Department of Education, 700 F. Supp. 2d 510 (S.D.N.Y. 2010); Anchorage School District v. D.S. and C.S., 688 F. Supp. 2d 883 (D. Alaska 2009); Troy School District v. Boutsikaris, 250 F. Supp. 2d 720 (E.D. Mich. 2003).

115. Jackson v. District of Columbia, 603 F. Supp. 2d 97 (D.D.C. 2009).

116. *See, e.g.,* Smith v. District of Columbia, 117 F. App'x (D.C. Cir. 2004); In re Conklin, 946 F.2d 306 (4th Cir. 1991); Hayes v. D.C. Public Schools, 815 F. Supp. 2d 134 (D.D.C. 2011); C.C. *ex rel.* Mrs. D. v. Granby Board of Education, 453 F. Supp. 2d 569 (D. Conn. 2006), *vacated and remanded on other grounds,* 580 F.3d 286 (5th Cir. 2009).

117. L.J. *ex rel.* V.J. v. Audubon Board of Education, 373 F. App'x 294 (3d Cir. 2010).

118. Howey v. Tippecanoe School Corporation, 734 F. Supp. 1485 (N.D. Ind. 1990).

119. King v. Floyd County Board of Education, 5 F. Supp. 2d 504 (E.D. Ky. 1998).

120. Teresa and Rusty R. *ex rel.* Patrick R. v. Madison Metropolitan School District, 615 F. Supp. 2d 860 (W.D. Wis. 2009).

121. P. *ex rel.* Mr. P. v. Newington Board of Education, 512 F. Supp. 2d 89 (D. Conn. 2007), *affirmed on other grounds,* 546 F.3d 111 (2d Cir. 2008).

122. Field v. Haddonfield Board of Education, 769 F. Supp. 1313 (D.N.J. 1991). *See also* Teresa and Rusty R. *ex rel.* Patrick R. v. Madison Metropolitan School District, 615 F. Supp. 2d 860 (W.D. Wis. 2009).

123. *See, e.g.,* Leticia H. *ex rel.* R.H. v. Ysleta Independent School District, 502 F. Supp. 2d 512 (W.D. Tex. 2006).

124. Wheeler v. Towanda Area School District, 950 F.2d 128 (3d Cir. 1991).

125. Board of Education of Downers Grove Grade School District No. 58 v. Steven L., 89 F.3d 464 (7th Cir. 1996); Salley v. St. Tammany Parish School Board, 57 F.3d 458 (5th Cir. 1995); Metropolitan School District of Lawrence Township v. M.S., 818 N.E.2d 978 (Ind. Ct. App. 2004).

126. *See, e.g.,* Nathan F. v. Parkland School District, 136 F. App'x 511 (3d Cir. 2005) (affirming that parents who entered into a private settlement agreement with a school board were not entitled to attorney fees).

127. Hunger v. Leininger, 15 F.3d 664 (7th Cir. 1994).

128. Linda T. *ex rel.* William A. v. Rice Lake Area School District, 337 F. Supp. 2d 1135 (W.D. Wis. 2004).

129. Fischer v. Rochester Community Schools, 780 F. Supp. 1142 (E.D. Mich. 1991).

130. Combs v. School Board of Rockingham County, 15 F.3d 357 (4th Cir. 1994); Claudia C-B v. Board of Trustees of Pioneer Valley Performing Arts Charter School, 539 F. Supp. 2d 474 (D. Mass. 2008); D.R. *ex rel.* Robinson v. Government of the District of Columbia, 637 F. Supp. 2d 11 (D.D.C. 2009).

131. Payne v. Board of Education, Cleveland City Schools, 88 F.3d 392 (6th Cir. 1996); Johnson v. Bismarck Public School District, 949 F.2d 1000 (8th Cir. 1991); W.L.G. v. Houston County Board of Education, 975 F. Supp. 1317 (M.D. Ala. 1997); Patricia E. v. Board of Education of Community High School District No. 155, 894 F. Supp. 1161 (N.D. Ill. 1995).

132. E.M. v. Marriott Hospitality Public Chartered High School, 541 F. Supp. 2d 395 (D.D.C. 2008).

133. Agapito v. District of Columbia, 477 F. Supp. 2d 103 (D.D.C. 2007).

134. Rapu v. D.C. Public Schools, 793 F. Supp. 2d 419 (D.D.C. 2011); Dickens v. Friendship Edison P.C.S., 639 F. Supp. 2d 51 (D.D.C. 2009).

135. Durkee v. Livonia Central School District, 487 F. Supp. 2d 318 (W.D.N.Y. 2007). *See also* T.B. *ex rel.* Debra B. v. Bryan Independent School District, 628 F.3d 240 (5th Cir. 2010) (denying fees to the parents of a child who had not yet been determined to be eligible for IDEA services); D.S. *ex rel.* Z.S. v. Neptune Township Board of Education, 264 F. App'x 186 (3d Cir. 2008) (affirming that parents who withdrew from a hearing prior to receiving an order that their child was eligible for special education were not entitled to fees).

136. *See, e.g.,* Daniel S. v. Scranton School District, 230 F.3d 90 (3d Cir. 2000); W.L.G. v. Houston County Board of Education, 975 F. Supp. 1317 (M.D. Ala. 1997).

137. Wenkart, R. D. (2002). Attorneys' fees under the IDEA and the demise of the catalyst theory. *Education Law Reporter, 165,* 439–445.

138. 532 U.S. 598 (2001).

139. Osborne, A. G. (2003). Attorneys' fees under the IDEA after *Buckhannon*: Is the catalyst theory still viable? *Education Law Reporter, 175,* 397–407.

140. *See, e.g.,* Doe v. Boston Public Schools, 358 F.3d 20 (1st Cir. 2004); John T. *ex rel.* Paul T. and Joan T. v. Delaware County Intermediate Unit, 318 F.3d 545 (3d Cir. 2003); T.D. v. LaGrange School District No. 102, 349 F.3d 469 (7th Cir. 2003); J.C. v. Regional School District No. 10, 278 F.3d 119 (2d Cir. 2002).

141. 20 U.S.C. § 1415(i)(3)(B); 34 C.F.R. § 300.517(a).

142. Osborne, A. G., & DiMattia, P. (1991). Attorney fees are available for administrative proceedings under the EHA. *Education Law Reporter, 66,* 909–920.

143. Moore v. District of Columbia, 907 F.2d 165 (D.C. Cir. 1990).

144. Moore v. District of Columbia, 886 F.2d 335 (D.C. Cir. 1989).

145. Osborne, A. G., & DiMattia, P. (1991). Attorney fees are available for administrative proceedings under the EHA. *Education Law Reporter, 66,* 909–920.

146. *Id.*

147. 20 U.S.C. § 1415(i)(3)(D)(i); 34 C.F.R. § 300.517(c)(2)(i)(A).

148. *See, e.g.,* Gary G. *ex rel.* G.G. v. El Paso Independent School District, 632 F.3d 201 (5th Cir. 2011); Hyden v. Board of Education of Wilson County, 714 F. Supp. 290 (M.D. Tenn. 1989); Olivas v. Cincinnati Public Schools, 171 Ohio App. 3d 669 (Ohio Ct. App. 2007).

149. *See, e.g.,* Woods *ex rel.* T.W. v. Northport Public School, 487 F. App'x 968 (6th Cir. 2012); Mr. L. and Mrs. L. v. Woonsocket Education Department, 793 F. Supp. 41 (D.R.I. 1992).
150. Springfield School Committee v. Doe, 623 F. Supp. 2d 150 (D. Mass. 2009).
151. Capistrano Unified School District v. Wartenberg, 59 F.3d 884 (9th Cir. 1995); Virginia McC. v. Corrigan-Camden Independent School District, 909 F. Supp. 1023 (E.D. Tex. 1995).
152. John M. v. Board of Education of City of Chicago, District 299, 612 F. Supp. 2d 981 (N.D. Ill. 2009). *See* also Gross *ex rel.* Gross v. Perrysburg Exempted Village School District, 306 F. Supp. 2d 726 (N.D. Ohio 2004) (rejecting a settlement offer because it did not include specific details).
153. Benito M. v. Board of Education of City of Chicago, 544 F. Supp. 2d 713 (N.D. Ill. 2008).
154. *See, e.g.,* Barlow–Gresham Union High School District No. 2 v. Mitchell, 940 F.2d 1280 (9th Cir. 1991); Shelly C. v. Venus Independent School District, 878 F.2d 862 (5th Cir. 1989); E.P. v. Union County Regional High School District No. 1, 741 F. Supp. 1144 (D.N.J. 1989).
155. *See, e.g.,* P.N. v. Seattle School District No. 1, 458 F.3d 983 (9th Cir. 2006); M.L. v. Sloan, 449 F.3d 405 (2d Cir. 2006); Salley v. Trenton Board of Education, 156 F. App'x 470 (3d Cir. 2005); Sanford v. Sylvania City School Board, 380 F. Supp. 2d 903 (N.D. Ohio 2005); Smith *ex rel.* Smith v. Fitchburg Public Schools, 401 F.3d 16 (1st Cir. 2005); Algeria v. District of Columbia, 391 F.3d 262 (D.C. Cir. 2004); J.S. v. Ramapo Central School District, 165 F. Supp. 2d 570 (S.D.N.Y. 2001).
156. *See, e.g.,* Walker v. District of Columbia, 798 F. Supp. 2d 48 (D.D.C. 2011); P.N. *ex rel.* M.W. v. Clementon Board of Education, 442 F.3d 848 (3d Cir. 2006); A.R. *ex rel.* R.V. v. New York City Department of Education, 407 F.3d 656 (2d Cir. 2005); Abraham v. District of Columbia, 338 F. Supp. 2d 113 (D.D.C. 2004); D.M. *ex rel.* G.M. and C.M. v. Board of Education, Center Moriches Union Free School District, 296 F. Supp. 2d 400 (E.D.N.Y. 2003).
157. Nathan F. v. Parkland School District, 136 F. App'x 511 (3d Cir. 2005).
158. *See, e.g.,* Eggers v. Bullitt County School District, 854 F.2d 892 (6th Cir. 1988); Yankton School District v. Schramm, 900 F. Supp. 1182 (D.S.D. 1995), *affirmed,* 93 F.3d 1369 (8th Cir. 1996).
159. Zirkel, P. A. (2007). Lay advocates and parent experts under the IDEA. *Education Law Reporter, 217,* 19–27.
160. Arons v. New Jersey State Board of Education, 842 F.2d 58 (3d Cir. 1988).
161. Heldman v. Sobol, 846 F.3d 285 (S.D.N.Y. 1994).
162. Connors v. Mills, 34 F. Supp. 2d 795 (N.D.N.Y. 1998).
163. *See, e.g.,* Van Duyn v. Baker School District, 502 F.3d 811 (9th Cir. 2007); Ford v. Long Beach Unified School District, 461 F.3d 1087 (9th Cir. 2006); Pardini v. Allegheny Intermediate Unit, 420 F.3d 181 (3d Cir. 2005); Woodside v. School District of Philadelphia Board of Education, 248 F.3d 129 (3d Cir. 2001); Doe v. Board of Education of Baltimore County, 165 F.3d 260 (4th Cir. 1998); Erickson v. Board of Education of Baltimore County, 162 F.3d 289 (4th Cir. 1998); Heldman v. Sobol, 846 F.3d 285 (S.D.N.Y. 1994).
164. Matthew V. v. DeKalb County School System, 244 F. Supp. 2d 1331 (N.D. Ga. 2003).
165. Weissburg v. Lancaster School District, 591 F.3d 1255 (9th Cir. 2010).
166. Osborne, A. G. (2005). Update on attorneys' fees under the IDEA. *Education Law Reporter, 193,* 1–12.

167. *See, e.g.,* Brillon v. Klein Independent School District, 274 F. Supp. 2d 864 (S.D. Tex. 2003); Pazik v. Gateway Regional School District, 130 F. Supp. 2d 217 (D. Mass. 2001); Mr. J. v. Board of Education, 98 F. Supp. 2d 226 (D. Conn. 2000); P.L. by Mr. and Mrs. L. v. Norwalk Board of Education, 64 F. Supp. 2d 61 (D. Conn. 1999); Aronow v. District of Columbia, 780 F. Supp. 46 (D.D.C. 1992), 791 F. Supp. 318 (D.D.C. 1992); Chang v. Board of Education of Glen Ridge Township, 685 F. Supp. 96 (D.N.J. 1988).

168. *See, e.g.,* Goldring v. District of Columbia, 416 F.3d 70 (D.C. Cir. 2005); Missouri Department of Elementary and Secondary Education v. Springfield R-12 School District, 358 F.3d 992 (8th Cir. 2004); Neosho R-V School District v. Clark, 315 F.3d 1022 (8th Cir. 2003); T.D. v. LaGrange School District No. 102, 349 F.3d 469 (7th Cir. 2003).

169. 548 U.S. 291 (2006). For a commentary on this decision, *see* Osborne, A. G., & Russo, C. J. (2006). The Supreme Court rejects parental reimbursement for expert witness fees under the IDEA: *Arlington Central School District Board of Education v. Murphy. Education Law Reporter, 213,* 333–348.

170. Murphy v. Arlington Central School District, 402 F.3d 332 (2d Cir. 2005).

171. Despite three attempts to modify the IDEA, the proposed amendments never proceeded. *See* H.R. 2740, 111th Cong., 1st Sess. (2009); H.R. 1208, 112th Cong., 1st Sess. (2011); S. 613, 113th Cong., 1st Sess. (2011).

172. *See, e.g.,* Fisher *ex rel.* Fisher v. District of Columbia, 517 F.3d 570 (D.C. Cir. 2008); A.W. v. East Orange Board of Education, 248 F. App'x 363 (3d Cir. 2007); Santy v. Charter Oak Unified School District, 220 F. App'x 712 (9th Cir. 2007); Friendship Edison Public Charter School v. Nesbitt, 752 F. Supp. 2d 1 (D.D.C. 2010).

173. Arons v. Charpentier, 828 N.Y.S.2d 482 (N.Y. App. Div. 2007).

174. 34 C.F.R. §§ 300.151–300.153.

175. Lucht v. Molalla River School District, 225 F.3d 1023 (9th Cir. 1999).

176. Upper Valley Association of Handicapped Citizens v. Blue Mountain Union School District No. 21, 973 F. Supp. 429 (D. Vt. 1997).

177. Megan C. v. Independent School District No. 625, 57 F. Supp. 2d 776 (D. Minn. 1999).

178. Vultaggio v. Board of Education, Smithtown Central School District, 343 F.3d 598 (2d Cir. 2003).

179. 20 U.S.C. § 1415(i)(3)(D)(ii); 34 C.F.R. § 300.517(c)(2)(ii).

180. *See, e.g.,* Brown *ex rel.* P.L. v. Barbara Jordan P.C.S., 495 F. Supp. 2d 1 (D.D.C. 2007); C.C. *ex rel.* Mrs. D. v. Granby Board of Education, 453 F. Supp. 2d 569 (D. Conn. 2006); Alfonso v. District of Columbia, 464 F. Supp. 2d 1 (D.D.C. 2006); E.C. *ex rel.* R.C. v. Board of Education of South Brunswick Township, 792 A.2d 583 (N.J. Sup. Ct. 2001).

181. Watkins v. Vance, 328 F. Supp. 2d 27 (D.D.C. 2004).

182. Fed. R. App. P. 38.

183. Caroline T. v. Hudson School District, 915 F.2d 752 at 757 (1st Cir. 1990).

184. Hiller v. Board of Education of the Brunswick Central School District, 743 F. Supp. 958 (N.D.N.Y. 1990).

185. 20 U.S.C. § 1415(i)(3)(B)(i)(II); 34 C.F.R. § 300.517(a)(1)(ii).

186. 20 U.S.C. § 1415(i)(3)(B)(i)(III); 34 C.F.R. § 300.517(a)(1)(iii).

187. District of Columbia v. Ijeabuonwu, 642 F.3d 1191 (D.C. Cir. 2011); District of Columbia v. Straus, 590 F.3d 898 (D.C. Cir. 2010); El Paso Independent School District v. Richard R. *ex rel.* R.R., 591 F.3d 417 (5th Cir. 2009).

188. R.P. *ex rel.* C.P. v. Prescott Unified School District, 631 F.3d 1117 (9th Cir. 2011). *See also* Hawkins v. Berkeley Unified School District, 250 F. Supp. 2d 459 (N.D. Cal. 2008) (stating that a board was not automatically entitled to fees simply because it prevailed in an IDEA case).
189. El Paso Independent School District v. Berry, 400 F. App'x 947 (5th Cir. 2010).
190. Bridges Public Charter School v. Barrie, 796 F. Supp. 2d 39 (D.D.C. 2011).
191. Ruben A. v. El Paso Independent School District, 657 F. Supp. 2d 778 (W.D. Tex. 2009).
192. Moser v. Bret Harte Union High School District, 366 F. Supp. 2d 944 (E.D. Cal. 2005).
193. Zirkel, P. A., & Osborne, A. G. (1987). Are damages available in special education suits? *Education Law Reporter, 42,* 497–508.
194. Garner, B. A. (Ed.). (2009). *Black's law dictionary* (9th ed.). St. Paul, MN: West.
195. Osborne, A. G., & Russo, C. J. (2001). Are damages an available remedy when a school district fails to provide an appropriate education under IDEA? *Education Law Reporter, 152,* 1–14.
196. Anderson v. Thompson, 658 F.2d 1205 (7th Cir. 1981).
197. *See, e.g.,* Barnett v. Fairfax County School Board, 927 F.2d 146 (4th Cir. 1991); Gary A. v. New Trier High School District No. 203, 796 F.2d 940 (7th Cir. 1986); Marvin H. v. Austin Independent School District, 714 F.2d 1348 (5th Cir. 1983); Powell v. DeFore, 699 F.2d 1078 (11th Cir. 1983).
198. 471 U.S. 359 (1985).
199. Charlie F. v. Board of Education of Skokie School District 68, 98 F.3d 989 (7th Cir. 1996).
200. Ortega v. Bibb County School District, 397 F.3d 1321 (11th Cir. 2005).
201. Marvin H. v. Austin Independent School District, 714 F.2d 1348 (5th Cir. 1983).
202. Barnett v. Fairfax County School Board, 927 F.2d 146 (4th Cir. 1991).
203. Gerasimou v. Ambach, 636 F. Supp. 1504 (E.D.N.Y. 1986).
204. Sellers v. School Board of the City of Manassas, 141 F.3d 524 (4th Cir. 1998).
205. Chambers v. School District of Philadelphia Board of Education, 587 F.3d 176 (3d Cir. 2009).
206. C.O. and Oman v. Portland Public Schools, 679 F.3d 1162 (9th Cir. 2012).
207. Padilla v. School District No. 1 in the City and County of Denver, 233 F.3d 1268 (10th Cir. 2000).
208. Wayne County Regional Education Service Agency v. Pappas, 56 F. Supp. 2d 807 (E.D. Mich. 1999); Sanders v. Marquette Public Schools, 561 F. Supp. 1361 (W.D. Mich. 1983). *See also* Long v. Dawson Springs Independent School District, 197 F. App'x 427 (6th Cir. 2006) (affirming that monetary damages are unavailable to remedy IDEA violations).
209. Finch v. Texarkana School District No. 7 of Miller County, 557 F. Supp. 2d 976 (W.D. Ark. 2008).
210. D.L., E.L., and L.L. v. Waukee Community School District, 578 F. Supp. 2d 1178 (S.D. Iowa 2008).
211. D.G. v. Somerset Hills School District, 559 F. Supp. 2d 484 (D.N.J. 2008).
212. Derrick F. v. Red Lion Area School District, 586 F. Supp. 2d 282 (M.D. Pa. 2008); J.L. *ex rel.* J.L. and C.L. v. Ambridge Area School District, 622 F. Supp. 2d 257 (W.D. Pa. 2008).
213. Edwards v. School District of Baraboo, 570 F. Supp. 2d 1077 (W.D. Wis. 2008).
214. Polera v. Board of Education of the Newburgh Enlarged City School District, 288 F.3d 478 (2d Cir. 2002).

215. Nieves-Marquez v. Commonwealth of Puerto Rico, 353 F.3d 108 (1st Cir. 2003).

216. 42 U.S.C. § 1983.

217. Mawdsley, R. D. (2002). A section 1983 cause of action under the IDEA? Measuring the effect of *Gonzaga University v. Doe. Education Law Reporter, 170,* 425–438. Osborne, A. G. (2002). Can section 1983 be used to redress violations of the IDEA? *Education Law Reporter, 161,* 21–32. Wenkart, R. D. (2004). The award of section 1983 damages under the IDEA. *Education Law Reporter, 183,* 313–335.

218. *See, e.g.,* B.H. v. Southington Board of Education, 273 F. Supp. 2d 194 (D. Conn. 2003); Cappillino v. Hyde Park Central School District, 40 F. Supp. 2d 513 (S.D.N.Y. 1999); Emma C. v. Eastin, 985 F. Supp. 940 (N.D. Cal. 1997); Brantley v. Independent School District No. 625, St. Paul Public Schools, 936 F. Supp. 649 (D. Minn. 1996).

219. Osborne, A. G. (2008). Can Section 1983 be used to redress violations of the IDEA: An update. *Education Law Reporter, 230,* 453–467.

220. Sellers v. School Board of City of Manassas, 141 F.3d 524 (4th Cir. 1998).

221. Padilla v. School District No. 1 in City and County of Denver, 233 F.3d 1268 (10th Cir. 2000).

222. Diaz-Fonseca v. Commonwealth of Puerto Rico, 451 F.3d 13 (1st Cir. 2006).

223. Alex G. *ex rel.* Stephen G. v. Board of Trustees of Davis Joint Unified School District, 332 F. Supp. 2d 1315 (E.D. Cal. 2004).

224. 544 U.S. 113 (2005).

225. W.B. v. Matula, 67 F.3d 484 (3d Cir. 1995).

226. A.W. v. Jersey City Public Schools, 486 F.3d 791 (3d Cir. 2007).

227. D.A. *ex rel.* L.A. v. Houston Independent School District, 629 F.3d 450 (5th Cir. 2010).

228. Jackson v. District of Columbia, 826 F. Supp. 2d 109 (D.D.C. 2011); Robinson *ex rel.* D.R. v. District of Columbia, 535 F. Supp. 2d 38 (D.D.C. 2008); B.R. *ex rel.* Rempson v. District of Columbia, 527 F. Supp. 2d 35 (D.D.C. 2007); Hinson *ex rel.* N.H. v. Merritt Educational Center, 521 F. Supp. 2d 22 (D.D.C. 2007).

229. Chambers v. School District of Philadelphia Board of Education, 587 F.3d 176 (3d Cir. 2009).

230. Russo, C. J. (2013). Negligence. In C. J. Russo (Ed.), *Key legal issues for schools: The ultimate resource for school business officials* (2nd ed.) (pp. 79–88). Lanham, MD: Rowman & Littlefield Education.

231. Mawdsley, R.D. (2010). Standard of care for students with disabilities: The intersection of liability under the IDEA and tort theories. *Education Law Reporter, 252,* 527–550.

232. White v. State of California, 240 Cal. Rptr. 732 (Cal. Ct. App. 1987).

233. Johnson v. Clark, 418 N.W.2d 466 (Mich. Ct. App. 1987).

234. Brooks v. St. Tammany Parish School Board, 510 So.2d 51 (La. Ct. App. 1987).

235. Hall v. Knott County Board of Education, 941 F.2d 402 (6th Cir. 1991).

236. Crocker v. Tennessee Secondary School Athletic Association, 980 F.2d 382 (6th Cir. 1992).

9

Section 504 and the Americans with Disabilities Act

The main focus of this book is on the Individuals with Disabilities Education Act (IDEA).[1] Even so, the IDEA is not the only federal law governing services to students with disabilities. Two other significant federal statutes protect the rights of students with disabilities. The first, Section 504 of the Rehabilitation Act of 1973 (Section 504),[2] which is codified as part of federal labor law, rather than as an education statute, states that "no otherwise qualified individual with a disability . . . shall, solely by reason of her or his disability, be excluded from participation in, be denied the benefits of, or be subjected to discrimination under any program or activity receiving Federal financial assistance."[3] Section 504 effectively prohibits recipients of federal financial assistance from discriminating against otherwise qualified individuals with disabilities in the provision of services or employment as long as they are able to participate in program activities with the assistance of reasonable accommodations.

In 1990 a second statute, the Americans with Disabilities Act (ADA),[4] was enacted "to provide a comprehensive national mandate for the elimination of discrimination against individuals with disabilities."[5] The ADA expands the scope of Section 504's coverage by protecting individuals with disabilities throughout society.[6] The ADA effectively extends the protections of Section 504 to the private sector. However, the ADA has not had a major influence on the delivery of a free appropriate public education (FAPE) in public schools since schools are subject to the mandates of both the IDEA and Section 504. Rather, the ADA's greatest impact has been on the employment of individuals with disabilities. Further, even though the ADA, like Section 504, prohibits discrimination against individuals on the bases of their disabilities, unlike Section 504, it does not specifically require the provision of a FAPE.[7]

In 2008 Congress enacted its first, and, to date, only, amendments to the ADA.[8] Importantly, the amendments expanded the definition of disability to include individuals who suffer from epilepsy, diabetes, cancer, multiple sclerosis, and other ailments, who in the past were denied protection if their conditions could be controlled by medications or other measures. The ADA amendments also include an exception so that officials of various institutions can consider the mitigating effects of ordinary eyeglasses or contact lenses in determining whether visual impairments substantially limits major life activities. In order to be covered by the ADA, individuals must inform school officials of their conditions and offer specific suggestions on how their needs can be met. The ADA amendments also apply to Section 504 so that the definitions of disability and major life activities in both laws are identical.[9]

The IDEA is the major statute governing the delivery of special education to students with disabilities in the public schools. Nonetheless, in view of the expansive protections that Section 504 and the ADA afford to students with disabilities, this chapter reviews their key provisions. Section 504 and the ADA cover students, employees, parents, and others who visit schools, without any age restrictions. Be this as it may, the focus of this book, and consequently this chapter, is on the rights of students.[10] Table 9.1 highlights major differences between the IDEA and Section 504.

Table 9.1   Major Differences Between the IDEA and Section 504

Points of Consideration	IDEA	Section 504
Age limits	3–21	None; all are covered
Identification	School officials must identify and assess	Individuals must/can self-refer
Disabilities/impairments	Covers only specified disabilities	Covers all who have, had, or are believed to have had impairments affecting major life activities
Limits/defenses	None: zero reject	Cost; significant alteration in nature of programs; health/safety
Funding	School boards receive additional federal aid	No extra funding for compliance
Dispute resolution	Must exhaust administrative remedies	Exhaustion unnecessary; may file suit directly

Eligibility for Protections Under Section 504 and the ADA

Section 504 defines an individual with a disability as one "who (i) has a physical or mental impairment which substantially limits one or more of such person's major life activities, (ii) has a record of such an impairment, or (iii) is regarded as having such an impairment."[11] The regulations guiding the implementation of Section 504 define physical or mental impairments as including

(A)   any physiological disorder or condition, cosmetic disfigurement, or anatomical loss affecting one or more of the following body systems: neurological; musculoskeletal; special sense organs; respiratory, including speech organs; cardiovascular; reproductive, digestive, genito-urinary; hemic and lymphatic; skin; and endocrine; or

(B)   any mental or psychological disorder, such as mental retardation, organic brain syndrome, emotional or mental illness, and specific learning disorders.[12]

An explanatory note accompanying these definitions suggests that the list provides examples of the types of impairments that are covered and is not intended to be exhaustive.

The regulations specify that in order to have records of impairment, individuals must have histories of, or have been identified as having, mental or physical impairments that substantially limit one or more major life activities. As defined by the regulations, individuals who are regarded as having impairments are those who have

> (A) a physical or mental impairment that does not substantially limit major life activities but that is treated by a recipient as constituting such a limitation; (B) a physical or mental impairment that substantially limits major life activities only as a result of the attitudes of others toward such impairment; or (C) none of the impairments . . . but is treated by a recipient as having such an impairment.[13]

"'Major life activities' means functions such as caring for one's self, performing manual tasks, walking, seeing, hearing, speaking, breathing, learning, and working."[14] After students are identified as having disabilities, the next step is to determine whether they are "otherwise qualified." In order to be "otherwise qualified," students must be "(i) of an age during which nonhandicapped persons are provided such services, (ii) of any age during which it is mandatory under state law to provide such services to handicapped persons, or (iii) [a student] to whom a state is required to provide a free appropriate public education [under the IDEA]."[15] Students who are "otherwise qualified," meaning that they are eligible to participate in programs or activities despite the existence of impairments, must be allowed to participate in programs or activities as long as it is possible for them to do so by means of a "reasonable accommodation."[16]

> In order to be protected under Section 504 and the ADA, the impairments of individuals must substantially limit one or more of their major life activities.

In order to be protected under Section 504 and the ADA, individuals must have impairments that substantially limit one or more of their major life activities. As illustrated by a case from Pennsylvania, the Third Circuit affirmed that a student with an identifiable disability that does not impact a major life activity is not entitled to reasonable accommodations. The court held that although the child had a bipolar disorder, which constitutes a mental impairment, absent evidence that it limited her ability to interact with others, care for herself, concentrate, or sleep, she was not entitled to an accommodation.[17]

Qualified students with disabilities are entitled to appropriate public education programs, irrespective of the nature or severity of their impairments.[18] In order to assure eligible children appropriate educations, Section 504's regulations include due process requirements for evaluation and placement similar to those in the IDEA.[19] When providing services to students with disabilities, as discussed in more detail later in this chapter, school personnel must provide aid, benefits, and/or services that are comparable to those available to children who do not have impairments.

In spite of the IDEA's least restrictive environment provision, students with severe disabilities may sometimes require special education classes and/or other services that are not offered in the general education environment in order to receive a FAPE. When students have to be removed from regular classes to receive appropriate programming, the services must be delivered in facilities that are comparable to those used for the education of children who do not have impairments. By way of illustration, a federal trial court in Pennsylvania ruled that the commonwealth's secretary of education violated Section 504 by not ensuring that the educational facilities for students with disabilities were comparable to those of children who did not have disabilities.[20] The court acknowledged that the facilities did not have to be exactly equivalent but found that in this instance they were considerably unequal. Thus, the court maintained that school officials violated Section 504 by relocating special education classes to lesser facilities for the purpose of accommodating classes for students without disabilities.

Along with Section 504, the ADA is a comprehensive federal mandate designed to eliminate discrimination against individuals with disabilities while providing "clear, strong, consistent and enforceable standards"[21] to meet this goal. The ADA's comprehensive definition of a disability is analogous to the one in Section 504: "(a) a physical or mental impairment that substantially limits one or more of the major life activities; (b) a record of such an impairment; or (c) being regarded as having such an impairment."[22] Moreover, also like Section 504, "major life activities" under the ADA include "caring for one's self, performing manual tasks, walking, seeing, hearing, speaking, breathing, learning, and working."[23] Neither the ADA nor Section 504 requires individuals to have certificates from doctors or psychologists in order to be covered by their provisions, but school officials can ask for verification of needs to support requests for accommodations.[24]

The Supreme Court has explained that persons are otherwise qualified for purposes of Section 504 if they are capable of meeting all of a program's requirements in spite of their disabilities.[25] Recipients of federal funds are required to make reasonable accommodations to allow otherwise qualified individuals with disabilities to participate in programs or activities unless doing so would create undue hardships on the programs.[26]

Consistent with Section 504, under the ADA otherwise qualified individuals with disabilities must be given reasonable accommodations so that they may participate in programs provided by public entities.[27] The term *public entities* includes state and local governments, agencies, and other governmental instrumentalities.[28] Since schools are public entities under the ADA, the statute prohibits educational officials from discriminating against individuals with disabilities in much the same manner as Section 504.[29] Even though the ADA includes extensive requirements to provide access to public transportation for individuals with disabilities, the statute specifically exempts public school transportation in its requirements.[30]

Section 504 protects students who have disabilities from discrimination who are ineligible to receive IDEA services. In order to be eligible for IDEA services, students must fit one of the categories of disabilities identified in the statute, and, as a result, need special education services and related services.[31] Since students who meet the IDEA's eligibility requirements are, under most circumstances, also covered by Section 504, the protections of the latter statute reach a much broader population. However, at least one court has indicated that eligibility for special education under the IDEA does not necessarily mean that a child is substantially limited in the major life activity of learning.[32]

> One of the best examples of the extensive reach of Section 504 involves students with infectious diseases, children who are entitled to special education services only if their academic performance is adversely affected by their illnesses.

One of the best examples of the extensive reach of Section 504 involves students with infectious diseases, children who are entitled to special education services only if their academic performance is adversely affected by their illnesses.[33] Nevertheless, pursuant to Section 504, students with infectious diseases such as HIV/AIDS cannot be discriminated against or excluded from schools unless there is a high risk of transmission of their diseases.[34] A case from a federal trial court in Illinois illustrates this principle. The court decided that school officials who forbade a student from attending regular classes and all extracurricular activities once he was diagnosed as having AIDS violated his rights under Section 504 because he was regarded as having a physical impairment that substantially interfered with his life activities.[35] Evidence had shown that there was little risk of transmission of the child's disease in a classroom setting.[36]

In considering differences between the IDEA and Section 504, the federal trial court in Massachusetts posited that school officials did not violate the latter when they offered special education services to a student with learning disabilities in a fashion that was not procedurally correct.[37] The court thought that insofar as school personnel did offer the services, the child was neither discriminated against nor denied services. Further, the court specified that the procedural errors had to be addressed via the IDEA's due process mechanism. Similarly, the Fourth Circuit rejected the claim that a school board in Virginia violated Section 504 by refusing to provide special education services in a student's neighborhood school when the services were available in a centralized location.[38] The court asserted that officials had not discriminated against the student because he was not denied services.

It should almost go without mentioning that when school boards provide services to students under Section 504 or the ADA, those services must be appropriate. In an illustrative case, a federal trial court in New Hampshire pointed out that a student, who alleged that he was not provided with educational services to address his learning disability effectively, presented a claim under Section 504.[39]

Not all students with disabilities are eligible for special education services under the IDEA. Yet, many students who are ineligible for services under the IDEA may qualify for accommodation plans under Section 504, a topic discussed later in this chapter. Since the different statutes have distinct purposes, the services that students are entitled to access may vary under each. A suit filed in the District of Columbia provides an example. The federal trial court sustained the school board's decision that a student with attention deficit hyperactivity disorder (ADHD) was ineligible for services under IDEA because his educational performance was not adversely affected by his condition.[40] Still, the court commented that a hearing officer could have ordered the board to provide special education services to the student who was designated as otherwise qualified under Section 504 in appropriate circumstances. The court remarked that Section 504 did not require affirmative efforts to overcome the student's disability, instead noting that it is designed to prevent discrimination on the basis of the disability. Under some circumstances, then, school officials may need to provide special education services to students with disabilities in order to eliminate discrimination.

Questions develop regarding whether incarcerated youths with disabilities are entitled to receive special education services.[41] In one such dispute, a federal trial court in Illinois declared that Section 504 is applicable to correctional facilities.[42] To the extent that correctional facilities receive federal funds to provide educational services to inmates, the court maintained that they fall within the scope of Section 504.

The major thrust of the ADA has been to extend the protections of Section 504 to the private sector. Still, the ADA has clarified other issues by codifying judicial interpretations of Section 504. Due to the similarities between the two statutes, compliance with Section 504 largely translates to compliance with the ADA.[43] Even though most suits are brought on the basis of both Section 504 and the ADA, students generally fare no better under the ADA than under Section 504. Certainly, in rare situations where the ADA has implemented stricter standards, school boards must meet those greater mandates. Thus, when school officials make diligent good faith efforts to comply with Section 504, they should not run afoul of the ADA.[44]

Discrimination in Education Prohibited

Section 504 and the ADA are antidiscrimination statutes designed to prohibit school officials and others from offering unequal opportunities to qualified individuals. In a case illuminating this principle, the federal trial court in Arizona stressed that a student did not need to prove that an act of discrimination was intentional in order to present an actionable claim under Section 504.[45] According to the court, the failure of school officials to correct a condition that resulted in the denial of access to educational programming resulted in an impermissible disparate impact sufficient to support her claim under Section 504. The court was persuaded that educators violated the student's rights by not correcting architectural barriers in the student's high school, which forced her to attend a school well over ten miles from her home and necessitated a commute over poor roads, aggravating her condition and forcing her to withdraw from school.

In a case from Vermont, the Second Circuit was convinced that Section 504 does not require school boards to provide identical benefits to all students with disabilities.[46] The court, conceding that jurists must allow for professional judgment, stated that a student would have to show that more suitable arrangements were available, but were not offered, to substantiate a discrimination claim under Section 504.

> School officials do not necessarily have to provide the exact accommodations students' request. Even so, educators cannot discriminate on the basis of the means by which students deal with their impairments.

School officials do not necessarily have to provide the exact accommodations students' request. Even so, educators cannot discriminate on the basis of the means by which students deal with their impairments. In a case contesting this issue, a federal trial court in California was of the opinion that as long as the means by which a student addressed her circumstances were reasonable, school personnel could not discriminate against her because of how she chose to address her condition.[47]

As discussed in previous chapters, courts are reluctant to become embroiled in disputes over methodologies used in specific placements, preferring to leave these matters up to educators as long as school officials can show that their selected approaches are appropriate. In Nebraska, the federal trial court posited that the ADA does not give parents an additional advantage over the choice of methodology.[48] The court emphasized that insofar as the methodology school officials selected to instruct students with hearing impairments was no less effective than the one preferred by their parents, it met the ADA's requirements.

In a noneducation case with implications for schools, a federal trial court in Pennsylvania held that even though a public entity was not forbidden from providing benefits, services, or advantages to individuals with disabilities or to a particular class of individuals with disabilities beyond those required by the ADA, its officials were forbidden from discriminating in the provision of affirmative services.[49] The court pointed out that providing services to persons with physical disabilities while not offering the same to individuals with physical and mental disabilities constituted discrimination since there was no rational basis for denying program benefits to those with physical impairments along with mental disabilities.

In another noneducation case of importance, a federal trial court in Florida acknowledged that the elimination of all recreation programs for individuals with disabilities violated the ADA since like activities were still offered to those who did not have disabilities.[50] When city officials abolished the programs due to fiscal constraints, the court insisted that benefits provided to persons who did not have disabilities had to be made available on an equal basis to those with disabilities. The court added that to the extent that city officials elected to provide recreation services to people who did not have disabilities, the ADA required them to furnish equal opportunities for persons with disabilities.

As stated throughout this chapter, many public school students with disabilities are covered by the IDEA, Section 504, and the ADA. Therefore, plaintiffs often file suits alleging violations of all three statutes. Commonly, courts agree that compliance with the IDEA with respect to the provision of a FAPE establishes compliance with Section 504 and the ADA.[51] By the same token, a violation of the IDEA does not automatically support a discrimination claim under Section 504 or the ADA.[52]

> In order to bring successful Section 504/ADA discrimination claims alleging the denial of FAPEs, parents must be able to demonstrate that school personnel acted either in bad faith or with deliberate indifference, or exercised gross misjudgment in failing to provide necessary services for their children.

In order to bring successful Section 504/ADA discrimination claims alleging the denial of FAPEs, parents must be able to demonstrate that school personnel acted either in bad faith or with deliberate indifference, or exercised gross misjudgment in failing to provide necessary services for their children.[53] For example, the federal trial court in the District of Columbia ascertained that a mother who claimed that school officials acted intentionally to deny her child a FAPE by fabricating documents and lying to a hearing officer stated a claim under Section 504.[54] In another illustrative case, the Fifth Circuit held that parents from Texas stated a plausible claim that officials committed gross misjudgment by failing to take steps to protect their daughter, who was intellectually impaired, from sexual abuse when their initial efforts at accommodation proved to be ineffective.[55]

Unfortunately, students with disabilities may be subjected to bullying at the hands of their peers. School officials can be liable if parents can show that officials acted with deliberate indifference in failing to take appropriate action with regard to the bullying incidents.[56] A federal trial court in Ohio was satisfied that school administrators who took appropriate disciplinary action against perpetrators who bullied a student with cognitive disabilities and devised a safety plan for the child were not deliberately indifferent to his needs.[57] Courts do recognize that the actions school administrators take to curb bullying may not always be effective. As long as educators respond to acts of bullying in an appropriate manner, courts are unlikely to find them deliberately indifferent even if their efforts are unsuccessful.[58]

A case from Colorado shows that educators also need to exercise caution when using restraints to control active children. Parents of a student with a seizure disorder and developmental delays alleged that their daughter had been placed in a restraint chair for a good portion of each day. While conceding that the allegations were highly disputed, the trial court decided that the parents established a prima facie case of discrimination since the restraint chair denied the child the opportunity to participate in classroom activities.[59] The court noted that two of the teacher's supervisors were deliberately indifferent to the discrimination since neither took action to investigate or remedy the teacher's alleged behavior after having been informed of the situation. In contrast, a federal trial court in Florida was satisfied that school personnel did not discriminate against a child with multiple disabilities by restraining him due to his own aggressive and self-injurious behavior.[60]

Otherwise Qualified Students With Disabilities

The Supreme Court, in *Southeastern Community College v. Davis* (*Davis*),[61] its first case interpreting the provisions of Section 504, maintained that in order to be considered otherwise qualified, individuals with disabilities must be able to participate in programs or activities in spite of their impairments as long as they can do so with reasonable accommodations. While *Davis* was set in the context of higher education, its implications for elementary and secondary schools are equivalent: Students must meet all of the usual qualifications for participation.

The student in *Davis* unsuccessfully contested her college's denying her admission to a nursing program because she was hearing impaired and relied on lip-reading to understand speech. In upholding the actions of the officials who denied the student's application due to safety considerations, the Court reasoned that Section 504 did not require educational institutions to disregard the disabilities of applicants or to make substantial modifications in their programs to allow participation. The Court was of the view that legitimate physical qualifications could be essential to participation in programs.

In Kentucky, a federal trial court applied *Davis* in explaining that a blind student who had other disabilities was not otherwise qualified for admission to the commonwealth's school for the blind.[62] The court indicated that inasmuch as the student did not meet the school's admission criteria, which required applicants to have the ability for academic and vocational learning, self-care, and independent functioning, he was not entitled to attend. The court also wrote that the IDEA still obligated school officials to provide the student with a FAPE. The Supreme Court of Ohio later affirmed the rejection of the medical school application of a student who was blind, observing that her requested accommodations were not reasonable since they would have required fundamental alterations to the essential nature of the program and/or imposed undue financial or administrative burdens on the school.[63] On the other hand, a federal trial court in Tennessee declared that a student who suffered from an autoimmune disease was otherwise qualified to attend a private school because she had the necessary academic qualifications.[64]

> Parents who have disabilities also may exert rights under Section 504 so that they may obtain accommodations to allow them to better participate in the educational programs of their children.

Parents who have disabilities also may exert rights under Section 504 so that they may obtain accommodations to allow them to better participate in the educational programs of their children. In one case, the Second Circuit affirmed an order directing a school board in New York to provide hearing-impaired parents with the services of a sign language interpreter so that they could participate in school related functions.[65] The court maintained that as parents of students attending the school, the plaintiffs were otherwise qualified to participate in parent-oriented activities but would have been unable to do so without accommodations. In another case a mother in Texas who used a wheelchair unsuccessfully filed suit alleging that the stadium at her son's school failed to meet the requirements of Section 504 and the ADA because its bleachers were not accessible. The Fifth Circuit affirmed that insofar as the stadium as a whole was accessible, it met the requirements of the two laws, even though the mother was not satisfied with the seating arrangements.[66]

Providing Reasonable Accommodations

Section 504 and the ADA do not require school board officials to disregard completely the disabilities of those who wish to participate in their programs and activities. Officials must permit participation when doing so would only require them to make reasonable accommodations. School personnel are not required to make substantial modifications or fundamental alterations to programs and activities.[67] The duty of board officials to provide reasonable accommodations to allow students with disabilities to participate in their programs does not obligate officials to lower their standards. Reasonable accommodations do mandate adaptations to permit access, but do not obligate officials to eliminate essential prerequisites.

> In making accommodations for students with disabilities, school personnel must provide aid, benefits, and/or services that are comparable to those available to children who do not have impairments.

Otherwise qualified students are entitled to appropriate public educations, regardless of the nature or severity of their disabilities. In making accommodations for students with disabilities, school personnel must provide aid, benefits, and/or services that are comparable to those available to children who do not have impairments. In other words, qualified students must receive comparable materials, teacher quality, length of school term, and daily hours of instruction. Likewise, programs for qualified children should not be separate from those available to students who are not impaired, unless such segregation is necessary for these children to be successful. Although school officials are not prohibited from offering separate programs for students with disabilities, these children cannot be required to attend segregated classes unless they cannot be educated adequately in less restrictive settings .[68] If programs are offered separately, facilities must, of course, be comparable.[69]

Reasonable accommodations may involve minor modifications such as giving elevator keys to students who are physically challenged,[70] providing a hearing interpreter or instruction in sign language,[71] permitting children to be accompanied by service animals,[72] or modifying behavior policies.[73] Further, it is fairly standard to provide accommodations such as using nonverbal signals to make students aware of inappropriate sensory stimulation and giving students preferred seating to minimize environmental influences that might disrupt their abilities to concentrate.[74]

At the same time, school officials do not have to grant all requests for accommodations. For example, a federal trial court in Missouri held that school authorities did not have to establish a "scent-free" environment for a child with severe asthma because she was not otherwise qualified to participate in its educational program.[75] The court was satisfied that the school's voluntary "scent-free" policy met Section 504's "minor adjustment" standard. Moreover, a federal trial court in New York decreed, and the Second Circuit affirmed, that school personnel did not fail to accommodate a diabetic student by refusing to warm up his lunches.[76] The trial court explained that he did not require hot food and school personnel were not required to accommodate his preference.

A federal trial court in Pennsylvania rejected claims that educators violated the Section 504 rights of a student who was classified as other health impaired by refusing to provide him with video teleconferencing equipment to allow him to participate in classroom activities when he was absent.[77] In agreeing with educators that the presence of the equipment was disruptive to other students in the class, the court observed that officials did not violate Section 504 because the plaintiff was not denied benefits that would have been provided to children who were not disabled.

In contrast, where a student in New York was unable to attend school due to a chronic illness, the Second Circuit ruled that the refusals of educational officials to provide her with reasonable accommodations, such as not requiring her to climb stairs if she felt too sick and allowing her to lie down on a couch if she needed to rest, presented actionable claims under both Section 504 and the ADA.[78] Further, when a teacher forced a student with asthma to perform physical exercise as a punishment, thereby triggering an attack of his illness, a federal trial court in Tennessee concluded that the educator violated the child's rights under the ADA.[79] The court reasoned that officials should have modified their standard punishment to accommodate the student's asthma.

Academic modifications might include giving children more time to complete examinations or assignments, using peer tutors, distributing outlines in advance, employing specialized curricular materials, and/or allowing students to use laptop computers to record answers on examinations. In modifying facilities, school officials do not have to make every classroom and/or area of buildings accessible. Instead, it may be sufficient to bring services to children, such as offering keyboards for musical instruction in accessible classrooms rather than revamping entire music rooms for students who wish to take piano classes.

> Section 504's only regulation directly addressing private schools specifies
> that officials in these schools may not exclude students on the basis of
> their impairments if the students can, with minor adjustments, be provided
> with appropriate educations.

On a related topic, Section 504's only regulation directly addressing private schools specifies that officials in these schools may not exclude students on the basis of their impairments if the students can, with minor adjustments, be provided with appropriate educations.[80] This regulation adds that private schools may not charge more for the provision of an appropriate education to students with disabilities than to their peers except to the extent that any additional charge is justified by a substantial increase in the cost of educating the children with disabilities."[81] Consequently, private schools may be able to charge additional costs to parents of children with impairments.

In a case from Texas that eventually made its way to the Supreme Court, *Irving Independent School District v. Tatro*,[82] the Justices interpreted the delivery of basic school health services to a student with physical impairments, allowing her to remain in a classroom, as a reasonable accommodation. The student needed to be catheterized approximately every four hours, a service that a school nurse, health aide, or other trained layperson was capable of carrying out. The Court agreed that when school officials refused to provide such a service, they violated the child's Section 504 rights.

Parents of students with severe disabilities have filed suits under the IDEA seeking programs for their children in fully inclusive settings. In ordering inclusive placements in many cases, courts relied on Section 504 as well as the IDEA. In an earlier case, the federal trial court in New Jersey remarked that excluding a student from a regular education classroom without first investigating and providing reasonable accommodations to facilitate education in that setting violated Section 504.[83] According to the court, a segregated special education placement may be implemented only when it is necessary for a child to receive educational benefit.

As discussed below in the section on defenses, accommodations that are disproportionately costly, create excessive monitoring burdens, or expose other individuals to unwarranted risk are not required. For example, the Eighth Circuit concluded that inoculating staff members in a rehabilitation facility in Missouri against the hepatitis B virus so that a carrier of that disease could attend their program went beyond the requirements of Section 504.[84] Conversely, a federal trial court in Kentucky declared that officials at a school for the blind could not be required to hire additional staff or modify the mission of the institution to accept a student who did not meet its minimum qualifications.[85]

Testing and Evaluation

Section 504 addresses the growing field of testing and evaluating students. Under the mandates of the No Child Left Behind Act[86] and similar state legislation, students are assessed at various points throughout their educational careers. Many students are also subjected to a barrage of diagnostic and evaluative tests to determine their eligibility for remedial or special education placements. Further, officials in some public and charter schools may require students with disabilities to take admissions examinations and/or be interviewed prior to being accepted. The statute's implementing regulations cover four areas: preplacement evaluation, evaluation, placement, and reevaluation.[87]

Regarding preplacement evaluations, the regulations require school officials to evaluate all children who, due to their disabilities, need or are believed to need special education or related services. These evaluations must be completed before school personnel act with respect to making the initial placements of children in regular or special education as well as prior to making later significant changes in placements.

> Section 504's evaluation provisions require school personnel to follow procedures similar to those under the IDEA.

Section 504's evaluation provisions require school personnel to follow procedures similar to those under the IDEA. These provisions require educators to validate tests and other evaluation materials for the specific purposes for which they are used and to ensure that they are administered by trained personnel in conformance with the instructions provided by their producers. These materials must also be tailored to assess specific areas of educational need and cannot be designed to provide a single general intelligence quotient. Additionally, these materials must be selected and administered in a manner that best ensures that when tests are administered to students with impaired sensory, manual, or speaking skills, the results accurately reflect their aptitude or achievement levels or whatever other factors the examinations purport to measure, rather than reflecting their impaired sensory, manual, or speaking skills, except where those skills are the factors that the tests purport to measure.[88] When school officials apply placement procedures to students under Section 504, their interpretations of data must consider information from a variety of sources, including the students' aptitude and achievement test scores, teacher recommendations, physical condition, social and cultural background, and adaptive behaviors that have been documented and carefully considered.[89] Further, not only must such decisions be made by groups of persons, including knowledgeable individuals, but all children must be periodically reevaluated in a manner consistent with the dictates of the IDEA.[90]

Under Section 504, schools relying on examinations or interviews may be required to provide reasonable accommodations to applicants with impairments. Although school officials are not required to alter the content of examinations or interviews, they may have to make accommodations in how tests are administered or interviews are conducted. Put another way, school officials are not required to make examinations easier so that students who simply lacked the requisite knowledge could pass, but they may have to alter the conditions under which tests are administered, or interviews are conducted, so that students with impairments who have the requisite knowledge and skills to pass or express themselves fully could do so despite their conditions.

The accommodations that educators provide for examinations may be as simple as providing quiet rooms without distractions for students who suffer from attention deficit hyperactivity disorder or procuring the services of a reader or Braille versions of examination for applicants who are blind. Additionally, students with physical disabilities may require special seating arrangements, or services such as those of scribes to record answers to questions, and/or permission to use computers to record answers on examinations. In like fashion, whether as part of examinations or admissions interviews, students who are hearing impaired might be entitled to the services of sign language interpreters to communicate directions that are normally given orally. At the same time, school officials may be required to provide students with learning disabilities with extra time to complete examinations or may have to make computers available to children who are more comfortable with them than with traditional paper-and-pencil tests.

Prior to receiving accommodations, students must prove that they have conditions such as learning disabilities[91] and that the extra time to take examinations is necessary due to their impairments. The purpose of providing the additional time is to allow students who might have difficulty processing information sufficient opportunity to show that they are capable of answering the questions.

In a major difference from the IDEA, which requires school officials to identify, assess, and serve students with disabilities, under Section 504, students, and/or their parents, are responsible for making school officials aware of their need for testing or interviewing accommodations. To this end, administrators should require proof that students have impairments in need of accommodation in order to demonstrate knowledge and skills on examinations. Students, through their parents, should additionally suggest which accommodations would be most appropriate. In considering whether students are entitled to accommodations, officials must make individualized inquiries. Educational officials may be liable for violating Section 504 if they refuse to make testing accommodations or make modifications only for students with specified impairments.

Most jurisdictions now require students to pass comprehensive state administered tests in order to graduate with standard high school diplomas. This prerequisite has become more prevalent in the wake of the No Child Left Behind Act.[92] Under Section 504 and the ADA, educators may be required to modify test-taking situations for students with disabilities. Even so, officials are not required to alter the content of the tests themselves.[93] By way of example, allowing a visually impaired student to take a Braille version of a test is a reasonable accommodation, but changing the content of an examination to make it easier would not be required.

Most of the litigation involving testing accommodations has arisen in the context of postsecondary institutions. Nevertheless, the legal principles that have emerged apply to elementary and secondary schools. These cases illustrate that accommodations in how tests are administered are required, but alterations to their contents are not mandatory. For instance, a federal trial court in New York ordered additional accommodations for a law school graduate with visual impairments who was sitting for the bar examination. While the Board of Bar Examiners granted some, but not all, of the examinee's requested accommodations, since her physician testified that the additional accommodations were necessary, the court ordered that they be provided since the purpose of the ADA is to guarantee that those with disabilities are not disadvantaged but are put on an equal footing with others.[94]

On the other hand, another case from New York involving a law school graduate confirms that candidates are not entitled to testing accommodations just because they have not been able to pass the examinations in the past without accommodations.[95] In this case the court was persuaded by the testimony of an expert that a student who claimed to have a learning disability did not need requested accommodations because he did not have such a condition. In like manner, the Tenth Circuit agreed that a student from Colorado claiming to have test anxiety, who fell asleep during an examination, was not discriminated against by an instructor who declined to give her additional time to finish the test since her condition is not recognized under Section 504.[96]

Participation in Athletics and Extracurricular Activities

The Office for Civil Rights in the U.S. Department of Education recently issued a *Dear Colleague* letter providing guidance on the obligations of school boards under Section 504 to ensure that students with disabilities have opportunities to participate in extracurricular athletics equivalent to those of their peers.[97] While such letters do not carry the same weight as statutes or regulations, they serve as guidance on how officials in the Department of Education expect requirements should be met. Specifically, the *Dear Colleague* letter provides instructions to those charged with implementing Section 504. As with all decisions under Section 504, school personnel must make individualized inquiries regarding the participation of athletes with disabilities.

As an initial matter, the letter advises school officials that they should not act on generalizations, assumptions, prejudices, or stereotypes when making decisions regarding students' abilities to participate in athletic activities. Second, the letter advises those charged with overseeing schools' athletic programs that activities must be offered in such a way that students with disabilities are given equal opportunities to participate in integrated manners. This may require school officials to provide athletes with disabilities with reasonable accommodations or other aids and services designed to allow their participation. As is discussed in the section on defenses below, schools are not required to provide accommodations amounting to fundamental alterations of their program. Further, officials may make decisions based on bona fide safety concerns.

In what is likely to become the most controversial aspect of the guidance, the letter counsels school officials to create separate or different athletic opportunities for those who cannot participate in existing programs even with reasonable accommodations. In this respect, the letter suggests that officials should consider forming districtwide or regional teams, mix male and female athletes together, or form unified teams of athletes with and without disabilities.

Students must be otherwise qualified to participate in athletic programs. In other words, students must have the skills needed to qualify for teams. A federal trial court in Indiana ruled that when a coach refused to select a student for his high school's basketball team, this did not violate the student's rights under Section 504.[98] The court acknowledged that although he had a Section 504 alternative learning plan, the student was not selected for the team because, in the coach's judgment, he lacked the requisite skill level.

The rights of students with disabilities to participate in extracurricular activities is not a new topic. Rather, this is a topic that was subject to litigation long before the *Dear Colleague* letter was issued.[99] In the past, litigation challenged school boards and athletic associations who refused to waive nonessential eligibility requirements to allow students with disabilities to participate.

At least two courts ordered athletic associations to waive age limitation requirements to allow students who repeated grades due to their learning disabilities to participate in sports.[100] These courts agreed that insofar as the associations granted waivers of other rules, waiving a rule barring students over the age of 19 from participating in sports was reasonable. Moreover, the Sixth Circuit decided that by preventing a transfer student from participating in sports after he changed schools solely due to his need to receive special education services, an athletic association in Tennessee violated his rights under Section 504.[101]

In a different factual context, the Sixth Circuit later determined that the Michigan high school athletic association's eight-semester eligibility rule did not violate either Section 504 or the ADA.[102] Earlier, the Eighth Circuit noted that a student from Missouri who challenged an athletic association's age restrictions was not otherwise qualified under either the ADA or Section 504 because he exceeded the age limit.[103] In both of these situations the rules were applied equally to all students, regardless of whether they had disabilities.

A federal trial court in Illinois, in a case involving a school's athletic conduct code, rejected the claims of a student who was suspended from his football and lacrosse teams for disciplinary reasons.[104] The court held that waiving the athletic code of conduct would have been an unreasonable accommodation under Section 504 and the ADA, suggesting that it could send the message to others that student-athletes could frustrate the enforcement of team rules by threatening litigation, making it difficult for administrators and coaches to sustain effective control over their athletic programs.

In Maryland a dispute arose illustrating that as important as it is for school policies to highlight the inclusion of student-athletes with disabilities in their programs, they are not required to make substantial rule changes to do so. A track and field athlete who used a wheelchair failed in her suit against state officials alleging discrimination because she was precluded from earning points for her team. In denying the plaintiff's request for a preliminary injunction, the court indicated that it was not discriminatory to preserve differences in the opportunity of wheelchair racers to earn points for teams where all but a small number of teams were significantly underrepresented in that class of competitors.[105]

The Second Circuit affirmed a jury verdict in New York that minor architectural barriers on school premises that forced a football team's manager, who had cerebral palsy, to make detours to and from the athletic fields denied him meaningful access to the programs provided to his peers.[106] The court explained that the detours effectively reduced the time the manager could spend in the activity and was convinced that this unnecessary usurpation of his time violated Section 504 and the ADA.

Section 504 Service Plans

As indicated earlier, students who are otherwise qualified under the Section 504 definition are entitled to reasonable accommodations allowing them to participate in and receive benefits from school programs. These accommodations may take on a number of forms. For example, students with physical challenges may require alterations to physical plants such as wheelchair ramps, curb cuts, or the removal of architectural barriers so that they may physically enter and navigate school buildings and grounds.

School boards may be required to make exceptions to policies, procedures, or requirements to provide students with academic accommodations in classrooms or testing situations. Even so, boards are not obligated to make accommodations that are excessively expensive, expose a school's staff or others to excessive risk, or require substantial modifications to the missions or purposes of programs.

Neither Section 504 nor its regulations mandate the creation of written documents outlining the accommodations to be provided, let alone specify the content of such documents. Nonetheless, educators in many schools meet with parents to formalize the accommodations and services that they will provide to eligible students. These written agreements are commonly referred to as Section 504 service plans. In practical terms, school personnel should be sure to include the following components in each written Section 504 service plan for each student:

- **Demographic Data**—the student's name, date of birth, school identification number, grade, schools attended, teacher, names of parents or guardians, addresses, telephone numbers, and the like
- **Team Members**—a listing of all team members who contributed to the development of the service plan and their respective roles
- **Impairment**—a detailed description of the student's impairment and its severity, along with an explanation of how it impedes the student's educational progress
- **Accommodations and Services**—a detailed description of the accommodations and services to be offered under the plan, including the frequency of services, where they are to be provided, and by whom they are to be provided

In addition, officials should attach the evaluative reports or assessments that helped to determine the nature of the student's impairment and the need for accommodations and services.

Defenses to Charges of Noncompliance

Even if students appear to be "otherwise qualified," school boards can rely on one of three defenses to avoid being charged with noncompliance with Section 504. This represents another major difference between Section 504 and the IDEA since no such defenses are available under the latter. These defenses emerged partly as a result of two Supreme Court cases not involving students in elementary and secondary schools.

In *Southeastern Community College v. Davis*,[107] the Supreme Court found that administrators at a community college did not violate the rights of an unsuccessful applicant to its nursing program. The Court clarified that inasmuch as officials denied the applicant admission based on their belief that her hearing impairment would have made it unsafe for her to participate, she was not otherwise qualified to do so.

Subsequently, in its first case on Section 504 in a school setting, *School Board of Nassau County, Florida v. Arline*,[108] the Supreme Court affirmed that board officials violated a teacher's rights by discharging her due to reoccurrences of tuberculosis. In finding that the teacher was otherwise qualified for her position, the Justices created a four-part test for use in cases involving contagious diseases. The factors that the Court considered in ordering the teacher's reinstatement were the nature of the risk, its duration, its severity, and the probabilities that the disease would be transmitted and cause varying degrees of harm. On remand, a federal trial court in Florida agreed that insofar as the teacher was otherwise qualified, she was entitled to return to her job.[109]

The first defense under Section 504 is that school boards can be excused from making accommodations that result in "a fundamental alteration in the nature of [a] program."[110] The second defense allows boards to avoid compliance if modifications impose an "undue financial burden"[111] on institutions or entities as a whole. The third defense is that otherwise qualified students with disabilities can be excluded from programs if their presence creates a substantial risk of injury to themselves or others.[112] Under this exception, a student with a severe visual impairment could be excluded from using a scalpel in a biology laboratory. Even so, in order to comply with Section 504, educators would have to offer a reasonable accommodation such as a computer program that could achieve an instructional goal similar to the one that would have been achieved in a laboratory class.

Finally, the Section 504 regulations, which are enforced by the Office of Civil Rights in the U.S. Department of Education, require recipients of federal financial aid to file assurance of compliance; provide notice to students and their parents that their programs are nondiscriminatory; engage in remedial actions where violations are proven; take voluntary steps to overcome the effects of conditions that resulted in limiting the participation of students with disabilities in their programs; conduct a self-evaluation; designate a staff member, typically at the central office level, as compliance coordinator; and adopt grievance procedures.[113]

FREQUENTLY ASKED QUESTIONS

Q: If students have disabilities, why are they not covered by the IDEA as well as Section 504 and the ADA?

A: The IDEA requires that in addition to having specifically identifiable disabilities, students must also need special education and related services as a result of their disabilities. By way of example, while students with physical challenges would have disabilities covered by Section 504 and/or the ADA, those students may not require special education services but they are protected against discrimination and are entitled to reasonable accommodations under the law.

(Continued)

(Continued)

Q: Do testing accommodations, such as those allowing students more time on an examination, give students with disabilities unfair advantages over their peers?

A: The purpose of testing accommodations is to level playing fields for students with disabilities, not to afford them unfair advantages. Thus, test administrators may need to modify how examinations are given but are not required to alter their content. Accommodations should remove unfair barriers that interfere with students' ability to show their knowledge on tests. For example, no one would disagree that it would be unfair to expect blind students to take paper and pencil tests. By the same token, many students with learning disabilities need more time to process information. The upshot is that affording students with disabilities extra time provides them with opportunities to demonstrate their knowledge; doing so does not grant them unfair advantages.

Q: Since athletics and other extracurricular activities are normally optional activities in which students may elect to participate, why must officials provide accommodations for students with disabilities?

A: If educational institutions offer programs or activities, they must do so on equal bases for all students, regardless of whether participation is required or optional. Many students with disabilities are capable of being contributing members of athletic teams if they are provided with reasonable accommodations similar to those provided in classrooms. For instance, students with hearing impairments who have the requisite skill levels could easily participate in sports with the assistance of interpreters.

Q: Does the failure to provide a free appropriate public education under the IDEA constitute discrimination under Section 504/ADA?

A: It depends on the circumstances. If educators make good faith efforts to develop appropriate individualized education programs for students with disabilities, but their efforts fall short, school officials are unlikely to be liable for discrimination. However, if educators egregiously and knowingly failed to follow the IDEA's mandates or acted with complete disregard for student needs, they have violated Section 504 and/or the ADA. Consequently, ignoring clear signs that students had disabilities, and refusing parental requests to evaluate their children, would constitute deliberate indifference to support a charge of discrimination. Similarly, school board policies that provide no more than five hours a week of special education for students with learning disabilities would violate Section 504 and/or the ADA.

Recommendations

Section 504 and the ADA are civil rights laws designed to prohibit discrimination against individuals with disabilities. In the context of elementary and secondary education, these statutes require officials to provide reasonable accommodations so that otherwise qualified students may participate in school activities and programs on an equal footing with their classmates who do not have disabilities. Although Section 504 and the ADA do not require educational institutions to provide accommodations that substantially alter the nature of their programs or result in unreasonable administrative or financial burdens, educators must take steps to ensure that students with disabilities are given equal educational opportunities.

School officials should

- Make individualized determinations regarding the identification of students with disabilities and their needs for reasonable accommodations.
- Establish, and regularly update, policies and practices to ensure that students with disabilities are neither excluded from participating in public school programs and activities nor denied services due to their disabilities.
- Designate a specific administrator as their school system's Section 504/ADA compliance officer and make sure that this person's role is made known to parents.
- Take steps to ensure that students with disabilities are not subjected to differential treatment due to their impairments or because they receive accommodations for their disabilities.
- Evaluate whether students with disabilities who do not qualify for special education and related services under the IDEA require reasonable accommodations under Section 504/ADA to access services and programs at their schools.
- Keep parents informed of the procedures they must follow to request accommodations for their children.
- Establish procedures, including timelines, to make individualized determinations regarding waivers of requirements for participation in extracurricular activities for students with disabilities who may not meet all usual criteria due to their disabilities.
- Request medical clearance before allowing students with disabilities to participate in sports or other activities if there are reasons to believe that they have increased risks of injury.
- Consider whether students with medical conditions require special accommodations such as reduced school days or testing accommodations even if their illnesses are in remission.

- Respond immediately and continuously to acts of bullying against students with disabilities.
- Exercise caution when using physical or mechanical restraints with students with disabilities.
- Make accommodations for parents with disabilities so that they can participate in school functions essential to the education of their children, such as parent–teacher conferences.
- Inspect facilities regularly to make sure that they remain free of architectural barriers.
- Provide regular professional development to teachers and other staff such as counselors and psychologists so that they are aware not only of the differences between the IDEA and Section 504/ADA but also so that they can be updated on changes in the law.

Endnotes

1. 20 U.S.C. §§ 1400–1482 (2012).
2. 29 U.S.C. § 794 (2013).
3. *Id.*
4. 42 U.S.C. §§ 12101–12213 (2012).
5. 42 U.S.C. § 12101(b)(2).
6. Vande Zande v. State of Wisconsin Department of Administration, 851 F. Supp. 353 (W.D. Wis. 1994).
7. Wenkart, R. D. (1993). The Americans with Disabilities Act and its impact on public education. *Education Law Reporter, 82,* 291–302.
8. ADA Amendments Act of 2008, P.L. 110-325, 122 Stat. 3553 (2008).
9. Russo, C. J., & Osborne, A. G. (2009). Update on the Americans with Disabilities Act. *School Business Affairs, 75*(3), 38–41.
10. For a review of Section 504 and the ADA as they apply to employees, parents, and others, as well as students, *see* Russo, C. J., & Osborne, A. G. (2009). *Section 504 and the ADA.* Thousand Oaks, CA: Corwin.
11. 29 U.S.C. § 706(7)(B).
12. 34 C.F.R. § 104.3(j)(2)(i).
13. 34 C.F.R. § 104.3(j)(2)(iv).
14. 34 C.F.R. § 104.3(j)(2)(i).
15. 34 C.F.R. § 104.3(k)(2).
16. 34 C.F.R. § 104.39.
17. Weidow v. Scranton School District, 460 F. App'x 181 (3d Cir. 2012).
18. Russo, C. J., & Osborne, A. G. (2008). Section 504 of the Rehabilitation Act of 1973 at 35: Implications for the educational rights of students. *Journal of School Business Management, 20*(1), 34–43.
19. 34 C.F.R. § 104.36. For a comprehensive discussion of Section 504's hearing requirements, see Zirkel, P. A. (2012). The public schools' obligation for impartial hearings under Section 504. *Widener Law Journal, 22,* 135–181.
20. Hendricks v. Gilhool, 709 F. Supp. 1362 (E.D. Pa. 1989).
21. 42 U.S.C. § 12101(b)(2).
22. 42 U.S.C. § 12102(2).

23. 34 C.F.R. § 36.104.

24. Kaesberg, M. A., & Murray, K. T. (1994). Americans with Disabilities Act. *Education Law Reporter, 90,* 11–20.

25. School Board of Nassau County, Florida v. Arline, 480 U.S. 273 (1987); Southeastern Community College v. Davis, 442 U.S. 397 (1979).

26. 34 C.F.R. § 104.12(a).

27. 42 U.S.C. § 12111(9).

28. 42 U.S.C. § 12131(1).

29. 42 U.S.C. § 12132.

30. 42 U.S.C. § 12141.

31. 20 U.S.C. § 1401(a)(1)(A).

32. Ellenburg v. New Mexico Military Institute, 572 F.3d 815 (10th Cir. 2009).

33. 34 C.F.R. § 300.8.

34. *See, e.g.,* Martinez v. School Board of Hillsborough County, 861 F.2d 1502 (11th Cir. 1988), *on remand,* 711 F. Supp. 1066 (M.D. Fla. 1989); New York State Association for Retarded Children v. Carey, 612 F.2d 644 (2d Cir. 1979); Doe v. Dolton Elementary School District, 694 F. Supp. 440 (N.D. Ill. 1988); Ray v. School District of DeSoto County, 666 F. Supp. 1524 (M.D. Fla. 1987); Thomas v. Atascadero Unified School District, 662 F. Supp. 376 (C.D. Cal. 1987); Doe v. Belleville Public School District, 672 F. Supp. 342 (S.D. Ill. 1987).

35. Doe v. Dolton Elementary School District, 694 F. Supp. 440 (N.D. Ill. 1988).

36. For a discussion of issues associated with HIV/AIDS in schools, see Russo, C. J. (2011). HIV/AIDS and K–12 education: Neither out of sight nor out of mind. *Education Law Reporter, 267,* 1–20.

37. Puffer v. Raynolds, 761 F. Supp. 838 (D. Mass. 1988).

38. Barnett v. Fairfax County School Board, 927 F.2d 146 (4th Cir. 1991).

39. I.D. v. Westmoreland School District, 788 F. Supp. 634 (D.N.H. 1992).

40. Lyons v. Smith, 829 F. Supp. 414 (D.D.C. 1993).

41. *See, e.g.,* Green v. Johnson, 513 F. Supp. 965 (D. Mass. 1982).

42. Donnell C. v. Illinois State Board of Education, 829 F. Supp. 1016 (N.D. Ill. 1993).

43. Vande Zande v. State of Wisconsin Department of Administration, 851 F. Supp. 353 (W.D. Wis. 1994).

44. Miles, A. S., Russo, C. J., & Gordon, W. M. (1991). The reasonable accommodations provisions of the Americans with Disabilities Act. *Education Law Reporter, 69,* 1–8.

45. Begay v. Hodel, 730 F. Supp. 1001 (D. Ariz. 1990).

46. P.C. v. McLaughlin, 913 F.2d 1033 (2d Cir. 1990).

47. Sullivan v. Vallejo City Unified School District, 731 F. Supp. 947 (E.D. Cal. 1990). Clark, S. G. (2010). The use of service animals in public schools: Legal and policy implications. *Education Law Reporter, 254,* 1–17.

48. Petersen v. Hastings Public Schools, 831 F. Supp. 742 (D. Neb. 1993).

49. Easley v. Snider, 841 F. Supp. 668 (E.D. Pa. 1993).

50. Concerned Parents to Save Dreher Park Center v. City of West Palm Beach, 846 F. Supp. 986 (S.D. Fla. 1994).

51. *See, e.g.,* Miller v. Board of Education of the Albuquerque Public Schools, 565 F.3d 1232 (10th Cir. 2009); Doe v. Alabama State Department of Education, 915 F.2d 651 (11th Cir. 1990); Cordrey v. Euckert, 917 F.2d 1460 (6th Cir. 1990); Barnett v. Fairfax County School Board, 721 F. Supp. 757 (E.D. Va. 1989), *affirmed,* 927 F.2d 146 (4th Cir. 1991).

52. Andrew M. v. Delaware County Office of Mental Health and Mental Retardation, 490 F.3d 337 (3d Cir. 2007).

53. *See, e.g.,* D.A. *ex rel.* L.A. v. Houston Independent School District, 629 F.3d 450 (5th Cir. 2010); Lucas v. District of Columbia, 683 F. Supp. 2d 16 (D.D.C. 2010); Taylor v. District of Columbia, 683 F. Supp. 2d 20 (D.D.C. 2010); Torrence v. District of Columbia, 669 F. Supp. 2d 68 (D.D.C. 2009); S.L.-M. *ex rel.* Liedtke v. Dieringer School District No. 343, 614 F. Supp. 2d 1152 (W.D. Wash. 2008).

54. Alston v. District of Columbia, 561 F. Supp. 2d 29 (D.D.C. 2008).

55. Stewart v. Waco Independent School District, 711 F.3d 513 (5th Cir. 2013).

56. For a commentary on this issue, *see* Conn, K. (2009). Bullying and harassment: Can IDEA protect special students? *Education Law Reporter, 239,* 789–800.

57. Doe v. Big Walnut Local School District Board of Education, 837 F. Supp. 2d 742 (S.D. Ohio 2011).

58. Long v. Murray County School District, 2012 WL 2277836 (N.D. Ga. 2012).

59. A.B. *ex rel.* B.S. v. Adams-Arapahoe 28J School District, 831 F. Supp. 2d 1226 (D. Colo. 2011). *See also* J.P.M. *ex rel.* C.M. v. Palm Beach County School Board, 877 F. Supp. 2d 1309 (S.D. Fla. 2012) (denying a school board's motion for summary judgment since officials had not shown that school personnel who restrained a child did not intend to discriminate); Ebonie S. *ex rel.* Mary S. v. Pueblo School District, 819 F. Supp. 2d 1179 (D. Colo. 2011) (denying a board's motion for summary judgment in response to a mother's allegations that the use of a wraparound desk raised a viable discrimination claim since it was used only to restrict children with disabilities), *affirmed on other grounds* 695 F.3d 1051 (10th Cir. 2012), *cert. denied,* 133 S. Ct. 1583 (2013).

60. J.P.M. *ex rel.* C.M. v. Palm Beach County School Board, 916 F. Supp. 2d 1314 (S.D. Fla. 2013).

61. 442 U.S. 397 (1979).

62. Eva N. v. Brock, 741 F. Supp. 626 (E.D. Ky. 1990).

63. Ohio Civil Rights Commission v. Case Western Reserve University, 666 N.E.2d 1376 (Ohio 1996).

64. Thomas v. Davidson Academy, 846 F. Supp. 611 (M.D. Tenn. 1994).

65. Rothschild v. Grottenthaler, 907 F.2d 286 (2d Cir. 1990).

66. Greer v. Richardson Independent School District, 752 F. Supp. 2d 746 (N.D. Tex. 2010), *motion for reconsideration denied* 752 F. Supp. 2d 759 (N.D. Tex. 2010), *affirmed* 472 F. App'x 287 (5th Cir. 2012).

67. Southeastern Community College v. Davis, 442 U.S. 397 (1979).

68. 34 C.F.R. § 104.4(b)(3).

69. 34 C.F.R. § 104.34(c).

70. D.R. *ex rel.* Courtney R. v. Antelope Valley Union High School District, 746 F. Supp. 2d 1132 (C.D. Cal. 2010).

71. Barnes v. Converse College, 436 F. Supp. 635 (D.S.C. 1977).

72. Sullivan v. Vallejo City Unified School District, 731 F. Supp. 947 (E.D. Cal. 1990).

73. Thomas v. Davidson Academy, 846 F. Supp. 611 (M.D. Tenn. 1994)

74. Molly L. *ex rel.* B.L. v. Lower Merion School District, 194 F. Supp. 2d 422 (E.D. Pa. 2002).

75. Hunt v. St. Peter School, 963 F. Supp. 843 (W.D. Mo. 1997).

76. A.M. *ex rel.* J.M. v. NYC Department of Education, 840 F. Supp. 2d 660 (E.D.N.Y. 2012), *affirmed sub nom.* Moody v. NYC Department of Education, 513 F. App'x 95 (2d Cir. 2013) (summary order), *cert. denied*, 134 S. Ct. 809 (2013).

77. Eric H. *ex rel.* John H. v. Methacton School District, 265 F. Supp. 2d 513 (E.D. Pa. 2003).

78. Weixel v. Board of Educ. of the City of New York, 287 F.3d 138 (2d Cir. 2002).

79. Moss v. Shelby County, 401 F. Supp. 2d 850 (W.D. Tenn. 2005).

80. 34 C.F.R. § 104.39(a).

81. 34 C.F.R. § 104.39(b).

82. Tatro v. State of Texas, 625 F.2d 557 (5th Cir. 1980), *on remand* 516 F. Supp. 968 (N.D. Tex. 1981), *affirmed*, 703 F.2d 823 (5th Cir. 1983), *affirmed sub nom.* Irving Independent School District v. Tatro, 468 U.S. 883 (1984).

83. Oberti v. Board of Education of the Borough of Clementon School District, 801 F. Supp. 1393 (D.N.J. 1992), *affirmed*, 995 F.2d 1204 (3d Cir. 1993).

84. Kohl v. Woodhaven Learning Center, 865 F.2d 930 (8th Cir. 1989).

85. Eva N. v. Brock, 741 F. Supp. 626 (E.D. Ky. 1990).

86. No Child Left Behind Act, 20 U.S.C. §§ 6301–7941 (2006).

87. 34 C.F.R. § 104.35.

88. 34 C.F.R. § 104.35(b)(3).

89. 34 C.F.R. § 104.35(c).

90. 34 C.F.R. § 104.35(d).

91. Argen v. New York State Board of Law Examiners, 860 F. Supp. 84, (W.D.N.Y. 1994).

92. No Child Left Behind Act, 20 U.S.C. §§ 6301–7941 (2006).

93. Brookhart v. Illinois State Board of Education, 697 F.2d 179 (7th Cir. 1983).

94. D'Amico v. New York State Board of Law Examiners, 813 F. Supp. 217 (W.D.N.Y. 1993).

95. Pazer v. New York State Board of Law Examiners, 849 F. Supp. 284 (S.D.N.Y. 1994).

96. Buhendwa v. University of Colorado at Boulder, 214 F. App'x 823 (10th Cir. 2007).

97. U.S. Department of Education, Office of Civil Rights (2013). *Dear Colleague Letter*. Available at http//www2.ed.gov/print/about/offices/list/ocr/letters/colleague-201301-504.html (accessed 1/26/13).

98. Doe v. Eagle-Union Community School Corporation, 101 F. Supp. 2d 707 (S.D. Ind. 2000), *vacated and remanded with instructions to dismiss as moot* 2 F. App'x 567 (7th Cir. 2001).

99. Osborne, A. G., & Russo, C. J. (2011). Interscholastic sports, extracurricular activities, and the law: Accommodating students with disabilities. *School Business Affairs*, 77(5), 30–32.

100. Hoot v. Milan Area Schools, 853 F. Supp. 243 (E.D. Mich. 1994); University Interscholastic League v. Buchanan, 848 S.W.2d 298 (Tex. App. Ct. 1993).

101. Crocker v. Tennessee Secondary School Athletic Association, 735 F. Supp. (M.D. Tenn. 1990), *affirmed* Metropolitan Government of Nashville and Davidson County v. Crocker, 908 F.2d 973 (6th Cir. 1990) (mem.).

102. McPherson v. Michigan High School Athletic Association, 119 F.3d 453 (6th Cir. 1997).

103. Pottgen v. Missouri State High School Activities Association, 40 F.3d 926 (8th Cir. 1994).
104. Long v. Board of Education, District 128, 167 F. Supp. 2d 988 (N.D. Ill. 2001).
105. McFadden v. Grasmick, 485 F. Supp. 2d 642 (D. Md. 2007).
106. Celeste v. East Meadow Union Free School District, 373 F. App'x 85 (2d Cir. 2010).
107. 442 U.S. 397 (1979).
108. 480 U.S. 273 (1987).
109. Arline v. School Board of Nassau County, 692 F. Supp. 1286 (M.D. Fla.1988).
110. Southeastern Community College v. Davis, 442 U.S. 397 at 410 (1979).
111. *Id.* at 412.
112. School Board of Nassau County, Florida v. Arline, 480 U.S. 273 (1987).
113. 34 C.F.R. § 104.5.

10

Conflict Management

IDEA Compliance

Key Concepts in This Chapter

- Practicing Preventative Law
- Resolving Disputes
- Hearing Preparation
- Selecting an Attorney

As this book has demonstrated, a major part of the Individuals with Disabilities Education Act (IDEA)[1] is designed to ensure that school officials comply with its provisions, which require educators to provide a significant array of substantive and procedural rights to students with disabilities and their parents. At the same time, the IDEA's due process provisions created a vehicle for the resolution of disputes regarding the delivery of the free appropriate public education (FAPE) it guarantees students with disabilities.

The IDEA's due process mechanisms are the most elaborate system that Congress has ever established for the resolution of disputes between parents and school officials. Unfortunately, although Congress intended for parents and educators to work together in developing individualized education programs (IEPs) for students with disabilities, there are times when the parties simply do not agree. Aware of the fact that parents and school officials cannot always agree about what is best for children, Congress saw the need to include dispute resolution processes in the IDEA.

This book provides information about many of the literally thousands of cases that have been filed since the IDEA was enacted. These suits involved numerous aspects of the statute and its regulations over the delivery of FAPEs. Moreover, the deluge of litigation in special education is unlikely to stop in the near future since the rate of cases continues to increase.[2]

Special education administrators have been heard to lament that it often seems as though they must be half lawyers to carry out their positions successfully. While having law degrees is certainly not a prerequisite for assuming leadership positions in education, the reality remains that the process for providing special education to students with disabilities is very much a legal one. Successful special education practitioners must therefore be knowledgeable about the law and understand how the legal system operates. The educators who are most successful are those who proactively manage the legal system rather than respond by allowing the legal system to manage their activities. Inasmuch as the purpose of this chapter is to provide information about how and when to access the legal system, it does not end with specific recommendations apart from this narrative discussion.

Preventative Law

The best way to deal with legal challenges is to prevent them from occurring, a practice known as preventative law, which focuses on increasing educator awareness of the dimensions of education or school law.[3] Even so, in recent years school boards have been forced to budget increased amounts of money for legal fees. It almost goes without saying that few will argue that this money would be better spent on educational programs. This is most true in special education, where litigation has increased faster than in any other area related to schools.[4] In addition to their own legal fees, school boards may have to reimburse parents who prevail in litigation for their attorney fees.

Aware of the need to avoid unnecessary litigation, many school officials have demonstrated an interest in the area known as preventative law. The goals of preventative law are to eliminate disputes before they can arise and to put school systems in favorable positions should litigation occur.

Aware of the need to avoid unnecessary litigation, many school officials have demonstrated an interest in the area known as preventative law. The goals of preventative law are to eliminate disputes before they can arise and to put school systems in favorable positions should litigation occur. In order to be most effective, educators must practice preventative law on a daily basis by seeking permanent solutions to situations that give rise to conflict in schools. Generally, it is less expensive to find permanent solutions by enacting proactive policies and procedures than to mount what essentially are reactive or after-the-fact defenses in potentially protracted litigation.

The first step in any program of preventative law is for school leaders and special education practitioners, including teachers, aides, and providers of related services, to be knowledgeable about the legal issues in special education. Reading this book and others like it should provide educators with a basic knowledge of the issues and the results of previous litigation. However, the law is constantly evolving as new cases that can alter its status are decided daily. Previous chapters cited examples of how these changes have occurred. Thus, school officials must take affirmative steps to stay abreast of legal developments.

Today numerous sources of information exist about issues and developments in education law. The Education Law Association (ELA), a non-advocacy group headquartered at Cleveland State University in Ohio, publishes *The Yearbook of Education Law,* often simply called *The Yearbook,* which includes a chapter on special education law. ELA also publishes a monthly newsletter, *ELA Notes,* and a reporter, *School Law Reporter,* as well as monographs to provide up-to-date information on school law. In the interests of full disclosure, we would like to point out that we are both past presidents of ELA. In addition, we have both worked on *The Yearbook:* Allan G. Osborne has written the chapter on students with disabilities in *The Yearbook* since 1990, and Charles J. Russo has been editor of *The Yearbook* since 1995 and was a chapter author before becoming editor.

Many special education and general education journals frequently contain articles on legal issues, especially those involving special education. Professional and academic organizations such as the Council for Exceptional Children, the National School Boards Association and its state affiliates, the American Association of School Administrators, the American Educational Research Association, the Association of School Business Officials International, and ELA generally include sessions at their annual conventions that address legal issues. In addition, the colleges or schools of education in many institutions of higher education offer courses on school law and/or the law of special education that can serve as excellent resources for educators. Workshops on special education law should be part of every school system's professional development program. In providing such ongoing professional development for staff, school officials should consider having their board's attorneys join in the presentations so that they can provide up-to-date legal perspectives. At the end of this book are additional helpful resources: Resource B includes the websites of all 50 state (or commonwealth) departments of education; Resource C provides a list of helpful special education websites along with brief descriptions of what they contain.

Working With Parents

Litigation frequently arises out of misunderstandings or small differences of opinion between parties. A great deal of costly and time-consuming litigation can be avoided if educators keep lines of communication open with parents and are willing to reach compromises when disagreements occur. When parents reject proposed special education placements and/or IEPs for their children, school officials should make every attempt possible to evaluate their reasons for doing so. The rejections may be due to misunderstandings over what proposals entail or disagreements with only minor aspects of IEPs. If educators do not communicate, or are unwilling to compromise, then litigation is sure to follow.

> One of the most important aspects of the communication process for school officials, especially with parents, is to be active listeners. When parents present counterproposals or make additional demands, educators must listen and give serious thought to what they hear.

One of the most important aspects of the communication process for school officials, especially with parents, is to be active listeners. When parents present counterproposals or make additional demands, educators must listen and give serious thought to what they hear. In the spirit of compromise, school officials should be prepared to make some concessions. If educators cannot meet parental demands, they should take great care in explaining why parental proposals cannot or should not be implemented as the parents wish.

Another common source of litigation, in addition to conflicts with parents, is the failure of school personnel to implement federal and state laws and policies as well as local school board policies. Put another way, although school boards typically have adopted appropriate and legally correct policies and procedures, their employees sometimes fail to implement them properly in all situations. This means that it is crucial for educational leaders to prepare new and continuing employees by providing ongoing professional development activities to ensure that staff members are aware of all policies and procedures as well as the importance of following these requirements.

At least three items can help educators to minimize conflict with parents.[5] First, educators should keep parents informed and offer their support by providing parents with information about the disabilities of their children. This includes directing parents to their central office personnel, to local support groups that can better help them to understand the disabilities of their children, and to useful websites such as those identified in the resources at the end of this book.

Second, educators should recognize that insofar as parents are part of the solution, not part of the problem, it is important to work with them in the best interest of the children with disabilities. Sadly, some school officials treat the parents of special education (and other) students as potential troublemakers rather than as valuable partners who can help address the needs of their children. Educators should keep in mind that because, unlike parents, they are temporary in the lives of children, they must work together with parents in the process of designing educational programming that best suits the needs of students with disabilities.

Third, educators should follow the law. Litigation involving special education can be contentious, and expensive, since prevailing parents can recover attorney fees. Because of this, one of the most important steps for school officials to take in the realm of preventative law is to conduct periodical legal audits focusing on board policies, procedures, and practices to ensure that they are legally correct. Since the status of the law is constantly evolving, it is important to complete legal audits at least every two years but preferably annually. School board attorneys, especially those who focus on special education, acting as part of teams with directors of special education and other central office personnel, should work together in conducting audits.

Dispute Resolution

Unfortunately, despite the best efforts of school officials to prevent it, litigation is a fact of life in today's school systems. Honest disagreements over what constitutes FAPEs are all but certain to occur between parents and special educators. Insofar as parents, for their own reasons, sometimes make demands or have unrealistic expectations that school officials cannot (and may not be required to) meet, compromise is not always possible. Further, sometimes litigation ensues because school district personnel make errors.

As described in Chapter 7, the IDEA contains a sophisticated system for dispute resolution. Rather than reiterate here the key points from Chapter 7, this section outlines steps that school officials should take when parents threaten to initiate or do initiate legal action.

Mediation

Sometimes communications between school officials and parents break down, making it difficult for the parties to sit down to work out their disagreements. Mediation can be helpful in situations such as these, and the IDEA now directs states and educational officials to offer mediation services at no cost to parents prior to scheduling due process hearings. Mediation is a viable alternative for the resolution of disputed IEPs but cannot be used to deny or delay parental rights to formal due process hearings. In fact, parents cannot be compelled to enter into mediation if they prefer to go straight to due process hearings.

> The parties involved in special education disputes may engage the services of impartial mediators who can attempt to bring them together through negotiation.

The parties involved in special education disputes may engage the services of impartial mediators who can attempt to bring them together through negotiation. Moreover, a variety of states have provisions in their own special education laws for formal mediation processes prior to litigation; also, the IDEA requires state officials to maintain a list of trained, impartial mediators. Successful mediation depends on the willingness of school officials to compromise. Educational officials must evaluate any reasonable proposals that are presented by either parents or mediators and be prepared to offer specific counterproposals.

There are many advantages to trying mediation before proceeding to due process hearings. The costs involved and the time spent on due process hearings certainly justify the effort to mediate and avoid the hearing stage. Perhaps most important, mediation can salvage the working relationships between parents and school officials. Unfortunately, even though it is not supposed to be so, due process hearings are often adversarial processes that do little to foster positive working relationships between parents and school officials.

Resolution Conference

A provision in the IDEA calls for resolution sessions to take place within 15 days of when parents file formal complaints about the education of their children with disabilities.[6] These conferences are designed to discuss parental complaints and all pertinent facts so that the disagreements can be resolved. In addition to the parents, relevant members of the IEP team should attend resolution sessions. School board attorneys may not attend resolution sessions unless the parents bring their attorneys along. As with mediation, this step is voluntary and does not need to occur if both parties either agree to waive resolution sessions or to proceed directly to mediation.

> Insofar as many disputes result from misunderstandings or unclear communication, resolution conferences provide one more opportunity to satisfy parental concerns in nonadversarial contexts.

School officials would be wise to take advantage of resolution conferences and should not agree to waive these sessions unless it is clear that parents will not participate. Insofar as many disputes result from misunderstandings or unclear communication, resolution conferences provide one more opportunity to satisfy parental concerns in nonadversarial contexts. As an added benefit, as with mediation, this process is far less costly than hearings.

Resolution conferences also provide opportunities for upper-level administrators, such as directors of special education, to become involved in the process of finding solutions to issues raised by parents. Insofar as administrators above the building level are often not involved in developing contested IEPs, they remain unaware of parental complaints until the complaints are filed. There are two benefits to having district-level administrators present at resolution sessions. First, because these administrators often have broader views of issues in light of their varied experiences, they can bring fresh perspectives to disputes. Second, since these administrators frequently have more authority to commit the resources of their school systems, they are able to offer options that IEP teams might not otherwise have considered. Consequently, it is often possible to resolve complaints simply by including persons with greater decision-making authority, since they bring something new to the table.

Preparing for Hearings

The best efforts of school officials notwithstanding, sometimes due process hearings are inevitable. If school officials have complied with all of the IDEA's provisions in making their placement decisions, they need not fear due process hearings. Even so, there is simply no substitute for proper preparation prior to hearings.

> Preparation for hearings must begin long before it is even apparent that hearings are to take place.

Preparation for hearings must begin long before it is even apparent that hearings are to take place. The key to success in due process hearings is for school officials to have all of the documentation handy to demonstrate their compliance with applicable laws, policies, and procedures. Documentation in this regard includes, but is certainly not limited to, copies of notice letters sent to parents, signed consent forms, copies of IEPs, and any and all other forms of written communication between the parties. It is impossible to create proper documentation after the fact if it does not exist. Accordingly, educational leaders should treat all special education situations as if they may culminate in hearings. In other words, school officials should begin documentation on the day they receive requests for services or referrals for evaluations. Simply stated, special education personnel should be trained to make the documentation process part of the routine of providing special education services.

Generally, the chief special education administrator in school systems, typically with the title of director of special education, is responsible for representing school boards at hearings. Insofar as these administrators usually become directly involved in cases only after problems have developed, they may be unfamiliar with the histories of the children involved. The first task for such administrators, then, is to gather all pertinent information. At the same time, administrators must become familiar with all aspects and details of cases, since the decisions that need to be made throughout the hearing process require thorough knowledge of the students.

In preparing for hearings, it is worth keeping in mind that the requirements and qualifications for hearing officers vary from one state to the next. In some states, such as Ohio,[7] hearing officers must be attorneys with some knowledge of special education practices. On the other hand, in states such as North Carolina,[8] hearing officers need not be attorneys and are typically faculty members from local colleges or universities who are versed in special education procedures. It would be a mistake to assume that hearing officers have detailed knowledge of a school system's programs or other available options. For this reason educators must inform hearing officers about the positive aspects of the school officials' proposals and any weaknesses in the parents' position.

One of the most important pieces of evidence that school officials must supply at hearings is proof that they complied with all relevant due process procedures. If officials cannot provide this evidence, or have not complied with the procedures, they should acknowledge their errors. While not all procedural errors are fatal to cases, evasiveness or intentional covering up of procedural errors can be very damaging to the cases of school boards since this can weaken their credibility.

During hearings it is important for the representatives of school boards to make complete presentations of the facts. It may be helpful to use visual aids such as charts, diagrams, or other graphic presentations to clarify points made during the oral argument or cross-examination of expert witnesses. Careful advanced preparation of these materials is necessary.

Those who testify or present evidence on behalf of school systems must also be well prepared in advance. This means not only that witnesses should be familiar with the information about which they are to provide testimony but also that they should be prepared by being given sample questions of the type that they are likely to face at hearings. While it is difficult to know in advance exactly what line of questioning the opposition is going to employ during cross-examinations, board attorneys should be able to prepare witnesses adequately for what is to come.

The task of school officials during hearings is to show that their proposed programs provide students with FAPEs. According to the IDEA, once educators have demonstrated that they have offered FAPEs, there is no need to examine alternative proposals. Even so, prudent school officials should be prepared to show why they do believe that the programs favored by the parents are unnecessary. Many school boards have succeeded in due process hearings by showing that the programs favored by the parents were inadequate.

The importance of school officials and their attorneys working together cannot be overemphasized because their communication is an important ingredient to success. The next section reviews factors to consider when choosing an attorney.

Selecting an Attorney

The party that is in the right in special education litigation is not automatically the victor. As in any legal contest, the party that presents the better case wins most often. This being the situation, having qualified attorneys may make all the difference between success and failure at due process hearings and/or in litigation. Thus, the necessity of having skilled attorneys in special education suits cannot be overemphasized.

> As an area of law, special education has become increasingly important due to the tremendous amount of litigation that has occurred since the IDEA was first enacted in 1975.

As an area of law, special education has become increasingly important due to the tremendous amount of litigation that has occurred since the IDEA was first enacted in 1975. School officials must be aware that the law in this regard has become so specialized that they cannot rely solely on their regular attorneys to defend them in special education suits. Put another way, as well qualified as school board attorneys are to handle most legal affairs, many may lack the specialized knowledge that is required to litigate special education cases adequately. To this end, school boards should consider retaining separate attorneys to handle their special education litigation. On the other hand, many boards retain the services of large law firms that focus on education law, firms that typically have attorneys on staff who devote significant portions, if not all, of their practices to the law of special education. Under these circumstances, school officials may need to look no farther than their present firms for special education counsel.

If school boards are not represented by large firms with special education divisions or lack their own counsel on staff, as is common in larger school systems, officials should locate and retain separate attorneys for special education litigation. These attorneys must be well versed in education law in general as well as in special education law and have experience in administrative hearing procedures since most litigation begins at this level. Further, attorneys should be familiar with educational issues and practices such as evaluation methods, teaching techniques, and various placement options. Naturally, experienced and talented attorneys cost more. There simply is no substitute for knowledge and experience.

In order to locate qualified attorneys to handle special education suits, school officials should solicit referrals from other knowledgeable parties. Since the persons representing school boards in special education litigation may need to confer with the regular attorneys that boards retain, the boards' attorneys would be a logical starting point. At the same time, board attorneys may have ready lists of qualified special education attorneys. Special education administrators from other districts can also serve as a good source of referrals. Finally, the national or state school board associations, in addition to county or state bar associations, should be able to provide lists of attorneys who specialize in special education litigation.

School boards should identify, and retain, attorneys long before they are needed. The point at which boards are under the pressure of litigation over a special education dispute is not the proper time to begin looking for qualified attorneys. It is better to retain, and form relationships with, attorneys well before litigation is pending. By adopting proactive approaches, school officials should be able to take the time necessary to make sure the attorneys they hire are the right persons for the job.

> Hiring attorneys, regardless of whether they are generalists or specialists in special education, is much like choosing professionals to fill any open positions in school systems.

Hiring attorneys, regardless of whether they are generalists or specialists in special education, is much like choosing professionals to fill any open positions in school systems. Educational leaders should first focus on the needs of their districts and consider, as many boards are already doing, putting out requests for proposals, sometimes referred to simply as RFPs, for attorneys who are interested in, and meet the qualifications for, the jobs at hand.[9] Once attorneys have submitted their applications, officials should examine their credentials, seek references from friends and colleagues in other systems that have used the attorneys under consideration, and interview the candidates that appear most qualified. Clearly, selecting attorneys is as important as filling any top-level administrative position in school districts. The process should not be taken lightly.

Conclusion

There is an old saying in sports that the best defense is a good offense. The same can be said of special education litigation except that unlike in sports, it is best to prevent a confrontation from occurring in the first place by engaging in preventative law.

The best way to avoid litigation is to be prepared constantly for such an eventuality. School officials can reduce their risk of suits by making sure that all employees are well aware of the law, and know and follow proper procedures. Employees who know and understand the law should be less likely to make legal errors. This is especially true in the field of special education where procedure plays such an important role.

When inevitable conflicts do arise, they do not automatically mean that litigation must follow since many disagreements can be resolved through more communication between the parties. Parents and school officials can clear up misunderstandings and negotiate compromises. The parties can also rely on formal mediation processes or prehearing resolution conferences to help settle disputes if communication between them breaks down.

Finally, when litigation is inevitable, school officials must not despair. If school employees have followed proper procedures and made placement decisions in good faith, then boards should have little cause for concern. Nevertheless, when entering the legal arena, school officials must come prepared by being able to defend their actions and recommendations while justifying all of their placement decisions. Moreover, qualified attorneys may be the greatest assets that school boards have when faced with the threat of litigation over providing special education to students with disabilities.

Endnotes

1. 20 U.S.C. §§ 1400–1482 (2012). The IDEA's regulations can be found at Assistance to the States for the Education of Children with Disabilities, 34 C.F.R. §§ 300.1–300.818 (2013).

2. Zirkel, P. A. (2005). The over-legalization of special education. *Education Law Reporter, 195,* 35–40.
3. For an article on this, see Russo, C. J. (2010). School law: An essential component in your toolbox. *School Business Affairs, 75*(9), 36–38.
4. Zirkel, P. A., & D'Angelo, A. (2002). Special education case law: An empirical trends analysis. *Education Law Reporter, 161,* 731–753.
5. Russo, C. J., & Morse, T. E. (2004). Working with parents of special education students. *Today's School: Shared Leadership in Education, 5*(3), 8–9.
6. 20 U.S.C. § 1415(f)(1)(B).
7. Ohio Admin. Code, § 3301-51-08(D) (2002).
8. N.C. Gen. Stat. § 115C-116(i) (1997).
9. Bennett, K. M., & Pole, K. M. (2005). Legal services: Getting what you need with RFPs. *School Business Affairs, 71*(8), 16–17.

Resource A

Glossary

Administrative appeal: a quasi-judicial proceeding before an independent hearing officer or administrative law judge.

Administrative law judge: an individual presiding at an administrative due process hearing who has the power to administer oaths, hear testimony, rule on questions of evidence, and make determinations of fact. The role of an administrative law judge in IDEA proceedings is identical to that of an independent hearing officer.

Affirm: to uphold the decision of a lower court or tribunal in an appeal.

Annual review: a yearly review of a student's progress in a special education program and an examination of his or her future special education needs. An annual review may repeat some of the original assessments for purposes of assessing progress but generally is not as thorough as the original evaluation. The student's individualized education program is revised and updated at the annual review conference.

Appeal: a resort to a higher court seeking review of a judicial or administrative action.

Appellant: the party who appeals a decision to a higher court.

Appellate court: a court that can hear only appeals and so has appellate jurisdiction.

Appellee: the party against whom an appeal is made to a higher court.

Case law: results from court opinions; this is also referred to as common law or judge-made law.

Certiorari, **(abbreviated** *cert.;* **literally, to be informed):** a writ issued by an appellate court indicating that it will review (*cert.* granted), or not review (*cert.* denied), a lower court's decision.

C.F.R. (Code of Federal Regulations): the repository of regulations promulgated by federal agencies to implement laws passed by Congress.

Civil action: a dispute between two private parties or a private party and the state to enforce, redress, or protect private rights that are civil (as opposed to criminal) in nature.

Civil right: a personal right guaranteed by the U.S. Constitution or a state constitution or by a federal or state statute.

Class action: a suit brought on behalf of named plaintiffs and others who may be similarly situated.

Common law: the body of law that developed as a result of court decisions and precedents.

Compensatory damages: a judicial award intended to compensate a plaintiff for an actual loss.

Consent decree: an agreement between parties to a suit sanctioned by a court and essentially settles the dispute by mutual consent.

Contract: an agreement between two parties creating a legal obligation to do or not to do something; a contract can be written or oral.

Criminal action: an action brought by the state to punish an individual who has been charged with committing a crime. Crimes are statutory only; there is no common law criminal law.

Damages: a judicial award to compensate an injured party; damages can be legal (or monetary), in the form of a payment by the party causing the injury, or equitable (see the definition of equitable, below).

Declaratory relief: a judicial decree clarifying a party's legal rights.

De facto (literally, by the fact): a situation in actual existence, regardless of whether it is legal.

Defendant: the party against whom a suit is brought.

De jure (literally, by law): a situation occurring by operation of law.

De minimis (literally, about the smallest matter): a small or unimportant item not worthy of a court's concern.

De novo (literally, from new): a court hears evidence and testimony that may have been previously heard by a lower court or administrative body.

Dicta (literally, remarks): a gratuitous statement in a judicial opinion that goes beyond the facts and issues of a case and is not binding on future cases; this is also referred to as **obiter dictum** (literally, a remark by the way). **Dicta** is the plural form; **dictum** is singular.

En banc (literally, in the bench): a judicial session where the entire membership of a court participates in a decision rather than a single judge or select panel of judges; a rehearing en banc may be granted if a select panel of judges has rendered a decision that is contrary to decisions rendered by similar courts.

Equitable relief: justice administered according to fairness; a form of relief that orders a party to do something or to refrain from doing something when monetary damages are inadequate to make an injured party whole.

Et sequor **(abbreviated as, and more commonly used as,** *et seq.;* **literally, and following):** a term generally used in a citation to indicate "and the sections that follow."

Evaluation team: a group of individuals who assess a student to determine whether the child has a disability and, if so, what special education and related services he or she will require. An evaluation team is composed of individuals such as the classroom teacher, a special education teacher, an administrator, a psychologist, the parents of the student (and in some cases the student), and other specialists. Different states have various names for the evaluation team such as multidisciplinary team, committee on special education, pupil personnel services team, or pupil placement team.

Ex parte **(literally, by or for one party):** an action initiated at the request of one party without notice to the other party.

Expulsion: a long-term exclusion from school, generally for disciplinary purposes; ordinarily, a disciplinary exclusion of more than 10 days is considered an expulsion.

Ex relatione **(abbreviated as, and more commonly used as,** *ex rel.;* **literally, upon relation or information):** a term in a case title indicating that the legal proceedings were instituted by the state or another party on behalf of an individual who had an interest in the matter.

Full inclusion: the practice of educating students with disabilities in a fully inclusive setting with children who do not have disabilities; this has also been referred to as mainstreaming.

Holding: the part of a court's decision that applies the law to the facts of the case, resulting in the common law rule of law from the case.

Independent hearing officer: an impartial third party decision maker who conducts an administrative hearing and renders a decision on the merits of a dispute.

Individuals with Disabilities Education Act (IDEA): the federal special education law, codified at 20 U.S.C. §§ 1400–1482.

Injunction: an equitable remedy, or court order, forbidding a party from taking a contemplated action, restraining a party from continuing an action, or requiring a party to take some action.

In loco parentis **(literally, in the place of the parent):** a term used in situations where school (or other public) officials act in the place of a child's parents.

In re (literally, in the matter of): a situation in which there are no adversarial parties in a judicial proceeding, only a res (thing) for the court to consider.

Judgment: a decision of a court with the authority to resolve a dispute.

Jurisdiction: the legal right by which a court exercises its authority; jurisdiction also refers to the geographic area within which a court has the authority to exercise its power.

Moot: when a real, or live, controversy no longer exists; a suit becomes moot if, for example, there is no longer any dispute because a student with a disability turns 21.

On remand: when a higher court returns a case to a lower court with directions that it take further action.

Opinion: a court's written explanation of its judgment.

Original jurisdiction: the power of a court, typically at the trial level, to assert jurisdiction at its inception; this is distinguished from appellate jurisdiction, whereby a court may hear only cases on appeal.

Per curiam **(literally, for or by the court):** an unsigned decision of a court as opposed to one signed by a specific judge or group of judges.

P.L. (Public Law): a statute passed by Congress; the IDEA was initially referred to as P.L. 94–142, the 142nd piece of legislation introduced during the 94th Congress.

Plaintiff: the party bringing a suit to a court of law.

Precedent: a judicial opinion binding on lower courts in a given jurisdiction; this is also referred to as binding precedent to distinguish it from persuasive precedent (such as *dicta*), which is not binding.

Preponderance of the evidence: the level of proof required in a civil suit; evidence that has the greater weight or is more convincing, meaning that it is just a bit more yes than no. Conversely, a criminal case requires proof beyond a reasonable doubt.

Pro se **(literally, for self):** a person who represents one's self in court.

Prospective: looking toward the future; prospective relief provides a remedy in the future typically by ordering a party either to do or to refrain from doing something.

Punitive damages: compensation awarded to a plaintiff over and above the actual loss suffered; such damages are designed to punish the defendant for wrongful action and to act as an incentive to prevent similar action in the future.

Reevaluation: a complete and thorough reassessment of a student. Generally, all original assessments are repeated, but additional assessments must be completed if necessary; the IDEA requires educators to reevaluate each child with a disability at least every three years.

Remand: to return a case to a lower court, usually with specific instructions for further action.

Res judicata **(literally, a thing decided):** the rule that a final judgment of a court is conclusive and acts to prevent subsequent action on the same claim.

Reverse: to revoke a lower court's decision on appeal.

Settlement agreement: an out-of-court agreement made by the parties to a suit to settle the case by resolving the major issues that initiated the litigation.

Sovereign immunity: a legal prohibition against suing the government without its consent.

Special education: instruction specifically designed to meet the unique needs of a student with disabilities.

Standing: an individual's right to bring a suit to court; in order to have standing, an individual must be directly affected by, and have a real interest in, the issues litigated.

Stare decisis **(literally, let the decision stand):** adherence to precedent.

State-level review officer (or panel): an impartial person (or panel of usually three or more persons) responsible for reviewing the decisions of an independent hearing officer from an administrative due process proceeding under the IDEA. The IDEA provides that if administrative due process hearings are held at the local school district level, provisions must be made for an appeal at the state level.

Statute of limitations: the specific period of time within which a suit must be filed.

Sub nomine **(abbreviated *sub nom.*; literally, under the name):** a situation in which a case was on appeal under a different name than the one used at the lower court level.

Suspension: the short-term exclusion of a student from school, usually for less than 10 days, typically for disciplinary purposes.

Tort: a civil wrong other than breach of contract; the most common tort is negligence.

U.S.C. (United States Code): the official compilation of statutes enacted by Congress.

U.S.C.A. (United States Code Annotated): an alternate version of the United States Code that includes annotations to federal and state cases, cross-references to related sections, historical notes, and library references.

Vacate: to set aside a lower court's decision in an appeal.

Resource B

Department of Special Education Websites, by State

Alabama: http://www.alsde.edu/html/sections/section_detail.asp?section=65&footer=sections

Alaska: http://www.eed.state.ak.us/tls/SPED

Arizona: http://www.ade.az.gov/ess

Arkansas: http://arksped.k12.ar.us

California: http://www.cde.ca.gov/sp/se

Colorado: http://www.cde.state.co.us/cdesped/index.asp

Connecticut: http://www.state.ct.us/sde/deps/special

Delaware: http://www.decec.org/index.php

District of Columbia: http://www.k12.dc.us/dcps/specialed/dcpsspecedhome.html

Florida: http://www.firn.edu/doe/bin00014/ese-home.htm

Georgia: http://www.doe.k12.ga.us/curriculum/exceptional/index.asp

Hawaii: http://doe.k12.hi.us/specialeducation

Idaho: http://www.sde.state.id.us/specialed/default.asp

Illinois: http://www.isbe.state.il.us/spec-ed

Indiana: http://ideanet.doe.state.in.us/exceptional

Iowa: http://www.iowa.gov/educate/content/view/574/591

Kansas: http://www.kansped.org

Kentucky: http://www.education.ky.gov/KDE/Instructional+Resources/ Student+and+Family+Support/Exceptional+Children/default.htm

Louisiana: http://www.doe.state.la.us/lde/index.html

Maine: http://www.state.me.us/education/speced/specserv.htm

Maryland: http://www.marylandpublicschools.org/msde

Massachusetts: http://www.doe.mass.edu/sped

Michigan: http://www.michigan.gov/mde/0,1607,7-140-6530_6598---,00 .html

Minnesota: http://www.education.state.mn.us/MDE/Learning_Support/ Special_Education/index.html

Mississippi: http://www.mde.k12.ms.us/special_education

Missouri: http://dese.mo.gov/divspeced

Montana: http://www.opi.state.mt.us [click on the "Programs & Services of OPI" menu in the upper right hand corner of the page; then scroll down to "Special Education"]

Nebraska: http://www.nde.state.ne.us/SPED/sped.html

Nevada: http://www.doe.nv.gov/edteam/ndeoffices/sped-diversity-improve.html

New Hampshire: http://www.ed.state.nh.us/education/doe/organization/ instruction/bose.htm

New Jersey: http://www.state.nj.us/njded/specialed

New Mexico: http://www.ped.state.nm.us/seo/index.htm

New York: http://www.vesid.nysed.gov/specialed/home.html

North Carolina: http://www.ncpublicschools.org/ec

North Dakota: http://www.dpi.state.nd.us/speced/index.shtm

Ohio: http://www.ode.state.oh.us/GD/Templates/Pages/ODE/ODE Primary.aspx?Page=2&TopicID=661&TopicRelationID=675

Oklahoma: http://www.sde.state.ok.us/home/defaultie.html [click on "Site Index" on the left side of the home page, then scroll down to "Special Education Services"]

Oregon: http://www.ode.state.or.us/search/results/?=40

Pennsylvania: http://www.portal.state.pa.us/portal/server.pt/community/special_education/7465

Rhode Island: http://www.ridoe.net/Special_Populations/default.aspx

South Carolina: http://www.myscschools.com/offices/ec

South Dakota: http://doe.sd.gov/oess/specialed/index.asp

Tennessee: http://www.state.tn.us/education/speced

Texas: http://www.mde.k12.ms.us/special_education

U.S. Virgin Islands: http://www.usvi.org/education/index.html

Utah: http://www.usoe.k12.ut.us/sars

Vermont: http://www.state.vt.us/educ/new/html/pgm_sped.html

Virginia: http://www.pen.k12.va.us/VDOE/sess

Washington: http://www.k12.wa.us/SpecialEd/default.aspx

West Virginia: http://wvde.state.wv.us/ose

Wisconsin: http://dpi.wi.gov/sped/tm-specedtopics.html

Wyoming: http://www.k12.wy.us/se.asp

Resource C

Useful Special Education Websites

http://idea.ed.gov

This is the site of the U.S. Department of Education; it contains updates on IDEA, IDEA regulations, articles, and other general information.

http://www.ed.gov/about/offices/list/osers/osep/index.html?src=mr

This site includes information from the federal Office of Special Education Programs.

http://www.csef-air.org

This is the website for the Center for Special Education Finance; it is easy to navigate and is to the point.

http://www.cec.sped.org

This is the website for the Council for Exceptional Children.

http://www.ideapractices.org

This site on IDEA practices provides articles, information, ideas, and links to other sites.

http://www.irsc.org/laws.htm

This site provides Internet resources for special children, as well as links and articles on the law of special education.

http://www.iser.com

This is the Internet Special Education Resources site; it provides links to many other sites.

http://www.napsec.org

This site contains material from the National Association of Private Special Education Centers, a nonprofit association whose mission is to represent private special education programs and affiliated state associations.

http://seriweb.com

This site for special education resources includes Internet-accessible information on special education.

http://www.specialedlaw.net/index.mv

This special education law site provides information on the law of special education.

http://www.specialednews.com

This site includes current news articles on special education.

http://www.wrightslaw.com

The Wrightslaw site includes articles, cases, newsletters, and other information about special education law.

Resource D

Useful Education Law Websites

Legal Search Engines

http://washlaw.edu
This website contains law-related sources on the Internet.

http://www.findlaw.com
FindLaw is an Internet resource that helps to find any website that is law related.

http://www.alllaw.com
AllLaw is another resource for locating law-related websites.

http://www.law.cornell.edu
This is a website sponsored by Cornell Law School; it provides free access to legal source materials online.

U.S. Supreme Court, Federal Courts, and Federal Government Websites

http://www.supremecourtus.gov
This is the official website of the Supreme Court of the United States.

http://supct.law.cornell.edu/supct/index.html
This website contains recent decisions of the Supreme Court. It also has free e-mail publication to distribute the syllabuses of the Court's decisions within hours after they are handed down.

http://thomas.loc.gov
This website was prepared by the U.S. Library of Congress and has links to the Federal Court System.

http://www.uscourts.gov
This is the U.S. Federal Judiciary website.

http://www.gpoaccess.gov/fr/index.html
This website contains the *Federal Register.*

http://www.ed.gov/about/offices/list/ocr/index.html?src=mr
This is the website of the Office for Civil Rights.

http://www.house.gov
This is the U.S. House of Representatives website.

http://www.senate.gov
This is the U.S. Senate website.

http://www.whitehouse.gov
This is the website of the White House.

http://www.ed.gov
This is the U.S. Department of Education website.

http://www.ed.gov/nclb/landing.jhtml?src=pb
This website contains the No Child Left Behind Act.

Index

CORWIN

A SAGE Company

The Corwin logo—a raven striding across an open book—represents the union of courage and learning. Corwin is committed to improving education for all learners by publishing books and other professional development resources for those serving the field of PreK–12 education. By providing practical, hands-on materials, Corwin continues to carry out the promise of its motto: **"Helping Educators Do Their Work Better."**